THE PRESIDENCY
AND THE POLITICS OF
RACIAL INEQUALITY

D0033818

POWER, CONFLICT, AND DEMOCRACY:

AMERICAN POLITICS

INTO THE TWENTY-FIRST CENTURY

ROBERT Y. SHAPIRO, EDITOR

POWER, CONFLICT, AND DEMOCRACY:

AMERICAN POLITICS

INTO THE TWENTY-FIRST CENTURY

ROBERT Y. SHAPIRO, EDITOR

This series focuses on how the will of the people and the public interest are promoted, encouraged, or thwarted. It aims to question not only the direction American politics will take as it enters the twenty-first century but also the direction American politics has already taken.

The series addresses the role of interest groups and social and political movements; openness in American politics; important developments in institutions such as the executive, legislative, and judicial branches at all levels of government as well as the bureaucracies thus created; the changing behavior of politicians and political parties; the role of public opinion; and the functioning of mass media. Because problems drive politics, the series also examines important policy issues in both domestic and foreign affairs.

The series welcomes all theoretical perspectives, methodologies, and types of evidence that answer important questions about trends in American politics.

POWER, CONFLICT, AND DEMOCRACY:

AMERICAN POLITICS

INTO THE TWENTY-FIRST CENTURY

John G. Geer, *From Tea Leaves to Opinion Polls: A Theory of Democratic Leadership*

Kim Fridkin Kahn, *The Political Consequences of Being a Woman: How Stereotypes Influence the Conduct and Consequences of Political Campaigns*

Kelly D. Patterson, *Political Parties and the Maintenance of Liberal Democracy*

Dona Cooper Hamilton and Charles V. Hamilton, *The Dual Agenda: Race and Social Welfare Policies of Civil Rights Organizations*

Hanes Walton Jr., *African-American Power and Politics: The Political Context Variable*

Amy Fried, *Muffled Echoes: Oliver North and the Politics of Public Opinion*

THE PRESIDENCY
AND THE POLITICS OF
RACIAL INEQUALITY

Nation-Keeping from 1831 to 1965

Russell L. Riley

COLUMBIA UNIVERSITY PRESS

NEW YORK

COLUMBIA UNIVERSITY PRESS

Publishers Since 1893

New York   Chichester, West Sussex

Copyright © 1999 by Columbia University Press

Library of Congress Cataloging-in-Publication Data

Riley, Russell L. 1958–

The presidency and the politics of racial inequality : nation–keeping from 1831 to 1965 / Russell L. Riley.

p. cm. – (Power, conflict, and democracy : American politics into the twenty-first century)   Includes bibiliographical references and index.

ISBN 0–231–10722–6 (cloth). – ISBN 0–231–10723–4 (pbk.)

1. Presidents—United States—Racial attitudes. 2. Political leadership—United States—History. 3. Racism—United States—Political aspects—History. 4. Afro-Americans—Civil rights—History. 5. United States—Politics and government—19th century. 6. United States—Politics and government—20th.

I. Title. II. Series: Power, conflict, and democracy.

E176.1.R56 1999

323.1'73'09—dc21   98–37018

To my parents,
who helped get me into this project,
and to Monique,
who helped get me through it

CONTENTS

"Every Society from a great nation down to a club," proclaimed Pennsylvania's Gouverneur Morris in 1787, "[has] the right of declaring the conditions on which new members should be admitted."[1] As Morris spoke, he and his colleagues at Philadelphia's constitutional convention were struggling with the establishment of qualifications for those who would serve in the new government, a vexing problem for a land with a relatively small native-born population. Yet the assembled delegates' brief encounter with that question—which ended, as so much did during that summer, in compromise—only hinted at the high tension commonly attending the exercise of that "right" Morris identified. Conflict over societal boundaries, over membership, over the distinction between "one's own" and the "other," is one of the most persistent and prominent features of human behavior, spanning social interaction from the level of "a great nation down to a club."

Indeed, there may be no better window onto the essence of a "Society" than how it deals with the *who belongs?* question. Decisions about membership often require a group to make explicit, and to consider explicitly, those characteristics of thought, nature, or conduct essential to belonging, but which often remain out of clear view for purposes of convenience or necessity. Thus, membership questions can illuminate group character by making the latent manifest. Moreover, open consideration of membership boundaries can precipitate conflicting interpretations within the group about who belongs, conflict avoided as long as the membership question remains dormant.[2] In consequence, active reflection by a society on its boundaries also affords a unique opportunity to watch that society's power structures in action, to discern which institutions and which personages ultimately direct the society's affairs. When conflict over membership questions arise, then, we can see not just *what* that society holds most dear (individual liberty?

adherence to some established group norm?), but also *who* has the power ultimately to settle disputes. Seldom do the defining attributes of a society appear in such bold relief.

These abstractions take on life in a host of everyday situations. Consider:

—the debate within modern-day churches about the place of openly gay communicants within their congregations;
—the routine in-law pressures that attend marriage decisions, and have done so since at least the days of the Capulets and Montagues;
—battles within civic and service organizations, country clubs, and military academies over membership privileges extended on the basis of race, sex, religious affiliation, or ethnicity;
—the strains within communities of all sizes occasioned by the arrival of new immigrants with social, economic, or ethnic traits differing from established norms; and,
—the familiar and often bitter disputes that erupt within academic departments over hiring and tenure decisions, and what they mean and communicate about the character of those departments.

In these instances, and myriad more, those who challenge the prevailing conceptions of group membership commonly precipitate vigorous debate (or outright antagonism) within the church, family, academy, community, or faculty, about who belongs, about the identity of the group. In many cases the very survival of the society is at risk. The outcome of those conflicts both identify who is ultimately acceptable to the society *and* who is responsible for guarding—or changing—it.

As it is with a club so it is with a nation. This book is premised on the notion that there is much to be learned about American political culture by examining how the United States has responded to challenges to its prevailing membership configurations over time, particularly on the question of race. These lessons about inclusion and exclusion, about a hierarchy of privileges, bear special poignancy for a nation founded on and animated by the proposition that "all Men are created equal." In this light, that phrase's author, Thomas Jefferson, appears as perhaps the quintessential American, one whose profound commitment to equality coexisted with his practice of keeping and exploiting the labor of chattel slaves. The nation's subsequent struggles over what Gunnar Myrdal would later call an "American dilemma"—the dissonance between a creed of equality and customs of inequality—are highly revealing, not just about the fundamental principles of membership in the American nation, but also about the role American political institutions play in dealing with disputes over who belongs. Nowhere is this more true than with the presidency.

It is within the presidency that racial equality has found among its most prominent authors—and its most powerful antagonists. It is accordingly that institution that is the focus of the study that follows. What I hope to illuminate here is the nature of an office long at the very center of the nation's efforts to cope with Myrdal's dilemma. Careful inspection reveals a paradoxical institution, equally indispensable as a guardian of the status quo and as a vital source of energy for change toward equality, making some of its incumbents—quite contrary even to their own expectations—great emancipators.

During the long course of writing this book, I have become an avid reader of acknowledgments, for now I understand how absolutely dependent writers are on those around them for guidance and encouragement. Although my name alone appears on the cover, this book would have been impossible without the efforts of a host of people who nurtured me through it. My name stands as proxy, then, for that group of individuals whom I gladly acknowledge in the paragraphs below. What passes for insight in these pages derives from their considerable influence. Any remaining flaws simply reveal my own limitations as a conductor of their collective wisdom.

I am most thoroughly indebted to James Sterling Young, whose fingerprints are on every page. It is a source of immense satisfaction to me that this book is brought to publication by the same press that published *The Washington Community, 1800—-1828;* that work set an impossibly high standard for Jim's student. That I finished this book at all, then, is testament to Jim's faith in the project and to his generosity with time and advice, joined to a willingness to forgive imperfections in another's work he would not countenance in his own.

Thanks also go to the other members of my dissertation committee at the University of Virginia. James W. Ceaser was on board, asking penetrating questions, from the earliest days, and his good humor and enthusiasm for the study of politics made the journey through graduate school an adventure. I am also grateful for the time Matthew Holden Jr. and William Lee Miller spent in reading this work in an earlier form, and for their encouragement to proceed toward publication with the results.

It gives me special pleasure to recognize, too, the contributions of two elder statesmen of the academy. Richard E. Neustadt not only helped me find my way into political science and the study of the presidency, he was a valued source of advice and inspiration as I labored toward the completion of a project that at times seemed endless. Kenneth W. Thompson was also a mentor, and the financial support he provided me through the White Burkett Miller Center of Public Affairs—and the intellectual environment afforded at Faulkner House—was an indispensable element in seeing this book to publication. This work is one meager contribution to their vast legacies.

I also benefited from the financial support of the Thomas Jefferson Memorial Foundation, the Earhart Foundation, and the University of Virginia, in various years as a President's Fellow, a Spicer Fellow, and a DuPont Fellow. My thanks to those who made that funding possible.

Many thanks also to my colleagues at Georgetown University and the University of Pennsylvania—especially Oliver Williams, John Skrentny, and Stephen Wayne—for their support as I labored on this project. My time helping direct Penn's Washington Semester Program was particularly fruitful because of Jack Nagel's constancy and friendship.

I am grateful to John Michel and Robert Shapiro at Columbia University Press for the confidence they showed the manuscript when others wavered. Joan McQuary's seasoned editorial advice helped me avoid some of the routine mistakes of a first-time writer. Sidney M. Milkis produced an extraordinarily thorough and meticulous reader's report on the manuscript, one that amazed the editors and kept the author busy for months. The end product has been immeasurably strengthened thanks to Sid's remarkable efforts.

No one labors on a project for over a decade without a personal-support network to make the professional commitments bearable. This book is dedicated to my parents and my wife, but I want also to thank my brother and sister—and their families—and my in-laws, the Hicks, for their patience as I devoted so much time away from other obligations. And my dear friends Mike Fowler and Julie Bunck know how indispensable they were as braces against all the vicissitudes of academic life in the 1990s.

To all these, and more, I offer heartfelt thanks.

THE PRESIDENCY
AND THE POLITICS OF
RACIAL INEQUALITY

In July 1987, *Time* magazine published a commemorative issue celebrating the bicentennial of the United States Constitution. Over sixty pages of text and pictures were devoted to the development of the Constitution and its place in American life, tracing the translation of the founders' words into a modern-day blueprint for republican governance.

The cover of that issue did not, as might have been expected, reproduce the familiar first page of the parchment document. In lieu of text—words of remarkable stability for over two hundred years—the editors substituted a collage of faces—a composite artistic portrait of "We the People," vividly attesting to what surely must be the most dramatic change in the nation's constitutional life during the past two centuries. That portrait—depicting Americans male, female, black, white, Asian, Latino, laborer, judge, minister, rabbi—powerfully demonstrated the social and economic diversity that 'We the People" have become. These the Constitution now embraces, securing the "Blessings of Liberty" to them and to their posterity.

The *Time* cover strikingly illustrates the scope of the Constitution in modern America. More importantly, however, it suggests what arguably is the central story line of American national development: the extension of the privileges and immunities of membership in the American nation to a people whose contemporary diversity was inconceivable in the late eighteenth century. Today, that which defines us as Americans[1] not only extends its protective reach to those unthought of by the framers, it embraces as well those the framers and their earliest successors purposely excluded from the full benefits of the original contract. Thus, the contemporary diversity of "We the People" emerged in ways at once consistent with and contrary to fundamental precepts embodied in the nation's charter.[2]

It is easy to identify the centrality to the nation's development of efforts to expand the horizons of American citizenship.[3] The quest for abolishing chattel slavery, terminating in civil war; the struggle for a more equitable distribution of political and economic resources for working men and new immigrants; the fight for equal rights for women; the crusade for civil rights for the descendants of freedmen and women—these clearly are defining episodes in American political development. Less clear, however, are the particular processes that resulted in changes in the polity in such instances, and the role certain individuals and institutions played in these processes. Perhaps even more obscure is how lessons of such episodes—what is collectively remembered or forgotten about them—are encoded into American political culture. These ambiguities are the motive force for the study that follows.

Arguably, the status of no single liminal[4] group has been as consequential for the nation's constitutional and political development as that of African Americans, witness one civil war and two constitutional reformations. Thus, this study focuses on the process of advancement toward first-class citizenship of this group.[5]

The central unit of analysis here, however, is one particular institution: the American presidency. This choice is not an arbitrary one. The presidency rests at the very center of American popular conceptions of the nation's movement toward political and social inclusion, especially in relation to the advancement of racial equality. For example, the story of emancipation without attention to the "Great Emancipator" seems at best half told. The same could be said of the successful advance of black civil rights and John Kennedy and Lyndon Johnson. These presidencies, and the place they now hold in the received culture, have created something of an air of primacy about the role of the presidency in extending equal citizenship to those previously excluded by law and custom. The conventional wisdom holds that major change in the nation's social structures or political regimes requires strong presidential direction.

Undoubtedly, there is something to this common perception. One as precise as Clinton Rossiter, in his now classic treatise *The American Presidency*, spoke of the "commanding position" the president maintains "in the ongoing struggle for [the extension of] civil liberties and civil rights." Indeed, he did provide evidence that supports popular conceptions of the president's centrality in this process. Yet Rossiter also conceded that his data were one-sided, presented, apparently, in exhortation for greater executive action on behalf of black Americans pushing that ongoing struggle as he wrote. By

Rossiter's own admission, then, a comprehensive picture of the presidency's role in extending the privileges and immunities of the Constitution may be more complex than the one he defined as "commanding," or what some might term simply "leading."[6] I contend that because of a now-longstanding inclination in American political culture to inflate presidential achievement, any claim for the centrality of the presidential institution in the production of change needs to be very carefully examined. There may be a cultural bias at work here that demands a high level of scrutiny in developing an accurate picture of what the presidency's role has been. The existence of a mythology—which arises in a political culture prone to attribute excessively all manner of good (and evil!) to the nation's presidents—should serve as a caution flag for those inclined to accept as a given presidential achievement where it is commonly taken for granted. The gravity of that mythology, to which I now turn, can unwittingly bend our conceptions of institutional performance and possibility.

The Monumental Presidency

Americans like to celebrate their presidency as a place of heroic achievement.[7] A people "dedicated to the proposition that all men are created equal" has proved itself remarkably adept at elevating selectively a few chosen figures above the status of citizen to that of demigod. Perhaps nowhere is this more in evidence than in the current arrangement of the nation's capital.

Originally, plans for the city of Washington reflected a scrupulous commitment to separated, equally independent political institutions, a notion at the very center of the Constitution that brought that city into being and gave it its purpose. Not one but two centers of activity were created by Washington's founders, in keeping with the national charter's premier operating principle that separated institutions provided the best guarantee against tyranny. Folkways of L'Enfant city reinforced the plan. Distinct legislative and executive villages sprang up within the Washington community, each meticulously jealous of its communal prerogatives and scrupulously guarded against overture or incursion from the other side. The symmetry of the city's map thus mirrored that of the nation's freshly minted political arrangements.[8]

But that symmetry, that balance between legislative and executive influences on Washington's landscape, is no more. The breadth and heights of the nation's capital now decidedly reflect a bias in favor of the executive.

Towering above the District's tidal basin flats, visible for miles as the capital's highest structure, is a granite and marble obelisk erected to the memory of George Washington, Father of His Country and her first president. The grounds spanning out from the base of the monument are generally free of obstructions, save for a ring of American flags, thus preserving space around as well as upward for Washington's memory. Not far off, directly away from the Capitol, rests the temple raised to honor the sixteenth president, Abraham Lincoln. And just across a tidal basin, at angles, sits the Jefferson Memorial.[9] Neither the tribute to Lincoln nor to Jefferson imposes itself on the skyline as does the Washington Monument, but, in a city where exponential growth has placed a premium on land values, the commitment of such spacious parkland to the memory of three figures remains remarkable. No comparable expressions of national gratitude exist in Washington for any who have served the country in the congressional branch of government alone, or for that matter for those who have provided exemplary service to the nation primarily through the courts, the military, or private professions.[10] Conspicuous by their absence are the likes of a Hamilton Monument or a Marshall Memorial on a scale matching the shrines to the first, third, and sixteenth presidents.[11]

The asymmetry of this devotion of public space is all the more notable when viewed in light of the original designs for the Mall area, where these presidential memorials now stand. Both of the primary, original plans for the city—one by Jefferson, the other by L'Enfant—included a large plaza connecting the gardens adjacent the President's Mansion with the Capitol. In the metaphoric scheme of the city as adopted, this plaza was analogous to the Constitution: the thoroughfare, opening to an expansive west, by which Americans could bring their petitions and grievances to a representative government, and an avenue, indirectly linking their separate villages, by which Congress and the president were to interact.[12]

The founding architects' metaphor suggests a unique alternative for mapping the course of the nation's political development. The earliest settlers of Washington struggled to carve a useful public space out of the forbidding Potomac wilderness, just as they labored to construct a working system of government from the tangled thickets of regional interests to be represented there. Later, troops bivouacked on the Mall during civil war, when the future of the Constitution itself resided in the tents of Union soldiers. Still later, in the Gilded Age, railroad tracks and boxcars traversed and cluttered the capital's central plaza, poignantly exposing to all those who controlled the switches of the nation's constitutional order.

Today, the landed representation of the Constitution no longer remains the equal dominion of two branches but is overwhelmed by the presence and memory of one. The presidency now transcends, unmistakably dominating the most recognizable public space in the country.[13] There is by no means an absence of democratic spirit on the Mall—lining both sides of the plaza are memorials to the American people, displaying their manifold artistic, technological, and social achievements. But the corridors of the Smithsonian rather meekly imitate in a thousand small ways monumental tributes to our presidential heroes. So eager, in fact, were Americans to raise an appropriate shrine to the memory of the Great Emancipator that they reclaimed a part of the tidal basin itself, lengthening the Mall to create space for Lincoln's memorial. A fitting monument indeed to a president who himself found it necessary to shape and extend the Constitution to meet the needs of the day.[14]

Americans may well be, as Clinton Rossiter has claimed, a nation of "constitution worshipers." But if the nation's temples can be taken as clues, its special brand of civil religion has its saints as well as its holy writ, and the worshipers seem to prefer personages to prose or impersonal institutional arrangements.[15] The Mall is not the only place where this is evident. Mt. Rushmore, carved out of the Black Hills of South Dakota, repeats the pattern nearly a continent away, in a fashion at least suggestive of the stone monuments keeping silent watch over Easter Island. Pilgrims flock to these hills just as they do to national sepulchres on the Potomac. Americans, it would seem, are also a nation of presidency worshipers.

Further evidence of a national inclination to elevate presidential heroes can be found by looking at the calendar. New Year's and Thanksgiving share billing among national days of commemoration with Presidents' Day, a joint remembrance of the birthdays of George Washington and Abraham Lincoln. The calendar also reflects decided democratic influences, including generic dedications to veterans, laborers, and, most recently, a tribute to the leader of the modern civil rights movement. Again, however, conspicuously absent are celebrations of the contributions of other prominent personages, especially those whose lives have been dedicated to public service in other national institutions.

The national tendency to extol presidential achievement extends as well to the coin of the realm, which remains the near-exclusive domain of the presidential countenance. Others have occasionally joined the roster of monetary honorees—Susan B. Anthony and Alexander Hamilton immediately come to mind—but this occurs notably not among the most widely circulated, thus most democratic, of American currency. Such memorials are age-old— "Render therefore unto Caesar the things which are Caesar's," Jesus taught after establishing whose image adorned the Roman penny—and are perhaps the most pervasive of the national tributes to the presidency. In a nation founded on political notions intended in part to avoid Caesarism, this practice merits special notice.

Most recently the tendency in Washington has been to establish so-called "functional" or "living" monuments to presidents, which memorialize their achievements while serving some useful public purpose. The John F. Kennedy Center for the Performing Arts and the James Madison Memorial Building of the Library of Congress are examples. Yet use of the term "functional" here is unfortunate. For clearly the shrines on the Mall, the national holidays, and the adornment of our coin and currency also were manifestly intended to serve a particular function: to hold up certain achievements as the zenith of public virtue.[16]

Thus, on public square, by public days, and on public tender—through devotions of public time and space—Americans honor presidents in ways and to degrees almost entirely denied other important actors and institutions in our national life.[17] It is this collectivity of commemoratives—and the popular perceptions it engenders—that I refer to here as the monumental presidency.[18]

Admittedly, the existence of this monumental presidency represents something of an anomaly in a political culture commonly given to the promotion of constitutional diffusion and the dispersion of political power. How, then, does this anomaly arise? In large part because monuments of stone and traditions of acclaim are enduring. Their accumulation tends to communicate lessons to posterity that may not have been originally intended. The creation of a triad of commemoratives around the Mall, for example, subtly alters what each individual monument alone might have signaled. Moreover, even absent the influence of complementarity, mute temples are imprecise conveyors of refined messages. Although George Washington's selflessness and Abraham Lincoln's humility may have been important considerations for those who moved to commemorate them, these personal attributes tend to be obscured rather than accentuated by the magnificence of marble memorials.[19] Indeed, there are certain identifiable patterns to what is and what is not commonly communicated about the practice of politics in America by these commemoratives. It is in this regard that the monumental presidency takes on its greatest significance for the current study.

The most obvious distortion by the monumental presidency is in its emphasis on the extraordinary. In some respects this is intentional, inasmuch as those who erect memorials to heroic figures such as Jefferson and Lincoln thereby mean to emphasize the *possibilities* of achievement by leadership figures. However, prospects for adverse comparison abound when Americans are conditioned, to whatever extent, to use the standards of the extraordinary as yardsticks by which to measure contemporary public servants. This may unintentionally undermine popular confidence in an institution incapable of routinizing the extraordinary.

More subtle (but equally powerful) is the distorting effect inherent in crediting to a single actor outcomes that were in actuality the product of a complex interaction of multiple actors.[20] A great virtue of attributing such occurrences to one individual is that it simplifies complicated events and facilitates the emergence of coherent historical narratives and lessons. Lost in such accounts, however, is a complex of nuances. The inclination to attribute to a single figure the preponderance of responsibility for the birth of a nation ("Father of His Country") or its decision to end ownership in humanity ("The Great Emancipator") obscures the contributions of other actors, whose roles may have been less prominent yet no less instrumental. Our popular portraits, then, tend not just to rely too heavily on instances of the extraordinary, but to overstate as well the degree to which those extraordinary presidents controlled their own destinies and the destiny of the nation. The overall effect of such distortions is a retrospective overstatement of presidential responsibility for the great success stories of American political development.[21] Consequently, the stories of those forces, people, and processes acting *on* presidents are often forgotten. Their recovery and elevation to equal standing may reveal significant lessons about the functioning of the American political system, lessons at odds with those typically derived from accounts stressing presidential performance. Such is the case with the long story of movement toward equal citizenship by African Americans.

Subject, Scope, and Method

This book is constructed on three working propositions. The first is that the conventional wisdom about presidential behavior in relation to racial advancement is dominated by the records and collective memory of three chief executives: Abraham Lincoln, John Kennedy, and Lyndon Johnson.[22]

These are the monumental presidents of what Kennedy called "the sustained struggle" for black equality in America.[23] The second proposition is that the prominence of these three figures produces a caricatured portrait of the institution, one exaggerating features commonly associated with leadership and positive change. The third and final proposition is that a faithful rendering of the institution requires drawing on details from a much larger pool of presidents than just these three. The following work is largely devoted to that task.

Justification for that broader examination comes from one simple piece of evidence: as Kennedy pronounced, the conflict he addressed had been a "*sustained* struggle," one waged for at least thirteen decades at the time he spoke. The politics of racial inequality—which confronted Kennedy in the form of one of the largest mass movements in American history—had been an active concern of his predecessors in the White House going back to the days of Andrew Jackson. From 1831 through the 1960s, in one form or another, with brief periods of quiescence, those disenchanted with the state of American race relations had organized for purposes of pushing their grievances onto the nation's political agenda. In so doing, they persistently threatened the stability of the American polity with demands for change in the nation's social, economic, and political structures. Accordingly, presidential intervention is not so much a part of this story because of a sudden moral epiphany by a few celebrated occupants of the White House, but because a long train of successive presidents was forced into the fray by social and political agitators. It is the relationship of these action-forcing activists to an enduring presidential institution—and the efforts of each side to shape the position and power resources of the other—that is central here.[24] As we will see, it is erroneous to assume that when the presidency was not heroically engaged in advancing racial equality, it was merely a benignly neglectful institution.

Although there now exists a large literature on social movements in general, and movements for black equality in particular, little comprehensive work has been done examining the presidential institution in relation to them.[25] The literature that does exist, and on which I rely heavily here, comes in three main forms.

First, presidential biographies commonly explore the many sources of domestic pressure operating on individual presidents, and, as such, racial tension is often included. Such studies are instructive, but they are of limited usefulness here, because their authors do not usually attempt to deal with the institution beyond the confines of the single president being examined.[26]

Second, some case studies of individual presidents and the movements they confronted exist, several of which have an analytic and institutional component.[27] However, these, too, have their shortcomings. In a seminal piece on the presidency and social movements published in 1981, Bruce Miroff, who focused solely on the relationship of the Johnson White House to the civil rights movement, acknowledged the limitations of such a restricted project. "A single case study cannot, of course, produce definitive generalizations. Its findings must be tested in analogous cases before generalized relationships can be confidently asserted."[28] My study is intended to fill that usual deficiency by looking at "analogous cases." I expand the relevant empirical sample by devoting substantial attention to multiple presidencies across a wide span of American history.[29] My understanding of the presidential relationship to abolitionism, for example, is not bound by Lincoln's presidency, but derives from extensive researches of the presidential institution from Jackson's first term—when abolitionism initially emerged as a national political concern—to the time of constitutional emancipation. Quadrennium-bound case studies are useful for laying groundwork, but broader conceptual models require putting chains of these together in an interpretive framework.

Third, there are a few works on the presidency and civil rights that do span the labors of several administrations, and thus that provide a broader analysis than the more time-bound case studies.[30] Yet these, too, commonly have limitations. The existing works usually focus on the so-called "modern presidency," the institution as it emerged in the wake of the New Deal. In trying to develop a comprehensive understanding of presidential role, I have looked also to the history of the presidential institution antecedent to Franklin Roosevelt.[31]

Although this approach remains somewhat unconventional for contemporary political science, a growing body of literature is emerging promoting the usefulness of historical approaches to the study of modern institutions. James W. Ceaser; Aaron Wildavsky and Richard Ellis; Jeffrey K. Tulis; Stephen Skowronek; and Sidney M. Milkis and Michael Nelson, among others,[32] provide theoretical justification for moving into the past to advance understanding of the presidency, "reclaiming history from the historians," as Ellis puts it. In social science terms, the object of these exercises is to increase the relevant "N," to overcome the severe handicap of idiosyncrasy presidential scholarship faces in relying on a population of eleven "modern" presidents to form institutional generalizations.[33]

However, theoretical justification remains merely a starting point. The success or failure of individual research projects rests primarily on the validity of specific comparisons of the past to the present, not on abstract generalizations. Informed judges will know if the history summoned is usefully or spuriously appropriated. In the final analysis, historic comparison must be an inductive process, measuring particulars against particulars. If done well, historic likenesses can reveal new lessons, and relevant historic differences can provide a critical vantage point for seeing our polity in a new light.[34] But as to success or failure, the devil is in the details.

The central finding of this study is that the presidency has routinely served as a *nation-maintaining* institution on the issue of racial inequality. Indeed, the evidence arrayed here strongly suggests that one of the enduring roles each president is required to execute is that of nation-keeper, a protector of the inherited political and social order and a preserver of domestic tranquillity.[35] There is, it should be noted at the outset, a duality to this role. It most commonly promotes presidential behavior intended to ward off or to moderate significant social change as a threat to the preferred status of the polity's prevailing interests. Yet nation-keeping presidents may also find, in some uncommon instances, that profound change is a prerequisite of preservation. As we shall see, an unusual confluence of events can lead to presidents becoming active advocates of significant change. Most conventional portraits of the presidency, especially those with monumental inclinations, all but ignore that first dimension, and tend to understate the conditionality of the second.

The nation-keeping role is only one of many the president fills, one whose salience varies over time. As one in a multiplicity of roles, it may or may not be the most prominently displayed at a given moment. Yet it is at the very core of presidential function in the American polity. Further, on the question of African-American equality, it has held a dominant position.

This role is not explicitly provided for in the Constitution.[36] But it is visible there as a constellation, appearing in outline through a connecting of the president's formally designated powers as commander-in-chief, the obligation to "take care that the laws be faithfully executed," and, perhaps most importantly, the sworn oath—unique to the president— "to preserve, protect, and defend the Constitution of the United States."[37] Moreover, careful examination of three categories of contextual evidence taken from the early American republic—relating to (1) the forces that brought the Constitution's framers together in the first place; (2) the authoritative claims of Publius in *The Federalist*; and (3) the behavior of the early governing community—further illuminate the subtle contours of that constellation, clearly highlighting the centrality of the institution's nation-keeping role at its very origins.

Nation-Keeping and the Constitutional Convention

The nation-keeping mission of Philadelphia's constitutional convention was plainly expressed in the framers' proclaimed intent to "form a more perfect Union." That assembly took extraordinary action to scrap the prevailing instruments of governance in favor of forms more conducive to defending the most basic political, economic, and social structures of the young nation from a host of external and internal threats. No development in Philadelphia was more significant in this nation-keeping effort than the crafting of a relatively strong, independent, unitary presidency to replace the discredited executive-by-consensus of the Articles of Confederation. An enfeebled and incompetent plural executive—a miniature legislature in the worst sense of that phrase—had left the young nation fatally vulnerable, many of the framers believed, to the continuing depredations of transatlantic powers intent on carving up North America for their own gain. A viable presidency promised to improve dramatically the nation's ability to deal with foreign affairs trouble, allowing it better to ward off the emergence of problems with nation-threatening dimensions.[38] The subsequent rise of the presidency as *the* dominant actor in American foreign policy merely reveals more clearly the nation-keeping responsibilities with respect to foreign threats which are visible in embryo in 1787.

The framers also recognized as a part of their mission, however, the crafting of a response to *domestic* disorder, a point best illustrated by the importance of Shays's Rebellion as a motive force for those who gathered in Philadelphia.[39] "Almost every important American leader," wrote Washington biographer James Thomas Flexner, "viewed Shays's Rebellion with extreme alarm."[40] That alarm, over efforts among debtors in western Massachusetts to alter fundamentally the prevailing conventions of economic life, largely explains why the feeble efforts at reforming the national government in Annapolis in 1786 grew to government-shattering proportions only one year later. Indeed, it is not unreasonable to claim that the Philadelphia convention would have failed had it not been for fears, of those like Washington himself, that the continuation of a weak central government threatened the nation's economic and social equilibrium. "What stronger evidence can be given," Washington asked James Madison, "of the want of energy in our governments than these disorders?"[41] Accordingly, the government framed in Philadelphia was one established largely to empower the governors to preserve the prevailing order against those who would undermine it from without *and* within, significantly through the presence of an empowered presidency.

Nation-Keeping and *The Federalist Papers*

These fundamental purposes, especially on the domestic side, are displayed and refined in a second contextual source, *The Federalist*. In those pages, Publius repeatedly asserted to his New York readership the superiority of the new-modeled Constitution for "the suppression of disturbances."[42] However, there is within *The Federalist* something of a schizophrenia about the precise way in which the national government would work toward this end. Unsurprisingly, two distinctive, if complementary, arguments emerge, one associated with each of Publius's two most prominent faces: James Madison and Alexander Hamilton.

The Madisonian argument appears most extensively in Nos. 10 and 51, and relates to Madison's claims about the value of an extended republic. This is an argument about benign structural barriers to collective action. In now-celebrated passages from No. 10, Madison maintained,

> Extend the sphere and you take in a greater variety of parties and interests; you make it less probable that a majority of the whole will have a common motive to invade the rights of other citizens; or if such a common motive exists, it will be more difficult for all who feel it to discover their own strength and to act in unison with each other. . . .
>
> The influence of factious leaders may kindle a flame within their particular States but will be unable to spread a general conflagration through the other States.[43]

The essence of Madison's case was that the very existence of the extended republic made it highly unlikely that those with factious intent would be able to muster sufficient power to threaten the nation's order. These protections were a felicitous product of size and diversity.

The Hamiltonian argument, however, is the more relevant here. The "preservation of the public peace," as Hamilton described it, arose less from the passive blessings of diversity than from the existence of an active, powerful and vigilant central government.[44] "A *firm* Union," he claimed at the beginning of No. 9, "will be of the utmost moment to the peace and liberty of the States as a barrier against domestic faction and insurrection." Hamilton's view was that the security of the nation against internal agitation was a function of purposive barriers to collective action, to be erected by those who control the nation's common forces. The new government, it was argued, would be vastly superior in this respect to its predecessor under the Articles of Confederation, which nearly disintegrated because of the stress brought by Shays's rebels and their like elsewhere.

What remains to be established is the place of the *presidency* in this general scheme, in the overall framework by which the Constitution was to achieve its first object, "the preservation of peace and tranquillity."[45] That the national government was empowered to respond vigorously to internal convulsions does not *necessarily* mean that the president was expected to be the central force for preserving the peace, and for guarding the sanctity of those inherited social structures on which peace depended. Yet the weight of the evidence indicates that this was indeed the case.[46]

In *Federalist* No. 8, Hamilton described the conditions under which armies "may *usefully aid the [executive] magistrate* to suppress a small faction, or an occasional mob, or insurrection" (emphasis added). He picked up the point again in No. 70.

> [Energy in the executive] is essential to the protection of the community against foreign attacks; it is not less essential to the steady administration of the laws; to the protection of property against those irregular and high-handed combinations which sometimes interrupt the ordinary course of justice; to the security of liberty against the enterprises and assaults of ambition, of faction, and of anarchy.

Finally, in No. 74 he explained why the constitutional convention took the unusual step of investing in the president special authority against the offense of treason.

> The principal argument for reposing the power of pardon in this case in the Chief Magistrate is this: in seasons of insurrections or rebellion, there are often critical moments when a well-timed offer of pardon to the insurgents or rebels may restore the tranquillity of the commonwealth. . . . The dilatory process of convening the legislature or one of its branches, for the purpose of obtaining its sanction to the measure, would frequently be the occasion of letting slip the golden opportunity.

There is an important inference here—to be discussed again shortly—of preemptive action, of grants of presidential authority to take advantage of "the golden opportunity" before a situation deteriorates into the kind of violent encounter that would, as a matter of course, precipitate military intervention under the commander-in-chief's direction. Energy—and dispatch—in the executive thus makes of it the superior instrument for dealing with those who directly threaten the nation's repose.[47]

It should be noted, however, that the existence of one related constitutional provision appears to contradict the interpretation offered here. For Article I, Section 8, provides that "*Congress* shall have Power ... To provide for calling forth the Militia to execute the Laws of the Union [and] to suppress Insurrections." This seems to undermine claims for the president's possession of nation-maintaining responsibilities, or at least for an exclusive or predominating executive role. Yet close inspection of a third, and final, category of contextual evidence reveals that consideration of this clause can actually buttress claims for the president's nation-keeping obligations. This evidence is found in the behavior of those who first gave life to the Constitution's provisions, those who made the new government a working reality.

Nation-Keeping and the Early Government

The best place to examine the early governors' behavior is in the years 1791 to 1794, when they had an opportunity to try out their constitutional designs in the case of the Whiskey Rebellion. How they responded to that challenge reveals much about their conceptions of institutional roles in the new republic.

THE WHISKEY REBELLION

President Washington was the government's leading actor in suppressing the rebellion of those in western Pennsylvania defying a new federal excise tax on whiskey. He used his powers as chief legislator successfully in recommending, and having enacted, modifications in the original tax act, so as to appease many of the more-moderate tax rebels. He intervened in the judicial process on at least one occasion to stop prosecution of alleged rioters, probably in part to maintain goodwill toward the national government in that locality.[48] He designated a panel of emissaries to go into the troubled region to bargain with the rebels, and even authorized the panel to waive payment of past taxes "if they could thereby secure compliance for the current year."[49]

He also sought to bring the force of his personal popularity—and the considerable weight of his presidential authority—to bear on the rebels by issuing strongly worded presidential proclamations, to "earnestly admonish and exhort all persons . . . to refrain and desist from unlawful combinations . . . tending to obstruct the operations of the laws."[50] Finally, he mounted a horse and rode westward for a time to direct personally the advances of the government force. This assured both that the campaign would be led by the nation's most proven warrior, and that rebels and onlookers alike would see unmistakably that no effort would be spared in enforcing federal law. This was a matter of the utmost moment, meriting what Washington reported to Congress as a "special interposition on my part."[51] In the end, the extraordinary display of force and authority pacified the rebels in a virtually skirmish-free campaign.[52]

During the course of the rebellion, Congress enacted two laws of special note for this discussion, both related to the powers granted Congress under Article I, Section 8, described above. Effectively these two acts, one in 1792, the other in 1795, transferred the power for "calling forth" the militia to the president.[53] In the former act, the president was empowered to issue a call for the militia "whenever the laws of the United States shall be opposed, or the execution thereof obstructed, in any State, by combinations too powerful to be suppressed by the ordinary course of judicial proceedings, or by the power vested in the marshals." The president could call forth militia aid after due notification of such conditions, notice issuing from either a district judge of the United States or an associate justice of the Supreme Court. Any troops so called could be legally deployed up to thirty days into the next congressional session.

The act of 1795—a revision to account for what the governors were learning about how best to respond to defiant dissent—contained a signal modification. It eliminated completely the requirement for judicial notice, making the president, according to a subsequent Supreme Court ruling, "the sole and exclusive judge" of the circumstances under which powers for suppressing insurrection could be exercised.[54] This is a highly revealing development, for it might otherwise be claimed, based solely on the language of the Constitution, that the president's duties with respect to managing internal agitation were derivative: restricted to directing military force only after such force was called into service by others. But Washington's behavior in the case of the Whiskey Rebellion, and the related deferential action by Congress and the United States Supreme Court, clearly indicate otherwise. Their collective response to internal agitation both affirmed the president's supremacy in the exercise of the government's highest power—its ability to coerce consent by use of military force—and indicated that that ultimate power encompassed as well within presidential discretion an almost unlimited range of lesser actions to respond to symptoms of disorder in the body politic.

In the final analysis, then, the experience of the Whiskey Rebellion was to clarify—both in law and practice—the nature of the president's nation-maintaining role, adding definition to the otherwise faint silhouette of the executive's constitutional responsibilities. Not alone were presidents needed to direct the militia, they were also expected, in the way of Washington, to use the sum of their lesser powers preemptively, to orchestrate public and private efforts to forestall insurrection. They were expected to use the wide latitude granted them by court and custom to be crisis preventers, to seek and to find the "golden opportunity" to avoid escalating internal conflict, perhaps using modest concessions to ward off more fundamental change.[55] (And, perhaps, by extension, to promote momentous change if the life of the nation depended on it.) Early intervention for purposes of preventive maintenance—just as an ultimate resort to the organized violence of the state when troubleshooting failed—was deemed a presidential responsibility, effectively defining a large part of the nation-keeping role. The experience of the Whiskey Rebellion, then, had confirmed that activist, Hamiltonian, *executive*-based defenses against internal agitation were essential for supplying deficiencies in Madison's extended republic.

THE ALIEN AND SEDITION ACTS, 1798

A final episode from this early period further confirms the early governors' reliance on the presidency as a nation-keeping institution, and reveals once again a connection between the foreign and domestic aspects of that role. This is the passage of the Alien and Sedition Acts in 1798, intended to protect the nation from what lawmakers perceived as a French-directed conspiracy aimed at splitting the country apart. The Alien Act granted the president extraordinarily wide discretion to monitor the behavior of resident aliens and to deport those suspected by the president of subversive behavior. The Sedition Act criminalized criticism of the government, even by U.S. citizens. Although its execution was left to the judiciary, it is noteworthy that the prosecutions pursued under color of the Sedition Act focused on attacks on the president, John Adams.

The adoption of these two acts serve as acknowledgment by those directing the councils of state that the presidency was the institution best suited for dealing with threats to the prevailing order, and thus that it needed both special powers and special protections. That Adams deported no one, and that the Jeffersonians rose to power on the strength of a popular backlash to the overreaching of the Federalists—subsequently undoing the most egregious violations of civil liberties under the Sedition Act (which, not coincidentally, had been directed at among their number)—indicates the existence of outer limits to the exercise of the nation-keeping role. However, that backlash should not obscure the fact that the enactment of these two statutes continued trends in presidential empowerment for nation-keeping purposes dating back at least to the summer of 1787.[56]

The relevance of this accumulated contextual evidence for the present project becomes clear by recognizing the longstanding, exceptional sensitivity—and explosiveness—of black-white relations in American society. Domestic tranquillity has been an especially fragile commodity on the dimension of color, with even hints of intended variance in established patterns of interaction often sufficient to register as a subversive act.[57] Accordingly, the threshold for upsetting the majority's sensibilities has been—on this issue—more easily crossed than on many others, tripping the alarm wire that sets into motion presidential reaction. This sensitivity on the question of race should come as small surprise in a nation that long countenanced the presence of a single drop of "colored" blood as sufficient to render an individual undeserving of the full privileges and immunities of American citizenship.

The potency and persistence of the nation-keeping role on this issue becomes readily evident when one examines presidential behavior over the extended sweep of American history. This study covers a span of time during which twenty-nine individuals served as chief executive. The range of personal interests, psychological traits, and philosophies, of partisan commitments, of program initiatives, and of political contingencies characterizing that broad span was immense. So, too, was the basic power position of the president. Yet on the question of greater inclusion for African Americans the response from the White House was almost uniform: the conservation of inherited structures of American race relations. Each of the incumbents described in this account certainly had the human freedom to act otherwise, to stake out an advanced position on the question of racial inequality. There were other *individuals* who actively did just that. But, the incentive structures governing activity in the presidential office—those formal ones embedded in the Constitution itself (related to elections and the sharing of political power) and those informal ones shaped by a political culture with a deep strain of racial prejudice—fostered a very different kind of behavior in the White House. These incentive structures made it extremely unlikely that someone fervently committed to racial equality would rise through the popularly based electoral process to the presidency in the first place, or that, once there, he or she would feel free (or compelled) to invest presidential power in that controversial enterprise. The American political culture did not positively sanction that kind of behavior in the presidency. It had a different role.

Instead, electoral forces and the politics of separated institutions, which give life to the nation-maintaining role, long constrained presidents as protectors of the prevailing order to oppose those who would organize threats to conventions that advantaged the white majority, and which that majority accepted as legitimate. The key point here is that the nation's white majority found it beneficial throughout most of the span of American history to keep a minority black population subjugated. Whites benefited economically and socially from this arrangement. Small wonder, then, that they wished to maintain it, and charged certain of their elected officials with exercising the coercive authority of the state and the informal power of the civil religion to that end. The evidence clearly shows that presidents often aggressively and creatively used their power in these pursuits, suppressing collective action by manipulating a variety of political resources to disadvantage those who promoted racial change.

It is from this kind of evidence—customary efforts to preserve and perpetuate the inherited constitutional order and its prevailing biases—that the change-resistant face of the nation-keeping institution emerges, the face that has tended to predominate on the question of race. This evidence further suggests that the president's oath of office— "I will to the best of my Ability, preserve, protect, and defend the Constitution of the United States"—is merely a legalistic manifestation of a broader duty imposed on the president by American political culture. Not only is a president called on to perpetuate the formal structures and processes provided for in the Constitution, he or she is also charged with defending the social and cultural institutions upon which the superstructure of that Constitution rests. Simply put, each president is expected not just to preserve the United States Constitution (large "C"), but America's constitution (small "c").[58]

Of course, a few presidents were instrumental in making significant changes in the national structures they inherited. What Lincoln, Kennedy, Johnson, and others, to a lesser extent, did cannot be ignored. Yet their embrace and promotion of racial change was perfectly consistent with the demands of the nation-keeping role. By the time these presidents invested their powers in the advancement of black equality, however, the second face of that role had become ascendant. In each instance, these pro-change presidents came to see that the only way for them to preserve the peace and security of the nation, at a time of great political instability, was to consent to demands for changes in the social and political structures that they and their predecessors had earlier worked to preserve.[59]

This reorientation of the nation-keeping role was occasioned in each instance largely by the success of racial activists in mobilizing mass support. As long as those efforts to mobilize had remained largely ineffectual— because of inherent or imposed constraints[60]—presidents had every reason *not* to cede ground on racial concerns; to have done otherwise would have courted repudiation, perhaps riot. However, when demographic and political conditions ripened so as to make extensive mobilization possible, the disruptive force of mass movements created powerful incentives for presidents to revisit the logic of the nation-maintaining role. To have done otherwise under these new conditions would have cultivated a continuing threat to the strained fabric of the American polity. Political signals issuing from the electoral environment and the policy-making environment communicated as much to these presidents. At bottom, on the question of African-American rights, the presidency became an agency of change only when movements for equality had successfully reoriented the incumbent's perception of those role requirements, by preparing public opinion and illuminating the risks of tolerating inequality in periods of heightened danger to the nation's peace and security. "The biggest danger to American stability," observed Lyndon Johnson, reflecting on his White House years, "is the politics of principle, which brings out the masses . . . , for once the masses begin to move, then the whole thing begins to explode. Thus it is for the sake of nothing less than stability that I consider myself a consensus man."[61] Only when "the whole thing" began to "explode" did Johnson (and those like him) reluctantly depart from the policy paths his predecessors had followed to help direct a constitutional reformation in service of "nothing less than stability."

This portrait of the presidency not only looks very different from the monumental one sketched above, it also sharply contrasts with the one detailed in

Stephen Skowronek's highly awarded interpretation of presidential history, *The Politics Presidents Make*.[62] Skowronek has characterized the presidency as "a prominent institution intimately and regularly engaged in changing things, one whose routine operation involves efforts to *reorder* things."[63] It is a "blunt, disruptive force," "*a governing institution inherently hostile to inherited governing arrangements*." The basic "institutional logic" of the presidency—shaping how presidents make their marks or fashion their legacies—impels them to do what they can to make anew the landscape they inherit, "shattering the received order." This is the *routine* of presidential life as Skowronek sees it.[64]

On the face of it, one would be hard pressed to imagine an institutional description more directly at odds with the one advanced in the present work. However, it is possible to reconcile partially the two portraits, despite the real differences remaining in our respective interpretations.

A complementarity can be detected by highlighting the fact that Skowronek takes as his subject the *politics* presidents make. His theory is generally constructed around presidential disruption of *political* institutions and practices, or "inherited governing arrangements" and "recast political possibilities." These are the realms of routine presidential change. My subject is something else, something deeper or more fundamental. This is the character of the *social* structures, broadly defined, upon which the superstructure of political institutions and practices are built. Included therein is the fundamental status of American race relations.

What is important to note here is that these deeper social structures are relatively impervious to the kinds of disruptions that may well be routine in more conventionally political arenas. Thus, political disruption at the level Skowronek describes cannot be equated with disorder of a more fundamental nature, that is, disruption in the nation's fundamental social, economic, and political structures.[65] Institutional disruption, that which Skowronek *has* identified as a routine of presidential behavior, usually proceeds without any commensurate disruption in the underlying structures upon which politics take place. The former is akin to weather, the latter to tectonics. The underlying social structures of the American nation—including its basic membership configurations—have proved to be remarkably resilient in the face of the politics presidents make.

Indeed, it should be noted here that *political* disruption often is pursued in service of *preserving* the fundamental status quo, a paradox best illustrated by a president Skowronek chooses to uphold as an exemplar of his theory.

Franklin Pierce, according to Skowronek, effectively "wrecked his presidency and sparked a revolution," because the order-shattering imperatives of his office compelled him to embrace the Kansas-Nebraska Act, a repudiation of the time-hallowed Missouri Compromise.[66] The disruptive influence of that decision on the politics of the day is easily seen: it ushered in civil war. However, as I argue later in this work, Pierce's decision, at its most fundamental level, was made in service of preservative, not disruptive, ends: the protection of slavery and existing North-South relations within the Union. I agree that Pierce's presidency serves as a metaphor for a larger class of presidential behavior; I disagree with Skowronek about what that behavior is.[67]

It is undeniably true that certain presidents do find the "institutional logic" of the office driving them ineluctably toward significant social change. Indeed the emergence of that logic, and its power on certain incumbents (moving them from one conception of the nation-keeping role to another), is a key part of the analysis that follows. But its development is anything but routine. The details of this study, to which we now turn, indicate how *rare* it is for a president to be directed by the American people, and to be empowered by them, to use presidential authority in ways that are fundamentally disruptive of the nation's established political, social, or economic practices. What subsequently emerges is a study in which the politics presidents make are routinely overwhelmed by the politics that make them.

PART 1

Abolition

CHAPTER 1

The Origins and Politics of Abolition

During the winter of 1820, Thomas Jefferson, then retired to the distant comforts of Monticello, anxiously watched as a nation founded largely on his democratic architecture wrestled with the disposition of slavery in the Missouri Territory. For a time it appeared that America would be sundered north from south as Jefferson's Republican children and grandchildren quarreled among themselves and with remnant Federalists over the fate of a "peculiar institution." That furor eventually dissipated in compromise, but not before deeply shaking Jefferson's confidence in the American experiment. He peered beyond the short-term settlement to omens of an intractable problem, and fearfully acknowledged, "[W]e have the wolf by the ears, and we can neither hold him, nor safely let him go."[1]

For over forty years after Jefferson wrote that sentence, his successors in the Executive Mansion found it the safer of the two options to hold the wolf, to sustain the institution of slavery, rather than to work actively toward the day of freedom. Abraham Lincoln eventually reversed that course, but only after repeated efforts to avoid emancipation, and only when the dictates of civil war confirmed for him that liberation was essential for the nation to endure.

Although before Lincoln's presidency emancipation had remained inconceivable to most Americans, the issue of slavery had been far from dead between the time of Jefferson and the Civil War. During that interval an organized movement of antislavery agitators arose—led by abolitionist publishers, lecturers and, eventually, politicians—pressing demands for liberation on a reluctant nation. With only minor exceptions they toiled without success, finding those in authority repelling their demands and conspiring to put an end to the agitation. Thus, when Lincoln eventually decided to array the vast powers of his war-enlarged presidency in favor of emancipation, he was not only conveying freedom to the slaves, he was also conceding political legitimacy to those who had worked for so long toward that end.

What follows is an examination of the sustained struggle for liberation that terminated with the civil war amendments to the Constitution. Much of the antebellum era was marked by passionate agitation, fervent reaction, and calculating adjustment, of which the war can be seen as merely an extension and culmination, the concluding act in an extended drama. The purpose of this part of the book is to treat the antislavery movement in its entirety as a single challenge to the nation's prevailing membership structures, and, more directly, to illuminate the presidential role in that episode. The specific purpose of this chapter is to explain in some detail *the nature of the threat* that a succession of presidents, beginning with Andrew Jackson, confronted.[2]

This was no ordinary political problem. It occurred along the deepest fault line in American politics, one whose fragility had been revealed as early as the constitutional convention in 1787 and as recently as the Missouri Compromise crisis. Moreover, it was being aggravated by a new and unusually menacing presence: a lot of uncompromising zealots with a flair for publicity and an evident capacity for attracting followers and sparking trouble. To understand fully why presidents of that day responded as they did—which is the subject of the succeeding two chapters—it is necessary to understand something of the ways and means of these agitators, and the popular reaction to them. This better enables us to view the divisive politics of emancipation "from over the President's shoulder," to see better why Lincoln's predecessors (and Lincoln himself, for a while) acted as they did to avoid the designation "Emancipator."[3]

Origins of a Movement: William Lloyd Garrison

I date the beginning of an *enduring* effort for the emancipation of the slaves to January 1, 1831. On that day, William Lloyd Garrison published in Boston the first issue of what was to become the most celebrated and reviled of antislavery periodicals, *The Liberator*.[4]

This event hardly merited special notice at the time, as both the message and the prophet were familiar to attentive New Englanders. The northeastern states had long since moved to rid themselves of chattelism, and small groups of Quakers and other religious bodies persisted in trying to generate enthusiasm for an assault on southern slavery.[5] Moreover, some small antislavery periodicals had occasionally arisen for the same purpose, yet none of these flourished.[6]

There probably was little reason to believe that Garrison's project would turn out any differently. He had already achieved a measure of ill-repute as something of a political crank, straining the patience of his fellow citizens in Baltimore and New England with short-lived publications railing against slavery and intemperance.[7] However, where other enterprises faltered, *The Liberator* did not. Either because of improved personal skill as a provocateur or because of good timing, Garrison emerged as an unparalleled force in generating pressure for antislavery reform. *The Liberator*'s publication endured through thick times and thin on a weekly basis from 1831 to 1865, establishing the newspaper and its editor as central to an unfolding debate over slavery in the United States spanning four decades.[8]

A careful examination of Garrison's writings and speeches reveals a more sophisticated political intellect than is conventionally accorded one whose name became "a grotesque of abolition fanaticism."[9] *The Liberator* was crafted in the pursuit of *three* specific aims, all with important consequences for how antislavery activism emerged as a nationally significant social and political force.[10]

The *first* aim was an assertion of unconditional, immediate emancipation as the only moral course for those who shared an aversion to slavery. *The Liberator* thus was presented as the gospel of a crusade, whose first purpose was establishing the tenets of the one true faith. Garrison's opening salvo in the paper's maiden issue made this abundantly clear.

> I *will be* as harsh as truth, and as uncompromising as justice. On this sub-ject [slavery] I do not wish to think, or speak, or write, with moderation. No! no! Tell a man whose house is on fire to give a moderate alarm; tell him to moderately rescue his wife from the hands of the ravisher; tell the mother to gradually extricate her babe from the fire into which it has fallen;—but urge me not to use moderation in a cause like the present. I am in earnest—I will not equivocate—I will not excuse—I will not retreat a single inch—AND I WILL BE HEARD.[11]

In effect, Garrison attempted to set the terms of debate by impugning the motives and means of those who sought more moderate avenues for dealing with the problem of slavery in the United States. Accordingly, he devoted great attention in his earliest issues to condemning heresy, i.e., those other major arguments then current for how slavery in America might be brought to an end—through gradualism, or compensation and colonization.

For those who counseled patience in awaiting a gradual evolution away from slavery—through economic advancement or gradual human improvement—Garrison offered only contempt. The evils of human bondage, he claimed, should not be allowed to remain in existence even one day longer in expectation of a painless course to freedom never to come. He harshly questioned the sincerity of those who repeatedly found excuses for not working for emancipation immediately.

He held an equally dim view of those who believed slavery would pass away only through the mitigating effects of compensation or colonization.[12] Financial recompense to slave owners for property lost under schemes of emancipation struck many northerners as a reasonable method of convincing slaveholders to give up their recognized property. Garrison vehemently rejected that option as both impractical and immoral. The costs would be astronomical, and compensation implied acknowledgment of human property as legitimate. Yet it was the idea of colonization—the shipping of slaves back to Africa or to Central America—that provided Garrison and those who followed him with perhaps their most difficult challenge.

Colonization appealed to an exceptionally wide audience, as it combined the moral strength of the antislavery argument with the baser power of social prejudice among whites who did not wish to share their free communities with blacks of equal standing. These forces took on an institutional manifestation with the emergence of an American Colonization Society, which, one later analyst noted, could boast the support of "just about every American political hero from 1790 to 1860."[13] During the earliest years of *The Liberator*'s existence, then, overwhelming space was devoted to criticizing the premises of colonization and to denying any sense of legitimacy to a half-measure that diverted energy away from the one true faith.[14]

The Liberator's contributing authors sought to undermine any latent sympathies toward the notion of colonizing freed slaves by claiming that such a course was at a minimum unfair, and at bottom immoral. Although slaves were brought into this country against their volition, the United States, it was argued, had subsequently become the homeland to hundreds of thousands who had been born here and knew no other country. In his presidential address at the inaugural meeting of the New England Anti-Slavery Society in January 1832, Arnold Buffum fluently articulated the Garrisonian sentiment toward the freedman: "He is, indeed, as really an American as any of us. This is his *native land*. It is the soil which has been sprinkled with his own blood, and which he has literally earned, perhaps a thousand times over, 'by the sweat of his brow.' To deprive him of this possession, is to deprive him of his *birth-right.*"[15] This charge was at the root of Garrison's aversion to the colonizationists, and its explication was a principal aim of his editorial labors.

Added to Garrison's intention to claim the moral high ground for immediate, unconditional emancipation was a *second* purpose for *The Liberator*: proselytizing. *The Liberator* was intended both to raise the level of awareness about the evils of slavery among its northern readership, and to assert northern complicity in sustaining the South's sinful behavior. Each week the paper reported accounts of the extent and brutality of slavery.[16] Often taken from southern periodicals—reviewing in graphic detail stories of retributive whippings, lynchings, and the physical inspection of female slaves in open markets—these accounts were reprinted as a means of awakening within Garrison's readers that same anguish which fueled his own passion to "be heard."

He did not, however, simply wish to stun his readers with tales of inhumanity. Garrison also sought to convey to his fellow northerners a sense of personal responsibility for those wrongs. In a piece penned in July of 1831 entitled "What Shall Be Done," written to answer inquiries about how those in the free states might act to bring about emancipation, he advised, "First of all, I want every man and every woman to discard their criminal prejudices, their timorous fears, and their paralyzing doubts. . . . The work of reform must commence with *ourselves.*"[17] Responsibility existed in a negative sense—because northerners *could* take morally derived action against slavery regardless of the limited extent of its immediate effectiveness, they were responsible to the degree they did not do so. As one abolitionist writer postulated: "[T]he people of the free states are morally responsible for the continuance of slavery, on account of the ten thousand channels of influence through which they may affect it."[18] "Every day we consent to live under a government which holds two million men in abject bondage," claimed one sympathetic minister, "we *consent* to live in a state of signal iniquity."[19] Given that logic, a leap from moral to political responsibility was small indeed.

This moral context explains why many early abolitionists concentrated on winning the support of institutionalized churches. If ministers could be convinced to attack slavery vigorously from the pulpit, an army of Christian soldiers would become available to do spiritual battle with the Southern Demon. In a response prefiguring what was to happen in the realm of political parties, however, the denominational ties between southern and northern wings of most churches proved stronger than the northern memberships' stomach for controversy. Church governing bodies declared slavery a political issue and urged their ministers to avoid it.[20] Garrison's subsequent condemnation of these churches heightened tensions among those who sought to bridge evangelical and political behavior.[21]

The *third* and final purpose of *The Liberator* was the development and execution of a distinctive plan of action for ridding the United States of slavery. It is here that the political dimension of the early abolitionists' labors is most clearly exposed.

Although the Garrisonians were motivated primarily by moral concerns, they did not fully eschew political activity, in its broadest sense, as a means of accomplishing emancipation.[22] "I know it is the belief of many profoundly good men," wrote Garrison in 1834, "that they ought not to 'meddle' with politics; but they are cherishing a delusion, which, if it do [sic] not prove fatal to their own souls, may prove destructive of their country."[23]

For those who took the step of moral commitment under Garrison's discipleship, *The Liberator* devised a precise, two-pronged strategic attack on slavery, intended to take advantage of the zeal of newfound converts. Garrison crafted a distinctive assault on slavery in each of the two primary jurisdictions within which it then operated: the states, and federally controlled territories, including the District of Columbia.

Of the two, the southern states represented the biggest problem. There the institution was more expansive and entrenched, and there northern protesters had little direct political leverage, as state sovereignty remained inviolate. "As a member of Congress I should think myself no more authorized to legislate for the slaves of Virginia, than for the serfs of Russia," explained William Jay, son of Chief Justice John Jay, and an early convert to the cause. Given the power of the doctrine of state sovereignty, emancipation in the southern states required something other than an externally-imposed solution. It required an internal conversion. "Constitutional restrictions," continued Jay, "forbid all other than *moral* interference with slavery in the Southern States. But, we have as good and perfect a right to exhort slaveholders to liberate their slaves, as we have to exhort them to practice any virtue, or avoid any vice."[24] The abolitionists adopted and extended this approach through a strategy of "moral suasion."

Viewed in retrospect, what Garrison and his followers had in mind for the South was one of the grandest public relations campaigns of all time.[25] Their intent was not to abolish southern slavery by convincing governments to change their policies and then to impose them against a reluctant people, but rather to persuade each individual slaveholder of the sinfulness of his condition, and thus to convince him, of his own volition, to free his slaves.[26]

According to the logic of this strategy, over time, with more and more individuals freeing slaves, the power of peer pressure would begin to work on those initially resisting. "We expect," Garrison wrote, "to conquer through the majesty of public opinion," a force at that very moment receiving the scrutiny of a French visitor who would become its most eloquent chronicler, Alexis de Tocqueville.[27] Thus, for the Garrisonians, a properly educated public opinion seemed to be the best approach for bringing about social change in the remote South. Abolitionist Robert B. Hall thus wrote:

> We should create such a public opinion against the [slave] system, that the Planter can remain no longer easy in his sins. If you ask then, how the monstrous evil can be remedied, you have my answer, by the force of public opinion. By public opinion sitting strongly against this abomination . . . Slaveholding will become unpopular, it will be considered infamous to persevere in it, and the planter must liberate his slaves.[28]

Under these circumstances, legislative activity in the southern states took on either an air of redundancy or of inevitability.

Through what mechanisms was this expected conversion of Southern opinion to take place? The churches represented one possibility, but the intransigence of the southern clergy, already noted, for the most part rendered this a dead option. Some efforts were made to proselytize in person by sending missionaries into slave areas, but southern reaction to these unwanted intruders made this a far too dangerous practice to continue.

The main institutional mechanism the early abolitionists looked to as a tool for moral suasion was a free press. They recognized the tremendous power of communications media in a society so reliant on the force of public opinion. "Without the agency of the press," Garrison noted, "no impression can be made, no plan perfected, no victory achieved."[29] He and others, however, found the existing presses, like the churches, largely closed to the message of emancipation, and thus largely responsible for fostering an enduring apathy toward those in bondage. "It is the profusion of superficial cant . . . poured from the northern presses which has almost persuaded the people of the free states, that they have no more concern with slavery at the south than with the institutions of the inhabitants of the moon."[30] Needless to say the southern press was at least as remote. This state of affairs led David L. Child to observe, "The customary avenues to the public mind are closed against us. The pulpit and the press, which enlighten, and which are relied upon on other subjects, intercept every ray which would shine on this."[31]

The Liberator, and its sister publications produced in later years, represented attempts to refract light into the darkness.

An active antislavery press became fairly widespread in the North. Yet the abolitionists labored with only marginal success to establish papers in the slave states.[32] Consequently, the strategy of moral suasion relied heavily on the postal system, mailing northern papers to influential individuals in the South. The northern abolitionist press thus performed double duty, addressing a local audience and working to create a southern one.

Moral suasion was also intended to effect slavery in the territories and the District of Columbia. However, because in these areas slavery was the direct responsibility of the central government, of which the northerners were constituents, additional efforts were deemed appropriate there.[33] While acknowledging "that each State, in which slavery exists, has by the Constitution of the United States, the exclusive right to legislate in regard to its abolition in that State," the abolitionists forcefully contended that Congress held the power "to put an end to the domestic slave-trade, and to abolish slavery in all those portions of our common country which come under its control."[34] In *The Liberator*'s initial issue, Garrison wrote:

> What do many of the professed enemies of slavery mean, by heaping all their reproaches upon the south, and asserting that the crime of oppression is not national? What power but Congress—and Congress by the authority of the American people—has jurisdiction over the District of Columbia? . . . Though it is the seat of our National Government,—open to the daily inspection of foreign ambassadors, - and ostensibly opulent with the congregated wisdom, virtue and intelligence of the land,—yet a fouler spot scarcely exists on earth.[35]

Such strong expressions violated southern sensibilities, less because of fears of losing slavery in the seat of government than because emancipation there would be taken as an ill portent. There were no guarantees that the abolitionists' respect for state sovereignty—already suspect—would endure if they tasted victory in the District.

The primary means the early abolitionists employed for influencing Congress was petitioning.[36] In so doing they consciously mimicked their English cousins, who successfully used petition drives, aimed at Parliament, to bring about emancipation in the British empire.[37] They intended to make a large show of force by inundating the United States Congress with prayers, signed by thousands of interested individuals, urging the immediate and unconditional emancipation of slaves in federal areas and an end to the domestic slave trade. Routinely throughout this period antislavery periodicals reprinted various emancipation petitions with encouragement for the reader to sign those circulated locally and to assist in getting others to do the same. The first page of *The Liberator*'s first issue contained a copy of one such petition, indicating the high priority Garrison himself placed on that activity. Introducing another memorial later, Garrison wrote:

> Seriously: we hope that the genuine philanthropists of this nation will now arouse, as the Lion from his lair, and pour into the Congress chambers the language of firm, unyielding remonstrance against the further toleration of the cruel system of oppression in the District of Columbia. . . . The members of that body *will* obey the voice of their constituents, in the case before us, when that voice is fairly expressed.[38]

Although the primary target of such petitions was the U.S. Congress, the abolitionists also directed petition projects (and other forms of communication, such testimony at public hearings) at northern state legislatures. These state assemblies at this time selected members of the United States Senate, so antislavery activists mounted efforts to have them issue formal instructions to their senators to support liberation in federally controlled areas. For the most part northern legislatures were reluctant to enter the fray, in deference both to southern states' rights and to those northerners who, for one reason or another—including racial sentiments many shared with southern whites—opposed action against slavery.[39]

In sum, the initial thrusts of antislavery activism under William Lloyd Garrison's influence were aimed primarily at creating a sea change in public sentiment toward slavery, both in the North—in order to create more foot-soldiers for the cause—and in the South—where conversion would lead directly to liberation. Political action, in its most common meaning of working directly and primarily through political institutions for change, was envisioned as important only insofar as Congress had power over federal jurisdictions, and even here the process of public education and motivation remained of paramount concern as the necessary tool for forcing Congress to act. These abolitionists thus had, from the first stages of their coordinated development, a plan of action for translating their moral convictions into reality.

Organizing for Change

As early as March 1831 Garrison had also suggested that a national organization would be an indispensable instrument to further abolitionist concerns.[40] Soon thereafter he explained:

The formation of an American Anti-Slavery Society is of the utmost importance; and it is now, I am happy to say, in embryo. The objects of this society will be, to consolidate the moral power of the nation, so that Congress and the State Legislatures may be inundated with petitions;—to scatter tracts, like rain-drops, over the land, on the subject of slavery;—to employ active and eloquent agents to plead the cause constantly, and to form auxiliaries;—to encourage planters to cultivate their lands by freemen, by offering large premiums;—[and] to promote education and the mechanical arts among the free people of color, and to recover their lost rights.[41]

That national society, the AASS, was to come into being two years later, in 1833.[42] The AASS experienced substantial growth in each of several years after its founding, and regional and state abolition societies existed in every northern state by 1836.[43]

The relationship between the national and state and local societies is not a clear one; little uniformity is in evidence.[44] The national society was a loosely constructed umbrella organization, a service instrument for all interested local units. It provided organizational guidance through its publications and communicated strategic advice concerning petition drives, mailing campaigns, and other matters of nationwide interest. The AASS did have some formal auxiliaries, often set up by commissioned agents who traveled throughout the North and West preaching abolition. However, in deference to local opinion, these had no uniform structure. Many community societies simply self-generated, organizing themselves on the basis of shared goals. "After your paper (the *Liberator*) had circulated some weeks in this settlement," wrote members of a Putnam County (Ill.) antislavery society to Garrison, "a few of the citizens undertook to form some kind of association, for the purpose of expressing to the world our abhorrence of slavery."[45]

In the AASS's annual statements, "auxiliary societies" and those societies unaffiliated but constructed "on kindred principles" were included in the same figure, because, according to one report, "We have not the means of distinguishing accurately between those which are constitutionally Auxiliary to the American Anti-Slavery Society, and others. . . . To those who signify a desire to become Auxiliary, and comply with the conditions provided in the Constitution, a letter of Recognition will be returned."[46] The national society's inability even to identify its formally affiliated chapters indicates at once an absence of effective centralized direction *and* the raw potential for antislavery action outside the South.

As early as 1835, the Society began directing special attention to organizational integration, to the need for having all state societies affiliate with the AASS for purposes of system-wide coordination. To facilitate this end, the Society requested affiliates to begin providing annual reports of their activities as a means of keeping abreast of events in each region. Even under these circumstances, however, a premium remained on local autonomy, as the Society adopted a policy of having its agents act "in concert with" state executive committees when in the field, rather than imposing centrally decided policy.[47] Further, membership in the AASS, according to the Society's constitution, was open to "any person who consents to the principles of this [Society's] Constitution, who contributes to the funds of this Society, and is not a slave-holder."[48] The "principles of this Constitution" were originally skeletal, requiring little but a commitment to unconditional immediatism.

Before 1836 there existed no central staff operation at the national level; until then, all administrative chores were performed in the New York headquarters by an Executive Committee of the Society. The national organization was never without some measure of internal turmoil, as certain key actors advanced competing visions of how the Society and its assets should be best employed. This later led to heated debate over what principles constituted the true abolitionist catechism. These fissures also made the annual meetings of the AASS—perhaps the most important service the Society performed, as they afforded guidance and fellowship for members—carnivals of dissent. Abolitionist Maria Chapman once remarked of her fellow reformers during this period, "The good Lord uses instruments for His purposes I would not touch with a fifty foot pole."[49] Yet through the mid-1830s internal dissonance did not appear disruptive of movement progress. To the contrary, by permitting entry to so many varied actors—anyone committed to the single goal of immediate, unconditional emancipation—the movement grew in a way unlikely under a more exclusionary policy. The ranks were not uniform, but their numbers were committed to the only outcome that truly mattered to the Society.[50]

Yet in those early years their success in making progress toward these goals was stymied by weak recruitment and a dismissive public attitude. Theirs was generally looked upon as a futile mission, yet another quirky manifestation of unbalanced prophets trying to bring heaven to earth.[51] Ironically, it took reaction and resistance from a sensitive South to awaken the North to the possibility that abolitionism might be other than quixotic.

Life was breathed into the movement by those very forces committed for so long to rendering it lifeless.

The Reaction

> Let us declare through the public journals of our country, that the question of slavery is not, and shall not be open to discussion—that the system is deep rooted amongst us, and must remain forever—that the very moment any private individual attempts to lecture us upon its evils and immorality, and the necessity of putting measures into operation to secure us from them, in the same moment his tongue shall be cut out and cast upon the dung-hill.
>
> From the Columbia (S.C.) *Telescope* circa September 1833[52]

New Englanders of the early 1830s commonly viewed Garrison and his associates as mere eccentrics. It probably appeared unlikely even to those with moral reservations about the "peculiar institution" that a small coterie of oddly mannered newspapermen, lecturers, and hyper-active women would dislodge from American soil such a deeply rooted constituent element. The Garrisonians, in their original state, hardly gave the appearance of a destabilizing force.

However, southern reaction was quick to change that perception. The first issues of *The Liberator* sent south were greeted scornfully in the slave states as dangerous intrusions into a misunderstood relationship between blacks and whites there. Southerners, familiar with the horror stories of violent slave uprisings in other societies, were, unlike their northern counterparts, extremely sensitive to the character of the abolitionist message.[53] Material that would not raise an eyebrow in Rochester—such as the publication of population statistics for southern states reflecting a high ratio of slaves to whites—aroused alarm in Richmond because of its potential there for breaking down the slaves' sense of isolation. As a result, southerners did not, as their northern brethren commonly did, dismiss Garrison out of hand. They recognized the inherent vulnerability of a socioeconomic system built on a massive, enslaved labor force, and thus they believed that anything which threatened to arouse a chained Leviathan could be calamitous.[54] This explains why the bloody revolt of Nat Turner, in Suffolk County, Virginia, in August 1831, only eight months after Garrison began publication, sent a shiver of terror through the slave states that eventually reverberated into New England.

Turner, a slave reputed to have been taught by his mother that he, like Moses, would lead his fellow bondsmen to freedom, convinced seventy fellow slaves to rise up against the white residents of the county. A violent rampage ensued, with angry slaves slaughtering fifty-seven men, women, and children. A volunteer force, supplemented by armed troops and a militia, eventually captured Turner and his confederates, and quickly thereafter meted out a brutal vigilante justice.[55]

There is virtually no evidence to indicate that the Turner revolt was in any way energized by northern abolitionist activity. However, many southerners refused to believe that the widely publicized Turner rebellion was merely coincident with recent circulations of radical papers in the South. The governors of Virginia and Louisiana reported to their legislatures that such revolts were fueled by misguided northern interlopers. These suspicions seemed confirmed by the fact that Garrison took what was perceived as an equivocal position on the rectitude of slave revolts, both before and after the Turner rebellion.[56] In January, well before that episode, he argued that the "possibility of bloody insurrection at the south fills us with dismay," but he noted further that no one was more justified in seeking revolution than the American slave.[57] His first editorial remarks about the Turner uprising itself were penned in a similar vein: "What we have so long predicted,—at the peril of being stigmatized as an alarmist and declaimer,—has commenced its fulfillment. . . . The first drops of blood, which are but the prelude to a deluge from the gathering clouds, have fallen."[58]

Almost immediately Garrison became the personal target of southern animosity.[59] Further, using the Turner revolt as evidence, white southerners argued that Garrison's work should not be allowed in slave areas, lest servile insurrection become epidemic. In October the *Tarborough* (N.C.) *Free Press* commented:

> An incendiary paper, 'The Liberator,' is circulating openly among the free blacks of this city; and if you search, it is very probable you will find it among the slaves of your county. It is published in Boston or Philadelphia by a white man, with the avowed purpose of inciting rebellion in the South; and I am informed, is to be carried through your co. by secret agents, who are to come amongst you under the pretext of peddling, &c. Keep a sharp look out for these villains, and if you catch them, by all that is sacred, you ought to barbacue [*sic*] them.[60]

Southern politicians quickly responded to this burgeoning pressure by strengthening laws regulating already-limited black freedoms in every southern state. In Atlanta, the state senate offered a $5,000 bounty for anyone capturing Garrison and returning him for trial under Georgia law; within four years such rewards, for a host of antislavery leaders, were commonplace in the South.[61] Additionally, state and local laws were enacted all over the region to prevent the distribution of *The Liberator*. In Virginia, a new statute was enacted making it illegal for anyone to circulate antislavery literature; a black found possessing it was punished with lashes for a first offense, death for a second. Many related statutes were intended to cut such material off at its first point of access in the South, the local post office. A Georgetown (D.C.) statute forbade free Negroes to take *The Liberator* from the post office under threat of fine and jailing; if the guilty party had insufficient funds to cover the cost of either, he was liable to be sold into slavery for four months.[62]

Not only did angry southerners act to expunge from their midst any trace of the agitators' influence, they also tried to stop the agitation at its source. Yet just as the internal affairs of the South were insulated from the direct influence of northern abolitionists, so, too, were the internal affairs of the North largely beyond the direct influence of southern reaction. Thus, appeals were issued from many points in the South for northerners themselves to put an end to a turmoil that threatened relations between the two regions.[63] Shortly after Turner's uprising, the *National Intelligencer* in Washington requested the mayor and people of Boston to act to silence abolitionist fanatics.[64] The Alabama legislature instructed the governor of that state to correspond with his counterparts in other states to find ways to suppress incendiary materials.[65] And during the summer of 1834 a public meeting was held in New York's Tammany Hall at the behest of southerners with northern connections to decide on a general response to the antislavery threat. Those attending considered calling a national meeting of delegates from slaveholding states to develop a strategy of reaction, but resolved instead to "rely with confidence on the intelligence of our northern brethren to frustrate and defeat the mischievous schemes of designing demagogues and deluded fanatics."[66] Since tension already existed in the relationship between North and South on other important fronts, preeminently on tariff and trade policy, southerners hoped that northern nationalists would willingly act to keep further rifts from opening.

The southern goal of enlisting a northern cadre to fight their cause was indeed attained, in part because of their success in painting the Garrisonians as a radical threat to public order, in part because of a northern sympathy for allowing the South to decide for itself the future of its own institutions, and in part because of northern racist reaction against radical "miscegenists."[67] Consequently, a private and public reaction set in against the early abolitionists on their native soil. This was forcefully brought home to Garrison when, in August 1832, almost one full year after the Turner revolt, Judge Thacher instructed a Boston grand jury to consider the possibility of bringing libel indictments against the local radical press. "I deem it my duty to express to you, at this time," charged the judge,

> my opinion, *that to publish books, pamphlets, or newspapers, designed to be circulated here and in other States of the Union, and having a direct and necessary tendency to excite in the minds of our citizens deadly hatred and hostility against their brethren of other States, and to stimulate the slave population of those States to rise against their masters, and to effect by fire and sword their emancipation, is an offense against the peace of this Commonwealth, and that it may be prosecuted as a misdemeanor at common law.*[68]

The "offense," it should be noted, was defined as against "the peace of *this* Commonwealth" (i.e., Massachusetts), plainly charging that the threat posed by antislavery literature was also being felt in the free states. This is a crucial point for understanding much of what subsequently occurs, for the existence of that apparent threat to the free states was claimed by northern reactionaries as justification for instituting a host of limits on the rights and freedoms of those participating in the antislavery movement. This early-set pattern lasted, with varying intensity, for over thirty years. Draconian restrictions were imposed on such rights as speech, press, and assembly, all in the interest of quashing an "offense against the peace of this Commonwealth." Some of these restrictions were the product of carefully reasoned legal processes in which the state's legitimate interests in preserving domestic tranquillity were asserted as a necessary balance against the individual's rights. Yet frequently these restrictions resulted not from reasoned, deliberative judgments, but from the passionate edict of mob rule. Abolitionist sympathizers were attacked—often tarred and feathered—and abolitionist meetings were routinely disrupted by groups of hecklers shouting down speakers, often forcing the attendees to adjourn elsewhere. Further, destruction of abolitionist-owned presses took place both in New England and in the western states. The extent and brutality of these violent reactions approached the level of hysteria in many areas across the nation, especially after New York's wealthy Tappan brothers began to fund vastly expanded leafletting campaigns, which (falsely) gave the appearance of a rising juggernaut. "Anti-abolition mobs," observes historian Leonard L. Richards, "saw themselves defending the established order against the encroachments of internal subversives and foreign agents," the latter being those English abolitionists upon whose experience and financing the Americans partly relied. Richards claims that in the summer of 1835, "Almost every major city and town in the nation held anti-abolitionist rallies."[69]

Ironically, the effect of this free-state crack-down, grafted onto the southern reaction which first mushroomed in 1831, was to *add* initially to the antislavery ranks to an extent perhaps unthinkable under other circumstances. Many otherwise disinterested or ambivalent northerners first joined hands with the movement not because of any vigorous commitment to freeing the slaves, but because they sympathized with a group of fellow citizens unfairly denied their civil and political rights.[70] The excesses of the mob mobilized many northerners who believed that slavery was indeed offensive, but who otherwise might have tolerated it as someone else's evil. During this era there was no model or theory available on which consciously to build such a strategy—formal conceptions of civil disobedience were a later phenomenon— but those who supported the abolitionists' right to be heard provided an unanticipated, invaluable ballast against the wave upon wave of political assaults the northern reactionaries later mounted.[71]

The case of Wendell Phillips illustrates well the general point. Phillips once commented wryly about the Boston of his youth: "The five points of Massachusetts decency were, to trace your lineage to the Mayflower, graduate at Harvard College, be a good lawyer or a member of an orthodox church,—either would answer,—pay your debts, and frighten your child to sleep by saying 'Thomas Jefferson.'" [72] By these standards few were more honorable or more deeply entrenched in the traditional Massachusett's establishment. But a mob assault Phillips witnessed in Boston violated his carefully cultivated sense of decency.[73] He much later spoke of the spectacle and its effect on him.

> At this hour, twenty years ago, I was below in the street.... I was not in the street as one of the mob, but as a spectator. I had come down from my office in Court Street to see what the excitement was. I did not understand antislavery then; that is, I did not understand the country in which I lived.

I remember saying to the gentleman who stood next to me in the street: "Why does not the mayor call out the regiment?" (I belonged to it then.) "We would cheerfully take arms in such a case as this. It is a very shameful business. Why does he stand there arguing? Why does he not call for the guns." I did not then know that the men who should have born them were the mob; that all there was of government in Boston was in the street; that the people, our final reliance for the execution of the laws, were there, in "broadcloth and broad daylight," in the street.

Such was the temper of those times. The ignorant were not aware, and the wise were too corrupt to confess, that the most precious of human rights, free thought, was at stake.[74]

A report of the American Anti-Slavery Society indicated that Phillips was not alone, however, in his conversion:

The exhibition of slavery, which has been made through all these anti-abolition meetings and mobs, has done more than could have been done by the arguments of a thousand lecturers, to convince the sober and disinterested, that slavery is a crime which cannot be tolerated in silence.[75]

What began in Boston as a simple, published declaration on the part of an eccentric newspaper editor had, within the span of only a few years, escalated into nationwide turbulence. Those years were characterized by a pattern of escalation. Northern abolitionist speech moved a South fearful of servile war to take action against the agitators' rights. Consequently, northern reactionaries, sensing the precarious stability of a Union already reeling from battles over tariffs and nullification, turned actively against the abolitionists in order to salvage national harmony. Reaction, and reaction to reaction, fueled the controversy to a point at which the very notion of emancipation became no longer just a moral goal for true believers, but a clear and present danger to public order. Debate on the matter was marked not by the mutual respect and common language one usually expects among fellow members of one nation, but by a mistrust and suspicion threatening to the consensus and comity essential to politics in a heterogeneous society. The fabric of the national polity was quickly weakening. Abolitionist Elizur Wright Jr. wrote in 1834:

Mightier elements are in agitation than have entered into any revolution in our country, moral or physical. Their action has been repressed by all the governing powers of society, till nature will no longer bear the restraint, and sympathy for the slave is gushing from a thousand rents in the opposing structure. The trick of tyrants will be unavailing. They might as well undertake to turn backward our glorious rivers, to check the swelling of the ocean, or hush its noisy tempests, as to stop the progress of this cause.[76]

It was the sound of those "noisy tempests"—the perilous straining of opposing powers one against the other—that first aroused in the presidency an urgency to action on the conflict between the pro- and antislavery forces.

CHAPTER 2

A Thirty Years "War": The Presidency and the Abolitionists

How did presidents from Andrew Jackson to James Buchanan respond to conflicts touched off by antislavery activism? The details presented in this chapter indicate that they worked overwhelmingly to suppress efforts to bring about that social change the abolitionists demanded. Indeed, some of the most vigorous exercises of presidential power during an era of "weak" executives came as antebellum presidents asserted themselves to strangle abolitionism, or to buttress its proslavery opposition. Those who have learned of an era of congressionally dominated politics—"In the nineteenth century, chief executives were chief of very little and executive of even less"[1]—may be surprised by the extent to which the historically obscure presidents of the 1830s, '40s, and '50s found creative mechanisms, in foreign and domestic policy, to keep abolitionist advances in check.[2]

Presidential efforts to suppress movement toward emancipation successively fell within four broad categories.[3] These are headed: Barriers to Political Access; Biased Expansion of Conflict; Execution of Legal Constraints; and Manipulation of the Decision-Making Process.

Barriers to Political Access: The Mails Controversy and the Gag Rule

The first issue of *The Liberator* was published at almost the exact midpoint of Andrew Jackson's initial term of office. Despite what was arguably a correlated escalation of political violence as early as 1833, however, official Washington took almost no notice of the abolitionists' earliest labors.[4] That inattention to the issue in the nation's capital signals the extent to which slavery was considered out-of-bounds as a concern of the national government, and suggests the general ineffectiveness of the agitators in fulfilling

Garrison's mission. These conditions abruptly changed in July 1835, when Washington policy makers were drawn into the fray over a matter they could not ignore. The controversy was delivered directly to Andrew Jackson's front stoop—by his postmaster general, Amos Kendall.

The Mails Controversy: Andrew Jackson

The abolitionist strategy for affecting a change in southern public opinion through a free press—that is, by mailing publications from the North—was well into implementation by the mid-1830s. This became an especially prominent part of their strategy in 1835, when the total number of publications produced by the American Anti-Slavery Society skyrocketed in one year from 122,000 to over 1 million copies.[5] Southern newspapers were subsequently filled with stories of an invasion of incendiary matter.[6]

On July 29, 1835, the packet ship *Columbia* docked in Charleston with a heavy cargo of antislavery publications addressed from New York to many of South Carolina's most prominent citizens. According to the local postmaster, Alfred Huger, the shipment "literally filled our office with thousands of Pamphlets and Tracts upon the question on which this community is too Sensitive to admit of any Compromise—the Emancipation of the southern slave." The contents of the delivery quickly became public knowledge, whereafter the post office was broken into and the offending materials seized and burned by a mob of 3,000 Charlestonians. Soon thereafter, the city council established a committee to screen out any further antislavery material transmitted by the United States Post Office.[7]

Amid this turmoil, Postmaster Huger penned urgent appeals to New York Postmaster Samuel L. Gouverneur and to Postmaster General Kendall in Washington, requesting instructions. Huger found a sympathetic audience in both places. On August 8, Gouverneur advised him that he would suspend shipping abolitionist documents pending official word from Washington on how to deal with the problem.[8] Two days later, the postmaster general's response arrived in Charleston.

Kendall's reply to Huger was a study in equivocation.

> Upon a careful examination of the law, I am satisfied that the Post-Master General has no legal authority to exclude newspapers from the mail, nor prohibit their carriage or delivery on account of their character or tendency, real or supposed. Probably it was not thought safe to confer on the

head of an executive department a power over the press which might be perverted and abused.

Kendall thus acknowledged the requirements of his office, displaying a sensitivity to the special importance of a functioning mail system to contemporary freedom of the press. However, Kendall's sympathy with the Charlestonians led him to temporize.

> I am not prepared to direct you to forward or deliver the papers of which you speak. . . . By no act or direction of mine, official or private, could I be induced to aid knowingly in giving circulation to papers of this description, directly or indirectly. We owe an obligation to the laws, but a higher one to the communities in which we live; if the former be perverted to destroy the latter, it is patriotism to disregard them.[9]

The policy thus established by the postmaster general of the United States, relying on his personal conception of higher law, was that the duty of the national government was only to transmit mail from city to city. Each individual postmaster, using community standards, could then determine a parcel's final disposition. In the South, this virtually assured that antislavery materials would never be delivered.

An ensuing protest against Kendall's decision came loud and fast, and even included some of the administration's most steadfast supporters. For example, the *New-York Evening Post* charged Kendall with "establishing a censorship of the press in its worst possible form, by allowing every two penny Postmaster through the country to be the judge of what species of intelligence is proper to circulate, and what to withhold from the people."[10] Notwithstanding the temper of this northern reaction, the postmaster general was sustained in his position by the only party that mattered: Andrew Jackson.

Kendall had written Jackson shortly after issuing his response to the Charleston postmaster, asking for Jackson's advice on how to proceed. He hoped for presidential cover for his actions, which Jackson readily provided. Although Jackson had until this time maintained an official distance from the emancipation controversy, he clearly had decided that the southern line about antislavery literature was correct: the intent was not education and reform, but destruction. "I have read with sorrow and regret," he told Kendall, "that such men live in our happy country—I might have said monsters—as to be guilty of the attempt to stir up amongst the South the horrors of a servile war—Could they be reached, they ought to be made to atone for this wicked attempt, with their lives." To Jackson, what the abolitionists took as an exercise of First Amendment rights amounted to a capital offense. He continued by acknowledging the administration's legal obligation to deliver papers which had been ordered, only to suggest that "few men in society will be willing to acknowledge that they are encouraging by subscribing for such papers this horrid and most wicked procedure; and when they are known, every moral and good citizen will unite to put them in coventry, and avoid their society."

Consequently, Jackson issued these instructions to Kendall:

> [W]e can do nothing more than direct that those inflamatory papers be delivered to none but who will demand them as subscribers; and in every instance the Postmaster ought to take the names down, and have them exposed thro the publik journals as subscribers to this wicked plan of exciting the negroes to insurrection and massacre. This would bring those in the South, who were patronizing these incendiary works into such disrepute with all the South, that they would be compelled to desist, or move from the country.[11]

Constrained by the law he was sworn to uphold, Jackson turned to the politics of public opinion on which his reputation was so brilliantly built.

With Kendall's orders standing, having the support and encouragement of the president of the United States, southern postmasters met with no official resistance in following the lead of Huger and closing their offices to the abolitionist presses. That same August, postmasters in Virginia, North Carolina, and Alabama, among other states, reported local backlashes against the flow of antislavery papers and a subsequent interruption of their delivery. A public meeting of concerned citizens in Richmond resolved, "That we have a just claim on all the non-slaveholding States for the enactment of suitable and efficient laws, to repress and put down by adequate penalties, all incendiary or seditious associations, whose avowed purpose is to disturb our peace, and to excite insurrection among our slaves."[12] Unwilling to await the action of the free states, the Virginia assembly in 1836 enacted a statute requiring postmasters to turn over incendiary materials to local justices of the peace, who were instructed to burn any mail deemed inappropriate and to arrest the addressee.[13] Southern mails accordingly became hostage to the fears of slave rebellion.

Less than a month after the Charleston affair, Kendall registered his official support for New York Postmaster Gouverneur, who had taken it upon himself, pending a ruling from Washington, to confiscate abolitionist literature headed south from his post office.[14] With Kendall's approval of this action, a circle of sorts was completed: individual postmasters throughout the country were granted the authority to make decisions about whether the government's postal services could be used to receive *or* to deliver mailed material, based on the nature of its contents. How such contents were to be determined, when a large portion of the mail traveled under seal, was never firmly established, but there was clearly an implication that concerns for public safety overrode any rights to privacy when one entrusted his or her parcels to the post office. Kendall's action may have been technically in conflict with that part of Jackson's order concerning delivery to known subscribers, but on the whole it was in keeping with the unmistakable spirit of the president's message. Further, the president made no effort to overturn Kendall's ruling.[15]

This formal intolerance toward abolitionist literature was matched—perhaps exceeded—by a spreading vigilante intolerance. In Philadelphia, for example, a mob seized a large box of antislavery publications on the city's wharf, took it into the middle of the Delaware River and dumped it overboard. Travel in the slave states became increasingly perilous for northerners, because fears had grown that distant travelers were channeling publications there to compensate for the closing of the mails. The *Little Rock* (Ark.) *Gazette* editorialized: "Some of Garrison's disciples declare themselves ready to suffer martyrdom even, in the *good* cause. If they will travel this way, they can be accommodated."[16]

When Congress returned to Washington in December 1835, Jackson had more harsh words for the agitators and a formal recommendation to Congress for dealing with problems in the postal service. In his seventh annual message, he continued to attribute to the abolitionists an intent to foster revolution. Literature sent south was depicted in his remarks as "addressed to the passions of slaves, . . . calculated to stimulate them to insurrection and to produce all the horrors of a servile war." Thus, all antislavery material was tarred with the same brush, notwithstanding the fact that most of it counseled abstinence from violence, and that most, if not all, of the mail in question was addressed to whites, including many slaveholders.[17] By characterizing the materials in the worst possible light, however, the president was in fact preparing his audience for further national action against the threat.

His recommendation was offered in the following terms.

In leaving the care of other branches of this interesting subject to the State authorities, to whom they properly belong, it is nevertheless proper for Congress to take such measures as will prevent the Post-Office Department, which was designed to foster an amicable intercourse and correspondence between all members of the Confederacy, from being used as an instrument of an opposite character. The General Government, to which the great trust is confided of preserving inviolate the relations created among the States by the Constitution, is especially bound to avoid in its own action anything that may disturb them. I would therefore call the special attention of Congress to the subject, and respectfully suggest the propriety of passing such a law as will prohibit, under severe penalties, the circulation in the Southern States, through the mail, of incendiary publications intended to instigate the slaves to insurrection.[18]

Jackson thus wanted to create a shield around the South through which no abolitionist material could pass, and the best way to accomplish this was to deny antislavery activists the use of the one conduit they, and other presses, most heavily relied on.[19] Further, his call for congressional action was intended to remove Jackson from an embarrassing conundrum: he now found himself a nullifier, unless Congress could provide him law he could execute in good conscience. The irony was not lost on Jackson's northern critics. The *Boston Atlas* wrote,

And pray what is the difference betwixt the *nullification* of a Post Office law and the nullification of a *tariff* law? Is it not about as much as the difference betwixt *tweedle-dum* and *tweedle-dee*? Will not the South Carolina nullifiers be mortified at being so outstripped in nullification by the President and his army of Post Masters?"[20]

Within weeks of Jackson's address, the executive committee of the AASS drafted a public letter to the president vigorously protesting his actions as unfair and prejudicial. They argued at length that Jackson's was a false characterization of labors entirely peaceful in intent. They especially denounced the sweeping publicity Jackson gave his accusations, protesting his use of official communications to bring public condemnation on their activities.

And is it nothing, sir, that we are officially charged by the President of the United States, with wicked and unconstitutional efforts, and with harboring the most execrable intentions? and this, too, in a document spread upon the Journals of both Houses of Congress, published to the nation and to the world, made part of our enduring archives, and incorporated in the history of the age? It is true, that although you have given judgment against us, you cannot award execution. We are not indeed, subjected to the penalty of murder; but need we ask you, sir, what must be the *moral influence* of your declaration . . . ?[21]

There is no record that Jackson responded.[22]

A new post office act was passed in July 1836. Contrary to Jackson's request, however, the new act contained a provision forbidding postmasters from interfering with the delivery of any matter submitted for transmission. Apparently fears of an overreaching executive, especially by Jackson's political opposition, stifled the effort to federalize a censorship law.[23] However, there was no express statement in the new law directing that materials reaching the destination post office be delivered, so southern postmasters continued to respect only local statute and vigilante law and refused to pass along antislavery publications. The administration commensurately refused to enforce delivery of such matter over southern objections. Congress thus indirectly sustained the president's actions. Jackson may have, as one biographer has suggested, believed it the government's responsibility to ensure the delivery of the mails, but one searches in vain in the available records for convincing evidence to support that claim.[24]

The mails question soon faded from the national political picture, for two reasons. First, the abolitionists, sensing the futility of dealing with obstinate postmasters north and south, greatly reduced the number of materials committed to the mails. They thereby acknowledged a strategic defeat.[25] Second, by early 1836, antislavery agitators began to turn their eyes increasingly to Washington, to wage war on slavery where they felt their leverage was greater.

By the fall of 1835, the second half of the early abolitionists' reform strategy—the petitioning of Congress for a termination of slavery in federally controlled jurisdictions—was well into implementation. Although petitions had trickled into the House and Senate chambers for years praying for federal action to mitigate the evils of slavery, these, like the publications sent south, dramatically increased as Congress reconvened in Washington in December 1835. These petitions exasperated southern members of Congress. "As often as they are presented to the House," wrote one first-hand observer, "the confusion of Babel follows and Bedlam itself, in contrast, becomes the headquarters of decorum and sanity. The effect is similar to the bursting of the light of heaven upon the darkness of pandemonium: nothing is heard but imprecations, and wailings, and gnashing of teeth."[26] A *Boston Daily*

Advocate correspondent characterized similar proceedings on the antislavery petitions as "the greatest serio-comico-farcico-nonsensico, donner and blitzer tragedy rehearsal, that was ever performed on any stage. From the external signs of inflammation and convulsion, I should think it a fair chance, that, to-morrow, it would be reported that about a dozen gentlemen had evaporated in self-combustion."[27]

The Gag Rule: Martin Van Buren

Both houses of Congress, led by their angry southern members, instituted "gag rules" of various forms, essentially denying abolitionists the right of petition either by refusing to receive or by immediately tabling antislavery petitions as a matter of course.[28] President Jackson did not formally stake out a position on the gag rules. Perhaps, given his widely known views on slavery, he considered a formal statement superfluous. However, Jackson's successor, Martin Van Buren, supplied any remaining deficiency as part of his first official act as president. At the very outset of the new administration—in the inaugural address—Van Buren moved to close completely to the abolitionists avenues of redress in the federal government.[29] That speech, "an indication of the general course of the administration," contained a formal pledge to veto any measures Congress might send him restricting slavery in the District of Columbia.[30]

Van Buren began his remarks by referring to the wisdom of the American founders in legislating for the country "as they found it," accepting the diversity of a nation with myriad domestic interests and building the structures of government "upon principles of reciprocal concession and equitable compromise." He then turned explicitly to slavery, calling it

> perhaps the greatest, of the prominent sources of discord and disaster supposed to lurk in our political condition. Our forefathers were deeply impressed with the delicacy of this subject, and they treated it with a forbearance so evidently wise, that, in spite of every sinister foreboding, it never, until the present period, disturbed the tranquillity of our common country.

The spirit of fraternity and patriotism which motivated the founders, and to which the growth and happiness of the Union could be attributed, was absent, Van Buren claimed, from the antislavery radicals. The maintenance of the nation thus depended on silencing them. As a step towards this end, he would, "in accordance with the spirit that actuated the venerated fathers of the republic," exercise his veto power against antislavery legislation.

The president's pledge is worth quoting at some length, beginning with his recollections of the campaign.

> I then declared that if the desire of those of my countrymen who were favorable to my election was gratified, "I must go into the Presidential chair the inflexible and uncompromising opponent of every attempt on the part of Congress to abolish slavery in the District of Columbia against the wishes of the slaveholding States, and also with a determination equally decided to resist the slightest interference with it in the States where it exists." I submitted also to my fellow-citizens, with fullness and frankness, the reasons which led me to this determination. The result authorizes me to believe that they have been approved and are confided in by a majority of the people of the United States, including those whom they most immediately affect. It now only remains to add that no bill conflicting with these views can ever receive my constitutional sanction. . . . If the agitation of this subject was intended to reach the stability of our institutions, enough has occurred to show that it has signally failed, and that in this as in every other instance the apprehensions of the timid and the hopes of the wicked for the destruction of our government are again destined to be disappointed.[31]

Van Buren issued his pledge as a calculated mechanism to put the issue off the public agenda.[32] He sent a clear signal that he supported closing all access to the instruments of the national government for those whose agitation threatened institutional stability. The veto threat thus became an extension of the gag by other means. As Thomas Hart Benton observed, the veto pledge was "not called for by anything in congress, but outside of it."[33] Anyone considering the investment of time or other resources in the antislavery cause found powerful agents of the government united in their refusal to give serious consideration to their grievances.[34]

The character of the president's actions take on even greater significance in light of the crucial role Van Buren believed political parties could play with respect to the slavery question. Since his earliest days in politics, Van Buren had been a sedulous advocate of the political party. As agitation over the slavery question began to stir the nation's politics, he argued that a carefully crafted two-party system provided the best hope for keeping the nation unified. Given the regional character of the American division over slavery, which made the country exceptionally vulnerable to disunion, Van Buren reasoned that the nation needed an alternative way of organizing political conflict, one which cut across regional lines. He asserted that the economic questions that emerged during the Jackson presidency provided just the right basis for organizing two enduring political parties, arrayed one against the other on such matters as banks and internal improvements. According to this logic, these issues were to displace the destructive one of slavery, permitting it to fade off the public agenda. Van Buren, motivated by these concerns, is commonly credited as having institutionalized two-party competition in the United States.

However, Van Buren's experience as a candidate, and as president, showed that his logic was terribly flawed. And that he knew it. Deeply rooted racial biases, often reinforced by regional prejudices and the very economic interests that Van Buren sought to exploit, proved to be highly resistant to the logical manipulations of even a "Little Magician." Tellingly, when the inclusive-oriented mechanisms of party failed Van Buren, he did not hesitate to resort to a policy of exclusion to deal with the problem. Nation-keeping ends here required a recalibration of suitable means, even though the embrace of this alternative—direct suppression through gag rules and preemptive vetoes—effectively amounted to a concession that his preferred option—the American party—was not up to the challenge.[35]

By the end of the 1830s, as Van Buren's presidency neared its conclusion, the initial movement for abolitionism had faltered. The momentum achieved by the AASS in the mid-1830s proved to be unsustainable through the end of the decade. A concrete sign of the movement's deterioration appeared in 1840 with the fracturing of the AASS into two competing organizations, one retaining the name, the other the assets, of the original society. The sources of this division are complex, rooted in such factors as a severe economic downturn that disabled financially the movement's main benefactors, and the mounting centrifugal forces inherent in an organization of reformers deeply committed to local autonomy and the individual's own sense of divine direction.[36] Yet severely restricted access to the nation's political institutions should not be underestimated as a contributing factor.[37] Indeed, the main point of contention among those who fought for control of the movement's future was politics. More specifically, the fight was over how best to respond to a political order that had been successfully closed to their previous efforts at moral suasion and petitioning.

Some activists reasoned that since their progress had been impeded by the obstacle-raising transactions of politicians in Washington, they had to enter more completely that arena to make their ultimate success possible. Garrison objected.[38] He believed the road into Washington was fraught with danger, and that the appeal of party politics was a mere Siren song. By 1840 he continued to urge action on the fronts already established, but he refused to endorse efforts to organize antislavery forces into a voting bloc. His rationale was straightforward: the life's blood of party politics is compromise, which is poison to a crusade.[39] Thus, the Garrisonians maintained a deeply held reformer's contempt for party politics, and for *organized* use of the franchise.[40] Better, as one purist wrote, to "Do *your duty*, and leave the event with God."[41]

However, other abolitionists became impatient with the Almighty's timetable. They recognized how effective those holding positions of public authority had been in retarding their efforts, and they sought to develop competitive political power as a necessary first step toward their more fundamental aim of emancipation. Their movement into the conventional channels of partisan politics required a public distancing from much of the perceived radicalism of the Garrisonians.[42] The result was a period of bitter in-fighting among those who previously had submerged their differences in common cause. Membership in northern antislavery organizations began to decline after 1840. By then, the editors of *The Liberator* found that the abolitionists had returned, in terms of progress toward their goals, "back to where we were in 1833."[43] Those barriers to the political marketplace erected by defenders of the status quo, within Washington and without, had served their purpose.

Biased Expansion of Conflict: Manipulation of Western Growth

Despite the decline in the abolitionists' fortunes, their opposition remained convinced that a potential for resurgence endured. A gradually emerging antislavery presence at northern and western polling places—bolstered by sympathizers who were more concerned about the Slavepower (i.e., the influence of proslavery interests in the councils of state) than the abolition of slavery itself—sustained anxiety in the South that the agitators of the mid-1830s might return, reinvigorated. This unease fed a continuing search for security, which manifest itself in at least two ways.

First, some proslavery spokesmen initiated efforts to recapture a portion of the moral and intellectual ground earlier ceded to the antislavery forces by developing and prominently publicizing for the first time arguments that slavery was something other than a necessary evil. As Richard Ellis and Aaron Wildavsky observed, "The unrelenting barrage of abolitionist criticism forced slaveholders to defend slavery as a humane, moral, and just form of social life— 'a positive good.'" Although the roots of this thinking predated organized antislavery activity, "Only after slaveholders were directly challenged . . . did a set of scattered ideas entertained by a few become systematic orthodoxy." Calhounite Duff Green explained this turn to positive propaganda: "We must satisfy [our people] that slavery is of itself right— that it is not a sin against God—that it is not an evil, moral or political."[44]

The second element in the South's quest for increased security, and the one of primary interest here, was an attempt to enlarge the national representation of the slave states, to tilt further the domestic balance of power in Washington in favor of the proslavery South. To do this, proslavery activists looked to Texas. Indeed, an unusually activist presidency was at the very center of these efforts to expand the bounds of conflict on slavery so as to bias its ultimate outcome against antislavery opinion.

Here we find a previously unrecognized example of E. E. Schattschneider's celebrated dictum of political conflict:

> Every change in the scope of conflict has a bias; it is partisan in its nature. That is, it must be assumed that every change in the number of participants is about something, that the newcomers have sympathies or antipathies that make it possible to involve them. By definition, the intervening bystanders are not neutral. Thus, in political conflict every change in scope changes the equation.[45]

The assertion made here is that the addition of new western "participants," as it was managed by the national government with substantial presidential guidance, was intended to change the equation of conflict over slavery significantly *against* those who sought emancipation.

The Annexation of Texas: Jackson to Polk

The relationship of Texas to the United States had long been touched with the politics of race. The literature of the early nineteenth century is riddled with expressions of Anglo-Saxon superiority over a dark-skinned native population. Also, slavery had been a constant matter of contention among those in the United States who sought to mold relations with their southern neighbor. Mexico declared independence from Spain in 1821, and fifteen years of schizophrenic domestic policy on slavery ensued there. Mexican lawmakers were torn between two competing impulses: the liberal inclination to abolish slavery throughout Mexican holdings, and the developmental urge to encourage further settlement and economic growth. These ambitions conflicted because American southerners were the most readily available pool of settlers. Thanks in large measure to the tireless efforts of Stephen F. Austin, who worked out a series of administrative compromises and improvised legal subterfuges, a flow of slaveholding southerners moved into Texas in the 1820s and early 1830s despite formal constraints on slavery by Mexican authorities. By 1835, a revolution for Texas independence from Mexico was underway, driven by proslavery forces and a generalized desire for self-government on the part of those settlers.[46] Because of the proximity of these developments to American soil, they drew the careful attention of policy makers in the United States.

Debate on policy toward Texas took on an especially passionate character because Texas was seen by many Americans North and South as "an empire for slavery." The geopolitical implications of a proslavery Texas nestled against the country's southwestern flank were impressive enough, but the ramifications of an *annexed* Texas were staggering. "Annex Texas to the United States," proclaimed Governor Albert G. Brown of Mississippi, "and you give to the South a degree of influence in the councils of a nation which will enable her to assert her rights with confidence, and maintain them with independence, and secure Mississippi peace in the exercise of her domestic policy, and a proud independence as a separate member of the confederacy."[47]

These prospects infuriated the abolitionists, who had long reserved for Texas a special enmity because of its zealous defiance of Mexico's decision to emancipate its slaves.[48] Moreover, their suspicions of a conspiracy to annex Texas seemed confirmed when, in early 1837, President Jackson discarded fears of war with Mexico and extended diplomatic recognition to the Texas Republic. On March 3, Jackson notified both houses of Congress of this action. A charge' d'affaires was confirmed by the Senate shortly before midnight, only twelve hours before Jackson turned the presidential reins over to Martin Van Buren.

Less than six months later, however, Van Buren announced his decision to reject a request by Texas for annexation.[49] He was undoubtedly mindful of the explosion of protest issuing from the North over the decision to extend recognition. *The Liberator* reported that, during this period, mounds of petitions on Texas had arrived on Capitol Hill, and were *"stowed away in the ante-chambers by wagon loads*[. E]re long there will be almost a sufficient quantity to erect a pyramid that shall vie with the proudest on the plains of Egypt, as a great moral monument of the expressed will of a free people."[50] Witnessing what had transpired from Jackson's term to Van Buren's (i.e., the progression from the mails controversy to the dispute over annexation), Thomas Hart Benton wrote, "We had just been employed in suppressing, or exploding, this [antislavery] annoyance, in the Northeast; and, in the twinkling of an eye, it sprung up in the Southwest, two thousand miles off, and quite diagonally from its late point of apparition."[51] Perhaps of greatest concern to the president was the fact that some leading northern politicians, who otherwise expressed little sympathy for the cause of abolition, were moved to oppose annexation on the grounds that further expansion of the influence of the southern states—the Slavepower—was simply unhealthy for the Union.[52] Sensing the import of this nonradical, free-state opinion, Van Buren wished to shelve the matter. All this changed, however, during the administration of John Tyler, who acceded to the presidency following the untimely death of Van Buren's successor, William Henry Harrison. Tyler sought Texas as the crown jewel of his legacy.

Tyler's decision to change course dramatically on Texas merits some special attention here because it provides a revealing window onto the character of the president's nation-keeping role. On the face of it, such an important reversal would seem to undermine my broad claims for the universality of the role requirements, their enduring presence from one administration to the next. However, Tyler's presidency—and his decision making on Texas—actually help illuminate some fine points about the character of that role not as clearly visible elsewhere.

First, we see here that there is a subjective element in how presidents interpret the requirements of that role at a given time, with respect to a specific issue. On an explosive problem, it is unsurprising that public decision makers—even those who share the same ultimate goal, who represent essentially the same people, and who are basically chosen to make common decisions through the same process—may differ on the efficacy of specific means. Accordingly, the essential historical *continuity* of presidential activity on the question of slavery (and directly related questions, such as expansion), is remarkable. It becomes even more extraordinary when we recognize that arguably the two most abrupt reversals of presidential policy in the entire antebellum era occurred as accidents.[53] Thus these nonroutine departures from the norm are better explained as the product of chance than of choice.[54]

Tyler and Millard Fillmore (whose reversal on the Compromise of 1850 will be discussed below) both rose to the presidency without having been elected to the office, as a result of the sudden deaths of their immediate predecessors. That they might perceive political reality differently from the presidents they replaced was virtually assured, if not by the unusual circumstances of their accession then by the peculiarities of partisan ticket-balancing. These seconds were originally put on national tickets precisely because of their *dissimilarities* to their principals. Small wonder, then, that after fate intervened, they would be inclined to strike out on a different path—albeit toward the same end—once the reins of power were handed over to them.[55]

Historian William J. Cooper has written, "In contrast to his predecessors in the White House, John Tyler felt no political impediments when he grasped Texas. Instead, political reality, as Tyler perceived it, propelled him toward Texas.... In the South, always the focus of Tylerite vision, Tyler could become the guardian of slavery and southern safety."[56] Tyler desperately needed to solidify the South because he had severely strained ties to his own Whig party by refusing to bow to that party's supreme congressional eminence, Henry Clay, whose principled Whig program was not one Tyler could make himself endorse.[57] Thus, very early in his presidential tenure Tyler found himself a political orphan, unable to lay claim to the support of the dominant wing of either party. This most unusual posture—indeed a position most unlikely for any elected president, given the role parties played in the nomination process—set Tyler off to cobble together a third, "Tylerite" party, based on the prospect of drawing to his standard southern Whigs and Democrats. In effect, he found it necessary to manufacture a political base *after* he reached the presidency. It was this strange confluence of circumstances, brought about by historical accident, that made a reversal on the Texas question so compelling for him.[58]

A second important lesson of Tyler's presidency emerges, though, from the fact that, despite his personal and political inclinations, Tyler felt compelled upon entering office *not* to take any immediate steps to annex Texas. In this he mimicked President Jackson, who evidently had shared his enthusiasm for embracing Texas, and Van Buren, who evidently had not. All three, however, recognized the explosiveness of that situation, and sought to avoid as best they could adding fuel to the fire by sponsoring official efforts to make annexation a reality. Here, then, we see the nation-keeping constraints of the office operating on Tyler contrary to what he saw as his own peculiar political interests, a point of major frustration both for the president and for pro-annexationist Texans. Tyler tried to explain to the latter the inescapable gravity of heightened northern irritability on the subject. As historian William W. Freehling reports it, "I wish 'to annex you,' Tyler whined to [Texas Minister Isaac] Van Zandt in April of 1843, '*but you see how I am situated.*'" This lament testifies to the nation-keeping constraints acting on even an accidental president who believed his political future depended on doing something else.[59]

A change in the face of the issue—effectively fashioned by shrewd Texans—eventually altered the character of the president's behavior, freeing him to follow his political inclinations. Recognizing that concerns about preserving domestic tranquillity were foremost in the president's thinking, the Texans (with important assists from their southern friends in Washington) maneuvered to appeal to the president on the one point best guaranteed to motivate him to favorable action: national security. What is especially instructive about this episode is that the matters of security and slavery were to become wrapped together so tightly in Tyler's thinking.

Under the influence of a number of southern "ultras" whom he had placed in important administration posts, Tyler became convinced that the Republic of Texas was preparing to establish a formal link with Britain. The president initially maintained a customary caution, but he grew increasingly worried by intelligence that suggested that Britain was insisting on emancipation as a condition of their support. During his period of uncertainty, Tyler penned a letter claiming that "American action would be mandatory only if the Administration received official confirmation that England had pressed 'abolition' as 'the basis of interference.'" His southern aides saw that he got what passed for such confirmation, although most of the evidence was constructed of vague suggestions in preliminary discussions by unofficial emissaries about possible openings. This, however, was sufficient.[60]

The Tyler administration's decision to pursue annexation of Texas, then, by the president's own hand derived entirely from concerns over threats posed by emancipation. "As in gag rule times," writes Freehling, "antislavery danger was still slight. But once again, the distant threat, if not early checked, looked capable of escalating. Only annexation would be an obviously effective check."[61]

Annexation, however, could not be accomplished by presidential edict; a supermajority of the Senate was required to ratify the related treaty. Thus, the administration set to work to sell confirmation to the Senate and to the American people, engaging in an aggressive lobbying and public relations campaign usually thought to be the sole province of the so-called "modern" presidency. Again, it is instructive that the effort was undertaken in large measure to afford additional security for the prevailing institutional structures of American politics, especially those in the South.

Given the obvious consequences of annexation—the buttressing of the Slavepower in the nation's government—this was no mean feat. The North was correctly expected to be very hesitant to pursue that course of action, despite its promise of denying England another toe-hold in North America. Consequently, the administration developed a two-pronged strategy for selling the treaty, one directed at the North, the other the South.[62]

The central component of efforts to market Texas to an extension-wary North was a lengthy missive written to a pro-annexation group in Carroll County, Kentucky, by then-Senator Robert J. Walker, a Mississippi Democrat, who was "enlisted by the President for the work of winning public opinion."[63] The Mississippian's letter creatively and forcefully described the benefits to be found in annexation for those *opposed* to slavery in the United States. This letter was published in pamphlet form, and is said to have circulated over a million copies, in addition to being serialized in a number of influential expansionist newspapers.

Walker, acting as the president's mouthpiece, argued that Texas was a "safety valve" for the American slave system. Although adding Texas to the Union as a slave state would have the immediate effect of extending the reach of the peculiar institution, in the long term Texas provided the only means for ridding America of slavery and the black race.

Slavery was, according to Walker's argument, a "soil-destroying institution." The southern states, after decades of depletion of their farmlands, were in the process of becoming economically unfit for the continued use of slaves. Texas, however, provided a vast area of largely virgin soil, which could benefit immensely from the application of slave labor. Thus, with Texas available to southern slaveholders, many would elect to relocate, or to sell their slaves to Texas landowners, to benefit from the comparative advantage inherent in a large region of previously unused farmland. A natural movement of slaves would result, first from border states and then from the deeper southern states. Eventually, Texas soil, too, would become depleted, and slaves would be moved further south, following their next most economical application. The end product would be equally beneficial to

American whites and blacks; the former would be freed from the burden of an onerous institution and the dilemmas of assimilating a freed race into the American mainstream, and the latter would eventually move into a Latin American clime more to their liking, among a people more favorably disposed to the idea of emancipation. These remarkable benefits were predicated on Texas being made available as a safety-valve for American slaves.[64]

Given the immediate political realities of Texas's annexation, the sales job in the South was relatively easy. Yet when Secretary of State Abel P. Upshur died as a result of a freak explosion just as treaty negotiations were getting under way, Tyler named as his successor one of the heavyweights of southern politics: John C. Calhoun. Tyler held up submission of the treaty to the Senate until Calhoun could enter into the record correspondence intended to instill southern confidence. Calhoun, apparently with Tyler's backing, acted on a long-held conviction that an open, aggressive assertion of slaveholding rights was essential for the protection of the South.[65] In two letters to Richard Pakenham, the British minister in Washington, Calhoun openly attributed responsibility for the administration's attempts to annex Texas to British efforts for emancipation there. Calhoun wrote, "It was not possible for the President to hear with indifference the avowal of a policy so hostile in its character and dangerous in its tendency, to the domestic institutions of so many States of this Union, and to the safety and prosperity of the whole." The British interest in a humane end "was equivalent, in Calhoun's mind," reports one student, "to the avowal of an aggressive policy." Calhoun's letters contained extensive defenses of slavery, arguing from questionable census data that the condition of blacks in the free states was substantially worse than conditions where slavery flourished.[66] These letters were voluntarily submitted to the Senate as part of the treaty proceedings, placing on the public record there an administration argument for slavery as a positive good. "Protecting slavery had always been a part of the Texas picture," concludes William J. Cooper Jr., "but with the Calhoun-Pakenham letters the prominence of slavery was dramatized. . . . After Calhoun's performance no one could possibly evade the equation: annexation equaled defense of slavery."[67]

Tyler was not initially successful in attaining either of his personal goals as president for grasping Texas; he was never seriously in contention for the 1844 presidential race, and the treaty he negotiated with Texas was defeated by a substantial majority in the Senate, well short of the two-thirds vote needed for approval. However, he did succeed in changing the complexion of the presidential election. The Democrats nominated James K. Polk of Tennessee, an avid annexationist. Polk defeated Whig nominee Henry Clay, who was caught in the cross-fire of his party's debate over Texas. Claiming that the election was a clear mandate that the American people wanted Texas brought into the Union, Tyler placed the treaty a second time before the outgoing Congress in December 1844. Relying on the questionable tactic of having simple majorities of both houses of Congress resolve to add Texas as a new state, Tyler finally succeeded. The lame-duck president took advantage of the joint resolution to extend a formal invitation for Texas to join the Union on his final full day in office. For all practical purposes, then, Tyler's goal for Texas was belatedly accomplished.

Picking up where Tyler left off, the Tennessean Polk quickly pursued the completion of annexation negotiations with Texas, efforts which came to fruition on December 29, 1845, when Texas was officially admitted as a state. The conditions of the annexation agreement were such that Texas could eventually create four additional states out of its vast expanse, with only that small area resting above the 36°30' parallel—the line of demarcation employed in the Missouri Compromise—being guaranteed as free in the event a separate state was created there. Under this arrangement the slave interests could be, in a nation composed at the time of only twenty-six states, markedly fortified.[68] Cognizant of the "sectional jealousies and heartburnings" inflamed as a result of acquiring Texas, Polk attempted to dismiss the impact of the change in his inaugural address: "Whatever is good or evil in the local institutions of Texas, will remain her own, whether annexed to the United States or not. None of the present States will be responsible for them, any more than they are for the local institutions of each other."[69] But the effect on sectional balances of power was unmistakable.

Annexation was a bitter defeat for the antislavery forces, both in immediate terms and because of what it represented for the country's future. Enumerating the specifics of the administration's unusually aggressive techniques for obtaining Texas, one historian has written: "[T]he clandestine opening of the annexation negotiation, the fraudulent justification for doing so contained in the diplomatic correspondence, the unscrupulous use of census errors to prove the beneficence of the institution of slavery, the hidden and illegal pledges of armed aid to the Texans if they should be attacked by Mexico, and the shabby recourse throughout to anti-British feeling to overcome reluctance in the North to accept an extension of slavery," all proved to the abolitionists, and to the antiextensionists, how far the Slavepower would go to protect itself. With the addition of that western empire, the South was in an even better posture than before to control the nation's destiny. A despondent John Quincy Adams, who represented the moderate antislavery forces in Congress, proclaimed Texas annexation "the heaviest calamity that ever befell myself and my country."[70]

Under three successive administrations, then, the power of the presidency had been aggressively asserted not to further liberty for the slaves, but to suppress the efforts of those who promoted liberty. The Chief Executive closed the mails to abolitionist tracts; the Chief Legislator pledged to veto antislavery legislation for the District of Columbia; and the Chief of State labored to bolster the power of slavery in the nation's councils of governance.

The West Beyond Texas: Polk, Taylor, and Fillmore

The annexation of Texas did not, however, have its anticipated effect. Although slave-state representation increased on Capitol Hill, those numerical gains were overwhelmed by a commensurate intensifying of free-state opposition to southern gluttony. Within eighteen months the editors of *The Liberator* proclaimed that a new day had dawned in Washington, in reaction to annexation and the resulting war with an angered Mexico: "Now any Northern senator or representative may rise in his place, and offer the severest denunciations against slavery in the South . . . and back up his word by his votes, and he is no longer in danger of being assassinated."[71] Thus, those who thought annexation would once and for all secure Slavepower supremacy in the national government were proved wrong. This new political reality was especially problematic for President James K. Polk, who rode into office on "an almost irrepressible movement to stretch the nation's boundaries" further, toward the Pacific.[72]

Here we find the intersection of the politics of racial inequality and of Manifest Destiny.[73] Though there was some overlap in the two, it would be erroneous to suggest that they should be wholly equated, at least as rationales for those who pressed for expansion. The general impulse toward the West, especially that of the post-Texas era, was sparked by a host of motives, including geopolitics and, in Sidney M. Milkis's words, "the Jeffersonian and Jacksonian commitment to protecting small landholders and artisans as the bone and sinew of the republic" by claiming for them more space.[74] Yet Tyler's legacy—his lasting bequest to the nation and to the presidency—was an entanglement of slavery and expansion so frustratingly inescapable as to vex even the most gifted of his successors.

Polk, commonly designated by historians as among the leading lights of the nineteenth-century presidency, seemed entirely confounded by this knotted mess, confiding once to his diary, "What connection slavery had with making peace with Mexico it is difficult to conceive."[75] Yet Polk was even *more* aggressive than his predecessor in pushing the nation's boundaries westward through Mexican holdings, driven by a belief that the nation's future security resided in Pacific lands and seaports.[76] He clearly articulated this conception of American geopolitics in his inaugural address:

> As our population has expanded, the Union has been cemented and strengthened. As our boundaries have been enlarged and our agricultural population has been spread over a large surface, our federative system has acquired additional strength and security. It may well be doubted whether it would not be in greater danger of overthrow if our present population were confined to the comparatively narrow limits of the original thirteen States than it is now that they are sparsely settled over a more expanded territory. It is confidently believed that our system may be safely extended to the utmost bounds of our territorial limits, and that as it shall be extended the bonds of our Union, so far from being weakened, will become stronger.[77]

The extent to which the slavery issue would effect his broader aims became clear in August 1846, when the House of Representatives passed the so-called Wilmot Proviso, a stipulation (added to a funding bill) that expressly forbade slavery in any lands gained as a result of a negotiated conclusion to war with Mexico. (Prospects at that time looked very favorable for the United States to add to its disputed Texas acquisition enormous Mexican lands, including a vast gateway to the Pacific in what is now the American Southwest.) The proviso manifestly revealed the growth of free-state frustration over the perceived excesses of the Slavepower and how potent a force that frustration had become in the most democratic of American political institutions.

Wilmot's initiative enraged many southerners. Historian William J. Cooper Jr. writes, "The proviso made the South the Ishmael of the nation that had to be banished and cut off because of its un-American social system."[78] One prominent Georgian claimed that it communicated to the world that the South deserved "public censure and national odium."[79] John C. Calhoun took it as evidence that the South was perilously close to losing control of its own destiny, and he consequently mounted a very public campaign, threatening regional secession, to secure the South against the proviso's backers.[80] These pressures—over how the expansion of slavery might bias the nation's constitution—threatened to tie up in endless debate Polk's push for expansion, jeopardizing his paramount policy desires as president.

Having the matter thrust on him in this fashion, Polk responded predictably. Although he had apparently been motivated by other impulses in moving the nation westward, once he was confronted with the issue of slaveholding in these new lands, he acted as had his predecessors: he categorically rejected the policy advocated by the antislavery activists, making denial of Wilmot's Proviso his sine qua non. He then lobbied aggressively to make certain that the Senate rejected the proviso's constraints, which it did.

The president's negative reaction, however, did nothing to convince the pro-proviso forces in the House that they should fold. Although Polk did successfully negotiate the acquisition from Mexico of California and New Mexico in early 1848, with the Treaty of Guadalupe Hidalgo, he still confronted a battle over the conditions under which those new areas would be affixed to the Union. The proviso controversy dimmed prospects that territorial governments could be provided those newly acquired western areas in the near future, leaving ajar prospects that the United States might lose them. Polk consequently sought another solution. His preferred alternative was an extension of the Missouri Compromise parallel to the Pacific Ocean, with all lands below the 36°30' latitude open to slavery, all above kept free.[81] This proposal had for Polk the virtue of making available to slavery the disputed Southwest lands (contrary to the intent of Wilmot's Proviso) while allowing him to say to disgruntled free-state representatives that he was merely following time-honored precedent. However, this proposal went nowhere. Newly invigorated free-state backers of the proviso were unwilling to cede *any* southwestern lands to the slave interests. Furthermore, increasingly hardline southern "ultras" also rejected the president's proposal as an unconstitutional artifice—the political atmosphere had become so electrified after the House's initial adoption of Wilmot's restrictions that many southerners were now following Calhoun's lead in embracing a novel argument that the Constitution guaranteed slavery in *all* federally controlled territories.[82] Thus the changed and charged environment of that era had corroded an option that a mere decade before might have been considered the perfect solution to the present dilemma. Going into the final months of Polk's presidency, then, the southwestern question seemed hopelessly deadlocked, and there appeared to be growing fervor North and South for disunion over it.

In December 1848, only three months before his scheduled departure from office, President Polk changed course and embraced another alternative for resolving the Southwest lands dispute. This represented a meaningful, unprecedented departure from prior presidential practice on the slavery issue.[83] Polk joined with Senator Stephen A. Douglas (D-Ill) in proposing that California be admitted directly into the Union as a state, bypassing completely the territorial stage. This meant that the decision about the status of slavery in California would be left up to that *state's* own citizens, rather than requiring some direct decision from Washington on the matter within a federally controlled territory. Since Mexican law had governed the area in question until its postwar cession, expectations were that any new state constitution would continue to outlaw slavery. In practice—but, importantly, not in form—the restrictions of Wilmot's Proviso would prevail. The great virtue of this plan for Polk was its apparent efficacy: many slave state representatives could be expected to join free state advocates, albeit grudgingly, because they believed that each *state* had authority over its own domestic institutions.

It is useful here to pause for a moment and examine *why* Polk—a slaveholding Tennessean serving in an office usually employed in the preservation of existing social structures—would depart from longstanding precedent and advocate a policy that promised to advantage those working to abolish slavery in the United States. The answer is that Polk believed that the short- and long-term security interests of the nation required some significant concessions.

In the most immediate sense, the nation Polk was pledged to preserve, protect, and defend was perilously close to disintegration over the status of the Southwest. Calhoun had visibly raised the specter of southern secession to deter the free states from excluding slavery in the common territories. Too, a small but vocal movement for northern secession had grown during Polk's term among those who believed that the annexation of Texas had nullified the nation's original charter.[84] In mid-1848, the president noted that the extension issue "was more threatening to the Union than anything which has occurred since the meeting of the Hartford Convention in 1814."[85] The problem only worsened thereafter. In earlier years Polk might have been able to side with the prevailing slave interests with impunity, outlasting his opposition. But the presence of a solid Wilmot Proviso majority in the House—and the emergence of the Free Soil party as a key electoral force in the 1848 election[86]—testified to the strength of free state opinion about slavery's extension. This was a force that could not be ignored.

Accordingly, some kind of delicately crafted accommodation—along the lines of the California statehood proposal—was in order, so that all sides in an increasingly acrimonious dispute could feel justified in maintaining peacefully their nationality.

Polk also believed that the long-term security interests of the United States demanded this accommodation; the nation needed to extend its borders to the Pacific Ocean in order to fulfill its Manifest Destiny. A significant step in this direction had occurred in early 1848 with the acquisition of California and New Mexico. Yet as succeeding months passed in gridlock over the establishment of governments for these territories, presidential satisfaction turned to alarm over prospects that the nation might lose the Pacific Southwest after all.

First, word reached Washington late in 1848 that gold had been discovered near Sacramento. That those southwestern lands were even richer than anyone had previously imagined both increased the risk that other nations might meddle with an unsecured territory and raised immensely the stakes associated with that risk. Second, persistent reports issued out of California that settlers there were becoming increasingly impatient with Washington's inability to provide territorial governments. This left them in a condition uncomfortably close to a Hobbesian state of nature. Small wonder that rumors mounted of an impending movement in California toward independence.[87]

Moreover, the president was furious to find that some in Washington, including Senator Thomas Hart Benton (D-Mo), were actually promoting that idea.[88] Polk's anxiety peaked after the 1848 presidential election, because he was convinced that the incoming Whig Zachary Taylor would gladly concede California's independence in order to circumvent the messy and politically troublesome process of holding on to that area.[89] All these developments energized Polk to do something he was otherwise reluctant to do: to compromise on the slavery question there as the price of securing for the nation the Southwest.[90] This was the most prominent pressure confronting a nation-keeping president. Commenting in his diary on his own frenzied activity for the California compromise, Polk wrote, "This is an unusual step for the Executive to take, but the emergency demands it. It may be the only means of allaying a fearful sectional excitement & of preserving the Union, and therefore I think upon high public considerations it is justified." Polk had been moved by the changed conditions in California to depart from the policy paths of his predecessors; a revised perception of his nation-keeping role required as much. As Polk himself soon thereafter announced to his cabinet, he sought California's admission as a state because he "had a country to save."[91]

In effect, then, what we see in Polk's presidency is a faint preview of the bolder presidential conversions associated with the 1860s and 1960s. For a brief time presidential concerns about the preservation of existing social structures became subsumed under broader worries about how racial politics might undermine the president's ability to meet his national security responsibilities, broadly defined. Polk did not abandon his sine qua non (i.e., a pledge to veto Wilmot's Proviso in that form), but he did promote modest accommodation with the antislavery interests as a means toward a broader goal: the procurement of a resource-rich California on the nation's western frontier. Toward this end he orchestrated an aggressive, personalized, "unusual" lobbying campaign of the type more commonly associated with the so-called "modern presidency" than with its mid-nineteenth-century forbear. This was, as he himself reported, required for "preserving the Union."

Since few of the combatants in the dispute were willing to move toward his compromise position on California—the unique perceptions by the president of his obligations, as Neustadt has observed, are not always shared by others[92]—Polk's job was unfinished when his term came to an end. He left office in deep despair. During a carriage ride to the Capitol for Zachary Taylor's inaugural ceremonies, Polk understood the president-elect to confirm that he found California and Oregon too distant from the East to be useful members of the Union, and that it would be better for them to form an independent government. The outgoing president bitterly confided to his diary that he found Taylor to be "uneducated [and] exceedingly ignorant of public affairs."[93] Polk died three months later, unaware of how the incentive structures of the presidential institution would conform his successor's behavior to his own.

Zachary Taylor's crucial southern Whig electorate had strong reason to believe that the slave interests had placed a friend in the White House, a president who would be unwilling to brook restrictions on slavery in the Southwest. Here, after all, was a Louisianan and a slaveholder, who had made his reputation in the Mexican War. But Taylor's status as a war hero had enabled him to move successfully into the presidency without making any public commitments on a number of key issues, including the Southwest

lands question. Once in office, the new president surveyed the situation carefully, and subsequently embraced the very position Polk had promoted: the
admission of California and New Mexico directly into the Union as states.
Further, he publicly announced to an audience in Pennsylvania that "The
people of the North need have no apprehension of the further extension of
slavery."[94] This turn of events baffled and infuriated southerners who
expected more from Taylor.

Why did this president, despite his personal sympathies with slaveholders
and his expressed disinterest in western statehood, move in this direction? It
is not clear that he had developed Polk's sense of geopolitical necessity, but
Taylor evidently *had* come to share his predecessor's understanding of the
explosiveness of the expansion issue, and accordingly, like the good soldier
he was, he sought to disarm it. Taylor wanted to take a fatally divisive issue
off the public agenda. He had seen the sectional controversy grow during his
lifetime to the point of threatening the Union, with each movement westward reopening old wounds. He reasoned, then, that if the disposition of the
last of the disputed territories could be settled, with a mild concession to the
North, then the long-burning battle over the slavery question could finally
be extinguished. One respected biographer has written,

> Taylor only desired to keep the nation free of slavery controversy. . . . By
> sweeping all Mexican Cession territory into two states, Zachary Taylor
> would leave no territories left to dispute. No Territory would kill agitation
> over slavery in territories, restore a Union where sections did not hate each
> other, [and] . . . make Whig nonpartisanship the saving reality.[95]

The trade-off was clearly defined: California and New Mexico would be
made free states—an admittedly painful concession for a sensitive South—
but that would spell the end of the protracted conflict over expansion. The
South stood to gain lasting security by putting to rest the agitators' best issue.

Taylor sought to secure these ends by making a most un-whig use of the
presidential institution. "Old Rough and Ready," writes William W.
Freehling, "was soon thrashing around Washington in a manner reminiscent
of Old Hickory. He threatened to veto any congressional plan not as pristine
as his. [And] he promised to march on Texas if that slaveholding state
refused to honor freesoil New Mexico's boundary claims."[96] Apparently
Taylor concluded (in the way that Richard Nixon much later did, believing
that his Cold Warrior credentials freed him to open relations with China)
that his stature as a war hero and southern slaveholder gave him space within

which to work momentarily against perceived southern interests for their greater long-term good.

Important southern leaders, however, refused to rely on the president's goodwill and judgment. With Calhoun fanning once again the flames of disunion from his seat in the Senate, Whig Henry Clay sought some kind of middle ground. He developed a package of eight, interrelated legislative measures, encompassing proposals on virtually every facet of the slavery controversy as it then stood. These were the basis for what was to become the Compromise of 1850. The eight measures provided for: (1) adding California to the Union as a free state; (2) organizing the New Mexico and Utah territories without federal restrictions on slavery (but with the general understanding that slavery could not readily exist there); (3) adjusting a disputed boundary between Texas and New Mexico, which amounted to establishing jurisdiction over a large area between a slave Texas and a probably-free New Mexico; (4) assumption of Texas's pre-annexation debt, offered as a sweetener for Texas to loose its claims on the New Mexico dispute; (5) a congressional pledge of noninterference with slavery in the District of Columbia; (6) prohibition of the slave trade in D.C.; (7) a more effective fugitive slave law; and (8) congressional disavowal of authority to interfere with the slave trade in the South.[97]

The central trade-off in Clay's compromise was essentially the same one Tyler promoted—land for security—but the two differed significantly on how specifically to satisfy southern security interests. The president proposed a very restrictive legislative agenda, believing that held the greatest promise for settling the dispute. "He had no wish to complicate [matters] . . . by confronting other disquieting issues, such as fugitive slaves."[98] Clay, conversely, proclaimed that the president's proposal merely patched one of the wounds "bleeding and threatening the well being, if not the existence of the body politic."[99] Clay's efforts at compromise—especially in promoting a vastly strengthened fugitive slave law and greater protections for the domestic slave trade—were intended to stanch the hemorrhaging at all points.

An intractable stalemate set in during the spring of 1850, with few signs emerging that either side would prevail.[100] Quite suddenly—quite unexpectedly—Taylor contracted a gastro-intestinal illness, and the second Whig to be elected to the presidency became the second Whig to die there.[101] The subsequent transition from Taylor to Vice President Millard Fillmore, in July 1850, became as dramatic as that from Harrison to Tyler had been.

Before Taylor's death, Millard Fillmore had confided to him that were he called upon to break a tie vote in the Senate on Clay's compromise, he would defy the president and vote for it.[102] Accordingly, after Taylor's death, Fillmore changed the course charted by Taylor and placed the White House squarely behind the work of Henry Clay. Taylor's cabinet was swept clean so that new officers could be brought in to ensure unity on the territorial issue. Most importantly, Daniel Webster, who had been closely in league with Clay in drafting his proposals, was named Secretary of State.[103] With this new-found support from the White House, Congress moved with dispatch to adopt, with some modifications, the provisions of Clay's compromise, finishing their work in the fall of 1850.[104]

"There never was such a metamorphosis," reflected one contemporary observer of the transition from Taylor to Fillmore.[105] The roots of this difference likely originated in both the personal perceptions and political histories of these two presidents, as well as in their own positions within the Whig party. Most prominently, Taylor's record as a war hero gave him the personal stature to stand apart from the recognized leaders of the party in a way that Fillmore could not comfortably do. Thus, the most proximate factor giving shape to Fillmore's inclinations on this matter was probably a difference in the political calculus he reckoned vis-à-vis that of his immediate predecessor.

Yet these forces should not be considered apart from the character of each president's nation-keeping role. As I have argued earlier, the general influence of that role is to incline presidents strongly to the protection of the nation's security and domestic tranquillity. It has the effect, then, of narrowing considerably a president's freedom to act on a host of issues that touch on questions of peace and defense, broadly defined. How those even-narrowed requirements are to be met in specific instances, however, may be highly subjective. How does a president, confronting an explosive issue that threatens to destroy the cohesion of a nation he is pledged to preserve, make judgments about which *specific* option within a limited array of alternatives to pursue? That the role exists does not mean that answers materialize out of thin air, any more than the president's role as commander-in-chief automatically instructs him as to where the nation's troops are best deployed or the role of chief legislator spontaneously informs him as to which bill ought to receive his highest priority. Neither do presidents come to understand the requirements of the role from some cryptic source, divulged to them after their swearing in like the secret code to the nuclear "football." Rather, they find in their political environment a host of everyday cues bearing on which course of action best leaves the nation and its institutions less vulnerable to strains and disruption. These include, but are not limited to, such things as the sum of the president's own political experience; his refined (and evidently effective) intuition about political behavior (mass, institutional, and individual); the face of issues as they appear through his partisan environment; his policy-making expertise; and his own subjective reading about the state of popular opinion and receptivity to various courses of action.

At times the signals emanating from the political system are more easily read than at others; at times the latitude to act is greater than at others. But the only way a president can determine the substance of what the role requires in practice is to consult these signals. Indeed, any president ignoring nation-keeping responsibilities—or seriously misreading them—would likely find the resulting, corrective signals in the political environment most bracing.[106]

Again, what is remarkable about the nature of presidential behavior on the question of slavery during the period under examination here is how infrequently significant departures from established courses of action occurred. This is evidence about the powerful place of racial inequality as a fact of social and political life during this era. But that substantial, abrupt changes did occasionally happen—albeit usually more the result of chance than choice—merely highlights the subjective character of how the broad demands of that role are carried out in practice. In this instance, we find that the nation-keeping role did not steer presidential action into a single, inescapable channel. Yet there are occasions, as we shall see, when a president feels bound—based on a reading of the signals in his environment—to follow a specific path of action because, in the fashion of Luther, he can "do no otherwise."

The broad incentive structures that give life to the nation-keeping role did not, then, undergo radical transformation at the moment Taylor's pulse stopped. Rather, successive presidents differed over which specific means promised most effectively to achieve commonly held goals—a securing of the West and an amelioration of the sectional controversy—goals they shared precisely because they saw their attainment as crucial to preserving the Union.

In 1850, most of the nation entered a period of great thanksgiving and relief that the cup of disunion had passed. Fillmore scrawled across the top margin of a letter about the compromise to New York's governor, "The long agony is over."[107] "Crowds thronged the streets of Washington," reports

David Potter, "and serenaded the Compromise leaders. On one glorious night, the word went abroad that it was the duty of every patriot to get drunk. Before the next morning many a citizen had proved his patriotism, and Senators Foote, Douglas, and others were reported stricken with a variety of implausible maladies—headaches, heat prostration, or overindulgence of fruit."[108] Years of turmoil, most believed, had finally been laid to rest.[109] The issue of slavery had been removed from the public agenda. With this, abolitionism fell to its lowest state in two decades.[110]

Execution of Legal Constraints: The Fugitive Slave Law

The abolitionists had very early voiced opposition to Clay's compromise, equating its effort to harmonize slavery and freedom with "an agreement by which Christ and Belial should jointly undertake to govern this world!"[111] Their preference had been for the kind of legislation Taylor proposed, in which the territorial issue would be settled satisfactorily with no concessions on collateral issues.

For the abolitionists, the joy at seeing the slave trade abolished in the District, and of bringing California into the family of free states, was as nothing in comparison to the sobering reality of the new Fugitive Slave Law and the empowerment of federal commissioners established to implement it. Although the Slavepower had been excluded from distant western lands, it had, as part of the bargain, extended its reach into the North, furthering there the complicity of free-state citizens in a crime against mankind. The abolitionists recognized that the compromise "placed the institution of slavery on a firmer legal basis than it had formerly possessed."[112] This bargain, they felt, had been made at far too high a price, and the "Godlike" Daniel Webster was as fallen as Belial himself for consenting to it. It was, then, this component of the compromise that the abolitionists latched onto as the key to their new assault against complacency.[113] The fortified Fugitive Slave Law was immediately denounced as "a bill to be resisted, disobeyed, and trampled under foot, at all hazards."[114]

Ironically, the new law worked in due time to Garrison's advantage, as it clarified the abolitionist position more than the thousand issues of *The Liberator* which theretofore had been published. Since the movement's very inception, the abolitionists had strained to convey to the people of the North that they shared responsibility for the continued presence of slaves in the

United States, that the sin of slavery was no respecter of Mason and Dixon's line. This abstraction became all too real once northerners were compelled into service under the new law to join the hounds and posses of federal commissioners in search of fugitives from the South. Such impressment, more clearly than Garrison's most lucid argument, exposed the extent to which the South depended on the North for sustaining its "peculiar institution." Abolitionists, and northern states righters, hoped to turn this sympathy into a means of building new support for their cause.

Once the new act was fully under implementation, northern publics were openly confronted with the raw facts of slavery as an American institution. The political climate in many free states became electrified as legal punishments escalated for those who gave aid and comfort to the fugitives, or who simply refused to be drafted into service of federal authorities.[115] The sight of respected members of local communities behind bars at the hand of the federal government for assisting runaways shocked the conscience of many an otherwise complacent citizen. Frederick Douglass subsequently commented, "The Fugitive Slave Bill has especially been of positive service to the anti-slavery movement."[116] A later analyst added,

> By their insistence on a Federal confirmation of the right to hold and recover slave property, southern leaders in Congress presumably had hoped to crush the growing abolition movement by opposing to it the powers, both legal and moral, of the Federal government. But in so doing, they ended the isolation in which the abolitionists had labored as nonpolitical reformers. Astute antislavery leaders now made common cause with the diverse forces arrayed against the government and the party in power.[117]

Of principal importance here is the part the presidency was expected to play in executing the agreements of Clay's compromise. In two significant ways, Millard Fillmore's job had just begun when he signed into law the legislation sent to him by Congress.

First, recognizing among some a residual hostility toward the compromise, Fillmore joined the ranks of those trying to put the slavery issue entirely in the past. In his annual messages of 1850 and 1851, the president appealed to Congress, and to the American people, to accept the compromise for what he saw it to be: the concluding chapter to a tumultuous epoch in the nation's history. In the first message, after acknowledging that many had quarrels with individual elements of the compromise, he stated, "The series of measures to

which I have alluded are regarded by me as a settlement in principle and substance—a final settlement of the dangerous and exciting subjects which they
embraced. . . . Most of these subjects, indeed are beyond your reach, as the legislation which disposed of them was in its character final and irrevocable." He
further suggested that adjustments to the compromise might be made, but
only should "time and experience . . . demonstrate the necessity of further legislation to guard against evasion or abuse." That final clause was pointedly
directed toward the fugitive slave provisions, and prospects that evasion might
require additional strengthening. One year later, Fillmore reminded his audiences of his claims for finality the previous year, and noted that he still subscribed to that view. His decision, he said, was based on an understanding of
his "duty to seize upon this compromise as the best that could be obtained
amid conflicting interests and to insist upon it as a final settlement, to be
adhered to by all who value the peace and welfare of the country."[118]

The president's claims for the finality of the compromise were clearly
more exhortations than objective statements of fact. Since the balance of
power in the Senate had shifted with the addition of California, Fillmore took
it as a major part of his duty to reassure the losing interest in the territorial
battle—those who desired the expansion of slaveholding in the Southwest—
that their concession to compromise would be fully rewarded. In effect, then,
Fillmore saw it as part of his presidential responsibilities to use whatever
rhetorical powers he had to nurture adherence to the agreement. He felt a
duty to argue in favor of a settlement that the abolitionists considered almost
completely without redeeming value.

Fillmore's second job was that of executing faithfully the compromise's
provisions, most prominently the Fugitive Slave Act. Here he became the
Chief Executor. It was in this position that the presidency was almost literally
placed in the path of emancipation. Not only did execution of the law evidence the government's intent to act in a general fashion against the interests
of northern abolitionists, it also physically barred efforts to spirit the enslaved
to freedom, the most fundamentally mass-based aspect of the movement.
Moreover, the Fugitive Slave Law is an unusually illuminating datum for this
study, inasmuch as it formally codified the requirements of the presidential
role under examination here. I have asserted that the central role relevant to
this study is that of the president as nation-maintainer, and that through long
stretches of American history that role constrained presidents to act against
movements for social change. In most cases, however, the requirements of
that role were imposed on the presidency in an informal fashion, according

to the push and pull of existing political incentive structures (i.e., prevailing electoral behavior, rewards and punishments within the system of separated institutions, etc.). The Fugitive Slave Law differs in that it imposed a *formal* obligation on presidents to take action against racial activism. It was a codified version of the prevailing wisdom about what presidents ought to do to preserve, protect, and defend national unity.

Although Fillmore himself had not personally approved of the strengthened fugitive slave provision, he recognized that there was a duty imposed on him as the nation's chief executive to see that the law was vigorously enforced. Members of Congress intent on upholding the compromise, and southerners intent on getting their just due, kept careful watch to make sure the president fulfilled his obligations. Test cases were not long in coming.

In February 1851, a number of free blacks conveyed to Canada a fugitive slave known as Shadrach, who had been seized in Boston by a federal marshal pursuant to the provisions of the new law. Upon learning of these events, the president issued an unusual proclamation calling on all citizens of Boston to assist in apprehending the escaped fugitive. This proclamation was treated with derision by the antislavery press. The *Portland Inquirer*, for example, editorialized,

> It was scarcely credible that the Chief Magistrate of the Republic would so forget the dignity of his office, and with such pompous, hasty zeal send forth his solemn *Pronunciamento* to the nation—to the world—as though war was to be declared, or some other dire calamity hung over the land, simply because a posse of official kidnappers had been outwitted by a handful of negroes. . . . Who ever expected to see the day when American citizenship would be thus outraged by a President of the United States! It was reserved for Millard Fillmore officially to summon 'well-disposed citizens,' in 1851, to play the bloodhound upon the track of human innocence agreeably to his own favorite law.[119]

The Shadrach case caused such a stir that the Senate formally requested the president to provide it with any information he had about the "recent case of a forcible resistance to the execution of the laws of the United States in the city of Boston," and to notify that body as to any additional legal measures he might need to get the job done. Fillmore responded, placing primary blame for the escape on Boston's unwillingness to provide jail space for housing fugitive slaves. He requested (but did not receive) new authorization by law for the use of additional armed force to compel execution of the law in such circumstances.[120] He closed by pledging "to exercise, whenever it may become necessary, the power constitutionally vested in me to the fullest extent," including the use of already authorized powers, to see the act rigorously enforced.[121]

The opportunity to prove himself came in April when another incident arose in Boston over the capture of fugitive Thomas Sims. This time, at great federal expense, Sims was returned to Georgia by the marshal and city officials—backed by a large militia force approved in Washington—for a public whipping. A Boston Committee of Vigilance had intervened to save Sims, only to face a courthouse door wrapped in chains to keep would-be liberators out.[122]

When Franklin Pierce moved into the White House in 1853—the product of an election during which both parties pledged allegiance to the 1850 compromise—the new president accepted the legacy of Fillmore. In so doing he also accepted the burden of the compromise's opposition, which was evidently growing. As David Potter has written,

> [B]eneath the surface, there were many little indications that the [compromise] . . . did not rest on broad or deep foundations. . . . The antislavery bloc in Congress, strengthened by militant recruits like [Charles] Sumner and [Benjamin] Wade, was no longer a little handful of isolated men. In 1852, for every four votes that Franklin Pierce received in the free states, one copy of *Uncle Tom's Cabin* was sold.[123]

The possibility loomed large, then, that what Pierce called the "repose and security" of "the public mind" was only temporary.[124] Indeed, as it would happen, Pierce contributed greatly to its disruption.

In both his inaugural address and his first annual message to Congress, Pierce—who had been pronounced by one Mississippian as being "as reliable as Calhoun himself" on slavery—reiterated a faith in the 1850 solution.[125] He professed "that the laws of 1850, commonly called the 'compromise measures,' are strictly constitutional and to be unhesitatingly carried into effect. . . . I fervently hope that the question is at rest, and that no sectional or ambitious or fanatical excitement may again threaten the durability of our institutions or obscure the light of our prosperity."[126] Pierce thus pledged to execute faithfully the laws entrusted to his care, and called on his fellow Americans to ensure that the compromise endured.

Pierce was also as committed as Fillmore to ensuring that the new Fugitive

Slave Law was implemented in the North. This placed him on a collision course with the abolitionists in New England.

In May 1854, the fugitive Anthony Burns was captured in Boston. An outcry went up among the abolitionists there, and as a result an antislavery mob moved on the courthouse to free Burns. In the course of the subsequent battle a volunteer deputy lost his life. The local United States marshal, sensing that he was losing control, called in U.S. military support from the surrounding areas. Upon learning of the turmoil, Pierce wired from the White House, "Incur any expense deemed necessary . . . to insure the execution of the law." Further, he dispatched military representatives to direct the restoration proceedings. Unlike the Sims case two years before, when the prisoner was spirited out of town in the middle of the night, the government made a major show of force in this instance. Burns was marched down to the docks in broad daylight as the city's entire contingent of armed forces lined the streets. The ship awaiting to deliver Burns back to Virginia was a revenue cutter, also provided courtesy of the president of the United States. Franklin Pierce, on behalf of the U.S. government, was intent on showing to the estimated 20,000 spectators that defiance of the Fugitive Slave Law would not be tolerated.[127] "At the cost of $100,000 (equal to perhaps two million 1987 dollars) the Pierce administration had upheld the majesty of the law."[128]

Pierce's action cemented his disrepute—and disrespect for the Fugitive Slave Law—in New England. A series of public meetings was called throughout the area to denounce all those who participated in the return of Anthony Burns to slavery and the laws that sanctioned their performance. The most notable meeting occurred on Independence Day, 1854, in Framingham, Massachusetts. Henry David Thoreau addressed the audience, casting his lot with the abolitionists after having theretofore avoided their company. But the most dramatic presentation of the day belonged to William Lloyd Garrison. Producing a copy of the Fugitive Slave Law, he held a flame to it and presented a burnt offering to the crowd: "And let all the people say, *Amen.*" Garrison then offered up a copy of the Constitution of the United States. Catching it, too, afire, he proclaimed, "So perish all compromises with tyranny!" For over a decade Garrison had denounced the national charter as a "covenant with death and an agreement with hell," but his burning of the Constitution punctuated the point unlike any other word or deed. *This* represented the extent to which the radicals would go in their quest to rid America of slavery.

Louis Filler has written of this incident:

Here was the acme of Garrison's defiance of constituted authority — the evidence his detractors would use to illustrate his irresponsibility and, less clearly, his insignificance. Yet it would seem that Garrison was, if anything, more important than he had ever been. True, the mass of spectators did not rally to his colors; they continued to invest others with authority. But Garrison's antislavery principles they made more and more reputable.[129]

As Filler notes, only a small minority were willing to join Garrison in his efforts to dissolve the Union, but the people of New England were increasingly attentive to that minority's message. Disunion was still too radical a step for most, but they were not nearly so hesitant to accept its first cousin, nullification. In the wake of the Burns episode, eight northern states adopted new sets of personal liberty statutes specifically intended to nullify the workings of the Fugitive Slave Law. The constant digging by the Garrisonians on that side of the political spectrum eventually guided the mainstream into a channel reminiscent of the one South Carolina followed twenty-five years before. In those earlier days, nullification had been roundly denounced in those same New England legislative halls as tantamount to disunion.

It was not alone the execution of those legal constraints provided for in the Fugitive Slave Law, however, that moved many northerners into sympathy with abolitionism in the 1850s. At least equally productive of new agitation—and new agitators—was Pierce's decision to reopen and reverse long-standing federal policy on the status of slavery in the Kansas and Nebraska territories. In so doing, he eviscerated over thirty years of compromise, partly in the interest of protecting the nation's political agenda from the influence of antislavery agitators.

Manipulation of Decision Making: Kansas, Dred Scott, and Concessions to the Rebels

The efforts of Franklin Pierce—and after him James Buchanan—to suppress the influence of abolitionism on national politics took the general form of manipulating the decision-making processes involved in disposing of issues related to slavery. In effect, both of these presidents looked to change the prevailing rules of the game that until then had governed public decision making on that issue. Such changes reversed those advances antislavery forces had gained in accordance with the old procedures. Here, then, suppression took the form not so much of impeding organizational capabilities as of selectively tilting the playing field against abolitionism on a series of crucial public choices in the 1850s.

The first appearance of this manipulation came with Pierce's decision in 1854 to reverse provisions of the Missouri Compromise of 1820, reopening the decision to outlaw slavery north of the 36°30' latitude in the lands of the Louisiana Purchase. Further, Pierce—and Buchanan after him—shifted the locus of subsequent decision making on slavery to those who were fully expected to make decisions hostile to antislavery interests. By the early 1850s, the U.S. House of Representatives had developed a sizable voting bloc against slavery—or at least against its extension—and thus Congress was no longer deemed by these presidents to be reliable in keeping antislavery opinion in check. As a consequence, Pierce and Buchanan looked elsewhere—to manipulated assemblies and executives outside Washington, and to the United States Supreme Court—for decisions on the extension of slavery. A shift in decision-making authority of this sort would relieve the political institutions in Washington from the unrelenting pressure of that issue *and* would restore Slavepower preeminence in the decision-making processes about the "peculiar institution." Given still-growing southern sensitivity on these issues, that restored preeminence was deemed essential by these administrations for preserving the Union.

The Plan for Kansas: Pierce

The main thrust for opening Kansas to slavery came in relation to the transcontinental railroad. Long a design of powerful Senator Stephen A. Douglas, the railroad was not an isolated matter. With it came hard questions about routing *and* about the nature of territorial organization throughout the routed areas. Douglas, for financial and political reasons, sought a northern route for the railroad, with the gateway to the West opening in his home state of Illinois. As a practical matter this required territorial organizations for the areas of Kansas and/or Nebraska, since these then-unorganized territories would contain a large portion of any northern-routed railway, and thus would experience a vast influx of people and property.[130] Herein lay a problem.

In both of these territories, according to the relevant provision of the Missouri Compromise, slavery was proscribed. When Douglas approached key southern senators to test their receptivity to his proposed route, he was told in no uncertain terms that they would oppose organization of those areas unless the Missouri Compromise restrictions were repealed. An added obstacle for Douglas was Missouri's Democratic Senator David R. Atchison, who had made a convincing argument that, with Missouri already bordered on two sides by free states (Illinois and Iowa), the addition of a free Kansas would make it impossible for Missouri to protect itself as a slave state. Atchison thus claimed that he would rather watch Nebraska "sink in hell" than have it organized free. Douglas accordingly moved out of committee legislation that was to lift congressional prohibitions on slavery in Kansas in favor of allowing territorial settlers there to decide the matter for themselves. By opening the question up at the territorial stage, Congress would effectively invite outsiders to cross the border to stake claims of authority to determine the character of the new territorial government.[131]

Nothing could have been better calculated to disturb the repose of the Union President Pierce had just recently praised than this completely unforeseen evisceration of the Missouri Compromise. Yet the president shortly found himself promoting that very plan as the centerpiece of his young administration.

Upon first hearing of Douglas's plan, the president sent to Douglas a counterproposal, developed by his cabinet, to refer the question of slavery in Kansas and Nebraska to the courts. He was convinced of the Missouri Compromise's unconstitutionality, and thus he fully expected the Supreme Court to invalidate the proscription of slavery in Kansas. Court action had the additional advantage of insulating Pierce from likely political fallout. In effect, however, the underlying aim of the two approaches was identical: to shift the matter to a venue less favorable to the antislavery interests.

Under duress from the South, Douglas rejected Pierce's plan. Then, sensing that the time was ripe for action, and fearful that a quickly building northern reaction might coalesce against him, Douglas met with the president and sought to convince him to join in supporting his measure. Pierce agreed. Douglas, recognizing the president's penchant for changing his mind, got the decision in writing, and subsequently brandished, in the president's own hand, a proclamation that the Missouri Compromise "was superseded by the principles of the legislation of 1850, commonly called the compromise measures, and is hereby declared inoperative and void; . . . the people [of a territory or state] are left perfectly free to form and regulate their domestic institutions in their own way."[132] He thus sought to remove congressional strictures against slaveholding in favor of turning the question over to the residents of the territory itself.

So pledged, the president placed the entire weight of his administration, such as it was, behind the Douglas bill, making especially pointed use of his powers of appointment.[133] A loud protest was raised in Congress, with several antislavery members issuing an "Appeal of the Independent Democrats," declaring that Douglas's action was the violation of a sacred agreement that had been long canonized in American politics.[134] An intense and bitter debate followed, but the measure passed the Senate handily. More formidable opposition arose in the House, but after heavy lobbying by Senate leaders and the president, the Douglas bill passed there, too. "Gradually," reports Stephen Skowronek of this episode, "the resources of the Jacksonian presidency—patronage pressure, newspaper propaganda, floor management—made themselves felt."[135] The appeal of popular sovereignty—joined to a committed proslavery bloc and the purposive wielding of the powers of the antebellum presidency—proved to be too much for the antislavery contingent to prevail.

David Potter concludes that "Few events have swung American history away from its charted course so suddenly or so sharply as the Kansas-Nebraska Act."[136] Given the explosion of free state protest detonated by the Act's passage, it may seem difficult, then, to reconcile Pierce's endorsement of it as consistent with a nation-keeping posture. How is it possible to hold the president's actions as nation-maintaining when the effect of his work was to rush a destabilized nation down the path toward disunion and civil war?[137]

The awful consequences of Pierce's decision, clearly visible in hindsight, rather easily obscure the basic rationality of what the president did. In fact, as he saw the problem, Pierce believed that his actions actually would contribute to preservation of the Union, not to its demise. To see this clearly, we must inspect carefully the problem through Pierce's eyes, allowing ourselves momentarily to be as ignorant of the ultimate consequences of his behavior as he was at the time.

First, as a preliminary matter, it should be noted here that Pierce shared with Douglas a general belief that the Kansas-Nebraska Act actually *fulfilled* the Compromise of 1850.[138] Indeed, the 1850 agreement had established, with respect to New Mexico and Utah, popular sovereignty as *the* central governing principle for determining the social and political structures of American states (explicitly) and territories (implicitly). There was, then, a certain symmetry in insisting that the same principle should obtain for the still-unsettled areas of Kansas, Nebraska, and Minnesota. That principle had the added virtue of being an indispensable component of a compromise widely judged as union-saving in intent and effect.

The most important factor, however, was Pierce's fear that inaction in 1854 might lead to disunion sooner than later, because southerners were showing signs of increasing frustration with the growing prominence of antislavery thought in the North—and in Washington. Although the South had just won major concessions in the Compromise of 1850, highly publicized northern resistance to the Fugitive Slave Law and the popularity there of *Uncle Tom's Cabin*, among other things, fostered a continuing, rational sense of vulnerability.[139] In Pierce's view, the South was being unreasonably provoked into contemplating a disunion he had the power to avoid by making reasonable concessions. Looking back, the president made abundantly clear in his 1855 annual message whom he believed to be the villains in this high-stakes drama, beginning with a reference to those undermining the Fugitive Slave Law.

> It has been a matter of painful regret to see States conspicuous for their services in founding this Republic and equally sharing its advantages disregard their constitutional obligations to it. Although conscious of their inability to heal admitted and palpable social evils of their own, and which are completely within their jurisdiction, they engage in the offensive and hopeless undertaking of reforming the domestic institutions of other States, wholly beyond their control and authority. In the vain pursuit of ends by them entirely unattainable, and which they may not legally attempt to compass, they peril the very existence of the Constitution and all the countless benefits which it has conferred. While the people of the Southern States confine their attention to their own affairs, not presuming officiously to intermeddle with the social institutions of the Northern States, too many of the inhabitants of the latter are permanently organized in associations to inflict injury on the former by wrongful acts, which would be cause of war as between foreign powers and only fail to be such in our system because perpetrated under cover of the Union.

The president then acknowledged the probable consequences of continuing agitation, and ultimately turned to ridicule in an effort to shame the offending parties away from their ongoing transgressions.

> It is necessary to speak thus plainly of projects [which are] the offspring of that sectional agitation now prevailing in some of the States, which are as impracticable as they are unconstitutional, and which if persevered in must and will end calamitously. It is either disunion and civil war or it is mere angry, idle, aimless disturbance of public peace and tranquillity. Disunion for what? If the passionate rage of fanaticism and partisan spirit did not

force the fact upon our attention, it would be difficult to believe that any considerable portion of the people of this enlightened country could have so surrendered themselves to a fanatical devotion to the supposed interests of the relatively few Africans in the United States as totally to abandon and disregard the interests of the 25,000,000 Americans.[140]

Small wonder, then, that the president chose to preserve the Union by supporting honestly aggrieved Americans rather than Africans and their fanatical partisans.

Not only was southern discontent perceived as extensive and merited, it came to Pierce through channels he could not ignore. The most powerful figures in the United States Senate—including Douglas and a group of senior Democrats known collectively as the "F Street Mess" (from the address of their common boarding house)—communicated unmistakably to Pierce the costs of a refusal to act. They "confronted the president with an ultimatum: endorse repeal [of the Missouri Compromise] or lose the South."[141] Historian Michael F. Holt asserts that they thus "*extorted* administration backing for the measure." The nation-keeping nature of Pierce's response is further established by Holt, who notes that Pierce "dared not offend the powerful Southerners who could wreck his program [of an expansionist foreign policy] by refusing to ratify his treaties." This president's concerns about southern rebellion in the short run, and about the nation's international security position in the long run, reinforced an inclination to back the pro-slavery South in this instance.[142] Thus, actions that, through the benefit of hindsight, seem to be nation shattering were in fact intended to have precisely the opposite effect.

Two other factors also help explain the character of the nation-maintaining pressures as Pierce experienced them. First, evidently the initial northern response to Douglas's Kansas-Nebraska proposal was muted. One free soiler attributed this unusual northern quiescence to a sense that "the Measure is so Enormously wicked—that it is supposed to be impossible to pass it." Another said that "We had no idea that it could become so formidable as to promise success."[143] This inertia may have confounded the president's political calculus, causing him to misjudge the costs of backing Douglas. But the second point worth noting here is that the virtue of popular sovereignty as a political matter was that it was expected to export whatever controversies arose out of Washington to the distant Midwest.[144] So styled, the Kansas-Nebraska Act actually conforms to both faces of the president's nation-keeping role: it promoted the preservation of the nation's prevailing social structures, and it served to remove from the *nation's* political agenda a source of constant friction and contention, leaving the whole more secure.[145]

Or so it seemed. Whether predictable or not, the intensity of the northern reaction to Kansas-Nebraska rendered all the supposed benefits of that option, like the clauses of the Missouri Compromise, "inoperative and void." The violation of a time-honored settlement—a biased change in the prevailing rules of the game—created a sense of unity among the opposition to an extent not before existing. Moreover, the president's political vision proved faulty on another count: Washington could not avoid the conflict, despite the fact that the locus of contention did shift westward.

When it became apparent that federal strictures against slavery in Kansas would be lifted in favor of "squatter sovereignty," an antislavery group formed in New England for the purpose of sending like-minded men and women into the area to decide the question against slavery. They would lead the charge into Kansas. The resulting New England Emigrant Aid Society was antiextensionist (not affiliated with abolitionism), but pro-slavery Missourians—who resided across a long common border with Kansas and who sought to populate the territory with slaveholders—viewed this "external" interference with alarm. Many thus used this as a pretext for moving across the border to counter the political influence of the easterners. For nearly two years, in 1855 and 1856, a series of violent clashes erupted between free and slave state advocates. Pierce attributed the trouble to abolitionist interference from New England. For months the nation's attention, and that of the administration, was riveted to "Bleeding Kansas."

As Kansas was under executive administration at the time, Pierce was required to keep a careful watch on his governmental overseers, who often found themselves acting as partisans in a small-scale civil war. Moreover, Kansas's explosion could be directly traced to a conspicuous act of the president of the United States. Accordingly, Pierce could not afford to let it run its course unattended. By the final days of his presidency he was able to still the turmoil in Kansas—through a series of deft administrative appointments and the threat of heavy U.S. military intervention on the side of the proslavery forces—but this was accomplished only by the sacrifice of much time and energy. He passed along a still-festering Kansas, as yet undecided on the fate of slavery, to his successor James Buchanan.

On the heels of his election in 1856, Buchanan announced that his primary

duty as president was "to arrest, if possible, the agitation of the slavery question at the North." He thus exposed as a manifest duty that which many of
his predecessors had accepted as implicit in the job.[146]

The Matter of Dred Scott: Buchanan

In fulfilling this obligation, Buchanan adopted the general approach of his
predecessor, and attempted to shift decision making on slavery to places
beyond the reach of the antislavery activists' growing political influence.
Since the solution of exporting the conflict to Kansas had proved unexpectedly nettlesome, Buchanan turned to the option Pierce had initially chosen:
the Supreme Court. He reasoned that if the highest court in the land were to
settle the territorial matter definitively (i.e., as a matter of constitutional
law), the entire slavery issue would be moved, once and for all time, beyond
appeal. Toward this end, Buchanan willfully ignored constitutional designs
for impartial administration of justice and orderly transfer of power, and
aggressively but quietly lobbied to have the Supreme Court render abolitionism completely moot. The case at issue was *Dred Scott v. Sandford*.

In the winter of 1857, the High Court was already preparing its decision in
this suit. Scott's attorney argued that his client's five-year residence with his
master in the free territories essentially rendered him free, despite the fact that
they had subsequently relocated to a slave state. The Missouri Supreme Court
had ruled against Scott, openly citing a political rationale: the need for discipline in an age of increasing instability in the holding of slave property.[147]

Buchanan believed that the case might be used as a pretext by a southern-
dominated Supreme Court to issue a broad ruling on the constitutional status
of slavery. Thus, in preparation for his inaugural address, he privately wrote his
friend Associate Justice John Catron of Tennessee. The president-elect
enquired of Mr. Justice Catron whether he, as president, might not skirt the
slave issue by announcing in his inaugural address that a judicial decision was
imminent. After a series of letters back and forth, Catron reported to
Buchanan that the Court intended simply to accept the Missouri court's narrow decision. Absent intervention, the Supreme Court was not expected to do
anything noteworthy in relation to that case. However, Catron suggested that
Buchanan "drop [Justice Robert C.] Grier a line, saying how necessary it
is—& how good the opportunity is, to settle the agitation by an affirmative
decision of the Supreme Court." Grier, a pro-southern Pennsylvanian, shared

Catron's views about the case, but did not wish to have the Court overreach itself politically. "[Grier] has no doubt about the question on the main contest, but has been persuaded to take the smooth handle for the sake of repose." Catron believed that the force of a presidential invitation would likely move the Court to decide the broader issues as Buchanan wanted.

Buchanan leapt at the opportunity. Grier responded quickly, taking Buchanan's letter to Chief Justice Roger B. Taney and Associate Justice James Wayne, who concurred, in Grier's words, that "an expression of the opinion of the Court on this troublesome question" was now essential.[148] On March 4, 1857, Buchanan announced upon his swearing in that the territorial problem was now before the Supreme Court, and he predicted it would be decided shortly. He expressed his personal preference for popular sovereignty at the statehood stage, but asserted that he and all "good citizens . . . shall cheerfully submit" to whatever the Court ruled. Forty-eight hours hence the decision came.[149]

Chief Justice Taney's majority opinion was not at all the narrow finding Catron had originally envisioned. Instead, at Buchanan's urging, the Court issued an epochal decision, at once declaring that members of the Negro race could not be citizens of the United States (thus, Scott had no standing to sue), and that no political authority existed—either with Congress or with territorial legislatures—to ban slavery from *any* United States-governed soil. Constitutional provisions protecting private property, especially slaves, took precedence over all other claims. All remnants of the Missouri Compromise were thereby junked, as the court outlawed any restrictions on slave property in the common territories.

Another Plan for Kansas: Buchanan

As consequential as that ruling was, it did not, however, end the matter. Although the Court had ruled that the Constitution provided for slavery in all U.S. territories, a battle still raged in Kansas (among those pressing for immediate statehood) over how slavery would be treated in the new state constitution. One might logically conclude that a president committed to popular sovereignty would refrain from intruding on the political process in a to-be sovereign state, but Buchanan labored mightily behind the scenes to secure there a proslavery constitution.

On taking office, Buchanan had dispatched a governor to Kansas with instructions to see that a new state constitution was drafted in a fair and orderly manner. That governor, Mississippi's Robert J. Walker (who had earlier been John Tyler's propagandist), took the job with the understanding that the new constitution would be submitted for popular approval, a position Buchanan assured Walker he was willing to "stand or fall" on. Despite heavy lobbying by Walker, the Kansas constitutional convention—tightly controlled by proslavery forces buttressed with Missouri interlopers—decided to offer only a restricted choice to Kansas voters. The ballots were to be marked "Constitution with slavery" or "Constitution with no slavery," but the latter option was riddled with loopholes, including a provision allowing slaves then in Kansas (and their offspring) to remain. As James M. McPherson has noted, "In effect, the constitution with no slavery merely prohibited the future importation of slaves into Kansas." Further, residents were given absolutely no choice on other specifics in the document, including a number of controversial economic provisions.[150]

Under pressure from southern state legislatures, members of Congress, and his own cabinet, Buchanan reversed his earlier position and allowed an election on restricted terms.[151] Despite the fact that most of the constitution's provisions were beyond the reach of the voter; the fact that even a vote for an "antislavery" version permitted slavery to perpetuate itself; the fact that the southern-born Governor Walker denounced the document as "a bare counterfeit"; and the fact that election officials had shown a remarkable creativity in manufacturing election returns to suit their own purposes, the "popular sovereignty" president found his personal requirements for legitimacy met.[152] Thus, writes Kenneth M. Stampp, "the President and his Cabinet joined . . . in urging the Congress and the country to endorse a fraud."[153] In December, the constitution was adopted by an overwhelming majority of the limited number of Kansans who consented to participate in the resulting election.

The president sent the so-called Lecompton constitution to Congress on February 2, 1858, recommending Kansas's admission into the Union.[154] "Kansas is therefore at this moment as much a slave State as Georgia or South Carolina," he proclaimed, suggesting that his efforts also paralleled those of a more distant predecessor, John Tyler, who sought to expand conflict to bias the nation's institutions in favor of slavery.[155]

Further, the president was just as unwilling to leave the statehood decision to free democratic choice in Congress as he was in the territory itself, lobbying aggressively for acceptance of Kansas statehood under the

Lecompton constitution. He demanded total loyalty from those in patronage positions, and extended jobs and printing contracts to friendly sources.
Some of the administration's backers even relied on bribery.[156] Commented
one contemporary observer, "[The] *thumb-screw* is being applied with much
force."[157]

In the end, however, the administration failed. The House of Representatives—by that time heavily populated with committed free soilers repre-
senting northerners fed up with the Slavepower's reach—refused to concede
to pressures brought to bear in Washington or Kansas. They forced the president to resubmit for a more representative vote a second, marginally different document. In August 1858, a much larger group of Kansas voters rejected
the revised Lecompton constitution by a 5-to-1 majority.[158] Despite this
stunning failure, Buchanan later said of his work on behalf of proslavery
Kansas, "In the course of my long public life I have never performed any official act which in the retrospect has afforded me more heartfelt satisfaction."[159] Kansas would enter the Union in early 1861 as a free state, only after
the United States had begun to disintegrate.

Perhaps the most important legacy of the Kansas controversy was the sun-
dering of the Democratic Party, north from south, and the outbreak of a
vicious rivalry between Buchanan and Stephen A. Douglas, who called the
Lecompton constitution "fraudulent."[160] This conflict intensified during the
remaining years of Buchanan's term, in no small measure because the southern wing of the party became increasingly radicalized. Despite frequent
southern threats of secession in the event of Republican victory in 1860,
however, neither Buchanan nor Douglas took meaningful steps to cobble
together a Democratic coalition to stave off that eventuality. The Democrats
went into the 1860 election season, then, with two candidates.

In that fragmented election, the Republican won a large electoral victory
while carrying less than 40 percent of the popular vote. Elbert B. Smith
observes, "A Democratic party united behind Douglas or some other popu-
lar-sovereignty candidate . . . might have beaten Lincoln, who clearly prof-
ited against both Democratic candidates by the foolish conduct of their
party . . . and by the warfare of their partisans against each other."[161] True to
their threats, southern extremists succeeded in the aftermath of Lincoln's
victory in pushing various deep southern states toward disunion. A nascent
confederacy was in the making, giving the South the ultimate bargaining
chip among a large population of union-lovers: secession.

Concessions to the Rebels

In the earliest stages, it was not at all certain how far the movement for secession would go. Buchanan, as a lame duck, sought to develop policy responses that would calm southern fears and limit the damage an incoming Republican administration could do. Although he denied the right of secession, he believed his duty as president required him to make the necessary concessions to keep the South loyal. He felt that if valid southern grievances against the North were accommodated, the South still could be convinced to remain in the Union. He took the occasion of his annual message of 1860, delivered shortly after his electoral loss, to promote a nation-keeping plan.

Buchanan began by identifying the problem. "Why is it . . . that discontent now so extensively prevails, and the Union of the States, which is the source of all . . . blessings, is threatened with destruction?," the president asked. He had a simple answer. "The long-continued and intemperate interference of the Northern people with the question of slavery in the Southern States has at length produced its natural effects. . . . [T]he incessant and violent agitation of the slavery question throughout the North for the last quarter of a century has at length produced its malign influence on the slaves and inspired them with vague notions of freedom." Thus, the president argued, resolution of the current crisis was not the vexatious matter some might imagine. "How easy it would be for the American people to settle the slavery question forever and to restore peace and harmony to this distracted country!. . . All that is necessary to accomplish the object, and all for which the slave States have ever contended, is to be let alone and permitted to manage their domestic institutions in their own way."[162]

Buchanan then proceeded to advocate passage of an "explanatory" constitutional amendment intended to "forever terminate the existing dissensions, and restore peace and harmony among the States." His amendment contained three parts.

1. An express recognition of the right of property in slaves in the States where it now exists or may hereafter exist.
2. The duty of protecting this right in all the common Territories throughout their Territorial existence . . .
3. A like recognition of the right of the master to have his slave who has escaped from one State to another restored and "delivered up" to him, and of the validity of the fugitive-slave law enacted for this purpose,

together with a declaration that all State laws impairing or defeating this right are violations of the Constitution, and are consequently null and void.[163]

Buchanan chose to ignore the fact that those promoting far milder versions of these sentiments had been overwhelmingly rejected in a nationwide election mere days before his message was delivered.[164] Evident in this attempt to recast the results of the election, in which the free soil Republicans had triumphed, was that same inclination earlier seen to manipulate the rules of the game on those occasions when antislavery opinion had prevailed. A president who had not been content to await his own inauguration before taking up the proslavery cause was now laboring diligently to exercise control beyond the end of his allotted four years for that same purpose.

The president's proposals went nowhere. Some members of Congress picked up his sentiments and tried to craft compromise packages granting concessions to the South. These, too, failed, despite Buchanan's efforts to have them adopted by Congress or a national convention convened for that purpose. Both southern extremists—who rejected compromise, sensing that it would deflate movement for secession—and Lincoln's Republicans—who cherished their electoral victory—were unwilling to give in.

In that final annual message, James Buchanan tried to place the impending civil crisis in historical context. "It can not be denied," he wrote, "that for five and twenty years the agitation at the North against slavery has been incessant." Having located a thread that tied current events to seminal protests nearly three decades earlier, Buchanan proceeded to identify his own endeavors as participation in a long tradition of respected presidential action aimed at producing harmony between the sections, and protecting the constitutional rights of American slaveholders. "In 1835 pictorial handbills and inflammatory appeals were circulated extensively throughout the South of a character to excite the passions of the slaves, and, in the language of General Jackson, 'to stimulate them to insurrection and produce all the horrors of a servile war.'" Although no explicit connection was made, Buchanan implied that his role as president had been as that of Jackson, to speak and to take action against those who would stir such antislavery passions. In this, his presidency was at one with that which helped close the mails to the circulation of such offensive materials. Indeed, Buchanan might have added, that thread ran through every presidency in succession from General Jackson's.

Buchanan further argued, however, that the present conflict had moved beyond the power of the president to restrain it; that power rested only with the American people.

> Without their aid it is beyond the power of any President, no matter what may be his political proclivities, to restore peace and harmony among the States. Wisely limited and restrained as is his power under our Constitution and laws, he alone can accomplish but little for good or for evil on such a momentous question.

That the American people, in sufficient force, were unwilling to "restore peace and harmony" on Buchanan's terms testifies to the ultimate success of the original abolitionist commitment to the process of moral suasion. What remained to be seen was how Abraham Lincoln would employ his powers on the momentous question then before the nation. "From the very nature of his office and its high responsibilities he must necessarily be conservative," predicted Buchanan.[165] Those pressing for immediate and unconditional emancipation ached on learning how accurate Buchanan's forecast would be.

From the tenure of Andrew Jackson through that of James Buchanan, the office of the presidency was routinely employed for purposes of quieting the agitation of those who sought immediate emancipation of slaves in the United States. This presidential activity came in a variety of forms intended to suppress the influence of abolitionists in the American polity, and to fortify the political order against their demands. Successive presidents, possessing a diversity of personal views on slavery, its desirability, and its allowable scope, almost uniformly worked toward a common end because they all perceived that they were elected in part to maintain the nation they served, and that antislavery agitation threatened the very stability of the nation's social and political structures. In order to maintain the nation as they inherited it, they were constrained to exercise their powers against the threat abolition posed. In the final analysis, however, they failed. The Union fractured.

In 1861, a president entered office refusing to exercise his nation-maintaining role as the South would have him. Lincoln was well aware of Buchanan's efforts to piece together some form of concessions package that would keep the Union intact. This Lincoln rejected. Yet he did not reject for himself the nation-maintaining role of his predecessors. He simply interpreted its demands differently. As he entered office, Lincoln plainly explained that making concessions to the South as Buchanan had suggested would have shattered the Union more thoroughly than the illegitimate secession indulged in by the South.[166] Two months before his inauguration, Lincoln wrote, "We have just carried an election on principles fairly stated to the people." For the integrity of self-government to be preserved, then, those principles must not be sacrificed to the losing side. "Now we are told in advance, the government shall be broken up, unless we surrender to those we have beaten, before we take the offices. In this they are either attempting to play upon us, or they are in dead earnest. Either way, if we surrender, it is the end of us."[167]

Neither, however, did Lincoln initially interpret his nation-maintaining role to include the emancipation of the slaves. The terms of the election demanded an end to expansion, but not, as Lincoln read them, an interference with slavery where it already existed. On this subject he later wrote to the abolitionist Horace Greeley,

> My paramount object in this struggle *is* to save the Union, and is *not* either to save or to destroy slavery. If I could save the Union without freeing *any* slave I would do it, and if I could save it by freeing *all* the slaves I would do it; and if I could save it by freeing some and leaving others alone I would also do that. What I do about slavery, and the colored race, I do because I believe it helps to save the Union; and what I forbear, I forbear because I do *not* believe it would help to save the Union. I shall do *less* whenever I shall believe what I am doing hurts the cause, and I shall do *more* whenever I shall believe doing more will help the cause.[168]

Lincoln thus announced the primacy of his nation-maintaining role. It was up to those who sought unconditional emancipation to make the case that this role compelled liberation. As the evidence clearly shows, however, Lincoln only belatedly came to that conclusion.

CHAPTER 3

The Making of a Great Emancipator

When Americans went to the polls in 1860 to cast ballots for the Republican nominee for president, they did *not* vote for a Great Emancipator.

Although Abraham Lincoln had repeatedly argued that slavery was a moral evil that ought not be allowed to spread, he was equally unyielding on another matter: the inviolability of slavery in those southern states where it then existed.[1] Throughout his campaign and during the transition period preceding his inauguration, Lincoln went to great lengths to emphasize to an increasingly mutinous South that the national government had no designs on slavery in the sovereign states. Further, he announced his intent to enforce vigorously the Fugitive Slave Act as a requirement of sustaining the Union. Lincoln had reasoned that limiting the expansion of slavery would eventually kill it, but he took pains to pronounce that such an eventuality was generations off, and he intended no extraordinary steps on the part of his administration to hurry it along.[2] He intended to contain the peculiar evil, but his respect for the Union, and his perception of the dictates of the nation-maintaining role of the presidency, demanded that he allow nature alone to determine how soon death would prevail.

Had Lincoln promised more than this, all evidence indicates he would never have been elected. His commitment to respect the dominion of the states on the question of slavery put him in the mainstream of American political culture, and also gave hope to many in the North and West that Lincoln's was a middle way that might preserve the Union while exerting some needed discipline over southern extremism—and, for many, northern extremism, too. Indeed, the Republicans had nominated Lincoln over presumed-nominee William H. Seward in part because Seward had developed a reputation of being a bit *too* bold on the issue of slavery.[3] Simply put, a Great Emancipator was unlikely to find much electoral support in 1860.

Lincoln later confirmed as much to Senator Charles Sumner: "I should never have had votes enough to send me here, if the people had supposed I should try to use my veto power to upset slavery."[4] State sovereignty mattered too much; Republican victory—which could be achieved on the basis of free soilism alone—mattered too much; Union mattered too much.[5]

Those who were entering a fourth decade of persistent attempts to rid the country entirely of its national sin, too, recognized in Lincoln a reformer of modest reach. They did not approve. Lincoln's willingness to admit the inherent evil of slavery made of him a hypocrite in their eyes, for illegitimate constitutional constraints had no call on the loyalty of those who saw God's laws clearly. Further, his record of support for vigorous execution of the Fugitive Slave Law brought from Wendell Phillips the appellation "Slave-hound of Illinois."[6] These abolitionists would continue to press the president during the balance of his days, in the interest of pushing him further down a road he did not gladly go. "Believing that he was called only to conserve," writes Richard Hofstadter of Lincoln, he "turned liberator in spite of himself."[7] That Lincoln would eventually arrive as the Great Emancipator is testament to the radicals' success in using the war to achieve what three decades of peaceful protest had denied them. As William Best Hesseltine observed, "In Lincoln's desk the Emancipation Proclamation would probably have remained had it not been for the increased activities of the radicals."[8] The cumulative weight of their efforts created political imperatives a nation-keeping president could not safely ignore.[9]

Lincoln and Disunion

Notwithstanding Lincoln's conciliatory rhetoric, states in the Deep South almost immediately began withdrawing from the Union upon Lincoln's election, making good on threats brandished intermittently for at least a decade. Their stature as equal partners in the enterprise of union had taken what they perceived to be an irreparable blow. Months before the election, the *Richmond Enquirer* asserted:

> The people of the fifteen sovereign [slave] States regard the Black Republican leaders as men hostile to their institutions: and, whether or not they have sufficient reason for that opinion, is immaterial; it is a violation of confederate faith in the Northern majority to insist upon the election of any man for whom so large a minority of the States have so decided a

distrust. And, when informed of this wide-spread distrust, the election of such objectionable men is an overt act of sectional violence, an indication of hostility, which only awaits the machinery of Government to carry out the bloody programme of negro freedom. To permit this sectional leader to possess himself of the Federal Government would be to acquiesce in an act violative of confederate faith.[10]

A Charleston paper resorted to the *ad hominem*: "He is a lank-sided Yankee, of the uncomeliest visage, and one of the dirtiest complexion and the most indecent comparisons. Faugh! after him, what decent white man would be President!"[11] Lincoln's inaugural, another paper said, would be an exercise in "humiliation and degradation."[12] Seven states seceded before that indignity could transpire, before giving Lincoln any chance to prove that they may have misjudged him. The polarization of preceding years truly had reached crisis proportions at this stage. The perception of dishonor would not allow the South to await evidence that Lincoln would indeed work "to carry out the bloody programme of negro freedom."

The period of post-election transition between Buchanan and Lincoln saw both men laboring to keep the Union intact consistent with their fundamental governing principles. Buchanan, as discussed in the previous chapter, put his efforts behind a series of constitutional and statutory proposals that would have effectively negated the Republican victory of 1860. Lincoln firmly asserted that he would not tolerate the adoption of any provisions intended to preserve the Union at the expense of principles his election stood for—especially the nonextension of slavery—lest the legitimacy of popular government be destroyed.[13] "By no act or complicity of mine," he declared, "shall the Republican party become a mere sucked egg, all shell and no principle in it."[14]

Lincoln generally avoided issuing public statements during the transition period, sensing that there was little he could do at that stage to stop the South's exodus. "What is it that I could say which would quiet alarm? Is it that no interference by the government, with slaves or slavery within the states, is intended? I have said this so often already that a repetition of it is but a mockery, bearing an appearance of weakness."[15] Yet he did sanction efforts to reassure the South of the security of its domestic institutions. He put his unofficial imprimatur on two measures he hoped might assuage some southerners—especially those in the border states—without compromising his standards. Lincoln apparently believed that if he could reverse the momentum on favorable terms, the Union might still be preserved.

Lincoln quietly passed along to a select House committee his endorsement of a resolution calling for strict enforcement of the Fugitive Slave Law and repeal of state personal liberty laws conflicting with it. He also communicated his support of a constitutional amendment forever prohibiting Congress from interfering with slavery in the states.[16] In so doing, Lincoln alienated some Republicans, who saw the concessions as excessive. Yet in the end they were fruitless. By the time they had been adopted, and a proposed constitutional amendment sent to the states, the confederacy was well on its way to becoming a reality.

There were those in the North—perhaps most prominently William Lloyd Garrison—who said "Good riddance!" "All Union-saving efforts are simply idiotic," claimed *The Liberator*'s editorialist on the paper's thirtieth anniversary. "At last, 'the covenant with death' is annulled, and 'the agreement with hell' broken. . . . Hail the approaching jubilee!"[17] Garrison and a host of abolitionists and radical Republicans contended that the nation had for too long been distracted by the arrogant immorality of southern planters, and thus that disunion was a moral, political and economic blessing. "Every four years," reported a Kentucky paper, "these Southern Quixotes swell up with bad whiskey and worse logic, and tell the balance of the people if they don't do so and so, that they (the Quixotes) will secede. Let them secede, and be— blessed. We are tired of their gasconade."[18]

Some of this rejoicing reflected smug satisfaction at finally being rid of those whose demands had long taxed their patience.[19] But their reaction was not alone a product of relieved irritation. They had long reasoned that the South required northern military and economic support to prop up their peculiar institution. Consequently, the southern decision to leave the Union was, they believed, a colossal miscalculation. Slavery might briefly survive— at last absent the complicity of the North—but the South could not long maintain slavery on her own. Disunion meant divestment of an essential reinforcement, and thus a hastened day of liberation.

Lincoln, however, chose not to bid the South farewell, but to try to maintain the nation.[20] And because the South had decided by that time that a political parting was in order, the Union could be preserved only with war.

As the conflict unfolded, what concerned abolitionists and many radical Republicans was not just that Lincoln intended to hold onto the South, but that the president's commitment to preservation of the union superseded all other considerations, *including resolution of the matter that had precipitated war: southern slavery*. Nothing seemed more incongruous to them than a president prosecuting war for the purpose of returning a slaveholding South to the Union, but that was precisely the direction Lincoln appeared headed.[21] They could be forgiven for not seeing a Great Emancipator in one who practically opened his first inaugural address by quoting himself saying, "I have no purpose, directly or indirectly, to interfere with the institution of slavery in the States where it exists. I believe I have no lawful right to do so, and I have no inclination to do so."[22] These same sentiments Lincoln essentially repeated in his July 4 message to the special session of Congress convened to deal with the war emergency.[23]

Much of the story of the early years of the Civil War is, then, of a president firmly committed to keeping the issue of slavery *out* of the conflict—politically and militarily—and of radicals within Congress and without trying to use the occasion of war to break the shackles of bondage once and forever. Immediate emancipation was certainly not the path Lincoln started down upon leaving the inaugural podium. Over a year passed in which he aggressively asserted his executive authority—for the first eleven weeks he effectively *was* the government of the United States[24]—to find some way short of emancipation to bring the South back into the fellowship of union. The generosity Lincoln voiced in closing his inaugural address— "We are not enemies, but friends. We must not be enemies"—was hardly shared by those northern and border publics tired of southern "gasconade."[25]

The incoming president encountered a double bind in trying to neutralize abolitionist-backed policy. First, deep southern congressional delegations, which for so long had sustained federal policy inclined toward the South against free-state attacks, were depleted through secession. Thus, the ranks of possible antiabolitionist allies in the legislative branch had been severely reduced because these southerners had decided to abandon the playing field.

Second, the elections of 1860 swelled the ranks of Congress with northern radicals intent on conquering the South and reshaping it to suit their own preferences. A well-placed group of radical Republicans, a political manifestation of cresting anti-Slavepower thought in the free states, proved to be a relentless source of pressure on Lincoln by taking a more advanced position than the president on promoting emancipation as a war aim.[26] They succeeded in electing one of their number Speaker of the House.

The radicals' power in Washington, however, derived in no small measure from the success advance agents for change could already claim in making emancipation politically viable. Further, the very fact of southern secession aided immensely the abolitionist cause. Many who theretofore had abided the Constitution's compromises on slavery no longer felt obligated to recognize the rights of property in mankind, because they perceived that the South had sacrificed any legitimate claims for northern acquiescence through its violence to the Union. Thus, as Carl Schurz wrote, "What we could not have done in many lifetimes the madness and folly of the South have accomplished for us. Slavery offers itself more vulnerable to our attack than at any point in any century."[27]

Lincoln's efforts to avoid direct attacks on slavery in the states, then, placed him in conflict with substantial publics in the North, and very powerful elements in Congress, who either wanted him to become a Great Emancipator or stand out of the way so that others could. For at least seventeen months he did neither. Indeed, he more than once interposed himself, as commander-in-chief, between the slaves and those who would have liberated them immediately. Early union military advances provided the administration a concrete test to show how slavery related to that war effort.

As northern troops worked their way gradually onto southern soil, fugitive slaves, at great personal risk and with little reassurance of security, escaped into Union encampments. The War Department made a point of openly discouraging this kind of activity, formally disavowing any intent to foment trouble among slave populations. Many of the commanding officers in the field were sympathetic to the practice of slaveholding, and thus readily implemented fugitive slave laws even against a declared enemy. General George B. McClellan announced to citizens of western Virginia that he had no interest in liberating their slaves. "We will, on the contrary, with an iron hand, crush any attempt at insurrection on their part."[28] Such action was deemed consistent with the president's overall plan for prosecuting the conflict, a plan ever sensitive to the political climate of the four slaveholding border states still neutral or loyal to the union: Missouri, Kentucky, Maryland, and Delaware.[29]

A policy of discouraging fugitives, however, did not instruct field officers as to how to deal with cases where slaves were successful in reaching Union lines. Should they be returned to their owners, or should they be granted asylum? Informally, many officers refused to accept them into camp. But the administration was directly confronted with the question when General Benjamin F. Butler, in May 1861, reported his refusal to surrender three fugitives to a southern commissioner at Fort Monroe, Virginia. Butler argued that since the slaves in question had been used in constructing enemy fortifications, he was confiscating them as contraband of war. Lincoln decided to support Butler's decision not to surrender the fugitives in the instant case, but he made no effort to generalize the policy. In other theaters commanders were ordered by the War Department to continue to do what they could to protect private property, including slaves.[30]

Butler's problems, however, had just begun. Fugitives swarmed to his fort when it became known that protection was being afforded, but the general did not know whether he was sanctioned to keep and support all comers, including women and children. When he requested further instructions from the administration, his calls were met with silence. Congress, however, responded.[31]

On August 6, 1861, Lincoln reluctantly signed into law a provision sent him by Congress that provided for the confiscation of any and all property employed "in aid of the rebellion." The radicals had specifically selected this vehicle from among a number of more extreme measures—including a call for immediate and unconditional emancipation—because they believed it would be accepted by the president; in effect, it was a limited measure. He hesitated, but approved the bill in large part because it helped him meet the pressing military problem brought to his door by black refugees. That Lincoln intended the so-called Confiscation Act to be strictly construed, however, became apparent quite quickly.[32]

On August 30, 1861, General John C. Fremont, the Republican's first presidential candidate and now commander of the Union army's Western Department (appointed by Lincoln), declared martial law in Missouri. Part of Fremont's order provided for the confiscation of property in the possession of all rebels. In effect, this liberated all slaves of the disloyal. Here was arguably a logical extension of the Confiscation Act, if one believed that slave labor always benefited the rebellion by aiding the southern economy. The president, however, objected. "I think there is great danger," wrote Lincoln to Fremont, "that . . . liberating slaves of traiterous [sic] owners, will alarm our Southern Union friends, and turn them against us."[33] When Fremont refused to modify his order according to Lincoln's suggestions—to bring it into strict compliance with the Confiscation Act—the president ordered the offending passage excised.[34] He later cited both legal and pragmatic justifications for so doing. He derided the notion that either "a General, or a President, may make permanent rules of property by proclamation," and he posited that the loyalty of the border states rested on his decision to countermand.[35] He could preserve more of the Union by acting this way than

by following Fremont's lead. Indeed, when Fremont's wife appeared before Lincoln to plead the general's case in person, the president averred that
this "was a war for a great national idea, the Union, and . . . General Fremont
should not have dragged the Negro into it."[36]

The radicals widely hailed Fremont's action as heroic, and subsequently
condemned Lincoln's contravention.[37] Charles Sumner proclaimed the
president's legalism sophistic, since he had shown little reluctance otherwise
to use his office dictatorially: "[H]ow vain to have the power of a god and not
to use it godlike!" The border states held firm, but this came at the expense
of support elsewhere in the Union, especially since McClellan's army was
showing little initiative in other venues. When Lincoln decided in late
October to relieve Fremont of his command—for a host of grievances,
including the emancipation order—radical discontent exploded. Lincoln
came under a storm of criticism in Congress, but with little immediate
effect, other than to add another item to a growing bill of particulars against
the administration on the question of slavery.[38] The storm raged even more
furiously in November when Fremont's successor claimed that fugitives were
being used as spies by the rebels, and thus ejected them from Union encampments, with no more admitted. This order the administration did not
remand.[39]

A second case of insubordination arose within Lincoln's own cabinet.
Secretary of War Simon Cameron, under executive and legislative pressure
for running a corrupt and poorly managed shop, sought to rally radicals to
his standard by publicly announcing, in a departmental report, that "it is . . .
clearly the right of the Government to arm slaves . . . and to employ their service against the rebels." Lincoln had the report recalled and effectively dis-
avowed its contents, and Cameron was subsequently forced out of office.[40]

Later, a similar case presented itself—to similar effect. In early 1862,
General David Hunter received command of the Union army's Department
of the South, which gave him responsibility for a limited number of coastal
enclaves under Union control in South Carolina, Georgia, and Florida.
"Please," wrote Hunter to Secretary of War Edwin M. Stanton in asking for
command, "let me have my own way on the subject of slavery. The administration will not be responsible. I alone will bear the blame; you can censure
me, arrest me, dismiss me, hang me if you will, but permit me to make my
mark in such a way as to be remembered by friend and foe." Stanton—one
of the radicals' friends in the cabinet—processed the appointment and
apparently signalled consent to the new commander's program.[41]

Within a few months Hunter issued an order proclaiming all slaves in his department "forever free." Hunter's initiative was clearly far in advance of the terms of the Confiscation Act. Once again, Lincoln would have none of it. Although at least one northern governor, hoping to offset the weight of the border states on Lincoln's mind, made a point of publicly promising that the decree would send New Englanders streaming southward to join the cause, the president voided the proclamation. In so doing, Lincoln reiterated the unacceptability of a field officer issuing such an edict, but in this case he suggested that such decisions would have to rest with the commander-in-chief. Perhaps the president was purposely opening a door here that he had shut in his Fremont decision, although it is just as likely that he stipulated his sole responsibility for such decisions as a means of cutting off similar problems with renegade generals in the future. But he was still unwilling at this stage to make a generalized, substantive concession to those who wished to use military necessity as valid justification for immediate emancipation in the South.[42]

Indeed, Lincoln's conception of military (and political) necessity impelled him in quite the opposite direction. In his thinking—undoubtedly shaped in part by his own Kentucky roots—the crucial balance of power in the entire conflict was to be found in those slaveholding border states that remained faithful to the Union, and in certain loyalist southern state enclaves similarly situated.[43] These Lincoln did not wish to alienate by taking precipitous action on slavery, especially action that might be of questionable constitutional provenance. The earliest months of the war had revealed to the president very harsh lessons about the limited state of the Union's military strength, and he thus felt compelled to do whatever he could to maintain the allegiance of slaveholding loyalists. In their hands, he believed the future of the Union lay.

Lincoln and the Radical Congress

As Congress convened in December 1861 for the beginning of its first regular session, Lincoln found himself constitutionally yoked to a governing partner he believed increasingly inclined toward impulsive and imprudent conduct toward the rebels. Conversely, the administration's inability to bring the war to a hasty conclusion left the president vulnerable to charges from Congress that he was being insufficiently daring in prosecuting the war. That legislative dissatisfaction had the effect of torpedoing the sense of high deference to presidential direction that had characterized the special session convened the previous July.[44]

The most concrete manifestation of Congress's intent to reassert its prerogatives as an equal partner was the creation of the Joint Committee on the Conduct of the War, a competing instrument of politico-military control that sought more directly to use the conflict for purposes of emancipation. "It became," wrote T. Harry Williams, "the spearhead of the radical drive against the administration."

> The radicals could never have initiated and carried on their struggle against Lincoln without the vital information which the Committee furnished in its jaundiced reports. . . . It investigated the principal military campaigns, worked to undermine Democratic and conservative officers, interfered boldly with plans of commanders, and bullied Lincoln into accepting the radical program. It was the most potent weapon wielded by the Jacobin cabal in the successful campaign to make radicalism instead of moderation the political faith of the nation.[45]

Further, one of the radicals, Thaddeus Stevens, "challenged Lincoln's contention that in war the president must become a temporary dictator." Stevens "admitted that one branch of the government should assume complete control of the direction of the war, but he insisted that Congress rather than the executive should be the dictator."[46] In consequence, Washington played host to a pitched struggle between congressional radicals and the president over control of war policy—including the inescapable question of slavery.

Contemporary commentators observed that, by this time, popular sentiment for liberating the slaves had reached unprecedented proportions. "Never has there been a time when Abolitionists were as much respected, as at present," claimed one of their number. Wendell Phillips ventured to Washington—"which he could scarcely have entered without danger to his life a year earlier"—and delivered a series of addresses to packed houses. "Given this mood," writes James M. McPherson, "antislavery bills poured into the congressional hopper like leaves dropping from trees in autumn."[47]

In the face of this mounting pressure to act boldly, Lincoln departed from his initial position—in his July 1861 message calling for a special session he had omitted entirely mentioning slavery as an issue of war[48]—and proceeded hesitantly down a path that Williams characterized as "timid."[49] Indeed, he sought refuge in those most traditional antidotes to abolitionist radicalism—colonization and compensation.[50] Perhaps, he reasoned, the fact of war itself had softened slaveholder opposition to these time-honored, if not time-tested, ideas.

Lincoln developed a series of proposals to lure slaveholders into ridding themselves—and ridding the nation—of the causes of the war. Yet his methods were decidedly noncoercive.[51]

Beginning in November 1861, he drafted two bills calling for use of federal money for compensated emancipation in Delaware, in hopes that a state with a minute slave population could be used as a pilot project. He did not, in the end, get the necessary cooperation from that state's authorities to execute the plan.[52]

In his first annual message in December, he promoted a universal plan, requesting that Congress authorize and fund a program colonizing (in Africa and Latin America) slaves freed under the terms of the Confiscation Act. In part, this plan was necessitated by the ever-increasing numbers of fugitives escaping into Union encampments, which could not simply remain there.[53] This recommendation, too, went nowhere, in large measure because congressional radicals and abolitionists were unwilling to adopt as war measures proposals they had deemed tepid even during a time of peace. "President Lincoln may colonize himself if he choose," the editor of *The Liberator* suggested, "but it is an impertinent act, on his part, to propose the getting rid of those who are as good as himself."[54]

Finally, on March 6, he sent to Congress a message intended to generate incentives for state-sponsored compensated emancipation.[55] The president asked Congress to resolve itself in support of funding voluntary state efforts, citing comparison cost figures suggesting that it was cheaper to compensate slaveholders than to continue fighting the war. Further, he couched his proposal in terms of military necessity, claiming that ridding the border states of slaves would reduce the temptation for them to join the already rebellious southern states.

This final measure Congress approved, largely because of the president's deft negotiations among radical leaders in Congress who had theretofore expressed strong reservations about buying slaves with tax dollars.[56] This action did prepare the way for legislation freeing (with provisions for compensation and colonization) slaves in the District of Columbia, but continued lobbying by the president produced no initiatives among the border states to take advantage of the law's provisions.[57] Ultimately, despite an impressive lobbying effort, the initiative came to naught. Lincoln's preoccupation with maintaining the nation by assuaging the border states led him to construct a voluntary program for which there were no volunteers. Border-state slave-holders proved to be no more willing to divest themselves voluntarily of that class of property than their Deep South brethren. And the president was unwilling at this point to use the war-enlarged coercive authority of the state—as the congressional radicals were inclined—to liberate absent the active consent of the masters.

The character of independent congressional activity at this time provides a useful backdrop against which to view the president's behavior. Lincoln's initiatives were in part defensive in nature, developed to moderate the advances of congressional radicals. Seven antislavery measures of various orders received favorable committee reports in January 1862, all of which became law before session's end. A brief discussion of a few of these bills will help illuminate the nature of the forces Lincoln was combating in Congress.[58]

First, as a symbol of its disaffection, Congress refused to readopt a resolution passed in the July war session that disclaimed slavery as an issue of war.[59] Then, on March 13, it passed a new article of war intended to stop the practice of U.S. troops returning fugitive slaves to their owners. Although Lincoln signed the bill, his execution wanted. Congressional radicals became incensed a month later to discover that the president had never even officially communicated the requirements of the new provision to the Army. In response, an effort emerged in Congress to have all fugitive slave laws repealed, thereby undermining the legal basis on which troops sympathetic to slaveholders were acting. This effort failed, however, until 1864.[60]

Congress also enacted a second Confiscation Act. In its initial form, this measure would have confiscated the slave property of anyone who *had* aided or abetted the rebel cause, and would have provided for forfeiture beyond the life of the offender. Lincoln opposed this bill, and threatened to veto it before its final passage.[61] Since the congressional session was nearing its conclusion, angry radicals had no choice but to accept the president's objections and to work around them. They sent him a bill, which he signed, that still went far beyond the first Confiscation Act.

To solidify control over army practices, Congress declared any slaves of active rebels free upon entering Union lines, and forbade their return by Union officials. Further, the act authorized the president to "to employ as many persons of African descent as he may deem necessary and proper for the suppression of this rebellion." The radicals hoped that freedman contributions to the war effort—including military service—would hasten the day of constitutionally sanctioned emancipation.[62] That, however, was an option a cautious Lincoln was still unwilling to exercise.[63] And enforcement of the bill faltered because it required proceedings by courts not then functioning in the rebellious states.[64]

The differences in the focus of the congressional radicals and the president merit some emphasis here. The radicals' legislative program centered on military action, on making of the northern war machine an effective instrument of emancipation as well as union. Some pressed for a simple declaration of martial law in the rebellious areas followed by a presidential decree of liberation.[65] They accordingly pushed Lincoln further and faster than he wanted to go in using the Union army to liberate southern property. The president's major efforts were devoted to crafting and selling what amounted to a diplomatic initiative based on voluntary emancipation. The former emphasized force, the latter persuasion. The former was more immediatist, the latter gradualist. Vigorous pursuit of the former complicated attempts to achieve the latter—the conversion of the war into an assault on slavery did not win friends among border-state slaveholders—which explains why Lincoln often got a case of the "slows" in dealing with congressional activists.[66]

Finally, the two sides differed on which approach best resolved enduring manpower problems with the Union military. The focus of congressional radicals was an expected explosion of voluntarism in the Northeast once the war became clearly a moral crusade, while Lincoln still believed in early 1862 that his best hope for saving the Union lay in the allegiance of the border-state loyalists, with whom he could reason to set aside the sources of so much trouble if the radicals would cease provoking them.[67] He was soon to find, however, that the essence of that logic was deeply flawed.

A Presidential Failure

On July 12, 1862, Lincoln called a group of border-state congressman to the White House to urge them once again to move ahead with a plan for gradual, compensated emancipation. He openly warned that if they did not take such an initiative, they might find themselves, through the uncontrollable "incidents of war," subject to even harsher loss of property later on. Popular dissatisfaction with the war's aims among free state residents was reaching proportions that could not be safely ignored, threatening to impinge on the president's ability to prosecute the conflict. Those gathered, however, spurned the president's plea.

> Two-thirds of the border-state representatives signed a manifesto rejecting Lincoln's proposal because it would produce too "radical [a] change in our social system"; it was "interference" by the government with a state matter; it would cost too much (a curious objection from men whose states would benefit from a tax that would fall mainly on the free states); and finally, instead of shortening the conflict by depriving the Confederacy of hope for border-state support, it would lengthen the war and jeopardize victory by driving many unionist slaveholders into rebellion.[68]

The border states' intransigence on what Lincoln considered to be a reasonable, moderate course of action finally revealed to the president in unmistakable terms the enormous—probably insurmountable—obstacles along his preferred path of action. Until that time, a key factor in his decision making on the question of slavery had been the strategic conclusion that his Union-saving war effort required the aid of the loyalist border states. He believed that he could not afford to alienate them, and thus he devoted extraordinary efforts to securing their continued support. "I think to lose Kentucky is nearly the same as to lose the whole game. Kentucky gone, we cannot hold Missouri, nor, as I think, Maryland. These all against us, and the job on our hands is too large for us. We would as well consent to separation at once, including the surrender of this capitol."[69] Yet, as matters unfolded, Lincoln found himself forced to revisit that logic, to examine new realities. He could either accommodate the border states and in the bargain further estrange an increasingly impatient population in the remainder of the Union, or he could energize the North through some dramatic reversal at risk of losing the slaveholding loyalists.[70]

As it happened, at about this same time pressures in the international arena were also coalescing so as to encourage Lincoln to think anew his direction. Union diplomats had been concerned since the war's beginning about how British reliance on southern cotton would dispose England to the conflict, but it was only in 1862 that surplus stocks of that staple had dwindled, threatening a key industry. By the summer, three of every four British cotton mill workers were either out of work or laboring part time, creating immense pressures on British policy makers to grant recognition and aid to the Confederacy in order to get cotton imports resumed and their economy moving again. "The British prime minister," James M. McPherson reports, actually "warded off a parliamentary motion for

Confederate recognition in mid-July, even though a majority in Commons clearly favored such a step."[71]

The cotton problem also affected the French, who had, however, other reasons for soliciting a southern alliance. Southern diplomats had tempted Louis Napoleon with Confederate military support in his quest to make of Mexico a French colony. Although these factors failed to move France in the South's favor, the temptations for alliance remained for the European powers. Further, the disincentives for European recognition of the South seemed to dwindle as the Union armies proved incapable of subduing Robert E. Lee's forces, leading those practicing Realpolitik in London and Paris to believe that a permanent independent state might indeed be established in Richmond. Moreover, as long as the Union position on the issue of slavery was indistinguishable in its essentials from the Confederate one, those European policy makers were free to craft positions without regard to the considerable antislavery sentiment prevailing on both sides of the English Channel.

Thus, with unsettling omens appearing on military and diplomatic horizons; with efforts to generate voluntary action for gradual emancipation stalled; with congressional radicals becoming increasingly hostile toward the administration; and with free-state opinion cresting in favor of immediate emancipation as a means toward and object of victory—Abraham Lincoln decided to alter the course of presidential history by embracing southern emancipation. The pressures of the war rendered perilous any other alternative. In the president's own words, emancipation had "become a necessity indispensable to the maintenance of the government."[72]

Lincoln apparently began moving decisively toward a decree to emancipate sometime during the late spring of 1862. He wrote the initial draft of an emancipation order during a series of sessions in the telegraph room of the War Department, escaping there the constant interruptions of the White House. After completing the draft, he revealed his plans to a few close advisers, and on July 22, ten days after his contentious meeting with the border-state representatives, he read the document to his gathered cabinet. The president indicated that his decision to issue the proclamation was firm, but he wanted consultations on particulars. Lincoln accepted some minor emendations, but only one major recommendation of note came forth. Secretary of War Edwin M. Stanton encouraged the president to delay issuing the proclamation. He was not at all opposed to the decision, but he felt that issuance at that moment would, given the low state of Union military affairs, communicate a sense of panic to the world. Better, Stanton argued, to await a substantial military victory, and then to greet the world with a symbol of American justice. Lincoln accepted the recommendation, which may have mirrored his own initial inclinations, and then settled into a difficult period of waiting.[73]

The proclamation Lincoln read before his cabinet took the form of a preliminary order, composed of two paragraphs. The first grounded the president's decision in the recently passed Confiscation Act. Lincoln ordered all confederates "to cease participating in, aiding, countenancing, or abetting the existing rebellion, . . . and to return to their former allegiance to the United States, on pain of the forfeitures and seizures" provided for in that Act.[74] The second paragraph offered a reward—and a threat. Lincoln therein announced his intent, upon the reconvening of Congress, to recommend again a bill establishing a program of federal aid compensating slaveholders for emancipation in those states reestablishing their loyalty. That was the carrot. The stick followed. He claimed that as a matter of military necessity, those slaves in states not reestablishing their allegiance by January 1, 1863 "shall then, thenceforward, and forever, be free."[75] Lincoln apparently hoped that this deal would be sufficient to lure back the rebellious South without further bloodshed.[76]

After Lincoln reported the proclamation to his cabinet, days turned to weeks, which turned to months, as the president awaited military conditions auspicious for the proclamation's public issuance. Further, he had the difficult task of shielding his intent from publics ever attentive to the slightest signal of change in policy during wartime. These difficulties were compounded by the ever-increasing momentum of the abolitionists, who continued to pound on Lincoln at every opportunity. Charges from this quarter so frustrated the president that he later told one group that a presidential proclamation—absent the wherewithal to enforce it—would have all the effect of the "Pope's bull against the comet!"[77]

Lincoln's drafting of a preliminary emancipation proclamation did not mean that he had turned entirely away from that which had long-distanced him from the abolitionists. The best evidence of this is found in the draft order itself, which endorsed as the preferred course of resolution gradual, compensated freedom. Further, he continued an active lobbying campaign in favor of colonization.

In August 1862, a month after he had apprised the cabinet of his emancipation plan, Lincoln invited a prominent group of free African Americans to the White House for the purpose of convincing them to leave the country, and to take others with them. The president, using blunt language and the psychological power of his office, urged free blacks to lead a movement out of the United States, where neither they nor their brothers in chains could ever really belong.

> You and we are different races. We have between us a broader difference than exists between almost any other two races. . . . [T]his physical difference is a great disadvantage to us both, as I think your race suffer very greatly, many of them living among us, while ours suffer from your presence. In a word we suffer on each side. If this is admitted, it affords a reason at least why we should be separated. . . . Your race are suffering, in my judgment, the greatest wrong inflicted on any people. But even when you cease to be slaves, you are yet far removed from being placed on an equality with the white race. . . . I do not propose to discuss this, but present it as a fact with which we have to deal. I cannot alter it if I would. . . . It is better for us both, therefore, to be separated.

The president also sought to inflict a sense of guilt on those who refused to depart "voluntarily." He asserted—and repeated—that the dreadful war then underway was made necessary only because of the presence on American soil of those of African descent. He further accused those freedmen who sought to remain in the "comfort" of the United States, instead of going to Liberia or Central America, of holding "an extremely selfish view." He lectured them on their responsibility "to help those who are not so fortunate as yourselves," and encouraged them to "sacrifice something . . . for the sake of your race."[78]

The president's plea fell on decidedly infertile ground.[79] The delegation that met with Lincoln returned to him a resolution that read, in part, "We, the few assembled, deem it inexpedient, inauspicious and impolitic to agitate the subject of emigration of the colored people of this country anywhere. . . . And furthermore, that we judge it unauthorized and unjust for us to compromise the interests of over four and a half millions of our race by precipitate action on our part." A more colorful response issued from one outside black observer, who was familiar with the publicized meeting: "We were with Warren on Bunker Hill, with Washington at Morristown and Valley Forge, with LaFayette at Yorktown, with Perry, Decatur, and McDonough in their cruisings, and with Jackson at New Orleans, battling side by side with the white man for nationality, national rights, and national glory. . . . Are you an American?" the author rhetorically asked of Lincoln.

"So are we!"[80] "This is our country as much as it is yours," another plainly announced, "and we will not leave it."[81]

The Proclamations Issued

On September 17, General George McClellan finally gave Lincoln the Union victory he had been anxiously awaiting for two months. At enormous loss of life on both sides—casualties four times greater than those suffered by Americans at Normandy—McClellan's armies repelled Robert E. Lee's advances into Maryland at Antietam Creek. Although disappointed that McClellan had refused to swallow Lee's army whole as it hobbled back to Virginia, the president immediately began final revisions on his order. On Monday, September 22, 1862, he issued what is commonly termed the "Preliminary Emancipation Proclamation."[82]

The order followed closely the model discussed with his cabinet in July. Its central feature was an expression of presidential intent to free slaves in areas not returning to the Union by January 1, 1863. Emancipation was to be conducted essentially under the president's war power; he would not return for additional congressional authorization. The order also contained, however, provisions calling for a program of voluntary, compensated emancipation in those areas not in rebellion. Here the president had to rely on the proposed creation of a financial incentive structure by Congress. He also pledged that, upon termination of hostilities, all slaveholders who had remained loyal throughout the conflict would be compensated for losses attributable to the war, including the dispossession of slave property. Moreover, despite the criticism he had recently weathered on colonization, Lincoln again suggested the development of plans for black emigration. Apparently at Secretary Seward's behest, Lincoln expressly made colonization voluntary.[83]

Although some looked on Lincoln's announcement as a gambit—after all it merely promised action *if* certain conditions were not met by New Year's Day—most of the nation was electrified by it. For the first time in American history a president was pledging to place the powers of his office—enormously magnified by war—in the balance with the slaves. A pledge to stand out of the way, to sheath the veto, would have been groundbreaking of itself. But here Lincoln promised not just to step aside, but actively to assert himself on behalf of those enslaved in the rebellious South.[84]

Horace Greeley called the pronouncement "the beginning of the new life of the nation." The *New York Times* offered that "no more important and far-reaching document ever issued since the foundation of this Government." "We shout for joy," exulted Frederick Douglass, "that we live to record this righteous decree." The hard-core abolitionists took issue with some of the particulars, but William Lloyd Garrison hailed the decision as "an act of immense historic importance." They remained vigilant, however, for assurance that the commander-in-chief would demand vigorous prosecution from an oft-irresolute military.[85]

The proclamation received a predictable reaction from the South. Confederates charged Lincoln with rank usurpation, and accused him of fomenting race war. The *Richmond Examiner* scored the president for his "call for the insurrection of four million slaves, and the inauguration of a reign of hell upon earth."[86]

The overseas audience—which Lincoln carefully watched for signs of rapprochement with the confederates—generally reacted less positively than expected. Some saw, as Seward had feared, the order as an act of political desperation. Some decried prospects of bloody servile war incited by a faltering commander-in-chief. And some, unschooled in the particulars of American constitutionalism, ridiculed the proclamation's scope. "The principle asserted," declared the London *Spectator*, "is not that a human being cannot justly own another, but that he cannot own him unless he is loyal to the United States."[87] Lincoln's parsimonious language in the proclamation fairly invited such charges.

The major question remaining was not whether the South would comply—reaction had been far too venomous, and Union military success far too modest, to believe any confederate state would surrender—but whether Lincoln would follow through with his threat. Speculation that he might not stand firm heightened after the mid-term elections of that fall, which severely reduced Republican majorities in both houses of Congress.[88]

The president had an opportunity to affirm the order with his annual message in early December. He did not do so unambiguously. He submitted a copy of the proclamation with the text of his message, but he raised yet another alternative for resolving the slave problem, thereby suggesting ambivalence about the course charted on September 22.

He recommended to Congress a constitutional amendment, yet again providing for gradual, compensated emancipation, with colonization.[89] Any state liberating its slaves before the year 1900 would be reimbursed with bonds drawn on the United States Treasury. Slaves freed by the circumstances of war would remain forever free, with their owners receiving no compensation; owners loyal to the Union would, however, be paid. It further included a specific constitutional provision allowing Congress to appropriate funds for colonizing freedmen outside the United States, with their consent.

The president acknowledged that advocates of immediate, unconditional emancipation would find such a program wanting, but he contended that gradual liberation "spares both races from the evils of sudden derangement—in fact, from the necessity of any derangement." At this late date—one month before he was to issue his final order—Lincoln was still searching for means other than unconditional liberation to resolve the disputes of war, evidencing a discomfort with that which the radicals had moved him to embrace. In effect, he asked Congress to relieve him of the necessity of proceeding with his earlier proclamation. Neither the war nor the "proceedings under the proclamation of September 22, 1862, [will be] stayed because of the *recommendation* of this plan. Its timely *adoption*, I doubt not, would bring restoration and thereby stay both" [emphasis in the original].[90] As David Herbert Donald has noted, " Lincoln foresaw the possibility that by January the war might be nearly over and the Union might be restored—but the United States would still be a slaveholding nation."[91] He would accept that result as the price of peace and a restored Union.

None of Lincoln's messages drew more ridicule from the abolitionists than this one. The *Boston Commonwealth* captured the spirit of most of the criticism.

> It is said that once there was a man who thought that if he should run two miles, he could jump over a mountain. When, after his run, he reached the base of the mountain, he sat down to rest. We are reminded of this individual by the President's Message. Taking a hundred days' start, he nears the base of the mountain; but, it seems, is very tired, and sits down to rest. He nods. Never did wide-awakes usher in a more heavy-eyed President. Here, evidently fallen asleep, he takes to dreaming of the year 1900! Is it that despairing of the present, he is turning his attention to future salvation? . . . [I]f the President means to carry out his edict of freedom on the New Year, what is all this stuff about gradual emancipation?

Lincoln's ambiguity led one *Liberator* editorialist to proclaim that "the President is not competent to write his own official papers." Another expressed sympathy for those of us now trying to decipher the president's method.

The vacillations of President Lincoln will greatly perplex the future historian. Why, having the war power in his hands, he did not proclaim emancipation at the beginning—why, having proclaimed a restricted measure of it, he did not push that with vigor—and why, when the time for the beneficent action of the Proclamation approached, he impaired that action by a Message, running counter to it—all these are difficult of explanation. At present, we have the amazing spectacle of the chief of a great country, attacked by a powerful and most dangerous enemy, having in his possession a bomb which would instantly scatter that enemy's forces, first letting that bomb remain more than a year inactive, then discharging it with a three months' fuse, and after two months, making special exertions to extinguish the fuse. . . .

It now remains to be seen if Congress also will disregard this last opportunity to save the nation.[92]

Congress did not. Led as much by Democrats opposed to emancipation in general as by Republicans in favor of a January 1 order, Congress rejected the president's appeal for passage of a constitutional amendment. Absent that escape, Lincoln was confronted with a decision to maintain the course proposed on September 22, or to delay action further in the interest of making headway on compromise. In this instance, he did not waver. On Thursday, January 1, 1863, Abraham Lincoln cleared the mountain. His approach run had taken three months. That of the abolitionists had been thirty-two years, to the day.

"Free at Last!"

The final Emancipation Proclamation, as written, bore "all the moral grandeur of a bill of lading," claimed Richard Hofstadter.[93] However, according to contemporary accounts, the order created a sensation. Pent-up tension north and south gave way to exuberant release upon hearing that Lincoln's order had been proclaimed. Nowhere was this celebration greater than in black communities, slave and free; the grapevine quickly carried news of the order to the far reaches of the South, such that spontaneous celebrations broke out in the most unlikely spots.[94] Yet Lincoln's proclamation initially liberated more spirits than people.

Secretary of State William H. Seward spoke honestly when he said of the proclamation, "We show our sympathy with slavery by emancipating the slaves where we cannot reach them and holding them in bondage where we can set them free."[95] Indeed the president's order again was more an expression of intention than of fact. The proclamation "freed" those slaves held in hostile, unsubdued territory, a peculiarity necessitated by the limits of the president's war powers.[96] But Lincoln set into motion an inexorable dynamic of liberation. Emancipation would thereafter not only follow the American flag, that flag would serve quite literally as a beacon to fugitives who now knew that freedom was to be found at its base.

Further, the president now made it known that the military was expected to comply firmly with his new commands. For the most part, he encountered little substantive resistance, as weary Union soldiers welcomed those who would support the war with manual labor in camp and, despite Lincoln's longstanding reluctance to use black troops, eventually with guns on the field of battle.[97] The depth of this welcome derived as much as anything else from the howls of protest issuing from their common southern enemies.

The Union armies, under the direction of Generals Grant and Sherman, made the freedom pledged in the president's proclamation a reality. Every troop advance thereafter took on new meaning, as an exercise in redemption of a promise. The evidence further suggests that the very process of military advancement itself moved more surely after the war's aims had been clarified, perhaps because of renewed vigor and purpose on Lincoln's part, perhaps because of the power and influence of fugitives at the front, and perhaps because of the effect on Union troops of endowing the war with the aspect of a crusade.[98] The impact of Lincoln's proclamation, then, is misreckoned by counting only those slaves freed from their masters on January 1, 1863.

Notably, however, even after the Emancipation Proclamation's issuance the president expressed a willingness to consider abandoning the path of liberation if the Union could be preserved that way. Nation-keeping concerns thus dominated the president's thinking on slavery to the very end. When confronted with subsequent overtures from a weakening South about calling off the war in exchange for restoring the Union to the *status quo ante-bellum*, Lincoln contemplated removing the most vexing road-block to re-union: abolition. In short, the emergency measures adopted by the president to win the war might, he suggested, be set aside as the permanent policy of the government in order to ease southern anxiety about reentry into the Union. The record is unclear about how serious Lincoln was in raising such prospects, but that his uncertainty became known to several prominent public figures, including Frederick Douglass, signifies that it was more than idle musings.[99] In the end, however, practical and moral considerations propelled him to stay the course.[100] Despite some private vacillations, Lincoln went into, and won, the 1864 election publicly committed to abolition as a nonnegotiable condition of peace.[101]

Freedom for those enslaved in the border states and in loyalist enclaves in the South, and the encoding of emancipation in the nation's fundamental law, awaited passage of the Thirteenth Amendment to the Constitution. This Lincoln made his own project, using his stature among his Republican and Union party partisans to have the amendment adopted as the centerpiece of the latter's 1864 platform.[102] The president then immersed himself entirely in the battle for that provision's passage in 1864–65. He used "all his powers of persuasion and patronage to get it through," including secret negotiations involving railroad monopolies and the release of rebel family members of wavering congressmen. Thaddeus Stevens said of this lobbying, "The greatest measure of the nineteenth century was passed by corruption, aided and abetted by the purest man in America."[103]

Although that amendment doubtless would have passed eventually, given the nation's prevailing opinion on slavery, Lincoln's role in pushing it through at that moment was indispensable. Thus, wrote Hofstadter, "Such claim as he may have to be remembered as an Emancipator perhaps rests more justly on his behind-the-scenes activity for the thirteenth amendment than on the Proclamation itself." Yet his work on behalf of that amendment in many ways was an extension of the commitment he made on January 1, 1863. And of that commitment Lincoln himself once acknowledged, "I claim not to have controlled events, but confess plainly that events have controlled me."[104]

The political calculus of Abraham Lincoln's tenure in office wrought, in the most literal sense, a role reversal for the presidency.

The central role relevant to the question of slavery for Lincoln, as it had been for his predecessors since Jackson, was that of nation maintenance, or preservation of the institutions and unity of the American polity. But where presidents before Lincoln's time found in that nation-maintaining role reason to suppress efforts to liberate the enslaved, Lincoln eventually found the demands of the role leading him to break with the past. He found himself confronting conditions that, he firmly believed, required him to work toward the liberation of the slaves, if the union he was pledged to preserve was to survive. To those who felt he was stepping beyond the bounds of constitutional propriety, Lincoln pointedly replied "that measures otherwise unconstitutional, might become lawful, by becoming indispensable to the preservation of the Constitution, through the preservation of the nation."[105] "Things had gone on from bad to worse," he elsewhere claimed, "until I felt that we had reached the end of our rope on the plan of operations we had been pursuing.... [W]e had about played our last card, and we must change our tactics, or lose the game!"[106] Only at that pass was the institution of the presidency converted to the course of emancipation.

If we borrow the definition offered by James MacGregor Burns, presidential "leadership" to free the slaves only became possible during the tenure of Abraham Lincoln. Burns defines leadership as "exercised when persons with certain motives and purposes mobilize, in competition or conflict with others, institutional, political, psychological, and other resources so as to arouse, engage, and satisfy the motives of followers."[107] There are two central elements to Burns's fundamental definition: motive (or purpose) and resources. Only in Lincoln's presidency did the proper motives and sufficient resources converge in that office for the exertion of leadership on behalf of emancipation. And arguably both arose less because of Lincoln's own volition than because of the circumstances surrounding his presidency, circumstances that owed much to thirty years' labor by the abolitionists. Thus, his acknowledgement "that events have controlled me."

Taking Lincoln's rhetoric as reliable evidence as to his motives, it is easy to see that he was not, before 1862, inclined to use his office to move toward immediate emancipation. Indeed, he quite frankly asserted in his inaugural address that "I have no inclination ... *no purpose* ... to interfere with the institution of slavery in the States where it exists." His purpose with regard to the slaves, however, changed. When it became evident to Lincoln that a war to retrieve the South required the conversion of that effort into a crusade against slavery, he made his break with the past. Thus, his purposes were subjected to a conversion, based on the changed perception of what his role as a nation-maintainer required. At the root of that change was a polity converted by the actions of, and reactions to, organized agitators.

That agitation also remarkably influenced in this instance the nature of Lincoln's resources. He was, by virtue of the war that emerged from the agitation, granted political power far beyond that usually conferred on a president of the United States. Indeed, Clinton Rossiter wrote that Lincoln assumed the position of a "constitutional dictator." The war created, in Rossiter's words, an "astounding expansion of the powers of the Presidency."[108] Presidential leadership toward emancipation, then, could only emerge when the president had the power resources sufficient to overcome the usual confinement of that office produced by separated institutions, federalism, and public ambivalence about the exercise of centralized authority. Of the presidents examined in this study, only Lincoln was invested with such powers.[108]

It might be objected that the real *institutional* leadership for the emancipation of the slaves in fact arose in Congress, given that body's early and persistent pressure on the president to move more boldly on behalf of the enslaved. After all, Lincoln actually vetoed some advanced legislation, suggesting that had the president simply stood out of the way, an earlier, corporate "Great Emancipator" would have arisen instead.

There is a certain simple appeal to this claim, based in part on the conventional inclination to associate leadership with a first-mover. Yet an emphasis on resources in the leadership equation adds an element of complexity to that claim. Undeniably had Congress been given free rein to wage the war, more individual slaves would have been freed earlier than under Lincoln's policies. But the consequences of those actions, as Lincoln argued, may very well have been devastating to the Union's overall resource position. Those actions may have solidified confederate resolve earlier; they may have caused northern moderates and conservatives to withdraw support for the war effort; and they probably would have alienated most if not all of the border states. Accordingly, the congressional radicals may have freed many slaves through piecemeal military action, but in the long run have saved southern slavery by weakening the eventual engine of its demise. In this light, Lincoln's Union-saving (his nation-keeping) efforts eventually provided him with an irreplaceable resource: a powerful, relatively unified war-making machine capable of dictating, of *commanding*, an end to slavery in the South.

Simply put, Lincoln's skilled efforts at holding together disparate fragments of the Union—his foremost concern—in time gave him *and his radical critics* the force necessary to wrest freedom from an unwilling South. Yet it remains true, ironically, that the success of Lincoln's project was ultimately dependent on his directing it where others pushed him. The leader's resources became fully functional *only* in service of a cause the followers defined. Hence, we see a president whose leadership was contingent on his following others whose successful followership was contingent on their leading the president to embrace the ends they desired.[110] These are complexities no simple construction of presidential leadership can explain. However, it is into such complexities that the obscured roots of leadership of the nation are deeply embedded.

The conversion of the presidency into an agency for racial equality did not last much beyond the war. That confluence of motives and resources that characterized the Lincoln presidency rather quickly dissipated. During Reconstruction, a divisiveness of purpose arose over what to do with free African Americans, and the political resources that had once been conferred on the national government, especially the president, withered. Under these conditions, new discontents emerged among those dissatisfied with the still-unequal standing of black Americans. Under these conditions, those committed to harmony and union—*and* those committed to white supremacy in the South—sought to still any further movement toward black freedom, and to quiet those pushing for it. And, under these conditions, the nation-maintaining role of the office once again constrained presidents to work against efforts at racial change. A time of further leadership from the White House for racial equality would await another conversion of that nation-maintaining role to favor black Americans.

PART II

Civil Rights

CHAPTER 4

From Reconstruction to the Great Depression: Latency Years

The Civil War wrought for African Americans a new standing in the American polity. They achieved, in Lincoln's phrase, recognition of the right to eat the bread they earned with their own hands without asking leave of anyone else.[1]

What they had not attained, however, was full civil and social equality with the nation's white majority—the ability to earn that bread and to break it wherever they chose. Thus, black Americans found themselves, after the war, needing to fight politically to receive that which they believed the newly recreated Constitution guaranteed them. As before, their challenges to prevailing social structures often sparked incendiary politics.

The post-Reconstruction responses by presidents to such challenges followed a now-familiar path, inasmuch as the nation had lost its zeal for change. White political elites, including those staffing the White House, actively worked to retard efforts aimed at advancing further racial equality. Some of these presidential exercises in nation maintenance mirrored those of the antebellum era, but evolving circumstances called for modifications. Two new realities were especially crucial in giving shape to presidential action during the long Jim Crow era.

First, the nature of the post-Reconstruction race issue was less clearly defined than the question of slavery. What was the best approach for securing that equality promised by the Fourteenth Amendment, when so much human behavior denying it seemed beyond the regulatory scope of the nation's peacetime constitution? Should economic advancement take precedence? Political action through agitation, publicity, or partisanship? Or social uplift through education and "moral improvement"? The efficacy of these proposed remedies was far from clear, leading to competition among those with differing visions for black America. This competition, in turn, created opportunities for presidential manipulation of the various factions, to diminish the threat to prevailing social structures.

Second, liberation and reconstruction had created within the United States an enlarged population of free blacks, which in some areas of the country became a significant political force. The costs of overt police-state or political suppression of black political action at the national level had commensurately risen, such that presidents of this era had to calculate them in trying to find the best means of keeping black activism in check. This usually meant a reliance on more benign methods of manipulation, often involving tokens of friendship offered to the select among the nation's black leadership. Even many of the nation's most ardent segregationists recognized that black votes, to the extent that they existed, could not be ignored completely by self-interested white politicians. In fact, they found that black Americans could be exploited in service of all manner of political ends— especially the winning and holding of elective office.

Thus, even before race became a consistently hot issue again in the 1950s and '60s, presidents had incentives to tend to it actively in order to preserve from change the social and political structures of a nation that found the "very presence of the Negro . . . a trouble."[2] Given the potential disarray inherent in that "trouble," presidents charged with maintaining the nation's security and its fundamental institutions were long attentive to how to prevent or curb agitation before it became a clear and present danger.

Finding a New Course for Black America

One of the most vexing questions that confronted those who pressed for the emancipation of the slaves was how a predominantly white society would treat freed blacks as they moved out of their stations as human chattel.[3] Those optimists who had envisioned liberation as leading directly to full civil and political equality for African Americans rather quickly found their hopefulness dashed.

For a brief time—some dozen years following the Civil War—those of egalitarian dreams joined with an assertive Republican Party to provide unprecedented opportunities for emancipated blacks in the South.[4] When postbellum political reality changed, however, the armed forces that had imposed greater equality on a reluctant South were withdrawn, opening the way to termination of the exercise of newfound civil and political rights there.[5] In the final decades of the nineteenth century, commitments north and south to national reconciliation overwhelmed devotion to racial equality. Thus, by century's end, the nation's social, political, and economic complexion bore marked similarities to its prewar condition. Only in the most constricted sense had equality emerged as a result of the Union victory, a couple of postwar civil rights acts notwithstanding.[6]

The relative deprivation that resulted among African Americans during that era met with a mixed response by southern blacks. "The Negro bred to slavery," writes C. Vann Woodward, "was typically ignorant and poor and was not given to pressing his rights to such luxuries as hotels, restaurants, and theaters even when he could afford them or was aware of them. So far as his status was concerned, there was little need for Jim Crow laws to establish what the lingering stigma of slavery—in bearing, speech, and manner—made so apparent."[7] Stigma most often induced political enervation.

"At the same time," Woodward continues, "the more confident, assertive, and ambitious members of the race had not forgotten the vision of civil rights and equality that Reconstruction had inspired. Still fresh in their memories was an exhilarating if precarious taste of recognition and power. The hopes and expectations aroused by these experiences had been dimmed but not extinguished by the Compromise of 1877."[8] The relative mix of these psychologies—the fatefully complacent and the actively optimistic—in each state produced a melange of racial advance in the South.

For a few years, then, African Americans could comfort themselves with successful experiments in social and political equality in scattered pockets throughout Dixie. But as the firm hand of Jim Crow finally established its supremacy across the region, those successes receded. It was under these conditions that leading African Americans, those Woodward designates "ambitious members of the race," began to contemplate the necessity of a coordinated response to renewed white supremacy.

The ambitious, however, confronted a variety of organizational and ideological barriers to collective action. The most fundamental of these—undergirding all others—was a widespread ideology of racism among a powerful white majority, an endemic popular belief in the essential biological inferiority of the black man and woman.[9] Southern whites, armed with such beliefs and newly freed from the compulsion of northern bayonets—lifted in part because the North shared that racist ideology—dismantled the political gains of the Reconstruction era by such contrivances as literacy tests and the poll tax. Organized violence, often publicly sanctioned, also remained as a resort against those too ambitious to respect less imposing political barriers.

Economic barriers endured, too. Although the formal structures of slavery had been toppled by war-related amendments to the Constitution, the political economy of the South emerged from the war largely unchanged, at least from the vantage point of those newly liberated. Tenantry and sharecropping—often the most desirable of the limited options available to the freedmen—afforded few practical advantages over the slave-master relation.[10] Thus it was that in that region of the country where overwhelming majorities of African Americans still resided, economic resources were so scarce that little in the way of organized political action could be easily mounted.

As important as a lack of physical resources was the absence of an ideological consensus among the discontented as to how best to proceed, how best to convert their numbers and their grievances into power. The ambitious could not agree on what steps or strategies would best lead toward full racial equality. Rather, between 1890 and 1930, a variety of competing notions emerged about the best route for black Americans to take. Unity of action proved elusive as long as disagreement prevailed concerning what steps were most likely to lead to racial progress. Three particular views—what might be termed schools of thought—drew the greatest followings.[11]

One developed in the 1890s around Booker T. Washington. Washington promoted a modest agenda constructed on the central premise that black sociopolitical progress first required economic advance. To Washington, prospects for economic progress for the masses of African Americans best lay in industrial education and manual labor, taking advantage of the economic space already ceded by the white majority to most blacks. Fundamental to this approach was a passive, largely conformist position on civil and political rights. Since industrial and agricultural education required the active financial patronage of whites, Washington counseled patience. White benefactors, he knew, were wary of giving money to those they saw as "uppity." Political passivity would thus reap long-term advantages; the meek would inherit the earth.[12]

An impatient W. E. B. Du Bois arose after the turn of the century to challenge Washington, providing a second ideological foundation for action.[13] Du Bois attacked Washington's thought at its heart, promoting political and social action, urging African Americans to rid themselves of the political complacency that Washington recommended. Where Washington sought patience, Du Bois instructed urgency. And where Washington embraced incrementalism, Du Bois pressed for immediate and substantial advances for African

Americans, politically and economically.[14] Gunnar Myrdal categorized the former as essentially accommodationist, the latter as protest-oriented.[15] From those who shared Du Bois commitment to protest sprang the National Association for the Advancement of Colored People, in 1910. Du Bois was hired as the NAACP's principal publicist, to edit the organization's newspaper *The Crisis*, a position from which he propelled himself into the forefront of the fight for racial equality.[16] The NAACP subsequently developed prominent efforts to advance racial equality both through publicity and litigation.[17]

A third school emerged to compete with the disciples of Washington and Du Bois. This was black nationalism. Henry M. Turner, an official of the African Methodist Episcopal church, and later Marcus Garvey, sought to convince black Americans of the folly of remaining dissipated among an oppressive white majority.[18] The black nationalists encouraged the constitution of a separate black nation, either in the United States or through mass emigration to Africa. According to one scholar, with the nationalists, "blacks could refuse to limit their choice to be[ing] either second-class Americans waiting for promotion, or men without a country."[19]

Although each of these schools attracted multitudes of adherents—and at times enjoyed relative ascendancy—none successfully prevailed over the enormous barriers to collective action among African Americans into the 1930s. As a result, protests over racial equality generally remained on a fairly small scale, seldom reaching the national agenda.

Presidents and Selective Preferment

Presidents of this era, from Rutherford Hayes to Herbert Hoover, did almost nothing to advance the cause of civil rights. Rather, aside from largely token efforts by Republicans in the final quarter of the nineteenth century to secure black voting rights in the South—a position that had the virtue of being self-serving—these presidents commonly used their offices to moderate or to stifle active movement toward racial equality.

In an extensive study of the presidency from 1861 to 1909, historian George Sinkler found that

> in attacking the problem of race, the Presidents, as Lincoln said about General McClellan, had the "slows." . . . If the Presidents of this period are judged only on their expressed intentions in matters of race, they make a good showing. When measured by actual accomplishment, with one or

two exceptions, their record is one of stark failure to enforce the federal laws involving matters of race, and an extreme reluctance to champion an unreserved racial equality in the full spirit of American democracy. When it came to a choice between vigorous action or inaction in matters of race the Presidents were paralyzed.[20]

More to the point here, however, presidents were not indifferent to the various parties to the internal conflict among African Americans. References to the "slows," and presidential reluctance and paralysis, imply a passivity in presidential behavior that is (unintentionally) deceptive and incomplete. Rather, American presidents, during this historical period, almost without exception, revealed an inclination to use their offices *actively* to retard movement toward substantive racial equality. The most persistent strategy adopted by successive presidents throughout this era was one of *selective preferment*, meaning that these presidents used their constitutional and extra-constitutional powers to favor certain of the contenders for leadership of black America.[21] The ultimate goal of selective preferment was to defuse radicalism by rewarding in general terms moderate to conservative political behavior. During the first three decades of the twentieth century, this meant showering Booker T. Washington and his heirs with tangible and psychological rewards from the White House.[22] These preferments were seldom controversial among southern whites, as they tended to encourage accommodating behavior among the region's black population.

After a famous "Atlanta Compromise" speech of 1895, in which he charted a moderate course for black Americans— "The wisest among my race understand that the agitation of questions of social equality is the extremest folly"— Booker T. Washington drew acclaim from white elites nationwide, including those in the White House.[23] President Grover Cleve-land—who had repeatedly defended the southern white position on race as justified by blacks' "ignorance [and] slothfulness"—read Washington's speech and sent him a message of high praise. "Your words cannot fail to delight and encourage all who wish well for the race. And if your colored fellow-citizens do not favor your utterances [and] gather new hope and form new determinations to gain every valuable advantage offered them by their citizenship, it will be strange indeed."[24]

Washington's passivity found an enthusiastic audience among whites who sought to protect their superior status. Thus, Washington became the White House's preferred channel for dealing with the question of race in America. By keeping the Tuskegeean's star ascendant, presidents at once could lay legitimate claim to honoring black America and could undermine the efforts of Washington's more aggressive detractors. Myrdal later observed of this dynamic, "*leadership conferred upon a Negro by whites rais[ed] his class status in the Negro community*" (emphasis in the original).[25] Washington's presidential sanction substantially bolstered his campaign to convince blacks that his way was the one most likely to bring measured progress.

Washington made the most of his conferred preeminence. Even otherwise-favorable scholarship has noted his "monopoly of leadership [that] prevented those with a different point of view from working effectively in their own way while he continued to work in his."[26] His penchant for intrigue, for secrecy, and for centralized control over resources available to the black community, was forcefully buttressed by the weight of presidential power and prestige.[27]

Perhaps the best example of this strategy of selective preferment surfaced during the presidency of Theodore Roosevelt. It was during Roosevelt's tenure that divisions within the black community over competing pathways to racial advancement first prominently emerged.[28] It was also during Roosevelt's tenure that Washington most prominently became the White House's chosen agent.

Booker Washington managed to ingratiate himself to Theodore Roosevelt by donning the hat of a political boss of a small but important Republican constituent group.[29] The common denominator underlying their relationship, historians seem to agree, was not an equal commitment to racial justice for all, but patronage. Even an unusual 1901 White House dinner for Washington, which created a rare and lasting furor within the South as a manifestation of undue familiarity, was arranged to discuss federal job vacancies in that region.[30] Roosevelt's reliance on Washington resulted in the elevation of worthy African Americans to a number of important federal positions, but little in the way of widespread social or political advance.

The president's support magnified Washington's relative position among potential black spokesmen. Many black elites, who otherwise may have been disposed to criticize Washington on grounds of principle, often found themselves holding their fire in fear of ostracism or because they wished to partake of the considerable bounty of government jobs and grant money under Washington's control.[31] Roosevelt apparently recognized his part in supporting such inclinations. He thought Washington's program of industrial education the proper focus of black energies, and he "had no use for loud-mouthed black agitators. He admired Booker T. Washington because he [in Roosevelt's words] 'was not led away, as the educated Negro so often is led away into the pursuit of fantastic visions.'"[32]

Du Bois hardly shared Washington's prominent embrace among the nation's political elite. Indeed, it appears that Washington's premier rival for leadership among African Americans was all but ignored by successive administrations, a situation that threatened completely to marginalize Du Bois politically. No one was more aware of this than Washington himself, who jealously guarded his near-exclusive access to the White House. At the hint—perhaps baseless—that Taft was mulling the prospect of nominating Du Bois to a ministerial post in Haiti, Washington actively intrigued to undermine his foe's credibility with the president. Washington had mutual friends warn Taft that Du Bois had "no strong following" among African Americans, and he moved to undercut any prospective support for Du Bois by having copies of anti-Taft material appearing in *The Crisis* forwarded to the president. One student of the conflict has written:

> The President had always been told [by Washington] that Du Bois attacked Booker Washington because the latter was a 100 percent Taft man. The Alabama educator was presented to Republican leaders as a martyr—crucified because of selfless service to the administration. Naturally this approach, minimizing the deeper causes of the dispute, made it difficult for Du Bois and his friends to receive much consideration from the White House.[33]

Virtually all that Taft heard, then, fortified a disposition to shun Du Bois. Washington helped craft a presidential response to Du Bois by reinforcing Taft's inclination to view Tuskegee as the safe alternative among the nation's blacks. Implied was that Washington's efforts on behalf of African Americans would not be waged in any way that created possible problems for the president.

On one occasion in the pre-depression era, established presidential relations with Tuskegee were interrupted. Washington's role as patronage adviser to Republican presidents created incentives for the Democratic administration of Woodrow Wilson to find some other avenue into the nation's black communities, and the NAACP appeared as the most likely option. However, less than two years into Wilson's first term, a combination of pro-segregationist policies by an administration steeply inclined toward its party's dominant southern wing, and the NAACP's unwillingness, under Du Bois's influence, to moderate its criticism, left the way open for an astute Washington to impress yet another president with his modest aims. In this he succeeded, largely insulating once again the White House from those arguing for more aggressive change. In the end, shared philosophy triumphed over partisan purity.[34]

To the extent that there was any change in the practice of selective preferment in the Republican administrations of the 1920s, it was in the direction of willful neglect of even the conservatives. Thus, those who anticipated major advances in racial equality with the departure of Wilsonian southern Democrats from the White House were disappointed. "Presidents Harding, Coolidge, and Hoover were either oblivious to minority rights or indisposed to invest their own political fortunes in support of minority causes. Republicans had little need for the still small black vote in the 1920s to assure their own political power."[35]

The last of this group, Herbert Hoover, perhaps responding to a perceived need to keep a small but by-then substantial force of disgruntled northern black voters in the Republican fold, did increase significantly the number of African Americans appointed to federal positions. But he also presided ultimately over a wholesale shift in the power structure of the Republican Party in the South, sacrificing the careers of long-time black partisans to burgeoning "lily-white" organizations. The Republican Party in the wake of Hoover's presidency was decidedly whiter than the party that nominated him in 1928.[36] Predictably, Booker T. Washington's successor as principal of Tuskegee Institute, Robert Moton, was perhaps Hoover's most relied-on source of support and information.

However, Hoover's nomination of Judge John J. Parker to the United States Supreme Court revealed vividly the narrow limits within which his black advisers and appointees operated. When statements from Parker's past, denigrating the capacity of blacks for electoral politics, were resurrected by an angry NAACP, the battle lines were quickly drawn. "Mr. Hoover," the Boston Chronicle observed, "seems to have gone far afield to add insult to injury to the negro. . . . [T]he president has stopped at nothing short of contempt toward the negro wing of the party." To such claims the Atlanta Constitution replied that "It is the hell-raising political vampires of New York and Boston who are fighting the Parker [nomination] purely on color-line contention."[37] Unsurprisingly, to quiet the storm the president sought out an endorsement for his nominee from Moton.[38] He naturally expected, given his previous relationship with Tuskegee, that one would be forthcoming. It was not.

"Personally I can forgive a great many things," Moton replied to Hoover.

"[B]ut when a man [Parker] sets himself up to publicly attack, revile or express contempt for my people for no other reason than that they belong to another race, he places himself in a position where I can have nothing less than an uncompromising and everlasting hostility." Moton then declared that the mutually beneficial relationship he had developed with the administration—control of patronage in exchange for a minority seal of approval—had reached its limit: "To have our friends ask us to palliate such hostility and to connive at a sacrifice of principle for political advantage is more than our self-respect can swallow."[39] In the final analysis, a policy of selective preferment, implemented by an administration that gave appearances of a willingness to retract even the limited gains then achieved by the nation's African Americans, betrayed to Moton the earmarks of a Faustian bargain.

Presidents and Selective Repression

The presidents thus far examined did not rely alone on an activist strategy of selective preferment. Beginning as early as Theodore Roosevelt, successive administrations found it useful to "carry a big stick" as well. Thus, the rewarding of compliant friends represented only half the equation. There also evolved a rather extensive—and sometimes severe—set of punishments meted out against those who promoted visions of racial justice too greatly exceeding the established conventions of the day. Political surveillance and persecution, especially by the FBI, were thus employed to keep the social, political, and economic advancement of African Americans within generally acceptable confines. Thus, the flip side of selective preferment was selective repression.

On July 1, 1908, Theodore Roosevelt's attorney general, Charles Joseph Bonaparte, established within the Department of Justice an investigatory detective agency, the Bureau of Investigation.[40] Bonaparte and Roosevelt almost immediately confirmed Congress's worst fears that such a police force would become an agency of political action. When angry members of Congress began to inquire into Bonaparte's administrative order, the Bureau's investigators were turned on Congress itself, with the president's blessings.

> Newspaper articles appeared, disclosing the fact that dossiers had been assembled for President Theodore Roosevelt containing information about the personal affairs of various Congressmen active in the campaign to investigate the Federal detectives. News accounts conveyed the

President's intention to publicize this collection if the Congressional investigation of Federal secret police were carried on to the length of provoking him.

On the question as to how and by what methods such data had been collected for the White House, Congressmen charged that Federal legislators had been shadowed and that their mail had been rifled. The President denied this, insisting that detectives whose job it was to ferret out criminals would not themselves violate the law by opening other people's mail packages. "But sometimes," he added, "through the accidental breaking of such [a] package the contents are exposed." With this explanation, he published the private correspondence of Senator [Benjamin] Tillman of South Carolina, who had been especially fiery in his opposition to the Administration.[41]

Thus, the FBI was at birth an agency with a political dimension. Although the first instance of the use of the Bureau for political purposes by the executive was against a coequal branch of the government, an instrument was thereby forged that gave subsequent administrations a powerful tool for surveillance and harassment of political agitators in the private sector, including black Americans.[42]

Concerns about domestic security escalated dramatically during World War I, leading to the emergence of a host of additional bureaucratic structures devoted to checking political dissent in the United States. President Woodrow Wilson presided over what has been termed "the birth of modern political surveillance in America." Theodore Kornweibel writes:

> During the late teens and early twenties of the present century, the Justice Department and its Bureau of Investigation (renamed the FBI in 1935), the intelligence branches of the Army and Navy, the State and Post Office Departments, and other agencies of the federal bureaucracy engaged in widespread investigation of those deemed politically suspect. Prominent among the targets of this sometimes coordinated, sometimes independent surveillance were aliens, members of various protest groups, socialists, Communists, opponents of World War I, militant labor unionists, ethnic or racial nationalists, and outspoken opponents of the policies of the incumbent presidents.... [B]lack radicalism was one of the major preoccupations and targets of the federal investigatory network during the Red Scare.[43]

Wilson's Attorney General, A. Mitchell Palmer, directed a widespread effort to combat a black activism that grew in magnitude and intensity as the incongruities between Wilson's international and domestic commitments to liberty became more conspicuous.[44] The Justice Department actively sought "to find any means to silence . . . The Crisis," as well as a number of other assertive African-American publications, including A. Philip Randolph's The Messenger.[45] Further, "By the end of 1919, [J. Edgar] Hoover had already defined political movements within the black community as a permanent field of investigation for his Radical Division."[46] Such activity elicited a bitter reaction from some African-American editors. Announced the Pittsburgh Courier, "As long as the Negro submits to lynchings, burnings, and oppressions—and says nothing he is a loyal American citizen. But when he decides that lynchings and burnings shall cease even at the cost of some bloodshed in America, then he is [labeled] a Bolshevist."[47]

Wilson's personal role in relation to these more intrusive government efforts to suppress black dissent remains obscure. At the time Palmer was escalating his efforts, Wilson was becoming increasingly preoccupied with the League of Nations, and then he suffered a severe stroke, removing him from active control of the administration. But the evidence does clearly suggest that if Wilson did not direct Palmer's work, he at least approved of it, occasionally cheered it, and refused to put a stop to it. A president who openly admitted his segregationist inclinations, and who shared with Palmer a fear of what Wilson himself once called "the poison of revolt," thus licensed an institutionalized effort to suppress the work of those who would challenge segregation and thereby incite dissent. The most aggressive exertion of this organized effort against political dissent took place, however, not against Du Bois and the NAACP, but against a smaller black socialist movement, and, more importantly for purposes here, against Marcus Garvey, the leader of the final of those three general channels of black protest described earlier.

It is understandable that the black nationalists would draw perhaps the government's heaviest scrutiny. Where others promoted racial equality—and even with that precipitated angry white reactions—Garvey and his flock openly advanced a brand of black pride easily interpreted as supremacy. Where other African-American leaders sought advancement largely through domestic diplomacy or reasoned intellectual persuasion, Garvey furthered his agenda with a personal flamboyance that even Du Bois termed "bombastic."[48] And where others made their inroads primarily among black elites, Garvey created what one student has called "the one truly mass based black movement" of that day.[49] Small wonder, then, that a young J. Edgar Hoover instituted an intensive Bureau of Investigation campaign to "cripple" Garvey's movement.[50]

During Wilson's presidency, Garvey's early labors were largely dismissed as failing to pose a substantial threat. This disregard was partly a function of Garvey's initial difficulty in attracting a significant following, and partly a function of his rejection of socialism—then Public Enemy Number One—in favor of a decidedly American "ideology of racial liberation through racial enterprise."[51] His Universal Negro Improvement Association (UNIA) developed around the task of building, through black subscribers in shares of stock, a black-owned and black-operated steamship line. Garvey argued, much as Booker T. Washington had done before, that meaningful social advance for black peoples had to be built on a foundation of economic independence. His enterprise, the Black Star Line, was be the first step in that direction.

Garvey's business, however, faltered almost from the start. An insufficient financial base among African Americans deprived him of ready sources of capital upon which to grow, a problem that was immensely magnified by the overall economic decline of the post-World War I era.[52] But since Garvey also hoped to use the success of his steamship line for political ends—intending financial conquest to establish him as the preeminent black leader of his time—he violated good business practices to make the enterprise appear more robust than it actually was. He formulated an elaborate Ponzi scheme, using proceeds from continuing stock subscriptions for dividend payments to old stockholders, generating an illusion of financial health—but real political power. In the early '20s, Garvey's charisma and his evident financial success secured for him an unmatched following. Thus, an ongoing contest between rival black factions for an acknowledged leadership role among African Americans grew especially acrid.[53]

J. Edgar Hoover recognized Garvey's unmatched potential for energizing black masses, and he escalated the surveillance effort against Garvey in hopes of finding grounds for deporting the Jamaican-born organizer. This reversal of tack seems to have been made both because of Hoover's own heightened sense of national vulnerability to radicalism in the postwar environment, and because some African-American challengers to Garvey's leadership—including prominent members of the NAACP—urged Warren Harding's attorney general, Harry Daugherty, to use the full force of the government to undermine the Jamaican.[54] Historian Judith Stein has noted here that one black faction succeeded in "enlist[ing] the government's aid to defeat a rival."[55] Some black leaders were apparently not completely comfortable with the decision to use the government to settle such an internal dispute, but the executive's willingness to play favorites—to help choose winners and losers—proved to be an irresistible weapon for those who felt they could count on the government's favor.

Garvey eventually was convicted of postal fraud in connection with charges that he had misrepresented Black Star fleet holdings in mailed fundraising brochures. "Although Garvey was indicted in 1922 for a commercial crime," Stein asserts, "his prosecutors were driven by the political goal of deporting the leading black alien agitator in the United States.... The Justice Department fastened upon the crime of mail fraud, accidentally and after a long search for a deportable offense."[56] Richard Gid Powers concurs, writing that "the desire to destroy Garvey as a black leader came first, the search for a crime came later."[57] Had the Justice Department failed to prosecute Garvey successfully on these charges, Hoover remained at the ready to pursue others until a conviction on something else was reached; he kept his widespread investigatory network busy finding evidence for charges that would stick. In one instance, Hoover trod into the local prosecution of a case in New Orleans, challenging area law enforcement agents to pursue extradition of an individual allegedly involved in the murder of a local black leader, because he felt the fugitive would render evidence linking Garvey to the crime. New Orleans police refused. After Garvey's ultimate mail-fraud conviction, both the Bureau of Investigation and the Immigration Service prepared additional charges, including counts of "radicalism" for the political content of his speeches, to thwart the possibility that Garvey might succeed in his appeal and thus remain in the United States.[58] No further efforts proved necessary.

Garvey's imprisonment, and his later deportation, testified to the power of a burgeoning surveillance bureaucracy in the United States. That presidents and their agents put to political use such domestic intelligence agencies would have come as no surprise to those present at the creation of the Bureau of Investigation and subjected to its initial foray into American politics.

Despite some attempts to restrict the agency's political activities, the Bureau of Investigation, under J. Edgar Hoover's direction, remained a principal source of domestic political intelligence for the White House. Of primary importance here is the fact that African Americans became one of Hoover's primary target groups. For example, when Herbert Hoover lost Judge Parker's Supreme Court nomination battle, he dispatched the Bureau to investigate the NAACP and its members.[59] Powers claims that Hoover's early investigations were generally "innocuous," but the fact remains that the nation's leading law enforcement agency was being put to political purposes, apparently under the active direction of the White House. "Political investigations," Powers adds, "had gotten the Bureau in trouble [occasionally], but there is no evidence that Hoover ever hesitated to do anything a president asked." "Eventually," concludes Powers, "Hoover could justify investigating almost anything on the grounds that the president might ask him for information on the subject, and that he had to be able to respond without delay."[60] That same desire to be prepared whenever the White House might call eventually helped justify the expansion of Bureau efforts from investigation to infiltration, and then to political sabotage.

The 1930 defeat of Herbert Hoover's nomination of Judge Parker to the Supreme Court was a signal event in the emergent history of the relationship of black America to the presidency. Parker's defeat was not wholly the work of African-American activists, neither did it usher in immediately an era of uninterrupted advance toward black equality. What that loss represented, however, was the beginnings of a slow evolution in the political calculus of race relations in the United States. Further, it hinted at the ultimate futility of presidential efforts to control fully those relations.

Parker's rejection can be traced, in part, to two interrelated developments in black America, both of which are significant in the overall movement toward racial equality: the ascendancy of the NAACP as the nation's preeminent racial protest organization, and the Great Migration.

Despite efforts by white elites—including those in the executive branch—to build up Tuskegee-based racial conservatism as the preferred avenue through which African Americans would pursue their economic and political interests, no clear successor of Washington's stature arose after his death in 1915. Instead, "the balance of power in the black world had moved from Tuskegee toward the small office on New York's lower Fifth Avenue where *The Crisis* was edited," under Du Bois's able direction.[61] Although at this stage in its development the association's reach was not extensive, the NAACP nonetheless became a persistent presence on the American political landscape, possessing at least the potential—as Herbert Hoover discovered—for progressing from nuisance to nemesis.[62]

The association's success with the Parker nomination also indicated the emerging political consequences of the Great Migration.[63] Beginning with World War I, and escalating in the postwar years, African Americans staged a mass exodus from the cotton fields of the South to the factories of the

industrial Northeast and Midwest. Census data show that between 1910 and
1930 the total number of African Americans in the northern and western
States nearly tripled.[64] These numbers, however, do not tell the whole story.
The significance of the Great Migration was immensely magnified by the
fact that black Americans were moving into areas where, for the first time,
political action became possible for them, a reality many cited as a reason for
heading north.[65] The social structures of urban life, and the relative openness of northern political processes, then, led to the growth of what
amounted to a new source of political pressure in the United States.[66] Black
Americans were able—with the assistance of the NAACP—to use their
numbers for political purposes, including influence among important urban
congressional delegations. These developments, and the manifestation of
their potential in the Parker fight, had enduring consequences for the relationship of the presidency to the community of racial activists. But there was
more.

    After 1930, the nation's peace and physical security—which rests at the
heart of the nation-maintaining role, as one of its central objects—entered a
state of heightened jeopardy spanning from depression through world war
to cold war. The destabilizing influence on the American polity of this series
of disruptions rendered the nation increasingly vulnerable to the kind of
internal agitation that racial activists frequently turned to in making their
cases. Thus, successive presidents became increasingly sensitized to demands
for racial equality, because the politics they confronted in Washington and
in the nation at large—the lenses through which the constraints of the
nation-maintaining role appear to them—required as much. These overlap-
ping pressures now imposed on presidents complexities that had not confronted their predecessors. Where selective preferment and selective repression alone had earlier sufficed to neutralize internal threats, new developments required of presidents movement into the more controversial domain
of concessions on policy. These forces were to emerge clearly during the
dozen years of Franklin Roosevelt's presidency.

CHAPTER 5

The Rise of Black Political Power: Roosevelt and Truman

The political and demographic developments of the 1920s materially altered the incentive structures governing presidential behavior toward African Americans. The costs of open antagonism or manipulation from the White House had risen considerably with a substantial growth in the black electorate, and prospects for directing black discontent into benign channels had dimmed with the NAACP's successful accession to preeminence.[1]

Notwithstanding the emergence of these pressures, the balance of incentives operating on the presidency still tipped decidedly in favor of segregated inequality. The duty most clearly presenting itself to a succession of presidents into the 1960s was that of maintaining the nation's economic, political and social structures against those who would fundamentally change them to benefit African Americans. Political signs inside and outside Washington loudly communicated these majority driven constraints, despite demands to the contrary from a significant and growing minority voice.

The pressure from these competing constituencies created a common dilemma for every president from Herbert Hoover to John Kennedy: how to keep secure the fundamental structures of white supremacy while satisfying the growing expectations of a minority population increasingly committed to their destruction. The common response was rather simple in design, if difficult in execution: modest concessions to black America in ways fashioned so as to avoid affront to the white majority. In other words, American presidents sought the path of least offense. One prominent New Dealer reasoned, "Where it was possible to make a gesture that might appeal to blacks without alienating more important supporters, why not do it?"[2] That logic drove most presidential action on black equality from 1933 to 1963.[3]

Yet during this period, presidents did occasionally risk offending their "more important supporters," sometimes taking high-profile actions that

clearly moved beyond the realm of gesture. The creation of a Fair Employment Practices Committee; desegregation of the American military; civil
rights legislation in 1957 and 1960; and the deployment of troops in Little
Rock—*all* occurred, without exception, because, under the prevailing
conditions a gesture alone ceased to be enough to satisfy racial activists.
Preservation of the essential character of American institutions, then,
required more than purely symbolic concessions. It necessitated taking the
rough edges off white supremacy, that inescapable fact of American life that
made a nation already endangered by economic chaos or threats from
abroad increasingly vulnerable to the embarrassments and convulsions of
racial unrest. These were forces nation-keeping presidents could not
ignore—and civil rights activists from A. Philip Randolph to Martin Luther
King Jr. knew it. The political environment had become after Hoover's presidency relatively more hospitable for African Americans, but they found that
new conditions merely constituted a new invitation to struggle for that
which they believed the Constitution guaranteed them—equal justice under
law.

Franklin D. Roosevelt

For all that was truly innovative about the presidency of Franklin Roosevelt,
he made rather conventional use of the White House in dealing with the
issue of race. Roosevelt possessed relatively orthodox notions about the state
of American race relations, and he comfortably became the chief of a party
whose major source of strength was a Solid South.[4] This was a Democratic
Party that revealed its attitude toward African Americans in 1928 by segre-
gating black alternate delegates to the party's national convention behind
chicken-wire fencing.[5] However, Roosevelt's political antennae—and several
people close to him who occasionally helped him fine-tune them—signaled
to him that in race relations, as in so much else, the conventions of the past
were not completely sufficient for the present. Thus, Roosevelt sought a
course of action that basically preserved the fundamental shape of race relations as he inherited them, but one that, not coincidentally, would make him
more attractive to a black constituency that was becoming an important factor in national politics. The hazards of that middle way he judged preferable
to the hazards, exposed during his predecessor's term, of relying exclusively
on the ways and means of the past.

Roosevelt's political calculations proved to be wildly successful. In the face of formidable obstacles—before the New Deal "a great mass of Negroes regarded white Democrats as the Devil's chosen children, and a Negro Democrat was a creature of such depravity that hell was far too good for him"[6]—FDR managed to wed to his party's existing southern base a realigned black voting bloc to create one of the most imposing electoral coalitions ever established in American political history. But the fact of that realignment can be misleading. The low estate into which the Republican Party had fallen established a relatively meager threshold for the Democrats to cross.[7] And although Franklin Roosevelt did not follow completely the conventions of his predecessors, neither did he engage in "bold, persistent experimentation," to borrow his own words, in the area of race relations. Indeed, bold, persistent experimentation on the question of race was inconsistent with the perceived constraints of his nation-keeping role.

Roosevelt's efforts to accommodate modestly the growing demands of black America came in three principal areas.

First, the president and other prominent New Dealers believed that their generic social and economic programs, intended to benefit "the forgotten man at the bottom of the economic pyramid," would alone resolve the problem of race in America by elevating to a position of self-help those disproportionately at the bottom: the African American.[8] This thinking—rooted in contemporary notions of class structure—largely relieved the New Dealers of any political or moral obligation to attend to the special grievances of a minority. The specific was subsumed under the general.[9]

Second, Roosevelt presided over a dramatic increase in the number of African-American appointees in the upper reaches of the executive branch; over one hundred black policy makers had served Roosevelt by 1940.[10] There emerged during the Roosevelt years what came to be called alternately a "Black Cabinet" or a "Black Brain Trust." Moreover, the black individuals invited to join the administration differed from the African Americans which preceded them under earlier presidents. The Roosevelt appointees commonly came from what was a growing mainstream in African-American life, composed of those professionals who, to an extent inconceivable by earlier appointees, sought purposive government action to remedy the ills of racial inequality.[11]

Finally, Roosevelt used increased symbolic action to solidify a connection with black America. He seldom spoke directly to the issue of race, but speeches laden with concern for the "forgotten man" and the "underprivileged," joined with attacks on "economic royalists," captivated poor black as well as poor white audiences.[12]

More than his predecessors FDR worked to show a greater connectedness between blacks and the national government. He was far more open to meeting with African-American groups professionally, to having his picture taken with them, and to having them participate in symbolic activities in the White House than had been previous presidents.[13] Further, he established an even closer personal connection by consenting to his wife's far more extensive involvement in matters of race. For a population so long stigmatized by the color barrier, these symbolic concessions were immensely meaningful and won for the president a large reservoir of popular goodwill among the nation's black communities.[14]

Yet as one historian has concluded, "symbolic gestures broke the prevailing pattern of racial conservatism in notable ways[, b]ut they did not betoken any growing commitment [by] the administration to the cause of civil rights. They were exceptional gestures, not the bellwethers of change in the making."[15] Indeed, there were limits to what could be done at that stage to accommodate the demands of black America. The force of those limits can be readily identified in each of the three areas of presidential action outlined above. "*Exceptional* gestures" remained, however exceptional, *gestures.*

First, the ability of the New Deal's generic relief and recovery programs to improve the lot of African Americans was significantly restricted because the execution of these programs was—by virtue of political and logistical necessity—decentralized. In consequence, local custom prevailed in the distribution of such benefits as jobs and subsidies.[16] This meant that in large parts of the nation where racial inequality was most pronounced, New Deal economic programs did not address equally the needs of black America.[17]

The racial mores of the South largely governed the administration of these programs there. In some circumstances, New Dealers aggressively pressed for equal treatment for African Americans, but to little avail, in part because of the president's own unwillingness to intercede. For example, Roosevelt ignored an explicit nondiscrimination clause in legislation creating the Civilian Conservation Corps, when he backed a controversial proposal by his CCC director to restrict the number of black enrollees. Internal documents indicate that afterward the president asked not to have his name "drawn into the [public] discussion" of the matter, which he called "political dynamite."[18]

One historian has documented in summary fashion the effects of this deference to southern conventions.

> More than a hundred NRA [National Recovery Administration] codes established regional wage differentials under which southern workers (which in many instances meant blacks, because of the job classifications) were paid less than people doing the same work elsewhere. The Blue Eagle did not even cover the occupations in which most blacks were employed: farm labor and domestic service. Eighteen NRA codes included what one NAACP official called the "grandfather clause of the NRA." It established wage scales for types of labor based upon what wages had been at a certain date in the past. Obviously this perpetuated pay discrimination based on racial distinctions in job classifications. . . .
>
> For blacks, the Agricultural Adjustment Administration served mainly to reduce their incomes . . . and force black landowners into tenancy, tenants into sharecropping, and many blacks off the land entirely. . . . Relief payments to blacks in Atlanta averaged $19.29 per month, while white relief clients in the same city received $32.66, nearly 70 percent more.[19]

In this environment, a rising tide lifted only those who possessed their own boats, or who were favored by the distributors of public life preservers.[20]

Second, despite the quantum leap in the number and character of black appointees in the Roosevelt administration, their influence did not appreciably exceed that of their few hamstrung Republican predecessors.[21] The role Roosevelt permitted African Americans to play did not match the expectations raised by their favored placement in the corridors of power. Although Roosevelt and his closest advisers did not actively pursue selective preferment in personnel decisions, neither did they appoint independent trustees of executive power. They chose instead a policy of co-optation: nominal apportionment of governing responsibility in the interest of winning favor among a growing black constituency.

Those African Americans helping administer the New Deal were generally kept under close watch and were rarely given positions of great power or authority. Black appointees commonly were deputed to—perhaps quarantined in—Negro affairs offices within various agencies. As John B. Kirby has written, "From the perspective of the Roosevelt administration, the race adviser's primary function was providing information concerning the needs of the black community to federal agency or department heads and performing as public relations spokespersons for New Deal programs."[22] There was little room for administrative innovation or aggressive pursuit of unapproved ends; these appointees were to become defenders of the administration's policies and pace. Some of the more independent minded—including the long-suffering Robert Weaver and the Justice Department's Robert Lee Vann—chafed under such constraints and resigned on principle.[23] Some stayed on while readily acknowledging their impotence, and stressed the need for aggressive *external* pressure to make the administration bend. One of Roosevelt's black advisers claimed:

> When [a black newspaper like] a Courier or Defender gives me hell in an editorial or [the NAACP's] Walter White writes me a stinging letter, I take it to my chief and tell him that I won't be any use to the agency unless I can produce[,] or if Negroes think I am an Uncle Tom. Then I can usually get some concessions that I have been after for weeks. I tell you the only way we can operate in Washington is for you to keep putting plenty of pressure on us.[24]

The influence of Roosevelt's black appointees was also restricted by the fact that many of the president's white advisers had little or no enthusiasm for advancing racial equality. "New Dealers who had solutions for almost every social problem," wrote Joseph P. Lash, "shied away from the color issue because they were themselves infected with prejudice."[25] This effectively neutralized those African Americans otherwise well placed to influence the course of public policy. Justice's Vann, for example, in two year's time never even met his boss.[26] Accordingly, one generally sympathetic student of the New Deal has written, "If President Roosevelt's record in race matters is to be faulted, it is not for failing to endorse a historically premature civil rights bill but for refusing to consider enlightened and fair racial attitudes an important prerequisite for all his administrative officers."[27] The influence of an unprecedented number of black appointees within the Roosevelt administration can be easily misreckoned if the context of their workplaces is not given sufficient consideration.

Finally, although Roosevelt's symbolic gestures helped generate a sea change in African-American partisan attachments, symbolism generally represented the outer limits the administration was willing to go specifically to advance racial equality.[28] Legislative initiatives, even to combat the widely acknowledged horror of lynching, were almost completely out of the question.[29] Further, the character of likely conservative reaction placed constraints on even symbolic concessions; certain speeches and public appearances were, for this reason, ruled out of bounds. In the aftermath of brutal race riots in Detroit in 1943, the president rejected multiple appeals to make a national address to promote tolerance, suggesting to reporters that he would not be moved to action unless war production faltered.[30] Roosevelt's warm demeanor toward certain African Americans, then, often masked the cool calculations of a skilled politician intent on doing what he could to steer clear of unnecessary conflict.

Roosevelt initially did not use as extensively as other presidents the services of the FBI in scrutinizing the actions of civil rights activists. However, as early as 1934 he ordered J. Edgar Hoover to keep an eye on possible racial agitation by the Nazis in the United States, and he apparently developed a taste for the vast political intelligence the director could provide. When black protest mounted during his third term, he sanctioned FBI surveillance of the NAACP and other black organizations.[31] Yet FDR had an even more intimate source of information than the FBI director, and one even better placed in some respects than Hoover to bend the direction of African-American activism: his wife.[32]

No prominent white New Dealer had a closer relationship with black America than Eleanor Roosevelt.[33] Her efforts to address racial inequality in the United States arose from a deeply held personal interest in economic and social justice, and she largely pursued these interests without direction from her husband. But, as Lash concluded, "By and large . . . she carried on in the field of welfare and race . . . with his knowledge and agreement."[34] Thus, his reliance on his wife in this area was not completely unsupervised. Indeed, it seems for the most part to have been quite purposive—and quite artful.[35]

Eleanor's ventures into the realm of racial justice provided the president an opportunity for political gain at a relatively low risk.[36] With Eleanor, President Roosevelt could keep channels open to a growing black constituency without being directly confronted by it, as he did in turning down a 1940 invitation to address an NAACP national conference where Eleanor did speak.[37] This arrangement afforded the president a unique form of plausible deniability— "I can always say, 'Well, that is my wife; I can't do anything about her.'" Socialist critic Norman Thomas later complained that this arrangement allowed the president to have it "both ways."[38]

Of course, the president *could* do something about her, and he sometimes did.[39] Although she was largely free to expend her time, energy, and talents as she saw fit, Eleanor was not completely a free agent. She was compelled by the nature of her role as First Lady to keep her husband's standing in mind as she worked, and on those occasions when she was perceived by Franklin to be insufficiently sensitive to his position, he did not hesitate to rein her in.

For example, he denied her request to attend a 1934 protest meeting in Carnegie Hall to speak against southern lynchings.[40] In effect, Eleanor's time and energies became for Franklin Roosevelt not merely a means of winning favor among an increasingly important electoral constituency, but also a lever into African-American politics, a modified exercise in the practice of selective preferment.[41]

The most important "preferred" client was the NAACP's Walter White. Eleanor kept up a "voluminous correspondence with White," and provided him a prized channel into the inner workings of the New Deal. That relationship significantly reinforced White's stature within black America, a development which had important consequences for how black activism emerged during the New Deal. According to John B. Kirby, Eleanor's friendship generally buttressed White's stature as the nation's preeminent black spokesperson, thereby substantially reducing incentives for him to ally the NAACP with other nascent efforts of the day to establish a more radical, mass-based black activism. White recognized these roots of his appeal to the White House, and he occasionally sought special concessions from the administration based on the idea that if it did not respond to him, more aggressive forces in the nation's black communities would emerge.[42]

The president's wife, in the final analysis, became a useful tool for the administration, as the trust she developed permitted her to become something of an honorary insider among black activists. Not only was she thus privy to information that might otherwise not have been available to the president, but she became a forceful presence for moderation on those occasions when activism became too threatening. In one such instance, in 1939, she exercised her influence with Walter White to help prevent youthful NAACP members from picketing a Washington meeting of the Daughters of the American Revolution.[43] Eleanor was also a central figure, as we will see shortly, in the president's effort to ward off a massive march on Washington in 1941. During the war years, she publicly took issue with leading black journalists who sought to make of the war an occasion for black advancement, and engaged in an often spirited correspondence with White on the same matter.[44] Her seat at the table during this on-going debate—which accrued palpable advantages to her husband—had been secured earlier by her willingness (with the president's active consent) to attend to a problem most other New Dealers willfully ignored.

Fair Employment and the March on Washington

The administration's approach to African Americans—avoiding substantive policy making on the basis of race, and, to the extent that it could, keeping racial activism in check through symbolism—served the president well in his first two terms. Early in his third term, however, Franklin Roosevelt felt it necessary to depart from nearly six decades of presidential precedent and to sign an executive order creating a federal agency—the Fair Employment Practices Committee (FEPC)—specifically to address the grievances of black America.

The FEPC was charged by the president with investigating and combating job discrimination in the defense-related industries. Not since the Freedman's Bureau had an agency of the national government been established expressly to advance the interests of the nation's African-American population. Indeed, the FEPC's birth was acclaimed by some at the time as a "second Emancipation Proclamation."[45] The truth in this assertion, however, proved to be more ironic than intentional.

Lincoln doubtless would have recognized the aptness of the analogy, as Roosevelt's order was the direct product of intense, organized, domestic pressures brought during a period of severe crisis. The president was forced to take this unconventional action because the political equilibrium he had earlier helped establish with respect to black America was failing. This failure grew directly from a conversion in the political attitudes and prospective political behavior of African Americans, during a time when, in the day's vernacular, Dr. New Deal was undergoing his transformation to Dr. Win-the-War.

The most proximate cause of Roosevelt's order was a threat issued, and apparently nearing execution, by A. Philip Randolph, to amass up to 100,000 African-American demonstrators to march on Washington. Some, including Roosevelt himself, were skeptical of Randolph's ability to organize such a march. However, presidential action seemed necessary for at least two reasons.

First, the stakes were extremely high. The threat was not just to Roosevelt's agenda or to the maintenance of domestic tranquillity, but also to the nation's ability to engage in a total war (which seemed a near certainty in the spring of 1941) with the requisite effectiveness.[46] Domestic turmoil would not only distract and divide Americans, it would also give potential enemies enormous propaganda advantages, threatening the national whole. In the words of

James MacGregor Burns, the march "seemed to offer a rude threat to the image of national unity [Roosevelt] was carefully fostering."[47] A nation-keeping president could not ignore such hazards.

Second, signals emanating from the nation's black communities seemed to indicate that the threat to march was not idly made. By that time, the relative quiescence that had for so long characterized most of the nation's African-American population seemed to be changing. Close observers of the period documented a shift in attitudes within the new black communities of the North and West, both as the war approached and as it was being conducted. James Baldwin claimed that the war represented "a turning point in the Negro's relation to America."[48] Essentially American blacks were energized, many radicalized. "[I]t now appears," writes Bernard Sternsher, "that the most important development in race relations during the war was the rise of mass black militancy."[49] This newfound militancy manifested itself in attitudes about the role of blacks in American society, and the value of that larger society itself. During a period when most citizens were rallying around the flag, many African Americans decided to point out openly the deceit they perceived in America's disparate standards at home and abroad. Emblematic of these sentiments was the claim of one black columnist that "Our war is not against Hitler in Europe, but against the Hitlers in America."[50] Roy Wilkins of the NAACP added that "it sounds pretty foolish to be *against* park benches marked 'Jude' in Berlin but to be *for* park benches marked 'Colored' in Tallahassee, Florida."[51]

Such malevolence was induced not alone by that exclusion in American society that had become commonplace over the years. Rather, sensitivity by blacks had been heightened because of new forms of discrimination that emerged with the war effort, and because of the obvious dissonance between this and the patriotic propaganda the government served up to encourage individual sacrifice. American blacks watched, but were largely prohibited from participating in, an economic expansion associated with industrial wartime build-up, which promised at last to lift the rest of the nation out of over a decade of depression.[52] Blacks could not get defense jobs, neither were their services usually accepted in the armed forces. Only rarely, then, could they contribute in ways that all "good citizens" were exhorted to offer.[53] Further, for the most part they could only watch in anxious silence as pressure built to dismantle New Deal relief programs whites no longer needed.

Additional indignities were legion.

Negroes, anxious to contribute to the Red Cross blood program, were turned away. Despite the fact that white and Negro blood is the same biologically, it was deemed inadvisable "to collect and mix caucasian and Negro blood indiscriminately." When Negro citizens called upon the governor of Tennessee to appoint some black members to the state's draft boards, he told them: "This is a white man's country. . . . The Negro had nothing to do with the settling of America." At a time when the United States claimed to be the last bulwark of democracy in a war-torn world, the legislature of Mississippi passed a law requiring different textbooks for Negro schools: all references to voting, elections, and democracy were to be excluded from the black student's books.[54]

Small wonder that African Americans would search for an outlet for their frustrations.

Presidential attentiveness to black concerns was also sharpened because of a new awareness that the organizational structures of black America were newly ready to exploit mounting frustration. The central figure in this organizational shift was A. Philip Randolph, who seemed poised to act on his own dictum, "Power is the active principle only of the *organized* masses, the masses united for a definite purpose."[55]

Randolph initially came to prominence as a racial activist during World War I, when he articulated a socialist critique of American racism as the editor of the New York-based magazine, *The Messenger*. His early writings occasioned Justice Department scrutiny and resulted in several instances in having the magazine's postal privileges withdrawn.[56] During the 1920s, Randolph moved from publicist to organizer, and started building what was to become the first black labor union, the Brotherhood of Sleeping Car Porters (BSCP). Although Randolph's politics were far more radical than those of the NAACP, his work arguably benefited more from the New Deal than that of any other African American, although quite unintentionally. The administration belatedly, and under pressure from Randolph, included the sleeping car porters within the orbit of Section 7(a) of the National Industrial Recovery Act, which guaranteed laborers the right to organize. Randolph's subsequent victory in having the BSCP recognized, in 1935, caused his stock to soar in black America. The prominence of what had always been considered a plum job among African Americans—sleeping car porters had relatively secure employment and traveled extensively[57]—increased further at decade's end, when war preparations elevated the place of rail transportation in the nation's economy. Randolph subsequently joined a select group of black leaders working with the white government in Washington to secure greater opportunities for African Americans.

In September 1940, during the height of the election season, the president met (at his wife's insistence) with several African-American leaders, including White and Randolph, to answer privately their complaints about discrimination in the military. These black leaders pressed for unqualified integration of the armed forces, but received instead a presidential statement outlining the restricted uses to which black servicemen would be put, then affirming specifically the practice of segregation that was at issue.[58] "The policy of the War Department," the president's announcement read, "is not to intermingle colored and white enlisted personnel in the same regimental organizations. This policy has been proven satisfactory over a long period of years and to make changes would produce situations destructive to morale and detrimental to the preparation for national defense."[59]

Insult was added to injury when a White House press release accompanying the statement (but thereafter clarified) implied that the president's policy had been preapproved by that group of black leaders. Their resulting anger was momentarily assuaged "with a barrage of symbolic racial gestures to counter some of the damage that had been done in the black community." One student of this episode notes, however, "It was impossible [given the proximity to the election] to miss the political motives behind Roosevelt's actions."[60] The transparency of these motives largely undermined the power of those symbolic acts.[61]

"Following the debacle of the September 1940 conference with the president," writes Herbert Garfinkel, "Negro leaders intensified their agitation," driven to more vigorous demands by an increasingly agitated constituency.[62] Roosevelt, relieved of the burdens of the election season and still smarting from that last foray into racial politics, refused for a time to contend again with black leaders. It was in this environment that Philip Randolph raised the specter of mass action.

Randolph understood—deriving lessons from his past immersion in socialist thought and the protest methods of organized labor—that the kind of elite level negotiations characteristic of Roosevelt's prior relations with black America held little promise for meaningful social change unless black elites could come to the bargaining table with something more than moral fervor. He sensed that organized mass action at last held promise of shifting the political scales Roosevelt so carefully balanced. Apparently Randolph read correctly the situation. As Garfinkel has noted, Randolph's plans to take advantage of this discontent "caught hold of the Negro-in-the-street," not just the elite organizer.[63] Virtually every student of the era echoes this observation, noting the rare receptivity which characterized the emergence of the March on Washington.[64]

Randolph's plan was quite simple: he sought a peaceful demonstration by African Americans in the nation's capital for purposes of conveying to white policy makers the depth of black America's resentment over their continuing economic exclusion. Few around him shared his initial confidence that such a rally could be effectively staged, but the force of his personal will and his organizational talents, in tandem with the rising tide of black expectations, established an inescapable momentum that converted many skeptics—including ultimately FDR.

"Dear fellow Negro Americans," Randolph wrote in his May 1941 call to march, "be not dismayed in these terrible times. You possess power, great power. Our problem is to hitch it up for action on the broadest, daring and most gigantic scale."

> In this period of power politics, nothing counts but pressure, more pressure, and still more pressure, through the tactic and strategy of broad, organized, aggressive mass action behind the vital and important issues of the Negro. To this end we propose that ten thousand Negroes MARCH ON WASHINGTON FOR JOBS IN NATIONAL DEFENSE AND EQUAL INTEGRATION IN THE FIGHTING FORCES OF THE UNITED STATES.
>
> An 'all-out' thundering march on Washington, ending in a monster and huge demonstration at Lincoln's Monument will shake up white America.
>
> It will shake up official Washington. . . .
> It will gain respect for the Negro people.
> It will create a new sense of self-respect among Negroes. . . .
> The Negroes' stake in national defense is big. It consists of jobs, thousands of jobs. It may represent millions, yes, hundreds of millions of dollars in wages. It consists of new industrial opportunities and hope. This is worth fighting for.
>
> Most important and vital to all, Negroes by the mobilization and coordination of their mass power, can cause PRESIDENT ROOSEVELT TO ISSUE AN EXECUTIVE ORDER ABOLISHING DISCRIMINATIONS IN ALL GOVERNMENT DEPARTMENTS, ARMY, NAVY, AIR CORPS AND NATIONAL DEFENSE JOBS.[65]

The march was to occur on July 1, 1941.

Randolph, of course, did not expect the demonstration to occur spontaneously. He relied on two organizational strategies to recruit marchers. First, he won the backing of several existing black activist organizations, all of whom agreed to form an umbrella March on Washington Committee for purposes of coordinating recruitment. The NAACP, under Walter White, joined as the most prominent coalition partner. White's consent came in part because he shared the concerns Randolph voiced—he had pronounced that "only those who continue to raise a racket in season and out . . . are going to escape being given the rawest of deals"[66]—and in part because he had come under heavy criticism in recent years for elitism, for allowing grassroots organizing to go unattended.[67] Also, although he respected Randolph, he thought it wise to keep an eye on a potential claimant to the mantle of black leadership.

Second, Randolph turned for grassroots organizing to the field structures of the BSCP. Local union leaders were requested to contribute a part of their salaries to get the march effort underway.[68]

A combination of popular fervor—manifest in a series of enthusiastically attended local protest meetings and parades—and the very visible emergence of an organizational structure to execute the march rather quickly caught the president's eye. Publicized estimates of the anticipated crowd moved from 10,000 to 50,000, and then up to 100,000 marchers. In response, the president tried a series of gambits, each unsuccessful, to deflate popular momentum for the march.

First, the president had New York Mayor Fiorello La Guardia (an occasional presidential adviser), Mrs. Roosevelt, and Aubrey Williams (considered by many African Americans a friendly face in the administration) meet with Randolph and White in New York to urge cancellation of the march. Randolph refused, and rebutted claims that the demonstration would reap no benefits: "In fact," he said, "it has already done some good; for if you were not concerned about it you wouldn't be here now."[69]

Secretary of the Navy Frank Knox, that same day, requested a conference with Randolph to discuss the march committee's demands. The president subsequently sent a memorandum to the co-directors of the Office of Production Management, encouraging greater efforts by OPM on behalf of black Americans. Black leaders read this as a meaningless half measure, and held firm on their demands for a formal executive order.

Finally, on June 18, as the march date neared, Roosevelt met personally with the committee's leadership. The president's purpose was, in typical Rooseveltian style, to use his personal charm to stop the march. One Roosevelt biographer has written that "FDR thought he could stall and sweet-talk the blacks."[69]

Randolph held firm, and received invaluable assistance from the more conservative White, who assured the president that 100,000 African Americans were indeed ready to descend on the District of Columbia. Only when compromise seemed completely out of the question, when the issue was clearly framed as capitulate or confront a mass of angry demonstrators, did Franklin Roosevelt concede in the issuance of Executive Order 8802, creating the FEPC. Details were worked out in negotiations involving both Mrs. Roosevelt and Philip Randolph. Essentially, the order called on employers and labor unions in defense industries to hire without regard to "race, creed, color, or national origin."[71] In return, the march was called off.

The way the president responded to Randolph's pressure is a useful indicator of the prevailing state of presidential power, suggesting further parallels with the Emancipation Proclamation. The FEPC order, too, was the product of an until-then unusual consolidation of powers in the presidency, which allowed for the crafting and execution of a meaningful, controversial policy initiative through executive order alone. Roosevelt, as Lincoln before, found that the prevailing emergency empowered the presidency toward that end. Significantly, a state of elevated readiness—a kind of on-going emergency—running from depression to cold war—kept the presidency in a position somewhat analogous to Lincoln's for decades to come, allowing presidents an unusual independence of action by historical standards.[72] This was an important institutional fact of life prevailing during the remaining years of the politics of racial inequality.

Yet the heightened state of empowerment did not mean absolute freedom from constraints on presidential behavior, especially on the question of race. The force of cultural and political institutions deeply committed to the preservation of white supremacy were not to be easily eluded. Roosevelt once explained these pressures to Walter White, who undoubtedly had voiced something like Sumner's lament about Lincoln: "[H]ow vain to have the powers of a god and not to use them godlike!" "I did not choose the tools with which I must work," Roosevelt replied, referring to the power of the South in Washington. "Had I been permitted to choose them I would have selected quite different ones." He added that presidential support for a civil rights initiative would endanger the rest of his program, which was dedicated to keeping "America from collapsing."[73]

It is with the execution of Order 8802, however, that radical critics of the Emancipation Proclamation might have recognized further parallels between it and the FEPC edict. For although the Committee's creation was, in James MacGregor Burns's assessment, "a sharp departure from tradition," the immediate effectiveness of Roosevelt's order was modest.[74] Indeed, the order excluded the one area most directly subject to presidential direction: government employment. Thus, its ultimate success in bringing about concrete change was nowhere near the Emancipation Proclamation's.

The FEPC proved to be largely an ineffectual agency. Observed Louis Coleridge Kesselman,

> Of unnatural birth as an involuntary gesture to America's minorities and unloved by its governmental midwives, [the FEPC] was ill-fated from the beginning. In the slightly less than two years that it sought to deal with the problems of discrimination in the defense industry, it was hamstrung by administrative frictions, financial malnutrition, and inadequate powers and personnel.[75]

When it held hearings in Birmingham, Alabama, and stepped on too many toes there, the FEPC was abruptly uprooted bureaucratically and moved under the umbrella jurisdiction of another federal office, which made it more vulnerable to the whims of hostile congressional budget-makers. The committee's first report, "on defense training by the Office of Education, was suppressed by Roosevelt on the advice of the War Department and [presidential adviser] Marvin McIntyre," undermining even its effectiveness as an instrument of publicity. In the final analysis, subsequent gains in black employment of the period could as easily be attributed to white manpower shortages as to administrative oversight, especially since the FEPC's only enforcement mechanism—cancellation of defense contracts—was, in a time of war, unusable. At bottom, Franklin Roosevelt did little to add bite to a relatively toothless agency, except on those rare occasions when larger conceptions of wartime necessity demanded it.[76]

In retrospect, then, the FEPC constituted a victory for Franklin Roosevelt as much as for Randolph, as it permitted the president effectively to disarm his opposition at a relatively low cost. The threat of direct action against his policies peaked at this point and never substantially materialized thereafter, largely because popular and official tolerance for dissent quickly faded with the onset of war.[77]

One sign of that growing intolerance was a correlation between the pressures brought by Randolph and White and re-invigorated FBI surveillance of African-American activities. Data indicate that the Bureau's attentiveness to black organizations heightened dramatically in 1941.[78] The FBI and White

House political operatives kept very careful watch on Randolph's organizational operations in the wake of the FEPC affair.[79] It is reasonable to conclude from this information that Roosevelt did not wish to risk being the object of political ultimata again, without accurate intelligence as to the intentions and capabilities of his challengers.

For a brief time the thrill of political victory motivated the nation's blacks to continuing action, and in so doing raised Philip Randolph to perhaps unprecedented heights as a spokesman for African-American masses. But this enthusiasm faded at about the same time its resurgence was most needed by Randolph, when it was becoming increasingly apparent that the FEPC was not going to attack vigorously workplace discrimination. Randolph wanted Roosevelt himself to press forward, but he recognized political realities. "The President will move," Randolph told his followers, "only when Negroes make him move. He is not going to take action on the Negro's problem unless he is compelled to."[80]

Randolph attempted to keep the momentum of his 1941 victory going, but his best efforts to institutionalize a March on Washington Movement— to develop a new, national organization for racial change—failed. The conditions of total war opened some avenues for black participation, but they also were not conducive to the kind of on-going campaign Randolph wished to wage, as challenges to the government under those conditions betrayed disloyalty to patriotic citizens black and white. He personally risked charges of treason in pursuit of broader goals, but recognized inevitably that the nuances of his internal critique of American social and political structures were swamped in that flood of nationalism that attended the war effort. Thus, in part because of the nationwide preoccupation with victory abroad, and a commensurate contempt for internal dissent under those conditions; in part because of the typical problems of bureaucratizing popular impulses; in part because of jealousies that emerged in such organizations as the NAACP once it became apparent that Randolph was intent on creating a permanent rival force; and in part because of Roosevelt's success in responding as he did with the FEPC, Randolph's so-called movement proved to be a paper tiger.

Nevertheless, the president's concession to those who threatened to march constituted what has been called "the thin edge of a wedge," providing precedent for those who followed.[81] Beyond anything else, Roosevelt's *pas de deux* with Randolph conveyed a lesson about the nature of political action and reaction in Washington. It helped convince a generation of young black leaders that mass politics among African Americans held the highest promise as a tool for destroying political complacency and segregated institutions. Randolph's brief success had resulted from the threat of mass action never executed; enduring success, this episode seemed to indicate, would call for the kind of mass organization Randolph could only threaten. In this sense, the march was a seminal episode in the evolving relationship of African Americans with the United States government, yielding powerful clues as to what the future would hold.

The Civil Rights Section

Roosevelt's legacy included one other "thin edge of a wedge," which merits brief attention here less because of its relevance to FDR's presidency than because of later developments. In 1939 Attorney General Frank Murphy created, on his own authority, a Civil Liberties Division within the Department of Justice, later renamed the Civil Rights Section so as to avoid popular confusion with the "radical" American Civil Liberties Union. The formal purpose of this office was to study the state of American civil rights law, constitutional and statutory, to determine what kinds of violations might be prosecuted by federal authorities, and to bring cases in those areas.[82] This was, on its face, a rather modest function, and one as much oriented toward the condition of laborers as of minorities.[83] But as Brian K. Landsberg has noted, the Section "was a sort of time bomb. Inevitably, as it started investigating and prosecuting civil rights violations, the need for more effective and comprehensive machinery would become evident."[84] That expanded machinery became instrumental under later administrations in the advancement of African-American rights.

Yet for Roosevelt the office seems, at best, to have been the product of a retreat. The most thorough student of its origins claims that "The creation of a civil liberties unit at that particular moment was [Attorney General Murphy's] idea and his alone," mentioning the president not at all.[85] Murphy may, however, have been moved to act by the president's public assertion less than a year before that the attorney general be authorized to investigate all cases of mob-related violent death.[86] If so, the president's actions are notable because of the context within which this suggestion was made. Roosevelt had just backed off pressing ahead with an antilynching bill he had earlier supported in the Senate, unwilling to continue tying up public business to break a southern filibuster.[87] Thus, a recommendation of more study was proposed in this instance as a substitute for legislative action, which would have required an expenditure of political capital the president was unwilling (or unable) to make.

Roosevelt's Justice Department did over time initiate some meaningful criminal prosecutions on behalf of abused African Americans, but it did not, it should be noted in conclusion, leap immediately to the cutting edge of the early civil rights movement. In part, this was a function of the natural conservatism of the legal process, in that the department could not get too far ahead of where the Supreme Court would let it go. There were also, however, political considerations. For example, when Thurgood Marshall approached a later Roosevelt attorney general, Francis Biddle, about having the government weigh in on the NAACP's side against white primaries, he refused. Added to concerns about the soundness of the case was an explicitly political dimension. Assistant Attorney General Herbert Wechsler explained that "we had to get along with the Senate Judiciary Committee, which was dominated by Southerners—and this seemed an unnecessary fight."[88] Marshall subsequently won what was perhaps the greatest African-American court victory to that moment, in *Smith v. Allwright*, absent the aid of Roosevelt's Justice Department. That decision—with eight Roosevelt justices voting against the Hoover-appointed Owen J. Roberts—suggests that any claims for FDR's having provided a "wedge" or "time bomb" on race are perhaps better rooted in the character of his judicial nominees, five of whom were still serving on the Supreme Court ten years later when it ruled on *Brown v. Board of Education*.

Harry S. Truman

One of the most striking contrasts encountered in an examination of the record of Harry Truman vis-à-vis that of his immediate predecessor is the dramatic increase in presidential time and energy devoted directly to civil rights. Although his presidency reflected a continued mix of efforts to co-opt and to accommodate the movement toward racial equality, Truman, far more than Franklin Roosevelt, employed executive orders, congressional relations, and presidential rhetoric to advance the interests of the nation's African-American communities. How do we account for this escalation? Simply stated, those demographic, organizational, and political forces that inclined Roosevelt toward concessions to black America had, by Truman's time, become even more irresistible.[89] Two related developments merit attention here.

First, there continued a significant out-migration of African Americans from the South into northern industrial centers, where defense-related industries, and organizational possibilities, flourished. Over a million black southerners moved into such cities as Chicago and Detroit between 1941 and 1946.[90] The consequences of this migration for the politics of civil rights—and for the political calculus of the presidency—are difficult to overstate.[91]

A book appearing just before the 1948 elections, entitled *Balance of Power: The Negro Vote*, succinctly described the new order within which Truman operated.

> The Negro's political influence in national elections derives not so much from its numerical strength as from its strategic diffusion in the balance-of-power and marginal states whose electoral votes are generally considered vital to the winning candidate. In the 1944 elections there were twenty-eight states in which a shift of 5 per cent or less of the popular vote would have reversed the electoral votes cast by these states. In twelve of these, with a total of 228 electoral college votes, the potential Negro vote exceeds the number required to shift the states from one column to the other. Two of these marginal states—Ohio with 25 votes and Indiana with 13—went Republican. The ten remaining states—New York, New Jersey, Pennsylvania, Illinois, Michigan, Missouri, Delaware, Maryland, West Virginia and Kentucky—gave to Mr. Roosevelt 190 electoral college votes essential to his victory. The closeness of the popular vote in the marginal states accented the decisive potential of the Negro's ballot.[92]

In the event Truman was not sufficiently attuned to these new realities, Walter White saw that a copy of this volume was sent to the president.[93]

Further, black organizational growth continued. That same NAACP that had for so long weathered complaints about its inability to reach the black masses, quickly experienced a remarkable membership surge. During the war years, their rolls expanded from 50,556 to 351,131, giving the association's leadership a potent weapon for display at the political bargaining table.[94] Clearly the disaffected were revealing an unprecedented inclination to organize, denying policy makers the luxury of ignoring them. Further, still-fresh memories of the mass pressures threatened by A. Philip Randolph testified to what might be resorted to in the event such grievances went insufficiently attended.

A second major transformation in the context of presidential decision

making on race occurred under Truman. The war's end left the presidency
newly exposed to pressures Roosevelt had largely avoided. Despite the generally weak record of the FEPC, African Americans had found themselves
out of sheer necessity invited into military service and production facilities
to an unprecedented degree—national survival had depended on the effective employment of every worker. Those who benefited from this necessity,
especially those who served under arms, were not at all disposed to return to
the *status quo ante* of race relations at war's end. Thus, they were newly
primed to protest. Moreover, when the shooting stopped, many no longer
felt compelled to abstain from open criticism of the government on grounds
that such protest gave aid and comfort to the enemy.

The combined effect of these pressures was to heighten Truman's sensitivity to the inferior place blacks held in the American polity. They informed
Truman's conception of his presidency and created incentives for him to
recalibrate the requirements of the president's nation-maintaining role. The
political calculus giving shape to that role had changed, placing great pressures on the president to accommodate rising demands by black Americans.[95]
"Out of that need," writes William C. Berman, "emerged the Truman administration's civil rights program."[96]

The President's Committee on Civil Rights

Unsurprisingly, Harry Truman's initial impulse as president was generally
toward continuity, despite signals of change in his political environment.
The unprecedented electoral success of his predecessor virtually
demanded as much. On the question of civil rights, however, Truman
could not perfectly replicate Franklin Roosevelt's example. Black America's
widespread acceptance of Roosevelt's largely symbolic commitment to
racial equality was grounded in a fundamental trust developed for the man
(and for Eleanor) that did not extend automatically to Harry Truman, and
in a host of New Deal domestic programs that no longer existed. Despite a
relatively progressive record on racial matters—the weight of black voters
in Kansas City had early attuned Pendergast politicians to the virtues of
racial liberalism[97]—Truman was skeptically viewed by African-American
leaders as a conventional product of a provincial state with essentially
southern values.[98]

Thus, Truman early recognized that he had to demonstrate openly to black

America that he was trustworthy. During the first two years of his presidency, he sought opportunities to establish that favorable relationship. He largely succeeded, relying almost exclusively on rhetoric, but strong rhetoric by historical standards. A *Pittsburgh Courier* editorial, penned in the spring of 1946, proclaimed that the new president had revealed "friendship for the Negro people," but noted further that the president "had produced but little in racial advancement."[99]

The final half of 1946, however, proved pivotal for Truman in deciding to pursue a more aggressive, substantive course on behalf of black America. Two circumstances produced this shift, both products of the fundamental changes in political context described above.

The first was a marked escalation in violence against African Americans following World War II. The new militancy among black civilians, and the return to a segregated America by black veterans liberated by their war experience, produced a backlash among American racists North and South. Overt activity increased among a resurgent Ku Klux Klan, and violence against blacks appeared to be on the rise.[100] These trends had the effect of shocking the conscience of many Americans otherwise disposed to complacency on the issue of race, especially since news of race-based violence evoked still-emerging images of the Holocaust.

In September, Truman agreed to meet in the White House with the National Emergency Committee Against Mob Violence, an umbrella organization directed by Walter White, composed of religious, labor, and civil rights groups intent on publicizing further the extent of racial violence in the United States. "My God," Truman responded to their reports of assaults and lynchings. "I had no idea that it was as terrible as that! We have to do something." The president announced to his audience—probably according to a prearranged plan—his intention to establish a special committee to investigate and to report back with recommendations.[101] "Here," reports William C. Berman, "was an ingenious solution that would serve Truman's political needs by allowing him through symbolic action to improve his standing among northern liberals while, conversely, avoiding the alienation of the South. After all, Truman's pledge to create this committee was not a commitment in advance to any legislative program the committee might recommend."[102]

The second pivotal circumstance of 1946 shaping the president's relationship with black America was the mid-term election, which produced a landslide victory for congressional Republicans. In many areas of the country,

Republican politicians successfully wooed black voters by raising the continuing specter of "Bilboism" as the controlling influence in a Democratic Congress.

The mid-term election sounded alarms throughout the Democratic Party, but perhaps nowhere as loudly as on Pennsylvania Avenue, where nervous attention was already affixed on 1948. The electoral debacle heightened attentiveness in the White House to the need to reaffirm African-American attachments to the Democratic Party, and probably resulted in Truman's decision to make a showcase of his commitment to racial justice.[103] On December 5, 1946, a month after the mid-term losses, Truman established the President's Committee on Civil Rights, fulfilling his earlier pledge to the Committee Against Mob Violence. The president directed his committee, in Executive Order 9008, "to enquire into and to determine whether and in what respect current law-enforcement measures and the authority of and means possessed by Federal, State, and local governments may be strengthened and improved to safeguard the civil rights of the people."[104]

Barton J. Bernstein has written of the committee, "by the standards of the forties it was a group of liberal, prominent citizens. Within the administration it was described as 'Noah's Ark' because it included [among its fifteen members] two Negroes, two women, two Catholics, two Jews, two businessmen, two Southerners, two labor leaders, and two college presidents."[105] However, despite the composition of the committee and the president's aggressive charge to it, the president's order did not initially incur any serious opposition among southern Democrats. They probably saw it as a generally benign exercise in the timeworn practice of substituting study for action. Some black Americans tempered their praise for the president's action for the very same reason.[106]

Throughout most of 1947, Truman did little to suggest to those skeptics that they were wrong. He sought opportunities to deepen his connection with black Americans through rhetoric, but he generally avoided action by claiming the need to await the committee's findings. As long as the committee met, Truman largely stepped away from vexing civil rights questions. "The president may be interested to see how his Civil Rights Committee is taking him off the hot seat," wrote presidential adviser David K. Niles in one internal memorandum in February 1947.[107]

The president did not, however, rely exclusively on the committee to win support in black America. In June, he delivered a nationally broadcast speech to an NAACP rally from the steps of the Lincoln Memorial, vigorously asserting that the "National Government must show the way" in protecting the civil rights "of all Americans."[108] This speech was widely viewed as the most open expression of support for equal rights issued by any president since Lincoln, although in the absence of vigorous executive action on behalf of civil rights the southern response was again notably muted.[109] That fall, Truman also consented to Attorney General Tom Clark's decision to have the Department of Justice enter *amicus* briefs in two civil rights cases before the Supreme Court, both dealing with the use of restrictive covenants to maintain residential segregation. Richard Kluger observes that Clark, often derided as a "political hack," saw valuable black votes in civil rights litigation, and thus sought to convert the civil rights section from the "Tinker Toy" it had theretofore been into a more activist operation.[110]

On October 29, 1947, the president's committee issued a final report, entitled *To Secure These Rights*. It extensively documented the effects of discrimination on American society and forthrightly asserted the incompatibility of discrimination with the fundamentals of American constitutionalism. It further set forth a specific, ambitious "program of action," including calls for abolition of poll taxes, enactment of antilynching legislation, legal proscriptions of discrimination in interstate transportation, and guaranteed voting rights in federal elections for qualified voters.[111]

"In all probability," Berman argues, "*To Secure These Rights* went far beyond anything Truman and his advisers had in mind when they initially commissioned the investigation of the problems created by the racial violence of 1945 and 1946." Thus, Berman continues, the report was "a political bombshell which had to be either detonated or defused" by Harry Truman.[112] The White House treated the report circumspectly, holding it at arm's length until a considered judgment could be made about how to proceed with a "bombshell" charged by the president's own hand. The costs of what had been a short-term solution to the problems of racial politics were becoming amply apparent.

A president largely recalled today as a model of decisiveness waffled. When the committee presented him a copy of its report he professed to them: "I have stolen a march on you. I have already read the report and I want you to know that not only have you done a good job but you have done what I wanted you to do." In a press conference less than a week later, however, he "equivocated," backing away from the committee's work through a claim that he had not read the report "carefully," and raising the prospect that it might not find its way into his approaching annual message to Congress.[113]

Richard E. Neustadt has written that "It is hardly credible that Truman could have ignored [the committee's] report, no matter what the politics of his own situation."[114] Indeed ignoring the report was not a credible alternative. But there were other options in the universe of possibilities that might have permitted the president to manage the report and, in so doing, effectively to neutralize it.[115] In the end, however, it *was* "the politics of his own situation"—as articulated by aide Clark Clifford (and manifest in intensifying pressure by African-American elites)—that virtually compelled Truman to embrace the civil rights committee's report as fully his own.[116] Truman's future political viability, he became convinced, depended on it.[117]

Clifford's logic—expressed in a mid-November memorandum to the president—actually reflected the consensus of a small but influential group of liberal Democrats who began meeting privately after the 1946 mid-term elections to salvage the Democratic Party's future.[118] Collectively, they projected the troubled contours of the 1948 presidential election for Truman, and from this deduced that the president's only possible avenue to victory was through a more activist friendship with labor and Jewish and African Americans.[119] A civil rights initiative was recommended as "the politically advantageous thing to do."[120] Three key political facts, as they understood them, led ineluctably to this conclusion.

First, the likely Republican nominee, New York Governor Thomas E. Dewey, would be a formidable opponent, and would bring to the election credible credentials on civil rights. This opened the way for crucial black voters to convey the entire elected government to the Republicans in 1948, extending what had happened with Congress in 1946. Second, Truman's liberal flank would be under enormous duress because of the third-party challenge of Progressive Henry A. Wallace. Unless Truman made a concerted effort to shore up this flank, he might well lose liberal Democrats to Wallace by a margin substantial enough in close states to throw important electoral votes to Dewey. Third, movement toward African Americans and labor, according to this group's logic, would be a relatively cost-free political maneuver, since the South would remain, through the strength of its historic partisan ties and reliance on federal patronage, solidly Democratic.[121] Southern objections, they reasoned, would not be sufficient to create a significant change in the region's voting behavior.[122]

Berman argues that "because Truman's political need dictated a fresh commitment to the Negro cause, he was receptive to Clifford's advice."[123] On February 2, 1948, the president submitted a message to Congress asserting the necessity of federal action in the field of civil rights, and asking of Congress ten specific actions, drawing directly on his committee's report. An omnibus bill was in preparation for these purposes, he claimed. Further, Truman announced that he would soon issue executive orders barring discrimination in federal employment and eliminating segregation in the United States armed forces. Tellingly, in closing he justified his action in terms of political necessity, but of the international variety. The nation's continuing struggle "to inspire the peoples of the world whose freedom is in jeopardy" first required, according to Truman, a correction in "the remaining imperfections in our practice of democracy."[124] Cloaked in the garb of commander-in-chief, Truman thus made the report of the President's Committee on Civil Rights his own.

Or so it seemed.

During the first two months of 1948, as Truman publicized his commitment to a civil rights agenda, Clifford's memorandum proved on one count to be increasingly—some feared fatally—flawed: southern opposition arose with an unpredicted ferocity.[125] The president thus found that a strategy billed as being relatively cost free threatened to destroy his party and his own electoral standing. In effect, this undermined perhaps *the* principal virtue of that strategy. Small wonder, then, that despite the presidential prestige already invested in a civil rights package, the president began to temporize.[126]

He decided against sending an administration bill on civil rights to Capitol Hill, despite his public pledge to do so.[127] Similarly, he decided to delay—perhaps permanently—the two executive orders also promised on February 2. On May 13, he retreated further, publicly denying that he was preparing an order to end segregation in the executive branch.[128]

Truman remained rhetorically committed to the principles of the report while precipitously scaling back his efforts to have its recommendations enacted. Even this, however, produced a net loss of support in a South now hypersensitive to Truman's initiatives. "[S]outherners who were inclined to revolt . . . failed to understand that Truman was [now] engaged in symbolic action, that his rhetoric was a substitute for a genuine legislative commitment."[129] Despite efforts by Walter White and Philip Randolph to return the president to his position of February 2, Truman remained focused on preventing a complete southern repudiation of his presidency before the 1948 election.

Indeed, the Democratic Party's famous 1948 civil rights platform—

adopted at the national convention in Philadelphia—passed over the strenuous objections of Truman and despite his best efforts to kill it. The president, through Clifford, initially labored victoriously with the platform committee to have the Democrats' relatively modest 1944 civil rights plank resurrected. Hubert Humphrey (then mayor of Minneapolis) objected, and initiated a successful floor fight, defeating Truman principally on the strength of urban Democrats who feared massive African-American defections to the Dewey ticket unless the strongest possible commitment to civil rights was recorded.[130] Southerners stormed from the convention and established Strom Thurmond of South Carolina as the Dixiecrat challenger to Truman, confirming the failure of Clifford's initial calculations to account fully for the political costs to the president of his civil rights strategy.

Perhaps, however, because that strategy was the only one realistically left to him after the events of the convention, Truman less than two weeks later finally issued Executive Orders 9980 and 9981, essentially making good on the promises of February 2 to outlaw discrimination in the federal government and the military.[131] Credit for Truman's decision to issue these orders when he did can also be attributed to the direct pressure brought to bear by a number of influential African-American figures.

When the president began to show signs of backing away from his earlier commitment, some black leaders recognized a need to bring counterpressure to keep the president in line. For example, once it became apparent that the administration intended to preserve *status quo* race relations in the military, a group led by National Urban League Executive Director Lester Granger informed Secretary of Defense James V. Forrestal that they would no longer consent to serve as advisers to the president, because their continued intimacy might be mistaken as consent to perpetuating segregation.

Additionally, A. Philip Randolph and Grant Reynolds—a one-time Republican candidate for Congress—announced preparations for a campaign of civil disobedience aimed at focusing public attention on the hypocrisy inherent in a segregated American military. Randolph told Truman of his intentions in March, to no avail, and then, five days later, appeared before an incredulous congressional committee to declare, "I personally pledge myself to openly counsel, aid and abet youth, both white and Negro . . . in an organized refusal to register and to be drafted." "No democracy, no arsenal," was a position with which 71 percent of draft-eligible African Americans concurred, according to an NAACP poll.[132] The

Randolph threat was reissued with increasing urgency throughout the summer, until Truman responded with his executive orders.[133] Senator Richard Russell (D-Ga), from the Armed Services Committee, reacted in disgust to Truman's action, claiming that the orders were "articles of unconditional surrender to the Wallace convention, and to the treasonable civil disobedience campaign organized by the Negroes, by A. Philip Randolph and Grant Reynolds." Truman's decision to desegregate the military "was not simply an exercise in good will, but rather the product of political pressure . . . at a time when a presidential incumbent needed all the support he could muster in states with the greatest votes in the electoral college."[134]

The South did not remain solidly Democratic on election day. Four states—South Carolina, Alabama, Mississippi, and Louisiana—turned their backs to the Democratic Party at the presidential level, and cast their electoral votes for the Dixiecrat ticket. But despite this crucial flaw in Clark Clifford's logic, his overall strategy for Truman's election succeeded.[135] Defying expectations, Truman won 303 electoral votes to Dewey's 189 and Thurmond's 39. Wallace won none.

The president's discernable—albeit halting—movement in favor of civil rights secured the lion's share of black votes in crucial areas throughout the country. One post-election poll conducted by the NAACP showed that Truman received 69 percent of African-American votes in twenty-seven major metropolitan areas. These ballots—arguably won by a fortuitous mistake (one wonders how Truman might have responded to Clifford's recommendations had he been assured in advance that the benefits of a civil rights initiative would actually be offset by significant southern losses)—helped spell the difference between success and failure for the Truman campaign.[136]

A Second-Term Reversal

That election, however, did little to secure those rights for African Americans contemplated by the president's committee. For black Americans the ensuing quadrennium became a time of promise unfulfilled.

The reality of the southern reaction against civil rights dominated Truman's second term. Although the southern backlash had been insufficient in 1948 to deny Truman's reelection bid, the politics of that presidential selection process proved to be dramatically different from the politics of separated institutions then prevailing in Washington. In the presidential arena, the electoral college amplified the importance of African Americans in the polity; in the legislative, the seniority system magnified the power of the southern states.[137] Ironically, that Truman's party recaptured Congress in 1948 complicated rather than simplified the process of dealing with the matter of civil rights. What had worked well to get Truman reelected, then, was not well-suited for defining a program of governance for the next four years.

Truman subsequently confronted a predicament. A meaningful part of his electoral base and of his party's political coalition, felt entitled—on the strength of its commitment to him, on the basis of its undeniable importance to his victory, and on the merits of the issue—to see civil rights as a focal point of a second Truman term.[138] Yet set against these forces was the equally undeniable power of segregationist opinion and its well-placed representation in Washington.[139] A composite of electoral politics and institutional politics, then, had placed the presidency at the very center of the nation's efforts to manage a growing confusion about the future of American race relations. This was the president's problem—perhaps his most acutely—but not the president's problem alone. And, in dealing with his own problem, the president—because of the unique place the institution holds in the political order—was inescapably central to the polity's ongoing efforts to resolve the nation's struggle over the status of African Americans. An American dilemma had become, in microcosm, Truman's dilemma.

The presidential institution in this light is in some ways analogous to a ship's captain, who, because of the importance of his decisions to the crew's future, is expected to be the sensory center of the ship's affairs. The captain, through a host of shipboard contrivances (physical and organizational), is made to feel the condition of ship and sea unlike anyone else on board. He is placed at the hub of a vast network of intelligence about the ship's condition, not alone because of his preeminent rank, but because the judgments the captain subsequently makes about his own position—based on what he knows about both his ship and the prevailing conditions of weather and water—are inextricably linked to the future of the crew. They are all quite literally in the same boat.

Although the metaphor falters a bit on one crucial dimension—shipboard hierarchies are seldom replicated in the American political arena—the notion of place and role here can be instructive. The place of the presidency in the political order is not merely a product of constitutional rank, but of function as well. The institution has been positioned, by constitutional design and cultural accommodation, to meet certain important obligations, none of which is more crucial than guaranteeing safe passage to the ship of state. The designers of the political order—meaning those present at the creation and those who have molded and shaped its institutions thereafter— have crafted a system that tends to ensure that the president, in the fashion of a captain, is made sensitive to those forces that both propel and possibly threaten the welfare of the vessel. So positioned, the president is more likely than not to find that, at this level, his own interests (institutional and personal) are inseparable from those of a polity whose peace and security is in his charge.[140] A presidency created without those kinds of useful pressures would be the equivalent of a captain asked to navigate a ship blindfolded from the hold.[141]

The conflicting forces on both sides of the issue of race during Harry Truman's second term created powerful crosswinds, which threatened at once to wreck the ship of state and to confound immensely the process of political tacking that is a skilled politician's stock-in-trade. Truman, recognizing both the futility and the peril of pressing on with a meaningful civil rights agenda, sought as best he could to steer the vessel out of harm's way. How he managed that feat in such troubled waters is a testament to Harry Truman's considerable talents as a political helmsman.

What Truman essentially did during his second term was to move the potentially devastating issue of civil rights off the upper reaches of the Washington agenda, to set it aside so as to avoid its attendant hazards. But he pursued this course in a novel fashion. Two battles during the 81st Congress (1949–1951)—one over Senate rules and the other over the establishment of a permanent FEPC—best reveal Truman's method. He publicly positioned himself in an advocacy role for the NAACP, but he did so in such a way as to serve his own purposes of subduing a growing civil rights movement. For some in that movement, Truman's actions bore signs of a hostile takeover.

The most crucial congressional decisions in relation to civil rights during Truman's second term came not on specific policy prescriptions, but on organizational questions, establishing the rules of the game for considering legislation. Most prominent was the reestablishment of a cloture rule in the Senate.[142] Senate liberals worked diligently to enact a rules change making it easier for that body to stop southern filibusters. Absent such a change, the Senate would continue to be a graveyard for anything the more liberal House passed. Roy Wilkins later termed consideration of the cloture rule in 1949 "the most crucial vote on civil rights in the past ten years."[143]

Truman publicly sided with the NAACP on the matter, but he did so—perhaps willfully—in such a way as to undermine completely the effort to rein in the filibuster.[144] The NAACP and the Americans for Democratic Action had been pushing for the most extreme version of change in Senate rules, one whereby cloture could be invoked by a simple majority of a quorum, a radical departure from the existing standard of two-thirds of a quorum.

The president's public endorsement of simple majority cloture during a March 3 press conference galvanized opposition among conservatives. It gave them powerful ammunition to convince moderates—who had been preparing a compromise substitute that bore some promise of enactment—that *any* concessions on cloture would put the Senate on a slippery slope to outlawing completely the venerable practice of extended debate. Southern legislators were buoyed by their good fortune in Truman's announcement. Senator Russell declared, "The President has now justified every statement that we have made that all this campaign [for rules changes] was but a step toward simple majority cloture. I saw in the beginning that they were opening a Pandora's box. It is now clearly opened." Indeed, Berman goes so far as to imply that Truman intentionally torpedoed the effort to change the rules, perhaps to provide a reasonable justification for not moving more aggressively on civil rights.[145]

After weeks of legislative wrangling, a rules change was forthcoming, but one which *raised* the threshold for invoking cloture. Having dared to challenge the southern congressional giants, racial activists found themselves further from their ultimate goals than when the term began. Truman had encouraged them, but provided little in the way of executive ammunition to fight the fight.

The president did consent, in general tacitly, to some low-key executive action on behalf of black Americans, including, for example, the expansion of the civil rights section of the Department of Justice and the intervention of his attorneys general with *amicus* briefs in some federal court cases with a civil rights dimension.[146] These unilateral exercises of executive authority had the political advantage of occurring in the relatively obscure backwaters of the fight for civil rights advances. They did not occasion much turmoil.[147]

Also, the president proceeded to have introduced as administration measures bills carrying out the recommendations of his Committee on Civil Rights. But the bills' spokesmen rather quickly announced that no effort would be forthcoming from the White House to have them enacted in the first congressional session. This inertia led to calls by the NAACP for a special session on civil rights, which the White House ignored, contributing to growing frustration among attentive African Americans. In July 1949, the NAACP annual convention resolved the following:

> It is our firm conviction that the 81st Congress of the United States presently in session has betrayed the mandate given it by the American people in the last election in the field of civil liberties. President Truman and the Congress must share responsibility for this betrayal. Both failed to pursue with vigor, persistency and strength a course of action which would have put into law the comprehensive civil liberties program which the President promised the American people.[148]

It was in this environment that the FEPC battle was waged.

Truman's position on an FEPC had been consistent throughout his presidency: there should be a permanent body, congressionally established, with the force of federal law behind it. In mid-1949 some southern Democrats, including Georgia's Russell, began to grow increasingly concerned about the party's prospects as it disintegrated over civil rights. Russell approached Truman with a compromise legislative package, including provisions for what was termed a "voluntary" FEPC—one without an enforcement apparatus—and mechanisms abolishing the poll tax by constitutional amendment and providing for greater penalties for those convicted of lynching. Truman refused to enter into negotiations toward compromise, accepting instead the NAACP position (and that of the Americans for Democratic Action and organized labor) that a mandatory FEPC bill was nonnegotiable. The administration declared the FEPC bill the starting point for all else; it had to be enacted before any other proposals could be considered.[149] The establishment of that bill as Truman's top civil rights priority angered some centrists, including Senate Minority Leader Kenneth Wherry (R-Ne), who charged the White House with holding all progress on racial questions hostage to "the one civil rights bill that they know will be the hardest to pass."[150] As earlier, Truman refused to invest significant presidential energies in advancing his proposals.[151]

What Truman was doing in these cases might be called engaged disengagement. He nominally accepted pro-civil rights positions as his own, but he neither invested significant presidential energies in advancing them nor did he use his stated positions as starting points in meaningful legislative negotiations to get as many concessions as the political environment would bear. The immediate political rationale for this kind of posturing was clear:

he had two powerful, polarized constituencies to try to keep happy, both of whom were inclined to see any movement in the direction of the opposition as capitulation. Accordingly, his claim, in the 1949 State of the Union message, "I stand squarely behind those [civil rights] proposals," was precise. The president did not back away from the earlier recommendations— indeed he maintained an impressive rhetorical commitment to equality— yet neither did he actively engage Congress in a full-scale effort to move them forward. This was decidedly not the "Give-'em Hell" Harry of the '48 campaign. As long as he stood squarely behind his proposals, he could keep the support of many African Americans (who were not accustomed to such advanced rhetoric from presidents) *and* those Democratic southerners who recognized and accepted words as a shrewd substitute for action. The president's claim that certain civil rights initiatives were part of his agenda did not mean, absent the use of the powers of the office, that those items were to become a part of the broader Washington agenda. Indeed, to the extent that Truman's favorable behavior encouraged civil rights activists to direct their energies through him—to rely on him—the president's actions had the opposite effect: draining a force that might otherwise have pushed others toward a more aggressive governmental response.

Truman's course, most fundamentally, was intended to avoid the substantial burdens of trying to engage the two sides in doing more when the perils of such an attempt were extraordinarily high. Truman could not, as president, put the genie of racial conflict back in the bottle. However, because those pressing civil rights advances had not ascended to the point of predominating political discourse in the American polity, the president *did* retain some considerable influence over the governmental agenda in Washington, if his powers were skillfully employed. Had he exerted the fullness of his powers, such as they were, in trying to reach some kind of accommodation on racial matters, he would have contributed significantly to inviting the full force of the growing conflict on race into the councils of governance in Washington, and thus would have effectively risked all else on the public agenda to either gridlock or belligerent atomization. Not only would this have generated turmoil in America, it would have threatened the prosecution of a hot war in Korea and a cold one worldwide. Actively working to place such an explosive issue at the top of the Washington agenda was not a job for a nation-keeping president, and Truman recognized as much.

When one African-American group urged him to do more, Truman effectively turned the matter back over to them, suggesting that the political soil needed more preparation: "[T]hat is possibly the only way we can get action," the president admitted.[152] Truman simply believed that conditions in the American polity were not ripe for doing more. Thus, he exercised his powers to rein what influence black Americans had come to exert. With no imminent prospects for success, he sought to avoid a prolonged and divisive fight by keeping civil rights off the active legislative agenda, all the while rhetorically reassuring black America of his goodwill. Truman was ultimately "reluctant to invest much executive capital in a legislative enterprise that could bankrupt the rest of his program."[153]

The power of the nation-keeping constraints as such on Truman's behavior is not, in general terms, as readily visible as it has been on many other presidents, because by Truman's day the force of these constraints were overwhelmingly mediated by—and thus obscured by—the prominence of electoral pressures and the politics of separated institutions sharing power in Washington. In other words, the beginnings of movement into the political mainstream of African Americans—as voters—tends to create an illusion that the president was now dealing *solely* with something very conventional, the management of competing constituencies in the electorate. Further, Truman, either through good luck or deft management , did not have to confront face-to-face the execution of mass politics or the specter of wholesale violence that afflicted his predecessor and successor, and which invokes nation-keeping behavior in its most easily recognizable form. Thus, it may seem more theoretically parsimonious to attribute Truman's stop-and-go behavior on the issue of race to something other than nation-keeping, something more conventional, like the reelection motive or the common transactional calculus of a legislative bargainer.

Yet it bears repeating here that these are among the kinds of forces that routinely communicate to presidents what the specific requirements of the nation-keeping role are at a given time. The prevailing condition of the electoral environment (especially as it becomes more inclusive and thus more representative of popular demands) and of the institutional environment are meaningful indicators of both the state of the Union and what kinds of presidential activity might contribute to its security, or its instability. That Truman would find it politically expedient to move with extreme caution on civil rights can actually be taken as an indication of institutional health; the warning signals of danger to the nation's tranquillity and security were being registered in ways that virtually any president would recognize.

It bears repeating here, too, however, that the politics of black-white relations in America has been freighted with an extraordinary explosiveness that did not wholly dissipate with the opening of some electoral channels. Significant racial agitation commonly brings to the surface nation-keeping concerns in the White House, but this does not mean that in the absence of protest in the streets or widespread violence, the presidential role disappears. As Publius anticipated, in such times the president will search for "the golden opportunity" to take preventive action, no doubt guided in part by the signals he reads in the electoral and institutional environment. So it was with Truman.

Moreover, the signs of the nation-keeping role *are* abundantly evident in certain aspects of Truman's behavior on the matter of race. An escalation of racial violence in the early post-World War II years—and the prospect that it might spiral into domestic wars of vigilantism and retribution—was among the chief reasons that Truman moved ahead with the Committee on Civil Rights.[154] The international dimension of the nation-keeping role provides even clearer examples. Truman's most consequential action toward racial equality was the desegregation of the armed forces. As Lincoln and Franklin Roosevelt had before him, Truman sought to fortify with the addition of black soldiers the state of American military might against those who would endanger the nation's peace and security. "Integration," Truman later held, "is the best way to create an effective combat organization in which the men will stand together and fight," a significant contribution to preserving national security at a time when the Communist menace was extending its reach across the globe.[155]

The propaganda advantages that same enemy possessed by virtue of American racial practices also moved a nation-keeping president to take more seriously than he might otherwise have calls for racial equality. "We could not endorse a color line at home and still expect to influence the immense masses that make up the Asian and African peoples," contended Truman in his memoirs, thoughts he had publicly voiced in his 1947 speech before the NAACP.[156] Truman found, in Kenneth O'Reilly's phrasing, that "if the Cold War is defined as a struggle between two rival empires . . . for the allegiance of the largely nonwhite third world and access to its resources, then America's racial baggage would prove a devastating handicap."[157] This reality created demands on presidential behavior quite independent of narrow concerns over electoral votes or the gamesmanship of partisan coalitions in Congress.

The dim hopes still harbored in black American communities that legislative advance might proceed under Truman's direction were shattered in November 1950 with the midterm congressional elections. Although the Democrats sustained majorities in both houses—a not entirely favorable condition for black Americans, given southern dominion of the legislative party—there was a marked backlash against liberal supporters of the president. Thus, the House and Senate Democratic caucuses became even more heavily southern in membership, with southerners holding a majority of Democratic seats in the House and falling just one short of that mark in the Senate.[158]

Moreover, civil rights increasingly came to be seen as destructive of the unity Truman sought in waging war in Korea. With manpower requirements filled by the addition of black soldiers, the administration was unwilling to go much further in abetting—even tolerating—internal dissent on the question of race. As O'Reilly notes, "Cold War issues always occupied center stage at the [Truman] White House, and when it came down to cases the demands of security always won out over racial justice."[159]

By late 1950, the momentum of the early Truman years seemed at best a distant memory. One commentator declared soon thereafter that the "civil rights program of the administration has been hidden so well in Washington that Sherlock Holmes couldn't find it."[160] "Suddenly," concludes William Berman, "it seemed civil rights was no longer the urgent political issue it had been. The postwar liberal tide was now receding, carrying with it the frustrated hopes of millions of American Negroes."[161]

It should not go unnoted here that Truman himself, in some important ways, participated in the rising tide of illiberalism that surged in the postwar era. His contributions to that swelling have been extensively documented elsewhere,[162] but what merits special attention here was the administration's "increasing tendency," in Walter White's words, "to associate activity on interracial matters with disloyalty."[163] How, White and others asked, could one in that environment reasonably bring charges of discrimination against the government without being branded "disloyal"? By granting sanction to efforts on the part of domestic intelligence agencies to investigate—and then to tarnish civil rights activists with charges of un-Americanism—Truman passively strengthened the hand of those conservative forces in Congress who obstructed the civil rights proposals he publicly embraced.[164]

Unsurprisingly, Truman's labors on behalf of civil rights became even more attenuated after the 1950 elections. He rejected direct calls from White to use the Korean War as the pretext for issuing a Rooseveltian FEPC order, and, with an eye on the 1952 elections, he began actively to seek out ways to restore comity with the southern wing of the party.[165] At a May 1951 conference organized by the NAACP, in the wake of what he called "an alarming administration trend toward appeasement of [dis?]credited Dixiecrats and other reactionaries," White castigated the president's declining visibility on the issue of civil rights and his recent appointment of men of questionable standing on racial matters. He declared that the president had "surrender[ed] on this issue."[166] Yet when Truman announced his intentions not to seek a second elected term in 1952, White, through all his frustrations, called the decision an "abdication." Overlooking for a moment Truman's latter-day softness on civil rights and his refusal to throw his presidency fully into the fray on questions of racial equality, White announced that "no occupant of the White House since the nation was born has taken so frontal or consistent a stand against racial and religious discrimination as has Mr. Truman."[167]

In part, White's pronouncement was born of that hyperbolic sense of forgiveness common to political eulogies. It also arose in part, however, from a realistic recognition of the advances made from 1945 to 1952, and further from White's grudging recognition of Truman's captivity to the political realities of his day, realities that would have to be reshaped by White's partisans before nation-maintaining presidents could be of much greater use to his cause. Yet beyond these factors was the cold realization that none of the viable claimants to succeed Truman held great promise for building on the Missourian's uneven legacy. Least of all, perhaps, was General Dwight David Eisenhower.

CHAPTER 6

Race Returns to Center Stage: The Eisenhower Years

When Dwight Eisenhower entered the White House, many African Americans despaired that their hard-won advances of recent years were in considerable jeopardy. The general's 1948 declaration to a congressional oversight committee of his opposition to "a complete amalgamation" of the races in the armed forces; his delight, during the 1952 campaign, in leading a cheering South Carolina crowd in clapping to the beat of "Dixie"; and his calculated ambiguity on most race-based issues, all suggested that the embers of hope that had faintly burned among civil rights activists during the preceding decade might be extinguished.[1]

Also fostering African-American distress was Eisenhower's plainly expressed conception of the federal government's limited role in the life of the nation. The new president entered Washington bearing a conservative public philosophy that had not prevailed in the nation's capital since the days of Herbert Hoover. Those who had grown to expect a more interventionist role for the national government in dealing with race relations could not help but worry, then, about the accession to power of one who pledged to diminish the intrusion of government in the private lives of the American people.[2] Moreover, Eisenhower's conception of the presidency seemed cramped in relation to the examples of his Democratic predecessors. Passivity in the White House did not appear to be a promising development for those who sought more, not less, from the national government.[3] The nation's voters elected a man evidently committed to maintaining America's prevailing social institutions, not to fostering action toward racial equality.

Once Eisenhower entered office, however, such fears initially seemed overwrought, as the incoming president took a number of steps supportive of African Americans' rights. The NAACP's 1953 annual report proclaimed that "President Eisenhower merits praise for taking effective steps" on a laundry list of matters, including the termination of "segregation in schools on military posts" and "the progressive elimination of segregation in the armed services."[4] The following year's report continued in a similar vein, noting that "President Eisenhower proceeded surely and steadily . . . to ban racial discrimination and segregation wherever the federal authority clearly extended. . . . [T]he end of the year saw improvement over the previous year."[5]

To what can we attribute Eisenhower's largely unexpected patronage? In the first place, the expectations themselves were faulty. They arose from a natural misreading of Eisenhower's own relatively moderate personal feelings about racial inequality, which had been obscured by the general's public conformity to the political realities of his prepresidential years.[6] More fundamentally, however, most of the basic constraints operating on Eisenhower's presidency were the same as those that confronted Harry Truman, irrespective of the differences in Eisenhower's partisan attachments and the distinct nature of his political commitments (i.e., the required loyalties to his distinctive partisan constituencies). Enlarged black voting blocs remained a reality of the political landscape, as did continuing possibilities for mass direct action on the model of Randolph's March on Washington.

Thus, although Eisenhower was not inclined—because of his personal disposition and the realities of southern predominance in the councils of state— to ratchet up significantly federal activity on behalf of African Americans, neither could he easily ratchet them down.[7] Substantial movement in either direction, under the prevailing conditions, threatened to disturb both the president's political standing and the tranquillity of the nation he was elected to sustain. Small wonder, then, that on this highly divisive issue, where the constraints looked so similar to those that confronted his predecessor, the new president proceeded in a Trumanesque path, making modest advances for black America while not alienating the white South. With this in mind, three specific characteristics of Eisenhower's early approach merit attention here.

First, Eisenhower indeed elected to act where "the federal authority clearly extended": military affairs, federal agency employment, and segregation in the District of Columbia, for example. Action-taking in these areas was perfectly consistent with Eisenhower's commitment to limited government, since all related essentially to the conduct of the national government itself. Action-taking in these areas also had the added virtue of rather quickly and easily scoring public relations points for Eisenhower in the growing

Cold War competition for Third World clients between the United States government and that of the Soviet Union.[8] During the 1952 campaign, Eisenhower had gone so far as to proclaim discrimination against people of color in Washington a national "humiliation . . . we can ill afford in today's world."[9] The national security dimension of the nation-maintaining role was very much on Eisenhower's mind as he directed these modest advances. Eisenhower wished the American people to know the centrality of Cold War competition in his thinking on civil rights.[10]

Second, most of what Eisenhower did on behalf of African Americans, broadly defined, derived directly from the momentum of the previous administration.[11] Truman had not exactly routinized efforts from the presidency for civil rights, but he had established precedents by word and deed that altered expectations within and without about that office. Having blazed a trail—albeit a narrow one toward a relatively modest destination—Truman revealed fully to his successors the consequences of civil rights initiatives, replacing the unknown with the known. Truman thus proved that the consequences of activism on behalf of a modest civil rights agenda could be weathered, indeed that the political advantages could largely offset any costs. Further, the trajectory of executive department involvement on behalf of civil rights continued after Truman's departure because of the weight of general public expectations. Eisenhower could not easily return the government to the *status quo ante* Truman without taking public steps to reverse the federal government's direction on a variety of fronts. Eisenhower could not begin at the beginning. Consequently, to turn away from Truman's positions was to incur the wrath not only of those who actively pressed for civil rights advances, but also of those political passives whose expectations had been raised that more was possible. Eisenhower could not ignore that more sizable constituency.

The third, and more direct, factor shaping Eisenhower's behavior was the growing pressure of civil rights activists. That same NAACP report that praised Eisenhower's "effective steps" on behalf of black America repeatedly emphasized that the president was reacting to their organized efforts. What the president had accomplished came *only* "in direct response to long continuing and persistent urging by the NAACP." Eisenhower's vast public popularity insulated him somewhat from the pressure brought on the margins by such organizations, but because the NAACP could legitimately claim to speak for steadily growing numbers of black voters and sympathetic whites, the Republicans could not afford to remain completely idle on the civil rights front.[12] Eisenhower, despite his hero's status, was not immune to enduring changes in the political calculus of the presidency.

The advances Eisenhower fostered during the early stages of his presidency, though welcomed and praised, did not satisfy completely civil rights activists. They charged that where the administration did act the results were too modest.[13] For example, activists remained critical of the president for not taking sufficient executive action to rectify race-based problems in federal housing programs and employment, and for being insufficiently sensitive to the need for appointing "only those persons who will faithfully administer the laws in a non-discriminatory manner."[14]

More importantly, they saw little promise in the president's self-proclaimed preference for resolving the American dilemma through private as opposed to public action. In his inaugural address, Eisenhower announced, "Much of the answer to the nation's racial problem lies in the power of fact, fully publicized; of persuasion, honestly pressed; and of conscience, justly aroused." But, his critics charged, Eisenhower himself refused to engage the government's single best instrument of public persuasion, the rhetorical presidency. Eisenhower frequently asserted the primacy of changing hearts as a prerequisite for social equality, but "He did not intend to use his moral authority as president to take the lead in changing racial attitudes."[15] In one revealing episode late in his first term, the president wrote to evangelist Billy Graham and encouraged him to urge the nation's ministers to speak out against racial violence, a request that under the circumstances suggested that the president was trying to privatize the bully pulpit.[16]

Perhaps most troublesome to these activists, however, was the president's notable unwillingness to deal with the nation's fundamental racial problems through aggressive legislative initiative. The membership of the NAACP was informed through the 1954 annual report that Eisenhower had "consistently refused to urge civil rights action by Congress."[17]

The early mixture of praise and censure of Eisenhower issuing from black activists matched fairly closely the treatment accorded his predecessor. But this hopeful, if uneasy, relationship to civil rights activists did not last. It turned decidedly sour about fifteen months into Eisenhower's presidency.

Eisenhower did not change, rather the character of the issue he confronted did. The president remained committed to the calculated, and largely passive, navigation of a slow-moving mainstream—content not to rock the boat—while dramatic changes in the current of events began to overtake him. The first of these changes was wrought by an epoch-making legal victory won by the NAACP before the United States Supreme Court in 1954. The president did not view favorably the character of this disruptive change, and he accordingly exercised his vast powers to ward off both the Court's decision and its consequences.

Finally, Eisenhower's presidency also coincided with the initial ripples of disruption springing from those in places like Montgomery, Alabama, who promised creative, assertive civil disobedience "until justice runs down like water, and righteousness like a mighty stream."[18] Those challenging the nation's prevailing social and political structures dramatically escalated their direct protests, in search of more than the modest accommodation they had theretofore received. For the remainder of his presidency Eisenhower was vexed by these changes and their bearing on his nation-keeping role.[19]

Brown v. Board of Education

When the inner circle of Eisenhower's Department of Justice first reviewed what they had inherited from Truman's attorney general on the school desegregation cases, the initial response was a collective wringing of hands. One participant at these early meetings later recalled the initial response as, "Jesus, do we really *have* to file a brief? Aren't we better off staying out of it?"[20] Neither did Eisenhower himself view warmly the unfolding drama at the high court.

Eisenhower had the distinction—perhaps the misfortune—of coming to the presidency at a time when a long-established strategy by the NAACP to pursue racial equality through the federal court system was finally coming to fruition.[21] In the early 1930s, joint efforts were mounted by attorneys at the NAACP and the Howard University Law School to train and organize a cadre of elite black lawyers to challenge the constitutional basis of segregation. Their goal was to establish incrementally a corpus of constitutional law favorable to African Americans. Initially, these efforts were relatively modest, involving prosecution of a series of cases intended not to overturn the logic of *Plessy v. Ferguson* (1896), but to fulfill it. As the Court had then declared that "separate but equal" treatment of the races was its constitutional standard, the NAACP worked on a case-by-case basis toward segregated equality, especially in the field of education.

However, having succeeded in the 1940s in getting the Court to assert "that separate-but-equal education was not a mere slogan," NAACP litigator

Thurgood Marshall decided to attack the very heart of the *Plessy* logic.[22] In a group of school cases jointly styled *Brown v. Board of Education of Topeka*, the NAACP sought a truly revolutionary ruling from the nation's high court: that segregated institutions were inherently unequal. Such a ruling would undermine in one fell swoop the constitutional underpinnings of racial discrimination.

The Eisenhower administration inherited these cases in an advanced state of pregnancy. Oral arguments were held at the Supreme Court only one month before the incoming president's inauguration. Of greater consequence was the fact that Justice Department officials, probably absent the lame-duck president's direct imprimatur, had submitted for the Truman administration an *amicus* brief on *Brown*. Although that brief explained how the Court might decide the case without revisiting *Plessy*, it claimed that the NAACP's position against the "separate but equal" doctrine was plainly justified.[23] That the outgoing government had taken such a position naturally led all interested observers to question how the incoming government would respond. This was the face of the issue as it first presented itself to Eisenhower and his attorneys.

The president himself clearly considered vigorous federal action to eliminate segregation in the southern states ill-advised. His preference was for a gradualist approach on the issue that accommodated the honest fears of southerners about social integration. "I do not believe that prejudices, even palpably unjustified prejudices, will succumb to compulsion," the president confided sympathetically to South Carolina Governor James F. Byrnes. "Consequently, I believe that Federal law imposed upon our states in such a way as to bring about a conflict of the police powers of the states and of the nation, would set back the cause of progress in race relations for a long, long time." A nation-keeping president feared that aggressive or precipitous federal action toward desegregation would be disruptive of the nation's peace and security, provoking "disaster" and mayhem in the South.[24] "He did not dwell long upon the possibility of riots" reported Eisenhower to his diary about Governor Byrnes's reply.[25] But the realities were unmistakable, whether spoken or not. The violence that erupted soon thereafter and continued for over a decade in response to federal efforts to promote racial equality did not spring forth unexpectedly. It did not take a Southern Manifesto to alert executive policy makers that federally enforced desegregation helped establish an "explosive and dangerous condition" in the South.[26]

Also, in a private "Memorandum for the Record," Eisenhower vented frustration over having himself drawn into a simmering dispute over school desegregation by a Supreme Court whose competence and motives he questioned. Addressing the fact that the Court had requested of the administration an *amicus* brief laying out the new government's case—a request that was virtually impossible to circumvent—Eisenhower wrote: "It seems to me that the rendering of opinion by the Attorney General on this kind of question would constitute an invasion of the duties, responsibility, and authority of the Supreme Court." Having dismissed a time-honored convention of federal jurisprudence, he continued: "It seems to me that in this instance the Supreme Court has been guided by some motive that is not strictly functional."[27] It is understandable, then, given Earl Warren's subsequent centrality in this entire process, that Eisenhower later would claim that his biggest mistake as president was that appointment.[28]

Attorney General Herbert Brownell convinced the president, however, that the Court's request had to be honored. Justice Department attorneys thus began drafting a reply, sensitive at once to their obligations to the Court and to a president whose "political views," Brownell admitted, led him in another direction.[29] Robert Fredrick Burk writes, "To ensure complete political control over the drafting of the Justice Department's 'Supplemental Brief,' writing supervision was removed from career officials in the solicitor general's office and placed in the hands of Assistant Attorney General J. Lee Rankin, . . . a trusted subordinate of Brownell." Rankin labored with the knowledge that the president himself had expressed a desire that the new brief be merely appended to Truman's own, and that it deal only with "fact and historical record."[30]

Despite the fact that the final draft of the brief complied with the president's instructions—it informed the Court that no "definitive conclusion" could be reached with respect to the intentions of the framers of the Fourteenth Amendment on the issue of school segregation—Eisenhower remained "eager to disavow any personal connection with the Justice Department's findings." Soon after the brief was filed with the Court, Eisenhower wrote to Governor Byrnes to share his personal reservations about federally enforced school desegregation, but concluded that "it is clear that the Attorney General has to act according to his own conviction and understanding." The president probably recognized that, during a Court-requested second oral argument, the evasions of the written brief could not be sustained.[31] Justice William O. Douglas assured this when he pressed Rankin, who presented the government's case, to state clearly a position on the fundamental question in *Brown*. "It is the position of the Department of Justice," Rankin responded, "that segregation in the public schools cannot be maintained under the Fourteenth Amendment." The president later made it clear to Brownell that he considered the attorney general's labors on *Brown* the work of "a lawyer, not . . . a member of the Eisenhower Administration."[32]

Eisenhower was not content to allow the formal briefs to be the last word on the matter, especially since they espoused positions at variance with his own sensibilities. Having privately accused the justices of acting in bad faith on the segregation cases, the president himself moved beyond the usual bounds of acceptable executive conduct and engaged in at least one instance of *ex parte* lobbying of the Court. During the deliberations on *Brown*, Earl Warren was invited to a small White House dinner with a number of other dignitaries, including John W. Davis, the lead attorney for the southern states arrayed against the appellants in *Brown*. Conversation turned to the school question, during which time the president "openly praised Davis in front of Warren, and, overstepping the bounds of propriety, raised the segregationist argument with the chief justice against placing white girls in classrooms with black boys."[33] There is no record of the chief justice's immediate reaction, but on May 17, 1954, he spoke for a unanimous Court in asserting the inherent inequality of separate educational facilities, thereby declaring school segregation violative of the United States Constitution. Eisenhower's clumsy attempt at judicial lobbying had failed.[34]

Once the Court's ruling was issued, the matter of implementation became of paramount public importance. How would the rest of the government respond to the ruling? Attendant to this question was heightened attention to the role the nation's chief executive would play in developing an implementation framework. Interested parties openly wondered whether the president would use the full authority of his office to see that the newly declared law of the land was faithfully executed, or if he would, mimicking Andrew Jackson, dare the justices to enforce the ruling themselves.[35]

The presidency's institutional environment had been altered with the Court's conversion, but the constraints of the nation-maintaining role still figured prominently. The public uproar that attended the *Brown* decision, especially in the South, encouraged the president to diminish, to the extent he could, the effect of the ruling on the American polity. The incentives against his leading the way in generating acceptance for the Court's decision overwhelmed any that might have encouraged him to do otherwise. The spark was too close to the powder keg.

After the original *Brown* ruling, the Supreme Court requested additional hearings for purposes of establishing implementation guidelines. At this stage, Eisenhower again encouraged moderation, to greater effect than before. In the Justice Department's original brief on *Brown*, the Truman administration had encouraged the adoption of a "reasonable period of time" for allowing southern states to develop their own compliance plans.[36] Eisenhower repaired to the same standard, proposing what Richard Kluger has termed a "hands-off-the-South" approach.[37] The administration submitted a second brief—including language evidently penned by the president himself stressing the need for the justices to consider the emotional impact of the ruling on the South—encouraging the Court to remand individual cases to federal district courts for final disposition.[38] Essentially the Court adopted that approach—in what has become known as the *Brown* II decision—eschewing an immediate, uniform, nationwide schedule in favor of local-based compliance regimens carried out "with all deliberate speed."[39]

The NAACP legal team responsible for the school cases, under the direction of Thurgood Marshall, was not at all pleased with the Court's implementation decision. Marshall argued that it denied protection to African-Americans' civil rights—rights the Court had just admitted existed—until it became convenient for those who routinely violated them to reverse their course. "[T]here is nothing before this Court," Marshall thundered in his closing statement, "that can show any justification for giving this interminable gradual adjustment. I am particularly shocked at arguments of the impotency of our government to enforce its Constitution."[40] Arguments stressing deliberateness rang especially hollow among observers who knew that the nation's executive establishment was under the management of one who had once directed the liberation of a continent from the armed forces of fascism. Frustration subsequently mounted with Eisenhower's apparent contentment in his self-proclaimed impotence.

Indeed, as the implementation process unfolded, Eisenhower continued to put as much distance as possible between himself and the Court's ruling, newly the supreme law of the land.[41] Despite his inaugural claims about the need for "persuasion, honestly pressed" and "conscience, justly aroused," the president maintained a purposive silence on the Court's ruling. When pushed at a presidential press conference for a statement endorsing the Court's action, Eisenhower refused, oddly claiming that an open endorsement would "lower the dignity of government" by raising "a suspicion that my vigor of enforcement would be in doubt."[42] However, as early as October

1954, the administration received requests from the NAACP and the American Jewish Congress to send Justice Department agents into defiant school systems in Delaware and the District of Columbia to execute the decision. Such requests were summarily dismissed.[43]

The president's restraint was not, however, rewarded with good faith efforts across the South, as he had hoped. Rather, a vigorous resistance emerged. With that resistance came increasingly urgent appeals from black Americans for the nation's chief executive to step in to ensure the faithful execution of the *Brown* decisions. Eisenhower still demurred.

The Civil Rights Act of 1957

It was in this environment, with the president's popularity in decline in the North and in black communities nationwide, that the politically sensitive within the administration initiated efforts to improve the president's image in the realm of civil rights. Most prominent among these initiatives was the Justice Department's production, under the direction of Attorney General Brownell, of a package of legislative proposals that eventually yielded the Civil Rights Act of 1957.[44]

The president's willingness to advance, however cautiously, a set of recommendations with the potential to become the first federal civil rights acts in nearly a century posed obvious hazards. Three associated factors explain why this particular path was chosen—why the costs of inaction were deemed to exceed those of action, carefully pursued. The first two items relate to the president's political calculus; the last one directly deals with perceived threats to the stability of a polity he was pledged to protect.

First, Brownell sought increased leverage with a growing African-American voting bloc. His interest in expanding Republican appeals to black voters came relatively early in relation to others in the inner circles of the Eisenhower White House, but his sentiments had been ignored both because his sympathies had not been shared by others (such as Sherman Adams), and because his argument from political necessity was seen as irrelevant.[45] Dwight Eisenhower was one of the most popular political figures of the American twentieth century, one who did not need to engage in risky political gambits to sustain his position. Yet when the president's popularity began to slip in 1955, some key administration officials became more receptive to Brownell's arguments. Crucial in creating a favorable environment for Brownell's case were fears that Eisenhower himself might not be available in 1956 to lead again the Republican ticket. A September 1955 heart attack suggested to the Republican Party that an electoral strategy bottomed on Eisenhower's personal appeal was perhaps fatally flawed. Consequently, the Brownell package came to be seen as wise insurance by those otherwise disposed to quiescence.[46]

Second, the Brownell package drew support within the administration in large measure because it was seen as an acceptable means for directing attention *away* from the president's growing problems in the vexing area of school desegregation.[47] In effect, the package became an enormous exercise in diversion. It tended to shift the terms of public debate away from the hot issue of schools toward the more ideologically and politically favorable terrain of voting rights. Moreover, the package provided for an expert commission to examine racial issues, thereby affording "the administration a respite from dealing [directly] with an increasingly acrimonious problem."[48] It was further hoped that concessions on voting rights protection would redirect the efforts of liberals and protesters.[49] With their energies poured into registering voters, the administration's critics would leave school desegregation to follow a slower, less impassioned course toward completion.[50]

The third factor suggesting to the president that a modest legislative initiative might pay dividends was the one that perhaps appeared most ominous. All the while that Eisenhower grappled with court orders, legal maneuvers, and southern resistance to school desegregation, there loomed on the political horizon prospects of a very different kind of conflict than that being pressed by NAACP lawyers. Beginning in December 1955, when African-American residents of Montgomery, Alabama, began to wage a mass boycott of that city's segregated bus system, real possibilities arose that those opposed to segregation would turn to mass demonstrations to remedy their grievances directly, rather than contenting themselves with the deliberate speed of the United States judiciary.

The Montgomery boycott's success elevated to the nation's attention—and to the attention of a nation-keeping president—both the potential power found in methods of civil disobedience and the eloquent determination of the boycott's chief spokesman, the Reverend Martin Luther King Jr. The Eisenhower administration could avoid neither questions about its interpretation of events there, nor appeals from some, including King himself, for intervention when violence erupted. But the White House kept a studied distance from that theater. Eisenhower's public statements emphasized the local nature of the problem, affording no pretext for federal intervention. Privately,

Eisenhower and some of his closest advisers worried that they were witness to an ill-portent.[51]

The tones of that omen darkened considerably on March 9, 1956. Eisenhower scheduled a cabinet meeting for that day, for purposes of developing an administration response to growing racial unrest in Mississippi and Alabama, and more generally to consider his own political standing with reference to the nation's African-American electorate. Featured on the agenda was FBI director J. Edgar Hoover. Taylor Branch describes Hoover's appearance, made at Eisenhower's request.

> Hoover arrived with a brace of aides, easels, and display charts. His peek into the inner world of Negro protest, though couched in the language of secret revelation, was superficial and riddled with error. Cursory remarks on Montgomery, for instance, misstated several dates and laws while distorting the nature of the bus boycott. No one in the Cabinet Room knew better, however, and the facts were of secondary importance anyway. . . . [Hoover] expressed no sympathy for civil rights and painted an alarming picture of subversive elements among the integrationists. . . . These comments hinted at political danger.[52]

Hoover completed his canvas with a relatively favorable depiction of the southern resistance, claiming that "In no instance have we been advised that any of the so-called Citizen's Councils advocate violence." The immediate influence of Hoover's briefing was grasped by Cabinet Secretary Maxwell Rabb, who, according to minutes of the meeting, voiced "the Cabinet's feeling that the conclusions advanced by Director Hoover are good starting points for any presidential statements on this subject." Undoubtedly Hoover's characterization helped give shape to the administration's subsequent dealings with King and his colleagues.[53]

At that meeting the president elected to proceed cautiously with Brownell's legislative package. As the cabinet meeting concluded, the president surveyed those around him, and claimed that "The great mass of decent people should and will listen to *these* voices, rather than to the extremists." His brand of "amelioration," as he termed it, had the great virtue of channeling energy away from those pushing for more.[54]

Brownell's original recommendation to the president contained four basic provisions: (1) establishment of a Civil Rights Commission to collect data and make recommendations on the state of race relations in America; (2) authorization for a new assistant attorney general, to be charged with management of civil rights; (3) authorization for the attorney general to intervene on behalf of private citizens to initiate civil rights lawsuits; and (4) a voting rights proposal, allowing the attorney general to seek injunctive relief immediately in federal courts when the right to vote was violated.

From the outset, however, the administration's presentation of its civil rights package bore the signature motion of a driver simultaneously pumping the accelerator and brake pedals. Some insiders, who early supported the initiative, backed off in relief once Eisenhower's health was restored and he announced his intent to seek reelection. By early April, the president—counseling Brownell against becoming "another [Charles] Sumner"—decided to allow him to proceed to Capitol Hill only with the first two provisions of the package as administration measures, those providing for a commission and a new assistant attorney general. Those parts immediately adding to the corpus of law guaranteeing federal protection of civil and voting rights were deemed too offensive to the South to pursue as administration initiatives.[55]

Brownell, however, deftly "bootlegged" the rejected proposals up to Capitol Hill, relying on cozy relations with legislators friendly to his case, and explaining his mission using semantic distinctions so subtle that even the Washington press corps largely missed them. Members of Congress thought they had a new administration package. Brownell succeeded in getting all four of his original provisions up for congressional attention.[56]

The attorney general avoided punishment for his actions, however, because there remained plenty of room for presidential maneuver. In the following months, legislators in committee and on each floor could argue legitimately that the president sought anywhere from none to four of the components of the package Brownell had proposed. The president refused to endorse the complete package, and on several occasions produced lists of "must" legislation that included only one or two of his favored provisions. Nonetheless, Brownell persisted in his course. Finally, in late October, as election day approached, and as fears endured that Adlai Stevenson's attacks on the administration's civil rights record might pay political dividends, the president endorsed Brownell's full four-point package. "This is the program of the Republican Party and I will continue to work for it until the free and full exercise of rights and privileges for every United States citizen becomes real and meaningful." Brownell's subterfuge had paid off. He got a belated presidential endorsement, and Eisenhower was reelected partly on the strength of a black vote not seen by Republicans since before the New Deal.[57]

Having experienced the electoral rewards Brownell promised, Eisenhower entered his second term invigorated to move a modest civil rights bill through Congress. He succeeded in getting the commission and the proposed alterations in the composition of the Justice Department, but in so doing he clumsily sabotaged (and subsequently lost) Brownell's injunctive relief measure, admitting publicly, during a crucial stage of congressional negotiations, that "I was reading part of that bill this morning and there were certain phrases I didn't completely understand."[58]

Further, the voting rights provision was effectively emasculated by Senate Majority Leader Lyndon Johnson, who orchestrated the addition of a clause requiring jury trials in instances of suffrage violations; southern juries, not judges, would decide guilt or innocence in the violation of civil rights. When Johnson's amendment was adopted—which at once weakened and salvaged the bill, a feat that has led to conflicting interpretations forever after about the credit LBJ should get for that act[59]—Vice President Richard Nixon declared, "This was one of the saddest days in the history of the Senate, because this was a vote against the right to vote."

E. Frederic Morrow, the White House's highest-ranking black official, fretted over rumblings among African-American elites that Eisenhower had "capitulated" to Johnson simply to get a bill he could claim was pro-voting rights. Morrow briefly found himself in odd alliance with administration conservatives in trying to convince the president to veto his own modified bill. The president signed it anyway, on the basis of a mild amendment to the jury trial provision.[60]

Although some leading African Americans welcomed the new law—the NAACP's Roy Wilkins quipped, "If you are digging a ditch with a teaspoon and a man comes along and offers you a spade, there is something wrong with your head if you don't take it because he didn't offer you a bulldozer"— the short-term effects of that act were not groundbreaking. Perhaps in recognition of the discomfort Harry Truman had faced in dealing with the report of his civil rights commission, Eisenhower was careful to designate the membership of this new panel so as to diminish the likelihood of future conflict. More to the point, for all the attention given voting rights in rationalizations for the new act, the federal effort to improve voting conditions in the South bore little fruit. Two years into implementation of the new law, southern registrars had increased by fewer than 3 percent the number of black voters on their rolls. Formal recognition of the act's failures came in the form of a second civil rights act, passed in 1960, in part to strengthen federal voter registration machinery. This time the response from black

America was decidedly more cynical. Thurgood Marshall called the 1960 bill a "fraud," and Wilkins, addressing the structures erected for blacks to seek relief, declared that "The Negro has to pass more check points and more officials [to secure the vote] than he would if he were trying to get the U.S. gold reserves in Fort Knox."[61]

Mansfield and Little Rock

Not only did the administration fail appreciably to advance voting rights protections in the South, it also misjudged the capacity of its congressional initiatives to divert attention away from school desegregation. Congressional discourse on the civil rights act itself seldom wandered far from the schools question, and Congress's refusal to grant the attorney general the right to initiate voting rights suits was derived from a fear among southerners that the same executive machinery could be used by the Justice Department to start school desegregation proceedings. But the primary reason the diversion strategy faltered was that high profile conflict over the execution of *Brown* continued to erupt across the South, despite the administration's desire to focus attention on other matters. The disputants refused to take a holiday while Congress debated.

In the face of burgeoning southern defiance of *Brown*, Eisenhower remained unmoved. His own brief in the *Brown* II decision had argued that "The responsibility for achieving compliance with the Court's decision in these cases does not rest on the judiciary alone. Every officer and agency of the government, federal, state, and local, is likewise charged with the duty of enforcing the Constitution and the rights guaranteed under it."[62] Yet the president offered little in the way of meaningful assistance to protect the rights recently guaranteed African Americans by the Supreme Court. The expulsion by the University of Alabama of a young black woman not yet formally enrolled; the formal adoption by a number of southern state legislatures of the doctrine of interposition; and the signing by one hundred congressmen of a Southern Manifesto, announcing the signers' intent to stop integration with congressional intervention—all met with passive equanimity in public by the White House. Eisenhower privately groused about the Court's ruling, suggesting an underlying sympathy with the southern resistance. He accentuated his unwillingness to bear the burden the Court laid down by actively working, behind the scenes before the 1956 Republican convention, to have his administration distanced from the *Brown* decision itself. He threatened to boycott the convention if the platform committee refused to take his language. What resulted was a civil rights plank that one prominent southern newspaper praised as "a victory for the South."[63]

Looking retrospectively at the 1950s, the Eisenhower record on *Brown's* implementation is dominated by the dramatic armed intervention in Little Rock. That episode can easily lead a casual observer to overstate the degree of commitment the president had to enforcing school desegregation—to mistake might for leadership. A less well-known episode in Mansfield, Texas, exactly one year before Little Rock exploded, however, provides a useful backdrop against which to examine Eisenhower's reaction to later events in the Arkansas capital. In Mansfield, the administration flatly refused NAACP requests for intercession, despite the fact that there were remarkable similarities to those conditions later present in Little Rock. A comparison of Eisenhower's responses to these two incidents highlights the ways in which the nation-keeping constraints influenced his behavior in office.[64]

In late August 1956, three black schoolchildren, with NAACP legal support, attempted to register for classes in the Mansfield, Texas, public school system.[65] Mansfield was under federal court order to desegregate that fall, and although appeals had been raised by the local school board to delay integration for one year, the appeals had been denied by the United States district court and the three-judge court of appeals in New Orleans. A request to the United States Supreme Court for an emergency stay was also filed with Associate Justice Hugo Black, who simply scrawled "No" across the front page of the prayer. The American judiciary, unanimous here in its voice, left no room for doubt or misinterpretation: the United States Constitution required Mansfield to cease its resistance and to educate its black citizens in integrated schools, *immediately*.[66]

Despite emotional appeals by local federal District Judge Joe E. Estes for the community to take "an attitude of prayerful obedience to the law," angry mobs of several hundred gathered at the school during the registration period to prevent the black students' entry. Effigies of the students were hanged about town, spattered with red paint and bearing signs reading "This Negro tried to enter a white school." As testament to the community's abiding standards, one such macabre figure replaced the American flag atop the school's flagpole. "I didn't put it up there and I'm not going to take it down," explained the principal.[67]

The NAACP attorney handling the case locally refused to subject the students to these conditions. His attempt to register them by telegram was rebuffed by the superintendent, leading to requests by the NAACP for assistance from Austin and Washington. Neither response brought relief.[68]

Governor Allan Shivers instructed the school board to transfer out of Mansfield any student whose appearance was expected to disrupt the local scene. This order in effect sanctioned efforts to deny the enrollment of any black student. The governor himself brashly asserted that if any charges of contempt of court were to be forthcoming, he expected them to "be laid against the Governor and not the local people."[69]

The NAACP telegram to Attorney General Herbert Brownell placed the administration on unfamiliar, and uncomfortable, ground. The administration had not before been confronted with a situation in which a state government had given its official stamp of approval to defiance of the federal courts on *Brown*.

Rather than asserting his executive authority, Eisenhower took the path of least resistance and refused to act. His inaction itself would have been sufficient to win the praise of southern resisters, but his public reasoning—revealed during questioning in a White House press conference—brought cheers in the white South and consternation among civil rights activists. "It is difficult," the president asserted, beginning in familiar fashion, "through law and force to change a man's heart," a change essential for integration to succeed. The president defended his public and private efforts at persuasion, and then laid the blame for the trouble in Texas equally at the feet of the obstructionists and the NAACP. Extremists on both sides, the president observed, including "the people who want to have the whole matter settled today," were responsible for the threatening atmosphere. "There is a question of leading and training and teaching people," he continued, "and it takes some time, unfortunately." Thus the president implied that the courts had erred in asserting that the rights of black children in Mansfield deserved protection without delay.

Asked if he endorsed the *Brown* decision, the president—overlooking the educative function such an endorsement might have served—declared, "I think it makes no difference whether or not I indorse [sic] it. What I say is, the Constitution is as the Supreme Court interprets it; and I must conform to that and do my very best to see that it is carried out in the country." Yet in Mansfield he actually adhered to a different standard. "In the Texas case," he continued, "the attorney for the students did report this violence and asked help, which apparently was the result of unreadiness to obey a federal court order. But before any one could move, the Texas authorities had moved in and order was restored, so the question became unimportant." The president elected to ignore any claims on his attention for enforcement of the court order as long as the peace was being preserved.[70] Small wonder that the *Dallas Morning News*, in successive editions, would trumpet the president's comments with headlines reading, "Ike Backs Action in Mansfield Row: State Use of Power Supported," and "Ike Backs Mansfield Edict: Cautions Against Federal Meddling." The paper reasonably concluded that "The President's statement made it appear he considers there's no necessity now for the Justice Department to act on [the NAACP call for intervention]."

Despite prevailing in the courts, the black students then decided to abandon efforts to register for the 1956–57 school year. With the situation there stabilized, and in the absence of any compelling factors beyond the open flouting of a decision of the United States Supreme Court, the president elected not to use his executive powers to protect the students' rights.[71] The presence of such compelling factors a year later in Little Rock, clearly in evidence by contrast, explains why the president responded so vigorously there to further the cause of racial equality.

In August 1957, just as the Little Rock Central High School was preparing to open, a group of parents and local segregationists filed suit in the state court system to have the school board's integration plan stopped. The school board, with the support of the NAACP, sought and received an order from the federal district court sustaining the integration plan, thus setting the stage for further conflict.

Actively monitoring events in Little Rock was Governor Orval E. Faubus. Faubus, who had by Arkansas standards produced a relatively liberal record on racial issues, nevertheless decided that Little Rock was not the place to indulge federal efforts to change southern racial practices.[72] Faubus called out the Arkansas National Guard to keep the black students away, in the interest, he claimed, of preventing violence; he was well acquainted with the precedents established by Governor Shivers in Mansfield.[73] The school board, faced with growing hostility and a governor who intended to keep the peace by satisfying the segregationists, decided not to enforce the integration order and requested of the court instructions as to how to proceed.[74]

As events were unfolding there, the Justice Department quietly dispatched to Little Rock a low-level functionary with Arkansas roots to meet with the governor. This official apparently conveyed in unmistakable terms the administration's strong desire to stay out of the school controversy, inelegantly reporting the administration's preoccupation with public order: "[W]e can't do a thing until we find a body," he allegedly professed.[75] The administration evidently did not calculate well the effects of this private confessional on Faubus's behavior. The governor, at once unhappy at the attempted imposition by the federal courts of an external solution that required him to do "their dirty work for them," and reassured that Eisenhower would find no reason to intervene as long as violence did not break out, escalated his efforts to preserve segregation at Central High.[76] It was Faubus's defiance, fueled by the administration's expressed reluctance to enforce desegregation, that soon brought court orders compelling the administration to become a principal actor in the drama.[76]

Eisenhower himself initially assumed a posture very much consistent with his behavior in the Mansfield case. On numerous occasions before Little Rock erupted, the administration flatly denied any responsibility for executing the Court's decision.[77] Indeed, as late as July 17, 1957, with an eye cast toward the opening of another school year, Eisenhower announced in a White House press conference, "I can't imagine any set of circumstances that would ever induce me to send Federal troops . . . into any area to enforce the order of a federal court." The president privately charged the agitation in Arkansas to "these people who believe you are going to reform the human heart by law." However, the administration soon found itself directly and formally entangled in the fray. United States District Judge Ronald Davies requested that the Justice Department investigate the validity of Faubus's claims of incipient insurrection. The judge subsequently took a number of legal steps drawing the administration deeper and deeper into the Little Rock controversy.[78] Eisenhower's initial reaction was predictable. He again questioned the judge's right to compel such intervention, contemplating defiance of the Court himself were that permissible. The attorney general again informed the president that he had a legal obligation to comply with the wishes of the Court. Otherwise, the president might well have dismissed Judge Davies's request just as he had done the NAACP's one year before.[79]

Once the Justice Department's reports on local conditions were submitted to Judge Davies, he requested of the administration "both a petition for an injunction and a supporting brief against the governor and two National Guard Officers" charged with obstructing the Court. Faubus, under duress directly from the Court and from mounting evidence that a Davies-directed Brownell was becoming an unexpectedly menacing presence in his state, sought and received a meeting with the president to work out a rapprochement.[80]

The two principals and their chief deputies met in Newport, Rhode Island, on September 14.[81] As a result of that meeting, the president believed that Faubus consented to end the impasse by altering his orders to the National Guard so as to protect the black students. But if Faubus did agree to that general course during the Newport meeting, he immediately began backing off it in public. He claimed that he would consent to change the National Guard's orders only if Eisenhower would agree to delay federal enforcement of desegregation until Arkansas's recently passed interposition law could be tested in the United States Supreme Court. Faubus then proceeded to attack Judge Davies, filing a motion to have the judge disqualified from the case on grounds of "prejudice."[82] These actions, all coming within days of the governor's very publicized meeting with Eisenhower, infuriated the president, who felt both personally betrayed and publicly humiliated.

Under a new injunction issued by Judge Davies—one which appeared to hold the threat of putting the governor behind bars—Faubus finally withdrew the guardsmen from Central High. The withdrawal, however, had a destabilizing influence on conditions at the school, as local police forces were both undermanned and ill-disposed toward protecting the black students. Eisenhower publicly encouraged the citizens of Little Rock to comply peacefully, hoping that events might turn. Any remaining hesitancy to send in the federal troops passed, however, when the president received a telegram on September 23 from the mayor of Little Rock, urgently requesting federal intervention: "Situation [is] out of control and police cannot disperse the mob. I am pleading with you as President of the United States . . . to provide the necessary troops within several hours." By the end of the day, September 24, 1957, United States paratroopers were on the ground in Little Rock to escort to class African-American schoolchildren.[83]

Not since Lincoln's tenure had the constraints of the nation-keeping role exacted such a stark reversal in presidential behavior. Twelve months before, under conditions virtually identical to those obtaining in Little Rock, the president had effectively conceded to Governor Shivers of Texas the right to determine whether a federal court order demanding immediate desegregation would be implemented. Two months before, the president had publicly claimed that it was inconceivable to him that he would ever resort to the path he followed in Little Rock. When violence erupted there, however, among those intent on a clear defiance of the United States Constitution and the duly constituted authority of the United States government, the president found it impossible to look the other way again.

With an unchecked mob descending on those the courts had said were in the right, and with the administration already forced into the conflict by those same courts, "the President's responsibility," Eisenhower told the nation, "is inescapable."[84] The president, then, was operating under a degree of compulsion that, in the most literal sense of the term, was unavoidable. It is precisely for this reason that Martin Luther King Jr. commonly credited Orval Faubus with being the political figure most responsible for advancing integration in the late 1950s.[85] Eisenhower did not willingly embrace the role of protector of minority rights, but under these circumstances, as Stephen Ambrose observes, "He could not have done otherwise and still been President."[86] These were conditions Lincoln would have readily recognized.

To have avoided action under these extreme conditions not only would have imperiled the lives of those individual citizens in Little Rock, it would have undermined the institution of the presidency *and* the sovereignty and security of the nation Eisenhower was pledged to perpetuate. "That situation," Eisenhower later wrote, "could lead to a breakdown of law and order in a widening area."[87] Taylor Branch thus claims that Eisenhower saw the Little Rock situation not as "an issue of racial integration but of insurrection, like Shays's Rebellion."[88] Tellingly, the formal roots of the president's intervention—traced by Attorney General Brownell in a memorandum for the record drafted just after the dispatch of troops[89]—reached all the way back to those statutes enacted in the wake of the Whiskey Rebellion to give President Washington the power to preserve the public order and the national sovereignty the Constitution establishes.[90]

Accordingly, as the president himself was to repeat frequently in the aftermath of that episode, he intervened solely because "Mob rule cannot be allowed to override decisions of our courts."[91] (Unless, we might observe in the wake of Mansfield, the mob's prey concedes without a fight.) "[M]y main interest is not in the integration or segregation question," he confided to his longtime friend "Swede" Hazlett.

> My opinion as to the wisdom of the decision has nothing to do with the case. The point is that specific orders of our Courts, taken in accordance with the terms of our Constitution as interpreted by the Supreme Court, must be upheld. . . . If the day comes when we can obey orders of our Courts only when we personally approve of them, the end of the American system as we know it, will not be far off.[92]

The preservation of that system is at the very heart of the president's nation-keeping function.[93]

One other point should be noted in this regard. A persistent concern of the president during the entire Little Rock affair was the terrible beating the nation's image was taking abroad, a worry Secretary of State John Foster Dulles had previously voiced in supporting a civil rights act.[94] "Overseas," noted Eisenhower, looking back, "the mouthpieces of Soviet propaganda in Russia and Europe were blaring out that 'anti-Negro violence' in Little Rock was being 'committed with the clear connivance of the United States government.'"[95] Further, in his televised speech to the nation divulging his decision to send in the troops, the president explained his actions in terms evocative of the foreign policy dimension of the nation-keeping role:

> At a time when we face grave situations abroad because of the hatred that communism bears toward a system of government based on human rights, it would be difficult to exaggerate the harm that is being done to the prestige and influence, and indeed to the safety, of our nation and the world.
>
> Our enemies are gloating over this incident and using it everywhere to misrepresent our whole nation. We are portrayed as a violator of those standards of conduct which the peoples of the world united to proclaim in the Charter of the United Nations. There they affirmed "faith in fundamental human rights" and "in the dignity and worth of the human person" and they did so "without distinction as to race, sex, language or religion."[96]

By these terms, the nation's ability to fend off its most menacing external threat was weakened without intervention in Little Rock. This virtually demanded an aggressive presidential response.[97]

The interjection of armed forces into Little Rock did not signal a complete reversal by the administration on the issue of civil rights. Indeed, Little Rock is best understood as an exception to a continuing trend by the administration against federal enforcement of desegregation; once the immediate insurrection was quelled, the administration reverted back to form, having marked one particular manifestation of resistance as unacceptable.[98] The president's rhetorical posture, after Little Rock, remained largely unchanged, although, if anything, his public and private signals reflected an increasing hostility toward federally imposed integration. "I personally think that the [Brown] decision was wrong," he openly confided to a speechwriter, and he publicly expressed a continued preference for a slower implementation process. Further, he refused to condemn a mushrooming massive resistance movement throughout the South, and turned aside requests that the FBI be employed more vigorously in the battle to uphold *Brown*.

Even the gains in Little Rock—advances that the administration made every effort to use for maximum political advantage, domestically and internationally—proved short-lived, as troop withdrawal in late 1957 and 1958 was followed by state-sanctioned efforts to impede integration by closing down public school systems. The courts eventually overruled those plans, only to see a pupil placement law enacted, which met Court requirements for integration by placing only a few black students in white school systems. Despite loud protests from the NAACP, Eisenhower's Justice Department endorsed such laws as acceptable progress. As Robert Fredrick Burk reports, "by the 1959–60 school year, only 6.4% of Southern black students in grade and high school attended desegregated classes, and only 0.2% did so in the Deep South."[99] The public record of the Eisenhower administration is barren of evidence indicating high-level dissatisfaction with this pace.

As NAACP legal teams continued to press the president for progress in the wake of *Brown*, other black activists sought to further the president's commitment to civil rights by building on A. Philip Randolph's legacy of direct action. Although these efforts bore little fruit during Eisenhower's terms, they became indispensable building blocks for the mass civil disobedience campaigns that would wrest advanced presidential action in the 1960s.

Eisenhower held this new generation of black leaders at arm's length, seeing little but trouble to be gained by consorting with activists on such a volatile issue. King's growing prominence—during Eisenhower's second term he appeared on both "Meet the Press" and the cover of *Time* magazine—did generate a problem for the White House, however, because he repeatedly sought audiences with the president.[100] This made it increasingly difficult for Eisenhower to ignore King's appeals.

On those rare occasions when King managed to force his way onto the White House's agenda, the president did his best to neutralize the threat to his own standing. Eisenhower got help in this not just from the FBI, but also from the more established civil rights veterans whose own status and methods stood to suffer as King's star rose.

In May 1957, for example, King activists organized a "Prayer Pilgrimage for Freedom," intended to commemorate the third anniversary of the *Brown* decision and to display mass support for an aggressive civil rights act. When the organizers asked permission to use the Lincoln Memorial for their rally, the administration initially balked. However, Adam Clayton Powell and NAACP representatives—including Thurgood Marshall, who called King a "first-rate rabble rouser"—intervened to have a permit issued, on grounds that they could keep the event respectable. Powell repeatedly brought intelligence back to the White House on the rally's preparations, and managed to steer the organizers away from their harshest criticisms of the administration. The turnout and press coverage for the event were more modest than the organizers had hoped, and a delegation from the pilgrimage to see the president was greeted at the White House gate and turned away.[101] In this instance the politics of selective preferment were recapitulated, as the White House worked through the "safer" alternative to moderate the more dangerous. Quite literally the gates to the White House were opened to the former, closed to the latter.

King was granted a long-awaited presidential audience a month after the pilgrimage, but the meeting was actually occasioned by the president's own need to compensate for verbal blunders made shortly before to an audience of black newspapermen.[102] Predictably, the meeting did not produce any new presidential commitments. The president spent much of his time inquiring why he should invest more energy in the cause of racial equality when his previous labors had been so underappreciated by black America. Afterward, when it became apparent that nothing new was planned by the White House, many black editors criticized the conferees, including King, as dupes.[103]

King believed, however, that a large share of the blame for the Eisenhower administration's inattention to civil rights belonged to African Americans themselves. The success of the Montgomery boycott raised tantalizing prospects for the usefulness of civil disobedience throughout the South, but the momentum of that victory carried but little in time or space. King and others wrestled uncomfortably with the immediate reality that they had not been able to spark a regional mass movement from the experience in Alabama.[104] The absence of that kind of mass pressure allowed Eisenhower to rest too easily in his complacency; its presence, properly applied, they reasoned, would reap political dividends.

On February 1, 1960, four black freshmen at North Carolina Agricultural and Technical College took seats at a whites-only Woolworth lunch counter in

Greensboro to protest the store's segregated food service, marking the emergence of a new chapter in the history of African-American political behavior in America.[105] News of that sit-in quickly spread across the South, sparking a host of copycat protests in North Carolina and beyond. Fred Shuttlesworth, a Birmingham-based minister who had been associated with King since the days of the Montgomery boycott, witnessed firsthand the energy of the student-led protest on a speaking engagement in North Carolina. "You must tell Martin," he urgently instructed the executive director of the Southern Christian Leadership Conference (SCLC) in Atlanta, "that . . . this can shake up the world."[106]

Although there was an element of spontaneity about both the initial Greensboro event and the immediate aftermath, the grassfire-like spread of the protests also owed much to King and Shuttlesworth and dozens of others who had prepared the tinder to accept just such a spark. In his treatment of the origins of the civil rights movement, sociologist Aldon D. Morris attributes the effectiveness of the early modern movement to two principal forces: what he calls "movement centers," which are community-based cells of activism, usually under indigenous leadership; and networking organizations, like the NAACP, the SCLC, and the Congress of Racial Equality (CORE), each of which provided useful connecting tissue for organizing on a regional and national level. The existence of these movement centers and their support organizations, developed in the final years of the 1950s, made it possible for an isolated outbreak of protest in 1960 to generate a nation-changing force in the realm of civil rights.[107]

"President Eisenhower and his . . . advisers," writes Robert Fredrick Burk, "were [initially] uncertain whether the rise of black civil disobedience and direct action was a positive development or not."[108] The virtue of direct action, from their vantage, was that it took the federal government off the front lines of the struggle for racial equality, as grievances were aired directly at their source. It did not take long, however, before any official ambivalence vanished, as local confrontations inevitably grew and reached Washington. King and other black Americans increasingly sought protection from Washington when their constitutionally guaranteed rights were not being protected at the local level.

Eisenhower characteristically refused intervention and meaningful public commentary on the backlash against the southern protesters. Some Justice Department officials did provide limited aid in trying to negotiate settlement of some of the grievances. Yet it is not at all clear that they acted with the president's knowledge or consent, although they generally restricted their efforts to promoting that which the president already endorsed—settlement by voluntary action. At bottom, the administration had no interest in 1960 in changing the pattern of behavior toward African Americans that they had established in the preceding seven years, regardless of how greatly the face of the civil rights issue had changed since 1953. That their inflexibility would cost dearly their party's nominee for president in 1960, Vice President Nixon, was powerful testimony to the magnitude of the changes by then underway.

CHAPTER 7

Emancipation, Act II: Pressures and Conversion, 1961–1965

Under the administrations of Presidents John F. Kennedy and Lyndon B. Johnson, decades of organized protest culminated in what historians have called a "second Reconstruction," the enactment of major civil and voting rights legislation in 1964 and 1965. However, that transformation of the presidency into an agency of racial equality did not flow immediately from the electoral returns of 1960.

The Kennedy-Johnson administration did take office with a more favorable disposition toward African Americans than Eisenhower had displayed. Yet they brought with them in 1961 only marginally more enthusiasm than their Republican predecessors for the social change Martin Luther King and others demanded. The struggle to convert the presidency into an instrument of social change, then, continued into the Kennedy-Johnson years. Indeed, much as had been the case with Abraham Lincoln a century before, this administration initially sought ways to avoid making major concessions on questions of race.[1] And once again, as with Lincoln, the transformation of the presidency came as a last resort, to stave off pressures that, left unattended, threatened the nation's domestic tranquillity and its international security.

Entering the 1960 electoral season, John Kennedy's *bona fides* on civil rights were actually less well-established than those of Richard Nixon.[2] Nixon, as a part of Eisenhower's pattern of keeping racial matters out of the Oval Office, had taken on the occasional task for the White House of letting civil rights activists know that the administration was not ignoring them. He probably was, by the terms of the day, more supportive of civil rights initiatives than anyone else in the upper reaches of the administration, with the exception of Herbert Brownell.[3]

Kennedy, on the other hand, had virtually no useful track record on civil rights, and by some accounts possessed the equivalent of a tin ear for racial politics.[4] Because he recognized the enormous potential to be found in solidifying black support at the polls, and, because he was so alarmed by his own ignorance, he tried to educate himself during the campaign season for that foreign world.[5] He sought out a private meeting with entertainer Harry Belafonte in New York, asking his support and quizzing him about the dynamics of black politics. A central part of Belafonte's advice to Kennedy was that he associate as closely as possible with Martin Luther King Jr. This recommendation puzzled Kennedy, who saw more to be gained by courting the endorsement of baseball great Jackie Robinson. Yet campaign aide Harris Wofford, selected by Robert Kennedy to work as liaison to African-American groups, shared Belafonte's reasoning, and labored behind the scenes during the course of the campaign to bring King and Kennedy together. They met in June 1960, an occasion that left King impressed with Kennedy's temperament but not by his grasp of racial issues.[6] In the closing days of the campaign, however, Wofford helped to engineer another contact, one that left a lasting impression on many black Americans and arguably constituted the difference between success and failure for John Kennedy that November.[7]

During much of 1960, King had devoted his energies to fostering the spread of civil disobedience, building on the momentum of Greensboro. On October 19, King was arrested in Atlanta for his part in arranging and conducting sit-ins at Rich's department store. A hostile judge, aware of King's history of operating against the law, sentenced him to four months hard labor for violating probation associated with a prior traffic citation. On October 25, upon learning that her husband had been sent to the state penitentiary at Reidsville, Coretta Scott King frantically called Wofford to see if he or the Kennedys could do anything to ensure her husband's safety there. Early the following morning, Wofford reached Sargent Shriver, who was traveling with candidate Kennedy in Chicago.[8] According to Arthur Schlesinger Jr., "Shriver waited for everyone else to leave the [hotel] room, fearing that general discussion would kill the idea." After hearing a description of the circumstances in Georgia, "Kennedy at once asked Shriver to get Mrs. King on the phone." The call went through and Kennedy expressed his sympathy and hopes that matters would be worked out positively. When Robert Kennedy later received news of the call by his brother, he was livid because of the potential adverse consequences in the white South. But less than twenty-four hours later, he, too, was on the phone, talking with law enforcement officials in Georgia to secure King's release.[9]

The boldness of the Kennedy response most clearly emerges when contrasted with what happened on the Republican side. Despite the fact that Richard Nixon found King's punishment excessive, he refused even to comment on the matter to the press. Sensing the likely political fallout in protesting King's treatment, he looked to lame-duck Eisenhower to respond more aggressively on behalf of the Republican Party. The president did not. Eisenhower never signed off on a staff-prepared statement protesting King's imprisonment and pledging the assistance of the Justice Department in having King released. In an extremely close election, Nixon's failure to intervene had catastrophic consequences for his campaign, symbolized by a decision by King's father—himself a prominent Atlanta minister—to reverse publicly his own endorsement from Nixon to Kennedy: "Because this man was willing to wipe the tears from my daughter[-in-law]'s eyes, I've got a suitcase of votes, and I'm going to take them to Mr. Kennedy and dump them in his lap." "This act," Eisenhower aide Frederic Morrow later wrote of Kennedy's intervention in Georgia, "won [Kennedy] the election."[10]

In discussing President Kennedy's early work in the area of civil rights, it is useful to turn to his own characterization of his presidency, not so much to define what it was, but what it was not: a New Frontier. Without question John Kennedy and members of his new administration adopted a friendlier posture toward African Americans than the previous White House had. The composition of their no-votes-to-spare electoral coalition virtually dictated as much, as did the increasing vulnerability of the race issue to international agitation. As Richard Reeves has noted, "Kennedy was most concerned about domestic racial troubles as a foreign policy problem," one which could not be ignored at a time when hot-spots such as Vietnam, Cuba, and Berlin threatened to boil over, undermining the nation's security *and* Kennedy's untested presidency.[11] However, Kennedy's administration distinguished itself to black Americans only in more extensively working in areas within the executive branch that predecessors of both parties had already legitimized. Thus, in Kennedy's idiom, the incoming Democrats of 1961 did not seek out a new frontier on the civil rights horizon, they simply worked more thoroughly within the established one.[12] This distinction goes beyond semantics, as it becomes useful in showing how Kennedy changed in office, adding necessary perspective in developing an accurate portrait of the Kennedy presidency and its legacy on civil rights.

The administration's initial efforts to sustain black favor developed in three areas: executive appointments, symbolic support (through rhetoric and recognition), and litigation.[13] In all three the administration's vigor notably contrasted with the relative torpor of the Eisenhower years. But it is instructive, again, that each of these centers of activity matches precisely those areas of endeavor that Eisenhower accepted, at least in principle, as permissible extensions of his own presidency, however grudgingly his execution came. Clearly, Kennedy's initial actions in civil rights flowed into what had by then become conventional channels.[14]

Kennedy consciously raised both the number and stature of black appointments in his new administration, giving African Americans a substantially higher profile in the Washington community than they had ever had. Indeed, Carl M. Brauer (whose work on Kennedy and African Americans is considered the standard text), writes that "The earliest signs that Kennedy would bring about genuine change [on civil rights] appeared in the employment of Negroes in government. . . . During his first two months in office he selected . . . forty Negroes for important posts." Most prominently, he successfully nominated Thurgood Marshall to the Second Circuit Court of Appeals in New York.[15]

The available evidence does not clearly indicate a conscious effort at selective preferment by Kennedy in his initial appointments. In other words, there was no readily apparent attempt to give shape to the internal politics of black America with the rewards of public office. However, the administration did draw its appointees almost exclusively from the ranks of a black elite with ties to organizations—such as the NAACP—that by that time had come to represent among the most conservative forces for change in black America. Perhaps indirectly, then, the administration subtly undermined with its favors those civil rights activists who sought change through the streets rather than the courtroom.[16]

Kennedy also won favor among black Americans—the activists as well as the politically inactive—through symbolism, especially with his words. Dwight Eisenhower had often said that a necessary precondition for achieving racial equality in the United States was a change of heart among Americans about race. Only rarely, however, did Eisenhower accept as part of his job the mounting of the bully pulpit to participate—in his words—in the "leading and training and teaching [of] people" essential to advancing race relations.[17] Here Kennedy was intermittently less reserved.[18]

> Evidently fearing an adverse reaction from southern Democrats, Kennedy avoided the "bully pulpit." He did not devote a major address to the racial issue.... Still, the administration, led by the President, substantially raised the level of rhetorical support for civil rights. During the first year, the President, among other things, endorsed school desegregation, congratulated several cities on their successful implementation of school desegregation, and participated in ceremonies marking the signing of corporate pledges to end discrimination through voluntary action.

His brother Robert also contributed, including a highly publicized speech at the University of Georgia in 1961, praising those who weathered opposition to integrate schools in the South.[19]

Further, the president generally gave the appearance of being relatively at ease with having civil rights activists into the Oval Office. John Kennedy not only had confidence in his own charm, he also recognized—with the help of those like Wofford—the considerable allure and power of the White House itself.[20] He thus saw that an important component of the equation in managing pressures from black America came in satisfying the personal needs of its leadership, which in part could be done through relying on his own charisma and on high-level dialogue.[21]

The third, and most substantive, form of action the administration engaged in was litigation. The Department of Justice, under the direction of Robert Kennedy, almost immediately after the inauguration moved to increase the number of civil rights lawsuits to which the United States government was a party. He built up the Civil Rights division and staffed it with eminent attorneys equipped with broad licenses to assist black complainants against unyielding school boards and voter registrars.[22]

The new administration's three-pronged approach to the issue of civil rights effectively carried over into 1961 much of the enthusiasm black America had manifest for Kennedy during the previous November's election. Official vigor cheered many African Americans, who took hope in signs emerging from the Kennedy White House. However, close observers sympathetic to civil rights increasingly found reason for concern, both in what they saw and in what they did not see.

What the Kennedy administration refused to produce were executive orders or legislative initiatives to change significantly the legal environment of segregation in the United States. The absence of activity in these areas raised questions about the administration's seriousness of purpose in the realm of civil rights, and heightened suspicions about the administration's motives. Martin Luther King Jr. later observed, "While Negroes were being appointed to some significant jobs and social hospitality was being extended at the White House to Negro leaders, the dreams of the masses remained in tatters. The Negro felt that he recognized the same old bone that had been tossed to him in the past—only now it was being handed to him on a platter, with courtesy." King increasingly gave currency to the word "tokenism" in his assessments of Kennedy's efforts, hammering away at an administration that hoped, through symbolic appointments, to "generate such a volume of pride that it could be cut into portions and served to everyone."[23] Even Harris Wofford, from his post within the White House, began to harbor doubts about Kennedy's enthusiasm for meaningful relations with civil rights activists. He subsequently explained, "What Kennedy liked best in my role, and I liked least, was my function as a buffer between him and the civil rights forces pressing for presidential action. . . . I got tired of his accosting me with a grin and asking, 'Are your constituents happy?'" Wofford unhappily recognized his own complicity in helping sell symbolic concessions to African Americans in lieu of substantive policy initiatives.[24]

Kennedy actually invited charges of hypocrisy because he had raised very specific expectations during the 1960 campaign. He had, for example, strongly criticized President Eisenhower's inaction in the area of housing discrimination, claiming that federally subsidized housing could be "desegregated by the stroke of a presidential pen." Justifiably, then, civil rights activists expected him to sign an executive order on housing early in his term. This he failed to do. Disgruntled observers, eager to deprive Kennedy of any excuse for inaction, showered the White House mail room with pens and ink. But he was unprepared at that stage to take strong executive action on civil rights, either administratively or legislatively.[25]

Kennedy's unwillingness to move boldly on behalf of black America was rooted largely in his perception of his own political standing in relation to the volatility of the issue. Ever mindful of Thomas Jefferson's admonition that great innovation should never be undertaken on the basis of slender majorities, Kennedy took his .3% popular vote margin over Nixon as a signal for extreme caution.[26] Further, the composition of the 87th Congress—elected with Kennedy in 1960—merely reinforced the interpretation that liberal activism would be successful only at great cost. The House of Representatives did possess a substantial liberal contingent eager to pursue an activist civil rights agenda, but the center of power in the Senate still rested mainly in the hands of southern Democrats. Their seniority deprived Kennedy of any advantage he theoretically gained from presiding over the party that controlled all the nation's elected government.[27] At bottom, John Kennedy had no plans in 1961 to sacrifice limited political capital on civil rights, when he had other initiatives—economic and international—he felt obligated to pursue. Neither the country nor the Congress, he reasoned, would willingly accept more than he was doing.

Once again in this instance the political realities of the day reflected significant cleavages in the nation's underlying social structures and deep divisions about the value of those cleavages and what might be done to preserve or to change them. These were divisions a nation-maintaining president had to approach circumspectly, or risk exacerbating or falling victim to them. Given the explosiveness of the race issue in the early 1960s, significant presidential engagement was as likely to aggravate one side of an explosive conflict as to ameliorate the fundamental condition. Kennedy's razor-thin margin of victory was not a manifestation of racial division alone, but it did instruct Kennedy's conception about his place in helping steer the nation through the prevailing hazards. Electoral, political, and social forces cautioned against quick or meaningful changes in course by the president. The circumstances of his time, then, strongly reinforced for Kennedy the notion that he should fill his nation-maintaining role in a conventional fashion: working to retard threats to the prevailing political and social structures, sometimes by offering modest concessions to the protesters. To do otherwise was to subject the nation to avoidable shocks.

Sensing the president's unwillingness to initiate on his own meaningful executive action in the area of civil rights, a number of activists began laying plans to stage protests intended to induce an executive response. They would manufacture conditions wherein Kennedy could not reasonably refuse to intervene on their behalf. In other words, if the president would not voluntarily exercise leadership, they would thrust it upon him.[28] Thus were born the Freedom Rides.

The Freedom Rides and the Kennedy Response

On May 4, 1961, thirteen civil rights activists boarded buses in Washington D.C. to begin an extended tour of the southeastern United States. Their purpose was a test: to discover how free interstate travel had become in the seg-regated South in the wake of the Supreme Court's *Boynton v. Virginia* deci-sion, which ostensibly desegregated interstate transportation terminals. It was a test they did not expect the South to pass.[29]

The Freedom Riders anticipated, however, that their failure to gain access would lead to a larger victory—publicity of the continuing horrors visited on African Americans in the home of Jim Crow. James Farmer, the trip's originator, later described his aims:

> We planned the Freedom Ride with the specific intention of creating a cri-sis. We were counting on the bigots in the South to do our work for us. We figured that the government would have to respond if we created a situa-tion that was headline news all over the world, and affected the nation's image abroad. An international crisis, that was our strategy.[30]

The precipitation of such a crisis was thus crafted precisely to provoke a reconsideration by the president of his nation-keeping responsibilities.

The strategy worked. Although the trip from Washington to Atlanta occurred for the most part without incident, mobs in Anniston, Birmingham, and Montgomery, Alabama, gave Farmer the crisis he had anticipated. One of the buses was completely burned out and the Riders severely beaten at these successive stops.[31] Press coverage of these atrocities immediately drew the attention of the administration, which weeks earlier had completely ignored a Farmer letter announcing plans for the Ride.[32] The president himself received detailed, off-the-record briefings from his brother Robert and other Justice Department officials on the worsening plight of the Riders. John Kennedy "was angry," reports Richard Reeves, because "this was exactly the kind of thing the Communists used to make the United States look bad around the world." The president subsequently impressed upon Harris Wofford and Justice representatives—using language clearly reveal-ing impatience—the need to stop the protesters from their provocations.[33] Efforts were begun toward this end, but a conscious decision was taken by this small group to keep the president as far removed as possible from the public aspects of their work.[34]

After the attacks in Anniston and Birmingham, Robert Kennedy sent a departmental emissary, John Seigenthaler, to Alabama to consult with the Riders. "Driving to ... Montgomery," Reeves continues, Seigenthaler reflected on the absurdity of his mission: "Here comes the United States government, a thirty-one-year old newspaper reporter in a rented car."[35] He did, however, successfully convince the Riders to fly to New Orleans from Birmingham so that the protest trip could be ended on schedule without further violence.[36] Yet that victory for the administration proved short-lived. Despite intensive efforts by Seigenthaler to turn them around, two of the original Riders returned to Birmingham only days later, reinforced with students from the Nashville movement center.[37]

The attorney general, who had already asked the FBI to gather evidence for federal prosecution of the attackers, subsequently worked with the Riders to ensure their protection on the next leg of the trip, to Montgomery. Aggravated over the Riders' inability to secure a bus driver to complete the trip—unsurprisingly, bus company employees were less than enthusiastic about taking part—he phoned the company's chief local official and spouted, "I think you should—had better be getting in touch with Mr. Greyhound or whoever Greyhound is, and somebody better give us an answer to this question. I am—the Government is—going to be very much upset if this group does not get to continue their trip."[38] Further, after repeated attempts by the president himself to get through on the phone, Robert Kennedy finally got an elusive Alabama Governor John Patterson to consent to guarantee protection to the Riders during the remainder of their travels in Alabama.[39] Patterson's assurances failed in the state capital, however, when local police did not show up on time to meet the buses at the Montgomery terminal. The Montgomery mob not only attacked the Freedom Riders, they also assaulted reporters covering the Ride, and seriously wounded Seigenthaler.[40] At this stage, the attorney general stepped up efforts to protect the Riders.

Federal marshals—supplemented with a congeries of plain-clothes civilian officers—moved into Montgomery to be available in the event further violence erupted. The attorney general also sought and received federal court injunctions prohibiting the Ku Klux Klan from interfering with interstate travel and compelling the Montgomery police to protect the Riders locally. One contingent of marshals was pressed into service when a mob gathered around a church where King was speaking; the attorney general was in direct telephone communication with King during that episode and assured him that the churchgoers' safety was being monitored. Finally, Kennedy's negotiations with Alabama and Mississippi officials proved instrumental in paving the way for the Riders to go from Montgomery to Jackson securely, under state police protection.[41]

While Kennedy's assistance with security in Montgomery was welcomed by black activists, his arrangements with Mississippi Governor Ross Barnett were decidedly less well received. The Justice Department conceded to Governor Barnett that once the Riders were safely in Jackson, the federal government had no grounds to challenge their arrest under local law there. Subsequently, the Riders were convoyed by heavy state police escort from Montgomery to Jackson, where they were promptly arrested on such charges as disturbing the peace. "In effect," writes Taylor Branch, "Kennedy agreed to let state officials defend segregation by making forcible, unconstitutional arrests of the Freedom Riders as long as those officials did not let mobs accomplish the same purpose by violence."[42] The Freedom Riders had been prepared for these arrests, but two other aspects of the journey into Mississippi precipitated a heated telephone exchange between King and Robert Kennedy.[43]

First, the Freedom Riders believed that the presence of a formidable police escort—Branch describes it as "worthy of a NATO war game"—effectively sabotaged their mission. It deprived the Riders of a true, publicized reaction from rural southerners. "We would rather risk violence and be able to travel like ordinary passengers," claimed one leading Rider. "We will accept the violence and the hate, [and] absorb it without returning it."[44]

Second, because of an imminent presidential summit with Nikita Khrushchev, Robert Kennedy pressured King to have the entire episode put behind them by working to have the protesters released from jail.[45] King resisted. The Riders intended to stay in jail, he asserted, because "Our conscience tells us that the law is wrong and we must resist, but we have a moral obligation to accept the penalty." King claimed that the jails of Jackson could be filled with thousands of protesters descending in sympathy with their confined brothers and sisters. Kennedy understood King's remarks as a not-so-veiled threat, and countered "That's not the way to deal with us." Although King ended the conversation by promising that the Riders would remain in jail, he apparently reconsidered almost immediately and joined Kennedy in counseling for a cooling off period.[46]

The aftermath of the Freedom Rides produced a number of important developments. Within the civil rights movement, those student leaders who had formed the backbone of the sit-ins and the Freedom Rides began a rapid rise in stature.[47] The Student Nonviolent Coordinating Committee (SNCC) had been formed in 1960 and had flourished with the events of 1961.[48] This younger generation of organizers came to prominence schooled in nonviolent direct action, and they harbored a manifest skepticism about the ways and means of their elders in the movement, especially in the traditional realm of politics. The students possessed an almost unlimited energy, an absence of inhibitions about accruing arrest records, and a patented resistance to entertaining counsels of patience. Among the most activist of the students, even Martin Luther King—barely thirty-two years old at the time—was suspect. It did not go unnoticed, for example, that King stayed out of harm's way when the Freedom Ride buses rolled.[49] These young activists held the potential for radicalizing the entire movement.

The Freedom Rides also sparked substantive developments within the Kennedy administration, although none that fundamentally changed the president's direction on civil rights. Most directly, Robert Kennedy, at King's request, petitioned the Interstate Commerce Commission for a ruling more vigorously combating discrimination in facilities under its jurisdiction.[50] That ruling came in September, confirming for the student leaders that only direct action would move the government to make desired change.

More generally, the administration considered the ascent of the students an ominous development, requiring an overall adjustment in how civil rights issues would be addressed. That process of adjustment began immediately in the wake of the Freedom Rides.

At the root of this adaptation was a newly gained understanding by the Kennedys of the incendiary nature of racial politics in the Deep South.[51] In early 1961, when Robert Kennedy ventured into Athens, Georgia, to beard the lion, he did so as essentially a neophyte. We read that his hands trembled as he addressed the University of Georgia crowd. "You may ask: will we enforce the civil rights statutes? The answer is: yes, we will . . . We will not stand by and be aloof. We will move."[52] Even then, however, he could not have fully appreciated the dread of racial politics, because he had only a passing acquaintance with the effects it could have on human behavior, a familiarity that became more intimate—and more powerful—with the violence in Alabama that victimized even members of his own staff. Thus, the daring of the attorney general's early foray into the Deep South gave way after the Freedom Rides to a compelling sense of caution about further intervention. This added circumspection led the administration to develop an aggressive program of conflict management, and to endeavor more actively to channel movement activity through mechanisms of selective preferment. Through these instruments the Kennedys hoped to gain a respite from the divisiveness of racial politics, to return the nation to repose by moderating the character of protest.

Although the Civil Rights Division of the Justice Department continued to work to gain voluntary compliance with a growing corpus of court rulings on racial equality, the division's director, Burke Marshall, increasingly found his time devoted to moderating specific disputes rather than removing generic racial barriers to equality of franchise and education. At Robert Kennedy's goading, Marshall rather quickly developed expertise in intervening early and quietly in potential controversies so as to keep them from erupting into something administration higher-ups would have to deal with. Marshall became the chief trouble-shooter in a trouble-shooting agency, feverishly working out of the glare of public attention to mitigate racial conflict before it flared into a reprise of the Freedom Rides.[53] The intent of Marshall's intervention was not lost on civil rights activists, for whom conflict was the essence of political creativity; they saw promise in civil disobedience precisely because it sparked publicity and the escalation of conflict, which were, their theories held, the handmaidens of progress. According to this reasoning, then, the modest advances Marshall and others helped broker merely undermined their efforts to agitate further for more significant change. Events in Albany, Georgia, in December 1961, seemed to confirm this assessment.[54]

The Justice Department became an important behind-the-scenes presence in Albany when that city became a test site for black activists in the desegregation of public facilities there. The intervention by the Kennedys was aimed principally at ameliorating conflict, not at breaking down wholesale the barriers to racial equality there. The so-called Albany Movement ultimately failed for a number of reasons, including internal dissension among African-American activists and the shrewd, nonviolent reactions of Sheriff Laurie Pritchett. Yet the Kennedy administration also played a crucial part in disarming conflict without producing meaningful concessions to the protesters. The attorney general, after consultation with representatives of the local white power structure there, agreed to keep the national government out of the conflict as long as there was no violence. Shortly thereafter, although he had promised in Athens, less than two years earlier, not to "be aloof" in enforcing civil rights, Robert Kennedy announced to a small group of friendly reporters that the administration was adopting a "hands off" policy on racial matters. "Real progress," Kennedy announced, unwittingly mimicking Dwight Eisenhower, required that "local leaders talk it out."[55] In effect, then, the administration renounced any intent to enforce aggressively desegregation on a defiant South.

The administration also worked surreptitiously to subvert the one tactic the protesters apparently thought would focus unbearable pressure on Albany's white leadership. When Martin Luther King Jr. and his associate Ralph Abernathy were imprisoned there for violating local ordinances, they decided to remain in jail as a means of attracting publicity. The city fathers saw the danger in King's jailing, and talked with the president by phone—and the attorney general in person—about devising a plan to remove the threat from their midst. They agreed on a course of action, and the two protesters were freed after "an unidentified, well-dressed Negro male" paid the city fines. Sensing something improbable in that cover story—the city fathers had gathered the money from among themselves—King remarked upon his release, "This is one time I'm out of jail that I'm not happy to be out." The effort to desegregate Albany quickly fizzled after King's departure, in part because of the administration's intervention in freeing the one celebrity best suited to drawing national scrutiny to that town.[56]

These efforts at conflict management did not always succeed. There were certain occasions on which the momentum of events moved beyond the administration's capacity to manage. The most prominent of these episodes was the enrollment of James Meredith in 1962 at the University of Mississippi.[57] Every effort was made by the administration to orchestrate quietly Meredith's admission, beginning with intervention by Justice Department attorneys, then by Robert Kennedy, and finally by the president himself. The administration could not easily have avoided action in Mississippi because it was working to implement a federal court order demanding Mississippi's compliance with desegregation rulings. In the final analysis, however, because of Governor Ross Barnett's insistence on walking the defiant path of Orval Faubus, John Kennedy found himself compelled—as he had promised he would not be—to act in the mold of Dwight Eisenhower.[58] He sent in U.S. troops to secure Meredith's safety only after rioting erupted. High casualties among law enforcement officers and civilians in Oxford, attendant to the administration's reluctance to send uniformed troops earlier, proved to be a sobering example of the potential downside to incremental intervention, a lesson that rested heavily on the president's mind during pivotal events in Birmingham one year later.[59]

In addition to creative troubleshooting, the administration also turned in the wake of the Freedom Rides to a more calculated engagement in the practice of selective preferment. The most important single exercise of this practice occurred not in relation to favoring a particular personage, but in aggressively, but confidentially, sponsoring a particular *activity*, into which African-American activism would be channeled. Thus emerged the Voter Education Project (VEP), an effort to finance and organize a vast voter registration initiative among African Americans in the Deep South.[60]

The plan to initiate the VEP was a Kennedy-driven effort to attract African Americans away from sit-ins and Freedom Rides.[61] Indeed, Doug McAdam claims that the VEP "offers perhaps the best and most significant example of the government's efforts to direct movement activity into channels it viewed as less threatening."[62] Democratic National Committee official and Kennedy confidante Louis Martin has confirmed that the origins of the VEP "were pure Democratic politics with the White House and Justice Department fully knowledgeable of where we were going."[63]

Burke Marshall and Harris Wofford met repeatedly with various civil rights activists—especially students active in SNCC—to convince them to turn to voter registration as an appropriate outlet for their protest. But the administration did not rely on the power of words alone. Marshall initiated contacts with wealthy funding sources—from foundations and such individuals as Harry Belafonte—to find private money where public funds could not be spent. Then, Robert Kennedy himself approached the head of the Internal Revenue Service to assure tax-exempt status for the effort, reminiscent, notes Taylor Branch, of the "clandestine pursuit . . . to secure tax benefits for those who helped ransom the Bay of Pigs prisoners."[64] At one crucial meeting with student leaders, Kennedy intimated that the Justice Department would selectively extend maximum physical protection to voter activists but not to those pursuing other means of protest. The phone numbers of Burke Marshall and John Doar were given those who agreed to work expressly on voter registration, with invitations to call the department collect anytime they encountered problems. Further, they confidentially promised to secure draft exemptions for those who cooperated. Robert Kennedy used virtually every formal and informal resource at his disposal to swing the movement in the direction of voter registration. "If enough Negroes registered, they could obtain redress of their grievances internally, without," the attorney general hopefully concluded, "the federal government being involved at all."[65]

The attorney general succeeded in getting the Voter Education Project up and running, and thus in directing a large number of African-American activists into a program that promised major political dividends for President Kennedy. As 1962 approached, the administration had good reason to believe that the diversions of the VEP would be successful and enduring.[66] King, and many SNCC activists, found merit in the program, because it provided funds that they used for organizational purposes beyond voter registration.[67] However, one activist claimed that, given the circumstances, SNCC had become "an arm of the Justice Department."[68]

Although the VEP itself helped the administration to win friends among a variety of African-American activists, the Kennedys, after the Freedom Rides, did work more conventionally in areas of selective preferment to solidify their reputation among African Americans and to give shape to black politics. Because Martin Luther King had emerged by this time as the most prominent among an upper tier of black leaders, the administration focused its efforts on sustaining a favorable rapport with him, although Robert Kennedy did flirt briefly with the more conservative NAACP.[69] On a number of occasions the doors of the White House were opened to King, and he and the Southern Christian Leadership Conference became perhaps the central conduit of administration communications back to black America.

Yet the relationship with King was not entirely a trusted one. The Kennedys used their increasing public association with King as pretext for sanctioning and escalating J. Edgar Hoover's massive surveillance campaign against the civil rights movement.[70] Relying on arguments that dated back to his salad days with the Bureau of Investigation, Hoover divined Communist direction of the movement and accordingly played on the Kennedys's sense of political self-preservation in gaining approval for telephone wiretaps, which he then converted into license for bugging. Hoover's case was helped by the fact that he could document Communist Party affiliation for two of King's close associates.[71]

Tension between the administration and the movement also existed because, by the Kennedy years, efforts to shape the internal dynamics of black political life through selective preferment had become problematic. The evolved internal dynamics of African-American politics had rendered such activity suspect.

In a *Harper's Magazine* article published the month after John Kennedy's inauguration, James Baldwin drew the curtain back on the character of political rewards typically passed along to prominent African Americans.

> The problem of Negro leadership in this country has always been extremely delicate, dangerous, and complex. The term itself becomes remarkably difficult to define, the moment one realizes that the real role

of the Negro leader, in the eyes of the American Republic, was not to make the Negro a first-class citizen but to keep him content as a second-class one. . . .

Whatever concession the Negro leader carried away from the bargaining table was won with the tacit understanding that he, in return, would influence the people he represented in the direction that the people in power wished them to be influenced. Very often, in fact, he did not do this at all, but contrived to delude the white men (who are, in this realm, rather easily deluded) into believing that he had. But very often, too, he deluded himself into believing that the aims of white men in power and the desires of Negroes out of power were the same.[72]

Baldwin's revelation was at least prescient, if not seminal. The critique he offered of conventional black leadership revealed a skepticism about those closely aligned with white "people in power," suspicion that resonated deeply among certain factions active in the struggle for racial equality in the early 1960s. The favors that a president might bestow on a preferred black leader, then, intended as always to convey honor and *gravitas*, increasingly generated the opposite among key African-American groups.[73]

Since the Kennedy administration had already established that it did not intend aggressively to attack the roots of segregation in the South, any general skepticism of African Americans toward white elites seemed completely justified in the instant case. Such a modest agenda conflicted dramatically with the vital spirits of a movement probing daily new frontiers in thousands of places across the nation. Those who had witnessed the fruits of victory flowing from mass civil disobedience; those who had finally been convinced that the very foundations of segregation would crumble like the walls of Jericho if the people would only march; those who had gone to jail in Mississippi and had emerged even more convinced of the strength of direct action, were indisposed to revert back to a situation in which their success depended upon the goodwill and good works of "an arm" of the government.[74] Small wonder, then, that the administration's hoped-for respite from protest did not appear.[75]

King's relationship with the Kennedys became increasingly problematic for him, because he was in competition with increasingly impatient activists for leadership among black elites and masses. This was to become a persistent problem for King, who sought to mediate the extremes of passion and indifference in the American populace.[76] King's reliance on a theology of nonviolent passivism had already earned him a derisive nickname among the more aggressive, who took to calling him "De Lawd."[77] Moreover, to the most radical, King seemed all-too willing to forgo the rigors of front-line protest in favor of the safety of the fundraising circuit and the television studio. The general skepticism to which Baldwin gave voice had in short order become pandemic. In the final analysis, King could hardly afford to give further appearances of dragging his feet—or of being captive to a foot-dragging administration—when others sought to force progress with direct confrontation. These pressures on King became irresistible by late 1962, when his attention was turned to the site of what would become a pivotal episode in the history of the civil rights movement: Birmingham.

Kennedy and Birmingham

In the aftermath of their failures at Albany, King and his associates had entered a period of evaluation and introspection. Where could they turn, they asked, to regain momentum for the movement, and to avoid the problems encountered in South Georgia? That they answered "Birmingham" reveals much about their overall strategy for pressing ahead.

Birmingham bore two traits not present in Albany: a relatively powerful central black spokesperson in Fred Shuttlesworth—a prominent member of the SCLC—and a passionately ruthless leader of the opposition in the person of Public Safety Commissioner Bull Connor. These ingredients made Birmingham, which King associate Ralph Abernathy later described as "the worst city this side of Johannesburg," an ideal location for directing the attention of the world on American racism. It held potential for the kind of focused, dramatic conflict absent in Albany.[78] Such conflict was to be desired precisely because of the effect it would have on the Kennedys. Birmingham was largely staged for them.

"The key to everything," King said of Birmingham, "is federal commitment," which could be wrought by "precipitat[ing] a crisis situation." David Garrow, capturing the thinking of the protesters, has written, "Two years earlier, the administration had responded to the heavily publicized violence that marked the Freedom Rides with federal intervention and a commitment to desegregate interstate travel facilities. In Albany, however, where there had been no photos of burning buses or beaten protesters, the Kennedys had shown no interest in bolstering the movement's cause." The logic, then, to selecting Birmingham was simple: Bull Connor was unlikely to keep a respectable face on segregation as Laurie Pritchett had. When, in King's phrase, "the *surfacing* of tensions already present" in Birmingham came to pass, the Kennedy administration would once again have little choice but to intervene vigorously on the side of the protesters. That logic proved to be eminently successful.[79] With the ugliness of southern racism openly exposed to an American public increasingly sensitive to violent injustice, the president's nation-keeping powers were necessarily deployed in favor of the African-American victims.

The protests in Birmingham actually began, as had matters in Albany, before King's arrival. Shuttlesworth and others had conducted peaceful demonstrations against downtown merchants who maintained segregated stores. Their inability to win meaningful concessions locally brought from Shuttlesworth appeals to King for his assistance.[80]

King and Shuttlesworth escalated protests in Birmingham in the succeeding months. Mass marches drew journalists from throughout the world, who reported on King's own jailing, as well as the arrests of nearly a thousand schoolchildren who volunteered to carry on the protests when insufficient numbers of adults were able and willing to demonstrate. The Kennedys monitored these events carefully and, as usual, labored with all parties in Birmingham to avoid bloodshed. However, it was only after highly publicized violence exploded in Birmingham and threatened to spread elsewhere—when pictures of local policemen turning dogs and fire hoses on peaceful demonstrators began circulating on press wires throughout the globe—that John Kennedy turned to action that legitimately constituted a New Frontier.[81]

Events in Birmingham had a riveting effect on the Kennedy administration. The prospects for continued violence in Alabama was cause enough for concern and attention, but what induced a near preoccupation with Birmingham were signs that the televised civil disobedience there was spreading. Louis Martin, from his post at the Democratic National Committee, passed along sobering observations to the attorney general.

> Events in Birmingham in the last few days have seemed to electrify Negro concern over civil rights all across the country. As this is written, demonstrations and marches are underway or being planned in a number of major cities, including Chicago. The accelerated tempo of Negro restiveness and the rivalry of some leaders for top billing coupled with the resistance of the segregationists may soon create the most critical state of race relations since the Civil War.[82]

J. Edgar Hoover confirmed Martin's assessment by passing along to the attorney general the contents of wiretapped telephone conversations between King and associate Stanley Levison. King asserted therein that "We are on the threshold of a significant breakthrough and the greatest weapon is the mass demonstration. . . . We are at the point where we can mobilize all of this righteous indignation into a powerful mass movement." The two discussed plans for using "the Birmingham pattern" across the country, perhaps in conjunction with a nationwide work stoppage or a mass march on Washington. Clearly Birmingham was conceived as just the beginning.[83]

Added to this King-directed unrest was another sobering prospect for the president. He had to consider that in the absence of action on his part, in the form of legislation, the movement would turn away from the likes of King and Roger Wilkins and increasingly toward even more immoderate elements. Here Kennedy picked up cues from both James Baldwin and King himself. Their highly publicized essays, "Letter from a Region in My Mind" and "Letter from Birmingham Jail," alerted white America to the appeal of violence among people who were afforded no other escape from despair.[84] As events in Birmingham festered, Baldwin attended a meeting with Robert Kennedy, where the attorney general was subjected by a former Freedom Rider, in the words of another participant, to "one of the most violent, emotional verbal assaults and attacks I had ever witnessed."[85] Kennedy sought support from the more mainstream members of the group, only to find that they empathized with his attacker. Moreover, the discontent expressed by elites in that meeting was increasingly finding popular outlet through the ever more contentious work of SNCC and the Nation of Islam. The Kennedys could see, then, that by their standards the black mainstream was becoming increasingly radicalized.[86]

Finally, the international coverage devoted to events in Birmingham threatened to overwhelm efforts the president was making to establish American supremacy in the struggle for friends in a world increasingly under the governance of people of color.[87] Carl Brauer reports that a quarter of Radio Moscow's transmissions were concerned with events in Birmingham.[88] This coverage, broadcast in over thirty languages, proclaimed that "American authorities cannot and do not wish to stop the outrages by racists." All this transpired as Vietnam was imploding over the deaths of nine Buddhist monks at the hands of the South Vietnamese police. King took note of the international pressures operating on the president and announced to one church congregation: "Mr. Kennedy . . . is battling for the minds and hearts of men in Asia and Africa—some one billion men in the neutralist sector of the world—and they aren't going to respect the United States of America if she deprives men and women of the basic rights of life because of the color of their skin. Mr. Kennedy knows that."[89] Indeed *President* Kennedy could not have ignored it, however much he may have wanted to.[90]

It was in this environment that Kennedy determined that he had to act decisively to deal with the problem of race in America, or risk being completely overwhelmed by the issue.[91] Absent a reversal of course and the embrace of an aggressive civil rights agenda, a course which many Americans were now seeing as justified based on their exposure through television to lurid scenes of reactionary violence, Kennedy could only envision an unbroken chain of Birmingham-like protests—one upon another—leaving both the nation and his presidency in a complete state of wreckage.

The president subsequently produced a revolutionary proposal. What leads Carl Brauer to term his actions a "Second Reconstruction" was the central feature of his contemplated legislation, a public accommodations bill outlawing by federal statute segregation in all places of public business.[92] Here truly was a "New Frontier" worthy of the name, an assertion of federal powers unprecedented since the days of that earlier reconstruction.[93]

On the night of June 11, 1963, President John Kennedy delivered a nationally broadcast television address in which he announced plans for a legislative initiative intended to eradicate segregation from American society. Kennedy chose this moment because earlier that day Governor George C. Wallace had defiantly blocked federal officials from registering African-American students at the University of Alabama. Kennedy's timing—intended to benefit from the fact that the governor's blockade had failed (the students enrolled at another site) and to demonstrate a forceful response to the governor's defiance—caught even his closest aides off guard. The proposed legislation was not yet ready, and some in the administration still sought to dissuade the president from pursuing such a radical course of action. He was still revising parts of the speech as he went on the air, and delivered much of it *ad libitum* where the prepared text failed.[94]

No presidential address on race since Lincoln's announcement of emancipation was as fraught with meaning as Kennedy's. He spoke in uncharacteristically moral tones, advancing the idea of a racial Golden Rule: "[E]very American ought to be treated as he would wish to be treated, as one would wish his children to be treated." He described in some detail the disparities of treatment facing children born to white and black parents in the United States, and he claimed that the actions of every American were essential to remedying that inequality. But he also proclaimed a need for congressional action, so that the laws of the nation would be sufficient to punish those who refused to comply. Included in his speech were three general legislative proposals: a public accommodations law, authorization for greater intervention in school desegregation suits, and tougher voting rights provisions. In the sum of these, and in his clarion enunciation from the bully pulpit of principles "as old as the scriptures and . . . as clear as the American Constitution," Kennedy set the stage for a clear break from the practices of his presidential predecessors.[95]

Kennedy and the Civil Rights Act of 1964

Although Kennedy's announcement drew an enthusiastic response from most civil rights activists—King termed the address "A hallmark in the annals of American history"[96]—it would be an exaggeration to claim that the Kennedys and the central leadership of the civil rights movement entered at that time a period of trusted friendship. Too much residual suspicion developed over years of conflict; too many unresolved internal tensions within the civil rights movement itself; and too many disputed questions about tactics, existed for harmony to arise in the aftermath of the president's decision. Indeed, in many ways the new period Kennedy entered looked very much like the one departed.[97]

A series of meetings between the president and various groups of civil rights leaders took place in the White House to work on developing strategies for cooperation. These became especially necessary given the profound backlash among southern congressional delegations to the president's civil rights initiative.[98] (The force of that reaction was so severe that the president privately expressed doubts about the prudence of his chosen course.[99]) Despite some efforts from both sides to extend hands of friendship to the other—based principally on the utilitarian concern that they could all accomplish more with cooperation—mutual distrust did not subside. Suspicion was exacerbated by genuine disagreements over the best route to take in achieving the legislative goals the president had established. The White House, claiming a superior feel for congressional politics, sought once again to channel African-American discontent into those conventional areas of political activity—like voter registration—that would have the most positive influence on congressional behavior. In this vein, the president counseled against a planned march on Washington, scheduled for later that summer. He argued that such a demonstration, coming as it would during congressional consideration of parts of his package, would be taken by members of Congress as a sign of intimidation, and thus would be counterproductive. Further, he privately doubted that such a march could be undertaken without at least collateral rioting.[100]

A large majority of the civil rights leadership rejected the president's thinking. They reasoned that their success to date had derived almost entirely from methods of mass action that had been considered inappropriate by the administration. "Frankly," King told the president, "I have never engaged in any direct action movement which did not seem ill-timed. Some people thought Birmingham ill-timed," and yet the president himself had earlier conceded that it was precisely the pressure of Birmingham that had brought him to his current position. The march on Washington would proceed over the president's initial objections.[101]

Planning for the march was closely monitored by the White House, with cooperation from most of the march's key organizers, who did not want the event to turn into a Kennedy-bashing affair. When the text of John Lewis's speech appeared to be too harsh— "We will march through the South, through the Heart of Dixie, the way Sherman did"—administration aides rewrote parts of it, which were delivered to the Lincoln Memorial by Burke Marshall riding in the sidecar of a police motorcycle. Lewis and his SNCC colleagues initially objected to making changes, but consented when King, Philip Randolph, and others made convincing cases about the need for unity. However, as a final checkpoint, two White House staffers gained access to the public address system's power supply, and were authorized to shut it off if anything unplanned began. After the march, which featured King's stirring "I Have a Dream" speech, the organizers were met at the White House by the president, who praised them for a successful, peaceful demonstration.[102]

Not all of the Kennedys' efforts to assume internal direction of the movement were so congenial. Based on a growing body of evidence provided by J. Edgar Hoover, obtained from previously authorized wiretaps, the administration brought heavy pressure on King to sever his ties with two close aides. Indeed, on the day that Kennedy first met with various civil rights leaders after his June 11 speech, King was privately pressured by Marshall,

Robert Kennedy, and—in an unprecedented display of high-level intrusive-ness into the internal affairs of the movement—by the president himself, to separate from the two suspected Communists. When King did not move as quickly as the administration wanted in firing the two, Robert Kennedy leaked a story to a friendly reporter detailing King's relationship with one suspect adviser, Jack O'Dell. Although that kind of story held prospects for damaging the administration itself, apparently Kennedy reasoned that a quick resolution of the matter would pay long-term dividends. "King," writes Taylor Branch, "could scarcely believe it." But the "message essen-tially was that you do not trifle with the president of the United States. When President Kennedy told King that the national interest required him to get rid of O'Dell, he meant now, *immediately*, without second thoughts or tender farewells."[103]

Not long after, having wrestled with the question for months, Robert Kennedy authorized wiretaps of King himself. (Previously, King's voice had been picked up from taps on Stanley Levison's phone.) In part Kennedy did this to assuage Hoover and to protect himself and his brother from bureau-cratic blackmail by the FBI director, whose files on the Kennedy brothers' social liaisons were growing.[104] But the carrot Hoover held out was that such taps provided exceptional political intelligence on the activities of individuals whose work could potentially devastate the administration. Hoover had long before learned that the attorney general had an appetite for such political morsels.[105]

Continuing tension between the administration and the movement also derived from the Kennedys' desire to avoid further executive intervention at racial flashpoints. In the fall of 1963, Birmingham teetered near the brink of disaster again, following a continuing impasse over segregation in public accommodations and the bombing of the Sixteenth Street Baptist Church, which resulted in the deaths of four children. When local law enforcement officials were deemed incompetent by King to deal with the problem, he and others requested federal assistance, including armed troops to protect black residents. Instead of the army, the president sent in a former Secretary of the Army and a former Army football coach to help negotiate a settlement. Some blacks in Birmingham welcomed any assistance, but for King the adminis-tration's response was taken as another in a series of acts of bad faith.[106] He publicly rebuked the president, and announced his intentions not to accept the administration's recently expressed goodwill as a sign that the struggle for equality was over. "Let them sabotage us with the evil of cooperation with segregation," he proclaimed. "We intend to be free."[107] Less than two months later, with relations not appreciably improved, John Kennedy was assassinated in Dallas, Texas.

The Johnson Transition and the Civil Rights Act

Perhaps no segment of the nation's population took news of the assassination with a greater sense of loss—and more anxiety—than black America. Two principal factors explain this distinctive grief.

First, Kennedy, after a tortuous personal journey, had at last taken an historic step toward remedying racial inequality in America. That he had invested the power of the presidency in the cause of civil rights, in a way unique in America history, drew unprecedented levels of admiration from both black elites and mass publics. Kennedy's sudden departure from American political life, then, jolted those whose expectations had begun to soar as a result of Kennedy's patronage. "I really think we saw two Kennedys," a grief-stricken Martin Luther King explained after the president's death. He had been happy to bid farewell to the first; the loss of the second shook him deeply.[108]

The second factor that gave rise to a special anxiety in black America was the matter of presidential succession. Lyndon Johnson's Texas roots, and attendant fears of his position on civil rights by party liberals, had nearly cost him the vice-presidential nomination in 1960.[109] As vice president, he had occasionally become an important advocate for civil rights within the administration, but these largely out-of-public-view initiatives did not dispel doubts about the nature of his fundamental commitments.[110] Anxiety endured into the period of transition from one president to the next, then, arising from fears that the advances John Kennedy had belatedly embraced would be set aside.

These worries were, as it happened, unwarranted. The social forces the movement had mobilized, which had imparted to John Kennedy a sense of urgency in moving ahead on civil rights, did not, to borrow Justice Cardozo's phrase, turn aside in their course and pass Lyndon Johnson by. At the moment he took the oath of office aboard Air Force One, Johnson inherited the various roles and responsibilities of the presidency and became subjected for the most part to the same kinds of social and institutional constraints that had operated on his predecessor. The realities of Birmingham concentrated overwhelming pressure on one filling an institution charged with preserving the order of the American constitution. These the president from Texas could no more ignore than had the one from Massachusetts.[111]

It is true, as we have seen elsewhere (most prominently in the transition from Taylor to Fillmore), that the death of an incumbent can open the way for a re-interpretation of the presidency's nation-keeping constraints by a successor. The *specific* path toward securing domestic order might be reconsidered and recharted. The irony of this particular transition was, however, that the pressures to move ahead on an agenda of racial change were even more acutely focused on the southerner than on his predecessor.[112] Because of the regional nature of Johnson's base constituency, it would be hard to conjure a presidential aspirant for whom civil rights was a more indispensable issue. If he wanted to win the respect and support of decisive elements in his own party—and he did—and if he wanted to be elected president by his own rights—and he did—he knew he would have to embrace the fallen president's civil rights agenda. He did.[113] In a quintessentially Johnsonesque moment, the new president pronounced to Harvard-educated aide Richard Goodwin from his perch on a White House toilet: "[N]o compromises on civil rights. I'm not going to bend an inch. Those civil rightsers are going to have to wear sneakers to keep up with me."[114] As Bruce Miroff observes, Johnson "wanted the course of civil rights to be shaped, as much as possible, from the White House."[115]

Less than a week after Kennedy's assassination, Johnson spoke to a joint session of Congress and left no room for doubt as to where he stood on the question of civil rights.

> No memorial oration or eulogy could more eloquently honor President Kennedy's memory than the earliest passage of the civil rights bill for which he fought so long. We have talked long enough in this country about equal rights. We have talked for one hundred years or more. It is time now to write the next chapter . . . to enact a civil rights law so that we move forward to eliminate from this Nation any trace of discrimination and oppression that is based on race or color.[116]

The president immediately drew leading activists into the White House to assure them further of his resolve, and to consult with them on tactics. As Kennedy had done, he encouraged a moratorium on mass demonstrations in the interest of keeping congressional attention focused solely on the merits of the legislation under review.[117] Evidence also indicates that Johnson worked to favor those in the movement who typically adopted the most conservative courses of political action. Records show that one White House aide "advised making it clear to [NAACP executive secretary Roy] Wilkins that the administration viewed him as *the* black leader" for purposes of advancing the administration's civil rights agenda.[118] Although Johnson adopted Wilkins as his preferred channel, he also met with King and James Farmer (of the Congress of Racial Equality) with some regularity to coordinate public work on behalf of the pending legislation. Johnson, however, avoided meeting with SNCC leaders, wishing not to reward that organization's perceived impetuosity with a presidential audience.[119]

Johnson succeeded in his effort to minimize movement provocations during the period of congressional consideration of the civil rights bill. However, his success in keeping the movement relatively quiet did not derive solely from the power of his political wisdom, the force of his will, or the carrot of White House privileges. To an important extent, the movement's quiescence was the product of internal disorientation occasioned by growing signs that the FBI had abandoned any pretense of neutrality on matters of civil rights.[120] Director Hoover, especially eager to discredit King, determined that no part of the movement leaders' lives were too intimate for exploitation, including their sexual behavior. He eagerly shared detailed reports of raw language and infidelities with the president of the United States, who apparently was an equally eager consumer of such information.

Although the most blatant exploitation of these materials began later, during 1964 King was well aware that his personal affairs were no longer his own secret, and that at any moment Hoover might see fit to ruin him publicly. Small wonder, then, that as 1964 progressed, King endured lengthy bouts of self-doubt, which severely undermined his capacity to direct the SCLC and to continue as the chief spokesperson for black America. King could never be certain that his phone calls and personal conversations were not being tapped, and he was deprived of his long-time reliance on the counsel of Stanley Levison because of White House insistence of Levison's Communist inclinations. These personal problems became problems for the movement, not just because its most prominent leader was distracted, but also because efforts at trouble-shooting FBI sabotage became an increasingly prominent feature of leadership strategy sessions. This disorientation, induced by presidentially sanctioned efforts by the FBI, seriously undermined the movement's ability to function during 1964, contributing to the creation of a period of relative calm as the civil rights act moved through Congress.[121]

While the street activists remained largely neutralized, the more established civil rights organizations moved on Washington to take the lead in convincing Congress to adopt the administration's bill. In his initial meeting with the NAACP's Roy Wilkins, President Johnson declared that the onus for passing the bill rested with his organization, and that he did not intend to get actively involved in lobbying Congress. "In effect, what Johnson was saying," Wilkins later remarked, "was, 'You have the ball, now run with it.'"[122] Wilkins's long history in coalition building among other liberal organizations, such as organized labor, proved indispensable in shepherding through the House and Senate the president's bill. True to his word, Johnson generally restricted his own lobbying efforts to a few crucial episodes, including a series of indispensable interventions to secure a cloture vote to end a Senate filibuster.[123] Nonetheless, his public and private rhetoric—and his steadfastness in refusing to bend to southern legislators and in keeping all other business off the Senate agenda until that bill got through—set the overall tone for the debate. A bill Senator Jacob Javits (R-N.Y.) called "the most momentous piece of legislation . . . which has come out of the Senate since the declaration of World War II" subsequently passed.[124] On July 2, Lyndon Johnson signed into law the Civil Rights Act of 1964.

In some respects the new law was more effective in bringing down Jim Crow than even its firmest supporters had imagined possible. Although pockets of resistance remained in the Deep South, the public accommodations section of the bill proved to be eminently successful. King and others in the SCLC had long planned to follow passage of the act with statewide challenges to anticipated defiance in the state of Alabama. David Garrow observes that King's plans crumbled when that state's expected resistance simply evaporated. To King's surprise,

> the first three days of testing for desegregated facilities at various restaurants, hotels, and theaters found almost complete compliance in Montgomery, Birmingham, Mobile, Huntsville, and Gadsden . . . [I]t was apparent that compliance with the public accommodations provision of the Civil Rights Act was so widespread throughout Alabama that no statewide action campaign could be built around continued segregation in public establishments.[125]

Just three years after personal representatives of the president had been savagely beaten while trying to protect Freedom Riders in Alabama bus stations, civil rights activists had difficulty, in that state's major cities, finding a place that refused to serve them. Perhaps on no other occasion in American history has the force of law as a modifier of human conduct been more conspicuous.

The Voting Rights Act of 1965

The Civil Rights Act of 1964 produced arguably the most dramatic change in the status of black Americans of any federal action since the Civil War.[126] In the following year, however, the United States government took action that promised to solidify the gains of 1964 and to make it possible for African Americans to move with greater certitude in the future toward a nation of social, political, and economic equality. This was the adoption of the Voting Rights Act of 1965. The story of the passage of that measure serves as a fitting conclusion to this narrative, as it so fully recapitulates in a single episode all the forces commonly at work when movements for racial justice effectively seek presidential action to advance their cause.

Lyndon Johnson did not enter the post-Civil Rights Act era with the intent of immediately striking another major blow for racial equality.[127] Johnson had already attained two central goals: official redress of major grievances of black America—which showed promise of defusing an explosive threat to the nation's peace and security—and, secondarily, an undeniable demonstration to blacks and northern liberals that this Texan was as progressive on race as anyone, including their beloved Kennedys. That accomplished, Johnson wished to consolidate his political gains, and to build an indestructible populist coalition for the Democratic Party, by investing his energies in a grand assault on poverty. Thus, his approach to black activists was rather simple. He privately continued to encourage a moratorium on demonstrations—he said the new civil rights law made them "unnecessary and possibly even self defeating"—and he sought to get African-American leaders to support his two mainstream projects.[128] He wanted them to sign on as footsoldiers in the war on poverty, and he sought their help in steering black organizational skills into party building enterprises. A major goal of each was to direct mass behavior immediately into relatively benign—or conventionally productive—channels.[129] In relation to these short-term goals he met with only marginal success.[130]

Ironically, it was the very success of the desegregation statute that initially put LBJ at loggerheads again with African-American activists. When it became apparent that the planned public accommodations protests in Alabama would be unnecessary, SCLC and SNCC activists searched for other venues for directing their energies. They decided to go into Mississippi to assist on-going efforts to organize the Mississippi Freedom Democratic Party (MFDP) there.[131] The MFDP originated as a protest mechanism to challenge the all-white Democratic regulars, who neglected that state's large black population. An initial goal of the MFDP was to send a delegation to the 1964 Democratic National Convention in Atlantic City, in hopes that the integrated delegation might be seated as the truly representative party of Mississippi.[132] This was not a development that made Lyndon Johnson happy.[133]

The passage of the Civil Rights Act had generated a predictable backlash against Johnson in the Deep South, one which the conservative Barry Goldwater was well situated to use to his maximum advantage. Accordingly, Johnson hoped that his existing record on civil rights would be sufficient to keep the liberal wing of his party on board, while he worked to regain the confidence of newly alienated southerners.[134] The MFDP challenge confounded for a time his planning, but the underlying political realities of the day supported what LBJ wanted to do. The emergencies that had precipitated the Civil Rights Act (e.g., the violence visited on protesters in Birmingham and a president in Dallas) had passed, lifting the direct nation-keeping pressures that had moved the White House to advance a social revolution.[135] Moreover, many African-American leaders were convinced by the president's logic that open protest just before the 1964 election would redound to Goldwater's immediate benefit, and thus would only hurt themselves in the long run. Accordingly, many of the most powerful black organizers were indeed forgoing street demonstrations during the election season.[136] The absence of these kinds of direct pressures, and the sense that black America had nowhere else to go on election day, left Johnson's supporters free to use a series of heavy-handed tactics at the national convention to keep white southerners happy.[137] The administration made a few minor concessions in order to allow some of the black leadership active in Atlantic City to save face, but Johnson's strong-arm methods in putting down the MFDP challenge bitterly offended African Americans there who witnessed their moral high ground bartered away for votes.[138] Wounds were opened that never fully healed.[139]

The MFDP's difficulties in organizing in Mississippi, and the party's effective dismissal by Johnson-led forces at the convention—highlighted against a backdrop of enduring movement concerns about the suffrage[140]—revealed to King and others what the next logical stage in movement development would be: demands for increased *political* power secured through improved federal protection of the right to vote.[141] One day after Lyndon Johnson won election to the presidency—ridding black America of the specter of a Goldwater (or Wallace) administration—Martin Luther King publicly announced demonstrations in Mississippi and Alabama to protest voter intimidation there.

Lyndon Johnson expressed sympathy with the movement's newly proclaimed aims, but he straightforwardly told King that he would have to wait for voting rights advances. "I'm going to do it eventually," said the president, "but I can't get a voting rights bill through in this session of Congress." Once again, the civil rights movement confronted a president whose personal calculations of the politically possible diverged from the movement's own sense of justice. Once again, black leaders undertook to move a president more rapidly than he would willingly go, to shift the president's understanding of what he ought to do.[142]

The focus of their renewed efforts was Selma. That west-central Alabama town had a long history of depriving the suffrage to black residents, and had been one of the few places in Alabama where public accommodations had remained largely unaffected by the provisions of the Civil Rights Act.[143] Equally important, that county's law enforcement officers were under the direction of Sheriff Jim Clark, whose relations with local African Americans bore a striking resemblance to those of Bull Connor in Birmingham.[144] Black activists hoped to replicate in Selma the publicized drama of Birmingham, to similar effect on the sitting president of the United States.[145] "Just as the 1964 civil rights bill was written in Birmingham," noted Andrew Young at the time, "we hope that new federal voting legislation will be written here."[146]

Johnson, as Kennedy before him, tried to negotiate a termination of hostilities in Selma before they exploded into something he would have to deal with publicly.[147] To do this, he made use of a little-noticed provision in the Civil Rights Act, which established a federal Community Relations Service (CRS). The basic purpose of the CRS was to institutionalize the troubleshooting function theretofore directed by Burke Marshall in the Justice Department. The administration sent two mediators into Selma under the auspices of the CRS, but they were ineffective, precisely because the essence of their mission clashed with the conflict-seeking objectives of civil rights activists. One of the mediators remarked, "If the CRS seeks to help Selma make steady progress in complying with the Civil Rights Act and to avoid lawsuits, violence and arrests, this may run counter to Dr. King's objective of creating a kind of confrontation."[148]

Periodic, publicized violence characterized the Selma protests, as the demonstrators refused to accept a rigged process of voter registration there. Once King himself was jailed, President Johnson issued a strong statement condemning the denial of the right to vote in Selma, and pledging in a general way to do something about the problem. "I intend to see that that right [to vote] is secured for all of our citizens." Johnson did not make specific commitments, and he evaded public suggestions by King that the two meet upon the latter's release from jail to discuss his experiences in Alabama. In this the president followed the counsel of presidential aide Lee White, who reminded Johnson that "You've gone that 'extra mile' with him quite a few times" already.[149] Indeed, King's announcement of a desire to meet infuriated the president as a manifestation of undue pressure. White later remarked of this incident, "No President, especially a very proud and vain one, wants to have some son of a bitch telling him who he's going to see. It took a little kind of skillful working with him to make sure that he, the President, didn't say anything and kept his own temper in check."[150] Public pressures prevailed, however, and King did see the president. Johnson instructed King that he intended that something be done about denial of the suffrage during his term, and he indicated confidentially that legislation might be forthcoming soon. King, however, sensing that the president's commitment to a strong, immediate bill was lukewarm—and recognizing that public outrage was needed once again to force support by other policy makers in Washington—returned to Selma to help manufacture an overwhelming pressure for voting rights reform.[151] Once again they would have to provoke the president's nation-keeping functions to their advantage.

The president's resolve was ultimately steeled when the eyes of the world turned to televised scenes of police brutality hauntingly reminiscent of the pictures that emerged from Birmingham a year before. Five hundred civil rights demonstrators, intending to march from Selma to Montgomery to petition the state government for redress of their grievances, were met on the outskirts of Selma at the foot of the Edmund Pettus Bridge by law enforcement officials of the state and county. The officers rushed into the marchers, using billy clubs, teargas, and charging horses to send them back into Selma. The melee spread to neighborhood bystanders who launched bottles and rocks into the battling mass. In the end almost eighty people were treated for injuries, with nearly twenty hospitalized.[152]

The press coverage of the attack was electrifying, generating a series of sympathy protests in a number of cities across the nation, including Washington.[153] "The news," writes Stephen Oates, "shook the country as had no other event in the civil rights struggle—not even the dogs and fire hoses in Birmingham." Ironically, ABC Television interrupted its telecast of the movie *Judgment at Nuremberg* to show footage fresh from Selma.[154] Outraged congressmen and movement representatives joined to condemn the attack and to demand that Johnson use his authority once again to meet the challenge at hand.

The president, cognizant of escalating public outrage and congressional restiveness, and of the civil rights movement's intentions to agitate until their demands for suffrage reform were met, effectively found himself with only one viable option. Two days after Selma's "Bloody Sunday," Lyndon Johnson announced through spokesman George Reedy that "The best legal talent in the federal government is engaged in preparing legislation which will secure [the right to vote] for every American. I expect to complete work on my recommendations by this weekend and shall dispatch a special message to Congress as soon as the drafting of the legislation is finished."

Under unrelenting pressure from continuing protests in Selma and from sympathetic members of Congress, President Johnson decided that presidentially backed legislation was again essential, including a powerful provision for federal registrars to intervene in counties where disfranchisement was most evident.[155] This was a turn of events that almost nobody had expected of Johnson in early 1965.[156] "As King had hoped, events in Selma— and the wide-scale outrage they had ignited—had convinced Johnson that he should draft a stronger voting bill than his administration had been contemplating, and had aroused moderate and progressive members of both parties in Congress, thus assuring Johnson of the support he needed to get the measure enacted."[157]

In a news conference announcing his decision to produce voting legislation, the president openly addressed the importance of what had transpired on the previous weekend.[158] "What happened in Selma was an American tragedy. The blows that were received, the blood that was shed, the life of the good man that was lost, must strengthen the determination of each of us to bring full and exact justice to all of our people."[159]

The president's most remarkable comments, however, came in his appearance before a joint session of Congress, convened on March 15, 1965, to introduce his voting rights package. Johnson called Selma a "turning point in man's unending search for freedom," a town whose name he proclaimed synonymous with Lexington and Concord and Appomattox. He asserted forcefully the justness of the grievances raised in Selma. "Many of the issues of civil rights are very complex and most difficult. But about this there can and should be no argument. There is no reason which can excuse the denial of that right [to vote]. There is no duty which weighs more heavily on us than the duty we have to ensure that right."[160]

Johnson then placed the current struggle in historic context, asserting as undeniable truths conclusions he had refused to embrace mere weeks before.

> We cannot, we must not refuse to protect the right of every American to vote in every election that he may desire to participate in. And we ought not, we must not wait another eight months before we get a bill. We have already waited a hundred years and more and the time for waiting is gone. . . .
>
> Even if we pass this bill, the battle will not be over. What happened in Selma is part of a far larger movement which reaches into every section and state of America. It is the effort of American Negroes to secure for themselves the full blessings of American life.
>
> Their cause must be our cause too. Because it is not just Negroes, but really all of us, who must overcome the crippling legacy of bigotry and injustice.

"And," the president then proclaimed, astounding King and others who had helped make the phrase the movement's mantra, "we shall overcome."[161]

Perhaps the apogee of Johnson's address was the extraordinary praise offered those who had effectively brought him, and the nation, to this pass.

> The real hero of this struggle is the American Negro. His actions and protests, his courage to risk safety and even to risk his life have awakened the conscience of this nation. His demonstrations have been designed to call attention to injustice, designed to provoke change, designed to stir reform. He has called upon us to make good the promise of America. And who among us can say that we would have made the same progress were it not for his persistent bravery, and his faith in American democracy.

Those whom the Constitution had pronounced three-fifths human—those who had provoked a recalibration of the president's conception of his responsibilities to the American people—had been elevated by dint of their own unrelenting labors of two centuries' time to the status of model citizen. Less than four months later, under Johnson's direction, the voting rights act passed—the second Reconstruction became a reality.

CHAPTER 8

The Presidency, Leadership, and the Struggle for Racial Equality

"The past," wrote William Faulkner, "is never dead. It's not even past."[1] Although the American polity is now more than thirty years beyond a protracted era of the politics of racial inequality, every contemporary president confronts the reality that Faulkner proclaimed. The past is not dead. It's not even past.

One of the central subtexts of this book has been that Americans' conceptions of the contemporary presidency are powerfully influenced by their perceptions of the institution's history. The expectations developed and standards of judgment employed about the office are commonly shaped by memories—personal and received—of those who have served before. Thus, presidential history is the stuff of which the culture constructs an organic job description for each incumbent, suggesting that the hand of the past is not nearly so dead as some might believe—and as some presidents might hope.

Presidents routinely are measured by the successes of their predecessors, perhaps nowhere more so than on the question of black-white relations. When Bill Clinton, for example, decided to withdraw his nomination of University of Pennsylvania Law Professor Lani Guinier to head the Justice Department's Civil Rights Division, a *Washington Post* columnist responded with these words: "If Bill Clinton had been president during the Civil War, blacks would still be in slavery. I'm not saying that the president is a racist. But clearly he lacks the strength of character and conviction that Abraham Lincoln had to stand up against opposition." In a later essay for the *New York Review of Books*, historian John Higham suggested inadequacies among all modern incumbents, citing as exemplary "Harry Truman's willingness to gamble his presidency in 1948 on the possibility that new black voters in a few northern states could (as they did) save him from a racist backlash in the impending election." By these characterizations, had the American people serving today presidents of Lincoln's "strength of character and conviction" or Truman's "willingness to gamble his presidency," the state of American race relations would be considerably more felicitous.[2]

The standards underlying these critiques are, as Richard Neustadt observed, a recipe for disappointment and failure. When the extraordinary realities of the institution's past get transformed into routine expectations, the president cannot, claims Neustadt, "be as small as he might like."[3] The job description will not permit it. Neustadt noted, for example, that the unusual activism of Theodore Roosevelt in the great coal strike of 1902 and Franklin Roosevelt in the Great Depression leaves little room for their successors to avoid economic intervention that was routinely avoided before.

Yet it is not alone the realities of presidents past that raises the bar of popular expectations. Today's presidents are also measured against the unreal, the mythic penumbras that seem to emanate from real historic accomplishments like auras in a Renaissance painting. The sum of the historical burdens weighing on modern presidents, then, is even more ponderous than Neustadt acknowledged.

Lincoln's example is perhaps the ideal case in point.[4] Anyone familiar with the essential elements of Lincoln's presidency finds ample evidence of an extraordinary figure exercising exceptional powers in office. He was, in the considered judgment of Clinton Rossiter, a "constitutional dictator."[5] Yet even that enlarged reality is merely a starting point in the popular culture, as it simply inclines Americans to exaggeration, to the construction of popular myths that are anything but benign. The accomplishments of an extraordinary president in an extraordinary time set virtually impossible standards for the "normal" president in "normal" times to meet. These standards move completely beyond the reach of mere mortals when they are subjected to the embellishment of popular memory.

Such myths are often highly resistant to contrary evidence. After Bill Clinton was attacked in the *Washington Post* for being no Lincoln (or at least no Lincoln of the writer's memory), one thoughtful reader penned a letter to the editor charging the columnist with "falling victim to a common misconception regarding" the sixteenth president, that he took the liberation of the slaves to be a wartime goal prior in importance to salvaging the Union. That letter, in turn, drew an indignant reply from another *Post* reader, who bristled at the inference that Lincoln did not deserve the designation "Great Emancipator." This correspondent, obviously well-versed in Civil War history, cited a variety of relevant details to further his argument. He sought to seal his case, however, by asking this simply styled question: "If Lincoln did not free the slaves, who did?"[6]

Inherent in this simple, rhetorical question is a veritable rat's nest of assumptions and inferences about the nature of cause-and-effect in American politics. The most fundamental assumption is that some *one* must be credited with the execution of a process so vast in scope that Charles and Mary Beard once termed it "the most stupendous act of sequestration in the history of Anglo-Saxon jurisprudence."[7] That such an assumption would find expression on one of the nation's most thoughtful editorial pages, however, is unsurprising, because the practice of attributing complex behavior to single individuals is such a common one. Wrote David B. Truman:

> The personification of events is a kind of shorthand convenient in everyday speech and, like supernatural explanations of natural phenomena, has a comforting simplicity. Explanations that take into account multiple causes, including group affiliations, are difficult. The "explanation" of a national complex like the Soviet Union wholly in terms of a Stalin or the "description" of the intricacies of the American government entirely in terms of a Roosevelt is quick and easy.

Thus, there is ever a tendency—at least, Truman claims, in liberal societies such as the United States—to "view . . . the isolated and independent individual as the 'cause' of complicated human events."[8]

Some sociologists have taken note of this inclination, and have concluded that much of what is regularly called *leadership* routinely derives from such attributions of causation. These students usually concede that, at the core, some concrete human activity may exist that can be legitimately distinguished as leadership, but they argue that frequently "leadership . . . is a residual category to which personal responsibility is assigned for events which would otherwise be unexplainable because they are, in fact, merely the point of focus in a stream of interacting and complex social forces."[9] In other words, observers may attribute something they call *leadership* to certain figures precisely because they seek a simple, quick-and-easy answer to our correspondent's question: "*Who* did?"

To the sociologists' general design of attribution theory, then, I will offer a single refinement, one which David Truman's passage coincidentally confirms: an enduring element of American political culture is the attribution of such leadership to the person of the president. Again, this does not mean that we cannot isolate a particular set of behaviors distinguishable as "presidential leadership." It merely means that quite commonly the use of the term goes insufficiently examined for precision, and that the term itself often substitutes for a host of complexities characterizing the practice of American politics.

Attribution of leadership to the presidency is a quite common phenomenon. Returning to our *Post* correspondent, we find that he does not simply suggest that a single individual emancipated the slaves, he identifies for us the responsible party: President Lincoln. However, not even scholars are immune from occasional reliance on this shorthand. In a 1991 interview, for example, eminent historian Stephen Ambrose explained to a *Washington Times* reporter that "Great presidents on the domestic side are measured by some lasting achievement that affects everyone's life, such as Teddy Roosevelt and conservation, Woodrow Wilson and the Federal Reserve System, Franklin Roosevelt and Social Security, Dwight Eisenhower and the interstate highway system, and Lyndon Johnson and Medicaid."[10] Ambrose undoubtedly knows that he oversimplifies in associating each of these domestic advances with the efforts of presidents alone, but his remarks are at once commentary on and participation in a tendency in American political culture toward ascribing political causation to presidents, and thus avoiding the complexities associated with reconciling the interaction of multiple actors in bringing public policy to fruition.

As a further refinement of this theory, I wish to reiterate here a claim made in my opening chapter, and underlying the entirety of this book: there is a strong cultural inclination to attribute to the presidency disproportionate credit for the nation's successful movement toward racial equality. This bias is commonly registered in two ways.

First, presidential contributions toward the processes of black equality have tended to be overstated. Claims for Lincoln's "strength of character and conviction . . . to stand up against opposition" on the slavery question ignore the pre-Emancipator who gladly would have preserved slavery to restore the Union. And Truman's exemplary electoral gamble resulted from a colossal miscalculation that, once recognized, occasioned an uncharacteristic set of presidential retreats.

Second, presidential contributions to the process of suppressing movements for racial equality have tended to go understated. Tellingly, this is one area where attribution tends *not* to take place. Accordingly, the quick-and-easy cultural portrait of the presidency on race has been routinely distorted to emphasize the role as champion of meaningful and difficult change.

I should note again that scholars have not been especially useful in countering the weight of popular misconceptions.[11] Matthew Holden Jr. properly observes in this regard, "Presidents are not 'natural' supporters of civil rights in the sense of supporting the interests and claims of African Americans," adding that "This would not be a necessary or interesting observation, except that for a certain period political scientists confused the contemporary facts with an underlying necessity."[12] To varying degrees Holden's assessment accurately characterizes the three most prominent works of political science on the presidency and civil rights.[13]

Perhaps because of his proximity to the era during which the civil rights issue was successfully kept off the federal agenda, Richard P. Longaker, in his *The Presidency and Individual Liberties* (1961), comes closest to acknowledging the absence of support for racial advance found in the White House during long stretches of American history. He mainly addresses the tools available to modern presidents for advancing and protecting civil liberties, broadly defined, but he does make a point early in his work of noting that the use of those tools on behalf of African Americans was only a recent phenomenon.[14]

Longaker's attentiveness to the time-bound character of such studies is not a feature of two other works. Ruth P. Morgan's *The President and Civil Rights: Policy-Making by Executive Order* (1970) focuses on the issuance of executive orders beginning with Franklin Roosevelt's administration. Steven A. Shull's *The President and Civil Rights Policy: Leadership and Change* (1989), examines the range of action-taking on the question of civil rights, focusing on the institution since 1953. While both Shull and Morgan address the political pressures operating on those presidents they examine, their projects were not designed to account for the place of the presidency over a longer scope of political time. Indeed, Shull claims that "Civil rights . . . received only minimal attention from presidents before Harry Truman." [15] In the most strictly construed sense Shull is generally correct, but his statement contributes to a misperception that those presidents before Truman who did not work in favor of civil rights merely assumed a benign posture on a benign issue. The evidence indicates otherwise.

Resource Mobilization and Presidential Behavior

The narrative produced in the text of this work details the range of specific actions American presidents have taken to manipulate movements for and against racial equality. The full extent of such manipulation will more clearly emerge by examining the evidence in a summary form, using a nonchronological, analytic tool.

Since the mid-1960s, political scientists and sociologists studying social movements have concentrated on the availability and mobilization of *resources* to explain the emergence and relative strength of various movements. Much of the work of these scholars has paralleled developments in interest group theory, and more generally in the study of political mobilization.[16] One school of thought in social movement studies, ascendant since the mid-1970s, has been resource mobilization (RM) theory, which focuses on the following kinds of questions: "where are the resources available for the movement, how are they organized, how does the state facilitate or impede mobilization, and what are the outcomes."[17] Although my general purpose here—according to these terms—has been to describe in a narrative fashion how one institution of the state has facilitated or impeded political mobilization for racial equality, the RM construction suggests a further refinement: an examination of presidential behavior on a resource-by-resource basis. In other words, if a central problem for those attempting to press for greater racial equality has been the identification, assembly, and mobilization of resources, then the relationship of the presidency to these movements can be analyzed in relation to that central problem. That analysis reveals in brief how thoroughgoing and intrusive presidential efforts to neutralize movement activity have been.[18]

Five general resource categories will be discussed here: leadership; membership; communications; monetary and material resources; and institutional allies.[19]

Leadership Resources

Perhaps the most persistent application of presidential power to manipulate activism for racial equality has come in relation to leadership resources. No activity in the presidential-movement relationship has been as prevalent over time as attempts to channel protest through management of the movement's leading elites.[20] Virtually no leading figure in the effort to mobilize mass opinion for racial equality has been immune from White House attempts to stop or to moderate collective action through selective use of political carrots and sticks. Cursory reflection finds Lincoln using the moral authority of his office in attempting to shame prominent black ministers into using their influence to initiate mass black colonization; Cleveland using his rhetorical and symbolic powers to channel support to Booker T. Washington; Wilson sanctioning the political application of federal police powers against Marcus Garvey; Franklin Roosevelt showing the charms of the White House to A. Philip Randolph to help stave off an impending march on Washington; the shunning and subsequent embracing by John Kennedy of Martin Luther King Jr. as the perception of King went from radical to moderate in relation to the rise of student insurgency; and Robert Kennedy promising draft deferments for SNCC leaders who ceased demonstrating and moved into voter registration projects. Further, all of the multiple exercises in the practice of selective preferment detailed in the foregoing chronological narrative serve as evidence of the effort to manipulate mass leaders.

Gary T. Marx raises two possibilities for why governmental elites typically focus on movement leaders. First, they are captive to an "undue reliance on an agitator theory of social movements: leaders and organizers, not social conditions, are seen as the key to movement unrest"; second, they have "an inability . . . to do much else: leaders offer tangible specific targets for intervention in a way that mass sympathizers (many of whom are unknown to the authorities) or broad social conditions do not."[21]

It is difficult to find evidence corroborating Marx's first point, because it addresses elements of perception and psychology on which few presidents have directly commented. However, American presidents have certainly *acted* as though they considered leaders to be an essential resource in the emergence and persistence of racial unrest. It is not necessary to assert that presidents have personified movements in certain key leaders (or have relied "on an agitator theory of social movements") to make a case that presidents have often recognized the considerable influence key individuals can have in the life of a movement. Accordingly, although movements may not have been perceived as strictly the product of organizers, organizers have been viewed as essential components of keeping movements going.

The second of Marx's points—based on the evidence of this study—is at once correct and incorrect in its construction. He errs in claiming that agents of the government—presumably including the president—have found few other ways to attack the problems of movement agitation; the discussion below on presidential efforts in relation to four other resource categories will amply illustrate this point. But Marx properly—even too weakly—asserts that leaders are "tangible specific targets for intervention" in the affairs of a movement. Presidents have often found movement leaders to be a smooth, if sometimes unreliable, handle on a host of nettlesome problems associated with collective action.[22] Presidents thus have tended to work on and with movement leaders from a recognition that such work offered the prospect of reverberating throughout the movement in a way no other single possibility afforded. By targeting leaders, presidents have had the opportunity to affect (and possibly to neutralize) not just a crucial resource in and of itself, but also to affect (and possibly to neutralize) secondarily each of the other major resources on which these movements relied.

A final point should be added to the two Marx offers. Presidential involvement with movement leaders also has been so prevalent because that interaction has frequently been perceived by movement leaders as useful for their own purposes. In the routine, enduring struggle among movement elites for preeminence as representatives of the cause, a presidential audience, or a continuing relationship with key actors in the executive branch, can be a powerful signal of recognition. The costs associated with that affiliation—increased susceptibility to capture or co-optation—are, at the stage where recognition is important, less prominent than the immediate, concrete advantage gained over other movement actors for public supremacy.[23] Few recognize at first the thorns in the Rose Garden.

Membership Resources

Just as they have manipulated movements' leadership resources, American presidents have also manipulated movements, or potential movements, in ways directly related to membership resources: their size, their unity of purpose, and their deployment. In effect, they have tried to deprive organizers of the aura of political efficacy that would motivate large numbers of potential sympathizers to rally to the cause.[24]

Presidents have acted as though they intuitively recognized the dynamic described by E. E. Schattschneider in his discussion of the contagiousness of conflict. Schattschneider directed the attention of those who would understand the unfolding of political conflict not to the roster of existing combatants, but to those on the immediate periphery who might be drawn into the fray. "[T]he outcome of every conflict," he wrote, "is determined by the *extent* to which the audience becomes involved in it. That is, the outcome of all conflict is determined by the *scope* of its contagion."[25] Weak combatants, in recognition of their relatively disadvantaged station under the status quo, thus have strong incentives to recruit additional combatants, as well as sympathizers among the larger class of noncombatants. Conversely, the stronger party, prevailing in the original arena, has every incentive to foil efforts by the weaker to mobilize more supporters. In the terms of this model, then, the presidency has typically been used as an instrument to thwart attempts by racial activists to change favorably this environment of conflict.

To accomplish this, presidents have often taken action to tip the cost-benefit calculations of potential movement participants against joining in the agitation. Presidents have worked to levy additional costs on those taking part in movement agitation, including Andrew Jackson's charge to Postmaster General Amos Kendall to publicize the names of those in the South who consented to receive abolitionist literature, so that they could be made to pay for their transgressions "with their lives."[26] Also, presidents have worked in a direct fashion to limit the rewards of movement activity. In this category we find Martin Van Buren's inaugural pledge that he would veto any legislation emerging from Congress on the question of slavery, a pledge intended to cut the Gordian knot of congressional warfare over gag rules and thus to subvert the then-preferred channel of activity for multitudes of abolitionist organizers.

The overall effect of such presidential interventions has been to undermine the sense of effectiveness organizers generally rely on to build their followings. In his groundbreaking work on *Collective Action and the Civil Rights Movement*, Dennis Chong asserts that the incentive structures of movement participation falter when participants and prospective participants judge the movement's labors as merely quixotic. Chong writes, "When collective action is widely regarded as futile, or as an ineffectual symbolic protest at best, these social and psychological incentives [to join in protest] vanish." He later adds about the civil rights movement, "For many blacks, the key word was involvement, but a particular involvement *in an enterprise that gave them a feeling of efficacy or accomplishment*" [emphasis added]. To underscore his point, Chong borrows these words from Brian Barry:

> Whatever the reason why a person may attach himself to a cause, more enthusiasm for its pursuit is likely to be elicited if it looks as if it has a chance of succeeding than if it appears to be a forlorn hope. Nobody likes to feel that he is wasting his time, and that feeling may be induced by contributing to a campaign which never looks as if it has a chance.[27]

Presidential efforts to manipulate the membership resources available to those pursuing racial equality emerged principally from an overall interest, then, in establishing a sense of futility among prospective participants.

Thus far I have discussed only one side of Schattschneider's contagiousness-of-conflict equation. However, presidents have not only acted to limit the appeal of racial activists among the relevant "bystanders," they have also worked to ally those "bystanders" with forces opposing change in race relations.

Perhaps the most literal exercise of this manipulated enlargement of conflict came with the presidentially promoted westward territorial expansion of the mid-nineteenth century. Although a complex web of motivations lay behind that expansionism, a central attraction of Texas, whose acquisition sparked much of what followed, was its political and economic potential as an "empire for slavery."[28] The admission into the Union of up to four states from the area of Texas itself promised to fortify proslavery forces in the nation as a whole, and, more importantly, to reassert southern dominance in the upper chamber of Congress, a dominance that was felt by southerners to be weakened by the gradual accrual of free states in what we now call the Midwest.[29] The dynamic of westward expansion, and presidential efforts both to exploit it and to avoid being crushed by it, became extremely complicated into the 1840s and 1850s—creating for presidents of the era a tale akin to that of the Sorcerer's Apprentice (i.e., a situation more to be managed than exploited). But it is well established that executive branch efforts to initiate southwestern expansion derived substantially from a concern with protecting southern slave interests. Again, this constituted a manipulation of membership resources for purposes of limiting the influence of antislavery organizers.

Finally, since, as Jeffrey K. Tulis contends, presidential rhetoric has increasingly placed presidents in a direct relationship with the American people, it makes sense to deal with rhetorical practices too under the rubric of membership or "bystander" manipulation.[30] Again, here, presidential rhetoric has been employed to diminish the efficacy of those mobilizing for racial equality.

In some instances, presidents have directly addressed the desirability of keeping racial agitation subdued. For example, Andrew Jackson both formally in his messages to Congress, and informally through published correspondence with his postmaster general, suggested that abolitionist activism constituted a capital offense. All sides to the controversy knew where the president stood on the issue, based on his own words. Later, we find Grover

Cleveland issuing public pronouncements praising the work of Booker T. Washington, in an overt effort to channel black America into adopting Washington's accommodationist posture.

However, the vast majority of presidential remarks relevant to racial equality have been indirect in nature. In part, this may be because of the doctrinal conventions Tulis asserts, according to which presidents before the turn of the nineteenth century largely felt confined by the formalisms of the office to avoid popular rhetoric. But general moderation in commentary prevailed long after the rhetorical practices of Woodrow Wilson—the seminal figure for Tulis in the emergence of today's "rhetorical presidency"—had become commonplace. There are very few instances in which post-Wilsonian presidents actively used the "bully pulpit" either to attack racial activism or explicitly to buttress the effort to thwart movements for racial equality. Indeed, in comparison to presidential efforts in a host of other areas, the character of presidential rhetoric on race has been remarkably moderate. How can this be explained? There are three possibilities.

First, because the impact of race on American political development has been so extensive, much presidential commentary on racial matters has been embedded in overt discussions of other topics, such as federalism, states' rights, and "law and order." Consequently, presidential efforts to subdue movements for racial equality have often taken the form of remarks on subjects other than race itself.[31]

Second, the issue of race creates special rhetorical problems for presidents. The notion of a "bully pulpit" is fraught with moralistic undertones, which effectively have entrapped presidents in a dilemma when it came to dealing with black America. Only a minority of American whites during the time-frame of my study ever found anything especially uplifting in the inferior status African Americans held in American society, or in the supremacy law and custom granted whites; even among many southern slaveholders much of the time, slavery was viewed as a necessary evil, not a positive good. It is unsurprising, then, that presidents, wishing to fulfill their obligations upholding through rhetoric the American creed, might avoid a subject that undermined the moral high ground of the nation's civil religion, and invoked feelings, at best, of strained ambivalence. Presidential circumvention of the topic thus mirrored the Constitution's own circumlocution in reference to the word "slavery."

Third, and finally, for much of the period under examination here presidents spoke moderately on the issue of race while simultaneously sanctioning executive action hostile to movement activity. In effect, rhetorical embrace of equality commonly was among the earliest concessions made to racial activists. The typical refusal to match policy with rhetoric suggests that, as the activists often claimed, "talk is cheap." As a matter of political cost-benefit analysis, that would seem to have been the case. Rhetorical concessions were probably the least costly presidential action that could have been taken, since astute presidential partisans hostile to equality often understood a president's purely political motives for speaking out, and since the overall policy direction of each administration seldom equalled its more-advanced rhetoric. Consequently, although words may be an important presidential tool in mobilizing or demobilizing certain interested publics on an issue, the specific circumstances surrounding race in America renders rhetoric a less useful datum about executive behavior than we might otherwise expect, at least in isolation.[32]

Indeed, the most profound influence of presidential rhetoric on the dynamic of membership resources among those fighting for and against racial equality came in an oblique, largely unintentional, fashion. In the main, such rhetoric was intended to satisfy momentarily the demands of racial activists; in the end it simply generated greater demands. Sociologist Doug McAdam convincingly asserts that even minor cues in the political environment that protest activity has reaped some unprecedented benefit—such as a rhetorical concession from the White House—can generate that sense of political efficacy essential to motivating marginal participants to join. As Frances Fox Piven and Richard A. Cloward have written, movements become energized when "there is a new sense of efficacy, [when] people who ordinarily consider themselves helpless come to believe that they have some capacity to alter their lot."[33] Presidential statements intended either as momentary diversions or as cloaks for executive malevolence elsewhere thus tended to create more problems than they resolved for the White House. But the trade-off was a classic one of certain short-term gains for potential long-term losses.

Communication Resources

One of the central problems of political mobilization is the dissemination of information essential to organizing would-be participants and to coordinating mass activity—the deployment of communications resources. Presidential efforts to manipulate the emergence of movements for racial equality, then, have often focused on thwarting effective communications, thus impairing the ability of movement sympathizers to organize.

Again Andrew Jackson's posture in the mails controversy serves as an ideal case in point. Early abolitionists had decided that their best avenue for pursuing emancipation came in communicating directly with southern slaveholders, in an effort to convince them of the sinfulness of their practices. Jackson, taking his cues from southern postmasters and from his postmaster general, adopted policies effectively blockading that avenue.[34] His successors through Lincoln followed suit. In a similar vein, much mob activity against abolitionism in the North and West took the form of destruction of antislavery literature and printing presses. Much of the destroyed material had already been entrusted to the United States government through the postal service, yet antebellum presidents did not assert their authority to protect materials deemed "incendiary."

Official publications of African-American organizations were frequently subjected to political intelligence oversight by such agencies as the FBI. On occasions, with presidential sanction, these publications were sabotaged in order to inhibit their effectiveness within the movement community.

Verbal communication has also been manipulated with White House approval or direction. The 1963 March on Washington was very closely monitored by White House staffers, who were given physical control over the loudspeaker system so that any unauthorized criticisms of President Kennedy could be silenced. The White House also significantly edited the speech given by SNCC representative John Lewis, having removed language deemed overly critical of the administration's work on civil rights.

Moreover, White House-approved wiretaps of the telephones of movement leaders in the early 1960s had the effect both of providing intelligence to the administration on movement strategy and of severely intruding on the freedom of communication organizers needed to direct protest activity. This recognized intrusion compromised the efficiency of the movement in a number of ways, requiring extraordinary efforts to locate secure telephone lines, compelling cryptic or vague telephone communications among activists (and thus increasing the risk of miscommunication), and necessitating networks of clandestine meetings in obscure locations for purposes of planning movement activity. All of this seriously undermined the efficacy of an operation that already had substantial operating inefficiencies by its very nature.

Finally, presidents have sanctioned efforts to use mainstream communications avenues—the print and television media—to undermine movement operations. For example, the Tyler administration went to extraordinary lengths to produce a public relations campaign—using mass-produced pamphlets—intended to win support for the annexation of Texas. Also, when Martin Luther King Jr. moved too slowly to suit the White House in distancing himself from alleged-Communist Jack O'Dell, Robert Kennedy called in a friendly reporter and gave him confidential information on O'Dell's background, so as to generate a story in the southern press that would force King's hand. This kind of specific manipulation of the media should be considered simply one component of overall administration-press relations, the very nature of which has been to propagate the president's own line of thinking. Press operations exist to manipulate the interpretation of media instruments on the entire range of issues on which a president is called to act. The question of race has been no exception.

Monetary and Material Resources

Although the ratio of financial resources to participants in social movements is typically quite low—because of the large number of volunteers involved—those who organize such collective action do need monetary and material resources for logistical purposes.[35] An organizer does not need to pay a volunteer, but she may need to write or telephone him, transport him, feed him, and perhaps provide him medical attention or bail. Money is also needed for payrolls to have organizers at work full time.

Some presidents have consented to their office's involvement in trying to restrain the financial capabilities of movements for racial equality, or at least to steer funds in relatively unthreatening directions. Although a number of alternatives were explored for undermining Marcus Garvey, the Justice Department in the Harding administration eventually pursued a tax case against Garvey, threatening his movement's financial base. During that same general era, much praise was directed at the labors of Booker T. Washington in Tuskegee, with attention given to helping him locate funding sources to make vocational educational a preferred channel for black progress.

During the 1960s, a number of efforts were undertaken by successive administrations to manipulate the financial needs of the civil rights movement. The most prominent of these was the Voter Education Project, which essentially was contrived and set in motion by the Kennedy administration to channel black activism into voter registration. Robert Kennedy's work to get funding commitments from private foundations for the VEP, and Kennedy's intervention with the director of the Internal Revenue Service to get the Project tax-exempt status, should be noted here. As these efforts were proceeding, the FBI was also involved in attempting—apparently with some measure of success—to cut off certain independent funding sources for the Southern Christian Leadership Conference.[36]

Institutional Allies

Finally, one of the most important resources organizers of political outsiders can have is friends on the inside, or institutional allies. Although my focus in this study has been on the institution of the presidency, racial organizers have also worked to win allies within state governments and the nation's legislative and judicial branches. Cognizant of the important part such friends can play in channeling movement activity, presidents have worked—often with a rare degree of assertiveness—to limit movement influence in those branches. Three particular episodes illustrate the point.

Martin Van Buren's decision to issue a preemptive veto pledge in his inaugural address was almost unprecedented. During that era, the presidential veto was widely deemed an acceptable instrument *only* in instances where the president believed a measure before him was clearly unconstitutional. The veto was not usually to be used to settle political disputes. Van Buren's message to the nation raised no such questions of constitutionality on the issue of slavery within the District of Columbia. He thus acted contrary to traditional practices in the use of the veto, in an attempt to restrict the advances abolitionists were threatening to make in the United States Congress.[37]

Second, James Buchanan made extraordinary uses of his proximity to the membership of the Supreme Court to lobby vigorously for a broad, definitive ruling supporting slavery in the case of *Dred Scott v. Sandford*. Evidence suggests that Buchanan's violation of the principles of separation inherent in the Constitution and in that era's political culture was instrumental in the Taney Court's decision to take a judicial sledgehammer to the legislative compromises of preceding decades.[38]

Third, in 1954 Dwight Eisenhower privately lobbied Chief Justice Earl Warren on behalf of the southern interests in *Brown v. Board of Education*, hosting a dinner with Warren and the main lawyer for the southern states in the case. That Eisenhower failed should not detract from the fact that he attempted to use the powers of persuasion at his disposal to deny civil rights activists an important ally in the Supreme Court of the United States. The pressure that Court later placed on Eisenhower to fulfill his pledged obligation to defend the Constitution (as they defined it) testifies to the stakes at risk when the president sought back channels to subvert the appeals of black America.

The foregoing survey is intended to make one basic point: presidents of the United States, during the long train of events in American history leading to the two major episodes of African-American liberation discussed here, have engaged in a wide variety of activities intended to defer movement toward racial equality. Not even those few who presided over what Lincoln called "a new birth of freedom" completed their tenure without at a minimum trying to slow the processes of change set into motion by activists and movements.

The Suppressive-to-Supportive Shift

Yet it is also true that some presidents were indispensable in translating the aspirations of black America into reality. If the historic predisposition in the presidency appears to be toward suppressing agents for change, what accounts for the eventual thrust toward racial equality? How do we explain the shift from a presidential posture essentially suppressive in nature to one predominantly—or at least significantly—supportive?

In part, the answer is that the incentive structures governing presidential behavior changed, because of the success of racial activists and movements in altering the nation's political environment. These changes were initially registered in quite ordinary ways, sufficient to encourage modest accommodation by presidents, but not the constitutional transformations racial activists sought. Two areas of such environmental change merit special notice.

The Electoral Environment

First, in both cases examined in this study, the presidential impulse toward accommodation was preceded by, or accompanied by, a transformation in the president's *electoral environment*. Lincoln's own election represented the culmination of such a shift, in that it brought into the presidency for the very first time an individual who had condemned the practice of slavery and who sought to stop its extension. In effect that electoral environment had become relatively inhospitable for candidates openly committed to the policy paths of the past. The impact of this shift in the electoral balance of power was so significant that it precipitated a rush to secession in the South. That electoral shift created prospects for a sea-change in presidential behavior by elevating to the presidency one whose fundamental sympathies were with the enslaved.

A similar shift occurred in relation to the latter struggle for equal civil rights. Because of the effects of the Great Migration on presidential electoral politics, presidents beginning with Franklin Roosevelt felt pressured to alter established relations with black America, to grant concessions so as to prevent the alienation of an increasingly important electoral constituency.[39]

Although a significant outward migration from the South had begun decades earlier, that migration dramatically escalated during the New Deal years as African Americans heeded the push of Jim Crow in the South and the pull of economic opportunity in the factories of the North and West. Net black out-migration from the South nearly quadrupled from the 1930s to the 1940s.[40] Although there might have been efforts to retard this migration— that was done during World War I by southern legislatures intent on preserving their states' economic institutions—the national government sought after the attack on Pearl Harbor to exploit efficiently every resource available in the fight against fascism abroad. Under cover of national preoccupation with winning the war, then, African Americans effectively staged a coup of historic proportions, enfranchising themselves by moving to those industrial centers where the nation needed their labor.[41]

This massive relocation, occasioned by the requirements of war, set in motion an immense change in the character of racial politics in the United States. Doug McAdam writes, "[T]he black migration was not so much a general exodus from the South as a selective move from those areas where the political participation of blacks was most severely limited." Further, sociological studies reveal that "87 percent of the total number of black immigrants from the South in the 1910–60 period settled in seven key northern (or western) states: New York, New Jersey, Pennsylvania, Ohio, California, Illinois, and Michigan"—states that by 1960 accounted for 197 electoral votes of the 269 needed for election.[42] The reversal of course in the presidency was not as precipitous in the twentieth century as in the nineteenth, but an essentially irreversible movement toward increasing sponsorship of civil rights was set into motion by this migration, ending a long era of near-total reliance on strategies of suppression.

Although a complete transformation in presidential action did not occur until three decades later, every president after Roosevelt followed his example in moderating suppressive behavior with modest accommodation, precisely because the changed character of presidential electoral politics demanded as much. Complete inattention to civil rights—or an unmitigated commitment to manipulating and suppressing black activism—would have been politically suicidal in that transformed environment. Election—or reelection—depended on keeping a black constituency (and its white patrons) mollified.

The Institutional Environment

A second change in the political calculus of the presidency came in the president's institutional environment, the milieu of separated institutions sharing power. Other institutions, for varied reasons, were converted to the cause of racial equality before the executive, and subsequently they began making demands on presidents to follow them.[43] In Lincoln's case, he was confronted throughout the early years of the Civil War with a radicalized Congress pushing him to go further toward emancipation than he believed otherwise advisable. In the second instance, presidents routinely found themselves under pressure from the United States judiciary to take more advanced positions on race than they thought wise. Eisenhower's battle with the courts over school desegregation is the ideal case in point.

Presidents under these circumstances increasingly found themselves in an institutional environment that encouraged them to make concessions to racial activists; were they to do so, they would not be alone, indeed they would be acting according to the legal and constitutional dictates of the office. So said Congress or the courts. Other institutions could not, however, compel unwilling presidents to lead the nation in a broad attack on racial inequality.

These two major shifts in the presidency's political calculus were necessary but not sufficient conditions to move presidents to embrace fully the transformational aims of the movements they confronted. The presidential electoral environment remained dominated by majorities unwilling to brook the minority's claims to equal standing, and the presidential institution remained largely insulated from those specific pressures that had converted Congress to abolition and the Supreme Court to equal civil rights.

The result was an institution moved to make marginal concessions at the expense of broader change, so as to balance competing pressures. It was not, however, until the president's perception of the institution's nation-maintaining role had been transformed that the presidency was converted to an instrument of transformational change.

Transformation and Nation-Keeping

In the Introduction, I posited two faces to the nation-keeping role, one oriented toward preserving the nation's fundamental social, economic, and political structures, and the second toward preserving the peace and security of that national whole. Why did presidents operating in a changed electoral and institutional environment—especially those basically sympathetic to the plight of African Americans—*not* throw themselves unreservedly into the effort to bring racial equality to fruition? The key is that their continuing perceptions of their nation-keeping role—gleaned from their continuing observations of the state of American political and cultural life— did not permit it. Their obligation to preserve the inherited constitution of the United States overwhelmed any competing claims to change.

Fundamentally, these presidents harbored enduring fears that more advanced change on the emotionally charged issue of race would endanger the security of the nation they were pledged to defend.[44] Despite their personal sympathies, whether latent or manifest, these presidents recognized the logic behind Andrew Jackson's retort to a British visitor in 1835, who suggested that the president advocate emancipation as a crowning achievement to his "great career."

> The President was standing with his back to the fire when I said this. He burst out laughing and addressing his guests on either side, said, "This gentleman has just come from the West Indies, where the British have been emancipating their slaves. He recommends me to make myself famous by following their example. Come here Donelson" (turning round to his private secretary), "put the poker in the fire, bring in a barrel of gunpowder, and when I am placed on it give the red poker to the Doctor, and he shall make me famous in the twinkling of an eye."[45]

Fame of that nature acted as an insurmountable deterrent to more advanced action by a nation-keeping institution.

The ultimate conversion of the presidency into an active agency of civil rights revolution came only when presidents became convinced that greater dangers accompanied preservation than change of the status quo. These presidents reasoned that the nation they had pledged to preserve would remain under a clear and continuing threat *unless and until* they acted to alleviate the grievances of black America. Under these conditions, presidents moved to direct the nation through two constitutional reformations, despite the absence of a clearly defined mandate for radical change. Under these conditions, the dictates of the nation-keeping role produced majority-creating rather than majority-following presidents on the matter of race in America. Armed with powerful arguments about threats to the American experiment, they found it their duty to complete the job of popular conversion movement activists had brought near to fruition but could not finish alone. Internal social structures could be reorganized because they had to be to preserve the nation as a whole. This presidents saw because of their special place in the political order; this presidents were empowered to do because of the nation's reliance on them as a nation-maintaining institution. Presidential leadership was offered to guide the nation through a moment of creative confusion. Presidential leadership was accepted to fill the interstices between a fearful present and a hopeful future, to bridge the narrowed but remaining gap between reality and ideal.

Lincoln moved toward emancipation when the future of the nation itself looked bleak absent that action. He feared continuing restiveness on the domestic front and the Confederacy's possible profit from the ambiguous difference in the northern and southern positions on slavery. An active southern alliance with Britain or France seemed quite possible. Lincoln thus saw as imperative a reversal of course—advocacy of liberation—based on the very rationale he had earlier cited as leading him to reject emancipation: "My paramount object in this struggle *is* to save the Union."[46]

Kennedy and his successor moved toward equal civil rights when it became apparent to them that African Americans intended to provoke disturbances to the nation's domestic tranquillity until their grievances were met, when they recognized that the illegitimacy of the status quo had been effectively exposed by the southern reaction black protesters had already provoked. The claims of justice that had long been made brought favorable presidential action only when the reestablishment of the nation's domestic tranquillity seemed to require it. And once again, the international arena was very much in mind. The Cold War, and the continuing competition in Third World nations for alliances against the spread of communism, placed a premium on the nation's chief diplomat resolving a domestic conflict that poisoned American relations worldwide among people of color.[47] Under these conditions, nation-maintaining presidents sought to embrace sociopolitical change. Indeed, they had, by the time that position was taken, every reason to believe that the enduring peace and security of the nation depended on that step.[48]

That the American people would turn to the presidency as a source of leadership in these instances is unsurprising, as they had already empowered that institution to deal with existing threats to the peace and security of the United States. Presidential leadership of the nation on behalf of racial equality was made possible in these episodes because there arose in the presidency a rare confluence of motive *and* power.

In the 1860s the security needs of the nation not only produced the incentives necessary to get Lincoln to move toward liberation, it also created an uncommon accumulation of resources necessary for him and the nation to pursue the course he had chosen. That exceptional merging of motive and power effectively brought about the termination of slavery in the United States.

In the second instance, the enduring international conflict of the Cold War effectively lengthened the commission of the presidential leadership regime licensed during World War II. The persistence of that regime conditioned the American people to defer to the presidency as the principal source of public problem-solving in the United States, especially on matters of international security. The necessity of having a single national leader in dealing with the turbulence of the Cold War heightened prospects that the president would be looked to as a source for resolving domestic security problems, too. Small wonder that presidents invested by the American people with the power to control a nuclear arsenal capable of destroying the planet would find themselves the focus of unyielding public attention in the struggle to resolve the nation's racial tensions.

Thus, no more than Lincoln could turn away from emancipation, could John Kennedy or Lyndon Johnson avoid major advances on civil rights. They embraced transformational change when they were convinced that, in the fashion of Luther, they could do no other. Certainly each of these presidents had the human freedom to act otherwise, but the pressures for them to do so—pressures that for so long had guided their predecessors to protect the racial status quo—had been re-formed by domestic and international forces such that rational actors saw contrary action as catastrophic. The pressures for them to act, as they felt them, were now overwhelmingly stacked in favor of advancing racial equality. From their special vantage point, this was the way to avert disaster. Accordingly, these second emancipators might well have echoed the words spoken by Lincoln as he reviewed his own course in freeing the slaves: "I claim not to have controlled events but confess plainly that events have controlled me."[49]

Nation-Keeping on Other Questions of Membership

The patterns of nation-keeping behavior presented in this study have not been exclusive, I believe, to the question of black-white relations. A brief examination of evidence from other controversies over membership config-urations in the American polity reveal episodes of presidential activity strik-ingly suggestive of those described here in relation to the issue of race. Thus, the theories developed here seem to have some broader applicability than to the question of race alone. Consider the following cases.

Women's Rights

The initial movement for women's suffrage in America did little to provoke concern among Washington policy makers, as early reform efforts focused on changes in the suffrage qualifications of individual states. However, once the momentum from those Progressive Era undertakings began to mount, gen-erating national repercussions, presidents sought to protect the established order by undermining the growing influence of the suffrage movement.

Theodore Roosevelt mounted his bully pulpit on several occasions to address the perils of women in politics. Ironically, he tied his warnings to the question of race. "As president," observes historian Thomas G. Dyer, Roosevelt frequently "used his position as moral and political leader to . . . exhort women to fulfill a special role as perpetuators of the race, and to encourage them toward even more plenteous reproduction." During a time when many women were striving to move out of domesticity, the president made it clear that he measured "the worth of a female as an American citi-zen by counting her children." Activities outside the home were, in the main, harmful distractions.[50] Roosevelt's concern over the breakdown in the American family—which he believed arose at least partly as a result of women's yearnings for broader horizons—led him to ask Congress for a constitutional amendment in 1906 federalizing all laws of marriage and divorce.[51] He would preserve the integrity of the traditional family unit through use of the federal police power.

William Howard Taft walked a similar path. He consented to address a Washington meeting of the National American Woman Suffrage Association, only to tell that gathering that most women were uninterested in voting, and that only those of a "less desirable class" were likely to exercise the suffrage.[52]

During Woodrow Wilson's presidency, the suffrage movement became increasingly radicalized, and Wilson's nation-keeping efforts became, accordingly, more aggressive. When Alice Paul organized picket lines around the White House, intended to embarrass a president whose concern about democracy abroad apparently did not match his commitment at home, she and her fellow protesters were not long tolerated. Wilson's White House worked with the local police force in having the picketers arrested, while ignoring the violence of counterprotesters. Moreover, the administration used Secret Service agents to help silence internal critics of its policy against Paul's protest, and it sought to deploy its censorship capabilities, enlarged by World War I, to manipulate media coverage of these events. That latter effort largely failed, as, in the words of Sally Hunter Graham, "the spectacle of government employees attacking gray-haired women at the White House gates" proved to be too sensational for most newspapers to ignore. Embarrassment for Wilson, at home and abroad, only became more intense, however, when Paul initiated a hunger strike while in the District of Columbia jail.

Wilson, seeking to protect American security interests in World War I by promoting democracy abroad, found himself deeply embattled. As Graham observes, "Wilson realized by late 1917 that in order to maintain the integrity of his demands for democracy abroad, he would have to acknowledge the right of women to democratic participation at home."[53] It was by virtue of these nation-keeping demands that he became a convert to the cause of women's suffrage, a point he made every effort to highlight as he vigorously lobbied for the Nineteenth Amendment. Evidently following an agreement with Paul for her to halt her protests, he made an extraordinary appearance before the U.S. Senate to appeal for adoption of a suffrage amendment. His expressed rationale was unmistakable—it was a "vitally necessary war measure." The president argued that the amendment was

> clearly necessary to the successful prosecution of the war and the successful realization of the objects for which the war is being fought. . . . The

executive tasks of this war rest upon me. I ask that you lighten them and place in my hands instruments, spiritual instruments, which I do not now possess, which I sorely need, and which I have daily to apologize for not being able to employ.[54]

Tellingly, Wilson successfully lobbied for final Senate passage of the amendment from Paris, while working to shape a postwar world more conducive to American national security interests.

Native Americans

"What description of Indians," wrote James Madison in *Federalist* No. 42, "are to be deemed members of a State is not yet settled, and has been a question of frequent perplexity and contention in the federal councils."[55] The presidency was to play a central role in the early nineteenth century in crafting a response to that vexing problem of membership, largely because of a common perception that the nation's internal health was at risk from Native Americans.[56]

White anxiety was born of two principle considerations. One was a persistent fear of domestic violence, which fed on a vivid folklore of Indian savagery. Assimilation was not generally deemed a viable option for an uncivilized "other." Second, there was a foreign policy dimension to this problem. Native Americans remained, because of a general unhappiness with their treatment by state and national governors, a ripe target for alliances with foreign powers interested in maintaining their political and economic leverage on the North American continent. Accordingly, American policy makers felt a continuing sense of vulnerability to international conspiracy.

Tensions over the Indian question heightened considerably by the late 1820s, driven by an increasing white migration into such areas as Georgia and Alabama where the Native Americans retained their greatest presence. The 1830s thus became a decade "matched by no other in American history as a dramatic period in the relations between the United States government and the Indians."[57] No one was more crucial in developing a response to these hazards than Andrew Jackson.

Jackson's very claim to the presidency was rooted largely in his previous career as an Indian fighter, a celebrated warrior who had defeated the Creek nation at Horseshoe Bend and had secured much of northern Florida from the Seminole. When Jackson ascended to the presidency, then, he took as central to his job a complete resolution of the Native American problem. In Jackson's mind, American "Security was possible only once the Indian threat . . . was finally stilled and whites did not have to coexist with independent realities unconnected to them and beyond their control."[58] Jackson believed the only way to meet that threat was to remove it—to relocate the Indian tribes to the western frontier, as far ahead of an advancing white population as possible. Nothing short of removal, Jackson believed, would be consistent with his nation-maintaining responsibilities.

In his 1831 annual message, the president proclaimed that "The internal peace and security of our confederated States is [a] . . . principal object of the General Government. Time and experience have proved that the abode of the native Indian within their limits is dangerous to their peace and injurious to himself."[59] Moreover, as Michael Paul Rogin has argued, Indian removal had two other aspects that commended it to a nation-keeping Jackson. At a time when the question of slavery threatened to divide the states North from South, Jackson was able to focus attention on ridding the nation of a common threat that transcended regional boundaries. Attention to the red menace diverted the nation from the more politically explosive question of the black one (and allowed Jackson to patch southern wounds opened by his rebuke to the nullifiers). Second, removal allowed for the kind of unencumbered expansion that was essential for the young nation to grow sufficiently to guarantee its self-defense. This was a precursor of arguments for Manifest Destiny.[60] "By opening," Jackson observed,

> the whole territory between Tennessee on the north and Louisiana on the south to the settlement of whites it will incalculably strengthen the south-western frontier and render the adjacent States strong enough to repel future invasions without remote aid. It will relieve the whole State of Mississippi and the western part of Alabama of Indian occupancy, and enable those States to advance rapidly in population, wealth, and power.[61]

Jackson pursued his removal policies with a vengeance. He began by indirectly manipulating conditions in the South so as to convince the tribes to accept removal voluntarily. He allowed state governments to extend their legal jurisdictions over the tribes—in some cases outlawing the tribal unit—in contravention of constitutional design. He refused to use troops to keep white interlopers out of Indian lands or to support Indian calls for state protection when violence against them erupted, but he did promise selected use of troops to keep tribes from coercing those who chose to leave. Federal agents, often acting under veils of secrecy, occasionally used bribery of tribal leaders as a means of fostering removal, with the president's passive consent. Further, Jackson made use of a policy of selective preferment, refusing to extend official recognition to duly elected tribal leaders in favor of others who consented to promote removal treaties. The administration's agents rigged tribal elections and closed opposition presses among the Indians who protested such treatment.[62]

All these developments left Native American tribes in a debilitated state, but many still refused to leave. Some officials in Georgia and Alabama urged the president to remove forcibly the remaining Indians, an alternative Jackson considered too extreme, given some sympathy in the nation for the Indians' plight and the remaining (if tattered) treaty structures between the tribes and the United States government. But the president's position rapidly changed as a series of Indian wars, provoked by the excesses just described, broke out across the country among those unwilling to tolerate further abuse. Here, as Secretary of War Lewis Cass wrote, was a "disturb[ance of] the tranquillity of the country," leading Jackson to reconsider what his nation-keeping responsibilities required of him—or would allow him to accomplish. Accordingly, Cass continued, "the law of necessity will certainly justify [the Indians'] transfer to the country provided for them west of the Mississippi."[63] By the end of the Jackson presidency, death or relocation had decimated Indian populations in most of the United States. Enforced removal had largely resolved—at least for a time—the perplexities of membership that sprang from encounters of a Native American population with an expansive white majority.

American Labor

Even brief reflection on the history of the American labor movement—and its efforts to secure a more equitable share of the nation's economic and political rewards—reveals an active presidency with features quite similar to those described throughout this book. Those traits appear most clearly in the record of presidential reactions to the central weapon of organized labor: the strike. That the right to organize and to strike was ultimately recognized by the United States government was a major transformation in the place of laborers in the nation's economic and political systems.

The response of late nineteenth-century presidents to organized labor indicated the overwhelming power of preservative (i.e., union-free) forces operating on that institution. Ulysses Grant once suggested that it would be appropriate for him to replicate "the effective tactics of the Wilderness on leaders of labor" in order to stop them from agitating for greater recognition. But the two most prominent instances of executive-labor relations occurred later, as railroad workers attempted to assert their powers of collective bargaining. Both Rutherford Hayes and Grover Cleveland—sensitive to the damage they perceived being done the nation's economic and political fabric by rail strikes—responded forcefully in ways that undermined labors' bargaining position and consequently its ability to sustain itself in the quest to enhance the standing of the American worker. Presidential concerns about domestic tranquillity prevailed in each instance.

As a result of a series of wage cuts, rail workers closed train lines from Baltimore to St. Louis in 1877, initiating the nation's first major labor conflict. The magnitude of the strike occasioned "near hysteria," with violence erupting in at least fourteen states.[64] The governors of many of these states, taking note of Article IV, Section 4 of the Constitution, formally requested that President Hayes send in federal troops to stop the violence and end the strike. Hayes acted accordingly.

The president had found himself at the end of a formal action-forcing process, one that had the effect of making him a partisan in settlement of the dispute. He "was painfully aware of the fact that the mere restoration of order did little to settle the quarrel between employer and employee." The president noted in his diary, "The strikes have been put down by force; but now for the *real* remedy. Can't something [be] done by education of the strikers, by judicious control of the capitalists, by wise general policy to end or diminish the evil?"[65] Hayes's confidential admission indicates a recognition on his part that his intervention had done nothing to resolve underlying problems in the existing system. Indeed, the most important long-term consequence of the president's actions was a retarding of growth in infant unions, preserving the prevailing imbalance in worker-business relations across a range of industries.[66]

In 1894, President Cleveland took the presidential role in labor disputes a step further, by directing an even more vigorous federal government intervention into another massive rail strike affecting twenty seven states and territories. The president followed the lead of his attorney general, Richard Olney, who wrote during the conflict, "I feel that the true way of dealing with the matter is with a force which is overwhelming and prevents any attempt at resistance."[67] The Cleveland administration then helped convince the federal court in Illinois to issue a blanket labor injunction declaring the work stoppage and all associated activity illegal. Over the objections of Illinois Governor John Peter Altgeld, the president sent in federal troops to enforce that court order, and had arrested a host of key labor leaders, including Eugene V. Debs. In this instance, the president was clearly interested in achieving the outcome he obtained: ending the strike in such a way as to send a message to labor organizers that such disruptions would in no way be tolerated in the United States.[68]

By the turn of the century, an evolution had begun in popular ideas about business and corporate interests (associated with the populist and progressive movements), which in turn altered the political environment shaping presidential responses to labor unrest. One sign of this was Theodore Roosevelt's response to the anthracite coal strike of 1902. Roosevelt initially sought to arbitrate between the two sides, but the obstinacy of the mine owners so offended the president that he threatened to use federal troops to operate the mines. This had the effect of reopening the mines and of bringing the owners to accept an arbitration panel. That panel rejected labor's central demand—union recognition—but the president's shift was an important signal of increased popular recognition of labor's legitimacy. This change in popular attitudes altered the terrain of nation-keeping behavior, as labor's presence on the political landscape—and the practice of the strike itself—had become significantly less incendiary than in earlier years.

The culmination of that evolving transformation would be registered during the New Deal. The economic emergency of the early 1930s moved the second Roosevelt administration—and industry leaders—to place a mild version of the right to bargain collectively in the National Industrial Recovery Act (NIRA), Section 7(a).[69] Full legal recognition of that right came with the passage in 1935 of the Wagner Act. President Roosevelt was not a prime mover of either measure, although his support ultimately had been a necessary condition of the passage of both. Again, popular acceptance of the place of organized labor in America had largely prepared the way for Franklin Roosevelt's support, but it remains notable that these New Deal advances occurred as the president wrestled with nation-preserving problems across a wide range of issues. Section 7(a) promised to help sustain the loyalty of a host of American workers who otherwise had ample reason to question the fundamental underpinnings of the American economic and political orders. And in 1935, the year of the Wagner Act and Roosevelt's so-called "turn to the left," the United States experienced a flood tide of political agitation that arguably represented the high-water mark of system-threatening radicalism in the twentieth century.[70] Such forces seldom go unattended by the White House.

Japanese Americans

We have seen several instances when presidents, through the forces of war, have found themselves compelled by nation-keeping pressures to help expand the horizons of American citizenship, to move toward greater inclusiveness. War has not always had that effect, however. The most prominent example of presidentially contracted horizons transpired during the Second World War, in relation to an episode that Edward S. Corwin termed "the most drastic invasion of civil rights in the United States by [the] . . . government that has thus far occurred in the history of our nation."[71]

On February 19, 1942, President Franklin D. Roosevelt issued Executive Order 9066, which effectively provided for the collection and internment of over 70,000 American citizens of Japanese descent on the West Coast. The racial aspects of this imprisonment were striking, as Americans of neither Italian nor German extraction met with the same treatment. The rationale for the Japanese internment was clear, and clearly stated: in the wake of Pearl Harbor and a raft of Japanese victories in the Pacific, Japanese Americans represented an immediate danger to United States security. The War Department official who initiated efforts to establish the internment policy maintained,

> In the war in which we are now engaged racial affinities are not severed by migration. The Japanese race is an enemy race and while many second and third generation Japanese born on United States soil, possessed of United States citizenship, have become "Americanized," the racial strains are undiluted. . . . [T]here are indications that these [Japanese] are organized and ready for concerted action at a favorable opportunity. The very fact that no sabotage has taken place to date is a disturbing and confirming indication that such action will be taken.[72]

The president accepted this logic, justifying the denial of rights to a multitude of American citizens (and resident aliens) on nation-keeping grounds.[73] Although some Justice Department officials vigorously protested internment, their voices within the administration were largely muted because it was a foregone conclusion that security concerns would trump any other claims on the president's attention in the instant case. As one

California public official proclaimed, "we must forget such things as the right of *habeas corpus* and the prohibition against unreasonable searches and seizures. The right of self-defense, self-preservation ... is higher than the Bill of Rights."[74] Shortly thereafter, Congress validated the president's actions by providing legal penalties for those who disobeyed the chief executive's order. And when the inevitable lawsuits arose challenging the government's right to a blanket denial of civil liberties, the United States Supreme Court upheld without exception the internment and related policies.[75] In effect, each branch of the nation's government had recognized that the status of membership privileges in the American nation may be contingent on the *president's* perception of how those group claims to the Constitution's shelter might relate to the nation's peace and security.

The Post-Civil Rights Era

Although none of the episodes just described occurred after the civil rights revolution of the 1960s, the president's nation-keeping role (with respect to membership questions) did not expire with the enactment of the Voting Rights Act of 1965. It was, however, exercised in a transformed environment.

The constitution each president is pledged to preserve, protect, and defend had been radically altered by the succession of events culminating during the Kennedy and Johnson years. A new American constitution came into being, with African Americans more fully integrated into the mainstream of the nation's social, economic, and political life. The *idea* of racial equality became a firmly fixed feature of the nation's culture. That legacy, at its most fundamental level, became a vital part of the constitution presidential guardians are expected to maintain.

Yet there persisted in the wake of that constitutional reformation a vast and volatile conundrum: How to fulfill in practice the promises of racial equality at the heart of the civil rights movement, how to make real King's widely shared dream of transforming the "jangling discords of our nation into a beautiful symphony of brotherhood."[76] That the nation had accepted explicitly as a part of its mission the abolition of race-based inequalities did not mean that there was widespread agreement about how specifically to proceed toward that end.[77] A continuing conflict, then, played out on a new constitutional tableau.

Clashes erupted over the pace and extent to which the vestiges of a protracted era of racial inequality would be eradicated. Civil rights activists attempted to consolidate gains and to move forward on new frontiers toward full equality in the workplace and the schoolhouse, while many whites vigorously objected that proposed remedies were too much too fast, or simply overreadings of the accepted legacy of the 1960s. Patterns of social behavior established over three centuries' time did not readily pass away, largely because of the thoroughgoing extent to which white supremacy had become interwoven in the fabric of the nation's daily life, *and* because the white majority was unwilling to divest itself completely of its preferred status, beyond the demise of Jim Crow and an extension of the right to vote. A more thoroughgoing and equitable division of the nation's economic and political resources required sacrifices outside the South and beyond the sharing of the ballot box that many whites were simply unwilling to accept. Accordingly, while in the new constitutional era the extremes of white supremacy had been discredited, the politics of black-white relations remained among the most volatile, and perhaps the most explosive, on the political landscape.

What have these developments meant for the presidency? In some respects the transformed constitution did serve to normalize the politics of black-white relations, leaving a wider latitude for presidential action beyond the usual nation-keeping concerns. Contributing to this was the fact that the extension of the suffrage to those previously excluded by law and custom generated a force vote-seeking politicians could not ignore. "The day the blacks got the vote in South Carolina," notes former United States Civil Rights Commissioner Morris Abram, "you saw Strom Thurmond referring to them no longer as 'niggers' but as 'our beloved brethren.'"[78] The race issue was, as a consequence, no longer the same, cost-free target for calculated demagoguery, moving even the likes of George Wallace to recognize the virtues of promoting racial equality, at least at some minimal level. Presidents, because of their nationwide electoral constituency, had since the days of the Great Migration found it necessary to consider black votes as a part of their routine political calculus. But the suffrage reforms of the 1960s removed from the political landscape a persistent source of irritation. So to some extent those suffrage reforms made the president's job more manageable. The high-profile provocations of a Wallace, or a Ross Barnett, or an Orval Faubus passed away, buried under an avalanche of black ballots. Black voters in a sense, then, became one more interest group, whose demands on the political order could be treated by presidents and other governing actors according to the typical ebb-and-flow of a pluralistic polity. Reinforcing this trend was the emergence of more mainstream black political actors—in the parties and as elected officials—and an inability on the part of civil rights activists in the post-King years to sustain the kind of social movement that changes politics-as-usual from the outside in.

This quasi-normalization means that overt exercises of the nation-keeping role are a less prominent feature of the post-civil rights era presidency than before. The polity is generally less susceptible than it once was to the kinds of racial paroxysms that brought forth conspicuous displays of nation-maintaining behavior in the White House. Yet the reforms of the 1960s did not constitute an absolute inoculation from racial unrest. The very same week he signed into law the Voting Rights Act of 1965, Lyndon Johnson received news of rioting in Watts, California, which was merely the first of a series of urban racial explosions he would be forced to confront during his remaining days in office. The civil rights advances he had helped guide through Congress had not, as he had hoped, routed black aspirations entirely into the conventional channels of American politics. Over two decades later, George Bush encountered a similar disturbance in Los Angeles following the acquittal of white police officers charged with assaulting Rodney King. In both cases, troops were dispatched to settle the immediate disturbance, followed by presidential initiatives to locate and deal with underlying factors that may have contributed to unrest. Though two decades separated their presidencies, Johnson and Bush found that opened avenues to political participation did not necessarily keep racial conflict from spilling into the streets. Andrew Jackson's powder keg was, given the right spark, as menacing a presence as ever.

These rare, overt exercises of the nation-keeping role, however, only partly account for its influence on presidential behavior in the post-60s era. Vastly more important has been the degree to which presidents have felt constrained, as a quiet matter of course, to conform their behavior on race-related matters to the requirements of that role. The perpetual volatility of the issue of race has ultimately bounded and grounded every president's pattern of response to the politics of black-white relations. The *possibility* of racial disturbances shaped behavior even when an immediate threat has not been present, especially among the more numerous Republican presidents whose electoral coalitions did not directly benefit from the civil rights revolution.

For those presidents inclined toward retrenchment—whether because of inclinations to build a popular base on white resentment or to scale back the use of the federal government as an implement of domestic reconstitution—the nation-keeping role established a floor not to be breached. His so-called "Southern Strategy" and "law and order" campaigns notwithstanding, Richard Nixon dared not tinker with the basic gains African Americans had made before he entered office. As Kenneth O'Reilly has observed, "Nixon wanted to manage school desegregation and other civil rights enforcement matters, not grind them to a complete halt. *Total noncompliance would raise security problems by increasing the risk to domestic peace.*" Some ideologues in the administration, including Patrick Buchanan, not burdened directly with the president's nation-maintaining responsibilities, promoted a more vigorous effort to undermine the structures of racial advancement the Republicans inherited in 1969. Yet "Where Buchanan saw glory and victory for the 'presidential party' in race riots and a nation torn in half, Nixon saw horror and defeat. Lacking the courage of Buchanan's convictions, he would not roll Buchanan's dice but instead throw the occasional bone to blacks and liberals *in order to preserve the peace and the Union.*"[79]

By Ronald Reagan's presidency "the occasional bone" was still being thrown—such as a belated presidential endorsement of the King holiday bill—but a much more thoroughgoing retrenchment in civil rights was inaugurated. The political environment was not nearly so charged as during Nixon's days, diminishing the risks to domestic tranquillity of federal initiatives hostile to African-American interests. George Bush generally continued on the same trajectory, only to recoil in the aftermath of the Los Angeles riots. The floor had once again been reached.

For those presidents inclined toward expansiveness, the fear of white backlash, which might endanger established advances in the nation's constitution, provided a ceiling beyond which it was imprudent to climb. It should be noted here that few presidents have found themselves abutting this ceiling, because the normal pressures in a democratic political system tend to favor majoritarian impulses. Thus, on the question of race, routine political pressures usually prompt presidents to stop advocating minority interests well short of the point at which a nation-threatening backlash might erupt, openly provoking a nation-keeping response. Indeed, these majoritarian strains put downward pressure on every president on the question of minority rights.[80] It is thus much more likely, because African-American interests tend to be underrepresented in conventional political channels, that presidents will find themselves unwittingly nearing the floor rather than the ceiling, as the usual signals on which presidents rely to warn them away from the extremes are not as dependable there.

An expansively inclined Bill Clinton, whom O'Reilly characterized as "arguably the least prejudiced of the forty-one men who preceded him," sought to make racial advance one of *the* central features of his historical legacy, setting forth a challenge to the nation: "America, we must clean our house of racism."[81] But Clinton chose to establish his legacy through the modest, timeworn practice of study and talk, establishing an independent commission and promoting a national dialogue on race. The president's actions were roundly criticized among civil rights activists who wanted, and believed Clinton was capable of, more.[82] Perhaps he was. But in a 1995 speech billed by the White House, and covered by the media, as a major address on the state of American race relations—and occasioned by Louis Farrakhan's Million Man March—the president proclaimed that "Law and order is the first responsibility of government." Not justice, not freedom, not equality, but order. That *this* president would make *this* claim in *this* context suggests the presence of an inescapable linkage in how presidents view race and the nation-keeping imperatives of the presidential institution.[83] It is unlikely that one can be raised to the presidency who possesses an immunity to those constraints.

Implications for the Study of Leadership

In these concluding pages, I want to offer some thoughts on the relevance of the foregoing analysis to leadership studies and to suggest some possible refinements in thinking about leadership and the presidency.[84]

I argued in my Introduction that the cases examined in this study have a gravity beyond their inherent importance as indicators of the scope of democracy in America. The story of the movement toward equal rights for African Americans also has been important in American political development because it has provided episodes of memorable presidential action, which loom large in popular conceptions about how the presidency can function to bring about meaningful political and social change. It seems perfectly natural to argue that Lincoln, Kennedy, and Johnson exercised presidential leadership in such a way as to benefit enormously black America. However, when prevailing conceptions of leadership are held up against and compared to the evidence arrayed in this study, at least two complications arise, rendering problematic the reconciliation of conventional notions of presidential leadership with executive behavior on racial advance in the United States. These two difficulties—the first relating to the subject of policy initiation, the second to policy direction, or change—suggest that we may need to revise conventional conceptions about the place of presidential leadership in the advance of racial equality. Moreover, our prevailing conceptions of leadership may need modification to account for relevant evidence that is often overlooked in conventional constructions of the term.

Many widely accepted definitions of leadership build on the notion that a personage or an institution may be designated a leader because he, she, or it *initiated* action—in effect the leader is the political equivalent of an unmoved mover, the actor that sets into motion an intended sequence of events among other actors toward some anticipated end. For example, one favorable biography of Ronald Reagan holds that he was an "extraordinary leader" because he was the "prime mover" of his times, "the architect of his own success."[85] Difficulties quickly arise in applying the term leadership, so characterized, in the case of racial inequality. Almost nowhere do we find a president initiating action in favor of black America without being forced by others to do so. Indeed, as we have seen, the adoption of policies toward racial equality only came at the end of extremely long action-forcing processes, at which time virtually every other option short of adopting a civil rights agenda had been exhausted. This evidence hardly leaves room for presidential initiative in its simplest form.

A more sophisticated approach to the leadership question emerges in the public policy literature, which holds that leadership can be exercised at various stages of a multileveled policy process. According to these constructions, public policy evolves through a number of phases—from problem definition through problem resolution to implementation and review—and various actors can play leading parts at various places in this process. This construction, too, remains problematic, because students of public policy also tend to look for presidential leadership at the earliest stages of the process.

For example, in one simple model crafted by Charles O. Jones, the presidency is assigned constitutional supremacy in these phases of the policy process: problem definition, priority setting, and program formulation.[86] If presidential leadership can be defined as aggressively asserting presidential influence at these stages of the process, we still have difficulty finding presidential leadership exercised in the advancement of black civil rights. Indeed, where presidents have actively been involved in program formulation for racial equality, it has generally been because they have been under enormous pressure by other actors—institutional and noninstitutional—who effectively defined the problem and who established racial issues as a public priority.

Parenthetically, it would seem that the notion of initiative as central to definitions of leadership severely constrains the assignment of leadership to *any* public institution in a republican political order. Except in those rare instances of purely Burkean trusteeship, in which a representative acts *against* the impulses of the community because of some independent judgment about what is in its best interest, the initiative for public acts generally arise not within institutions of governance, but among the governed themselves. Thus, focus on the act of initiation actually alerts us to what might be called the tyranny of institutionalism, or the routine crediting to governmental institutions of features best found among noninstitutional actors. Our correspondent with the *Washington Post*, for example, could conceive of leadership on the issue of slavery only in terms of such institutional actors as Abraham Lincoln. That more appropriate designations of leadership might have been found outside those institutions—among the ranks of William Lloyd Garrison, or Wendell Phillips, or Harriet Tubman, or John Brown, or even among a myriad of unknown slaves who directed unwanted "contraband" into Union encampments—escaped that writer. Yet the correspondent's inclinations are so common—and so commonly powerful—as to go generally unremarked.

The second complication encountered in reconciling conventional notions of presidential leadership with the story of racial advance revolves around the concept of change. Simply stated, according to many conventional definitions, leaders produce change, often toward some preferred end. For example, Barbara Kellerman writes that "political leadership implies some kind of partisan (or ideological) leadership, *a personal push for particular changes* in group goals, activities, or structure."[87] Bert A. Rockman develops his working conceptions of leadership in a chapter entitled "Leadership and Change," and offers that "A natural way of thinking about leadership is to see it as relevant to the process of producing significant change—that is, intended adaptations meant to lead to a significant alteration in the status quo."[88] In *The Politics Presidents Make*, Stephen Skowronek styles his work as "a general study of presidents as agents of political change," an examination of "[f]aith in the transformative capacities of the presidency."[89] Leadership, according to these authoritative voices, is about change.[90]

Further, inherent in many conceptions of leadership is a subjective element, which holds the exercise of leadership as a positive good by definition. In other words, leadership is often not defined as purely instrumental—because an instrument can be employed toward negative ends—but is defined as the exercise of power in a given direction, toward a certain kind of change. In perhaps the most popular form, the end is one of elevation or improvement.

In his award-winning book *Leadership*, James MacGregor Burns develops what he offers as a definitive model that expressly conveys a positive valence on the notion of leadership. For Burns, "true leadership" moves the leader and the led to higher and higher planes of purpose and morality. Leadership is change-oriented, change in a positive direction. "*The ultimate test of practical leadership is the realization of intended, real change that meets people's enduring needs* . . . The function of leadership is to *engage* followers, not merely to activate them, to commingle needs and aspirations and goals in a common enterprise, and in the process to make better citizens of both leaders and followers."[91] The directional component of Burns's definition seems to be deeply embedded in popular conceptions of leadership in the United States, as Americans loudly and persistently call for it from the White House.

By these conventional standards, however, it is impossible to apply the term "leadership" to presidential behavior on matters of race throughout most of American history. American presidents were only rarely change oriented, and they certainly did not labor to extend common avenues of participation or citizenship building to many who now share the name "American."

The directional component of conventional definitions of leadership fails, then, to account for a great deal of presidential behavior on race, behavior that might, based on a purely instrumental definition, qualify as leadership. Arguably presidents other than Lincoln, Kennedy, and Johnson as aggressively, as creatively, and as pro-actively as this trinity used the powers of the presidency to craft public responses to movements for racial equality. These others occasionally molded popular opinion and governmental policy to suit their broader purposes. Yet these powers were applied in service of ends no longer considered politically legitimate. Subsequently, the term leadership does not comfortably apply.

There are consequences to such freighted use of the term leadership. One is a misallocation of confidence in the presidential institution's inclination toward political or social change. After all, we expect our presidents to be "leaders," and change is what "leadership" is all about. But perhaps no lesson more clearly emerges from this study than that the presidency is—at the most fundamental level—supremely a place of conservation. Through long stretches of American history presidents worked effectively to diminish chances for political advancement by those of African descent, and when such change did come about it was only belatedly embraced by the White House. The evidence strongly indicates that presidents heed first demands for security and stability. Only when those are disrupted, and when their reestablishment appears to require a change in prevailing social or political structures, do other demands generate favorable action. The requirements of the Constitution for the establishment of justice and the insurance of domestic tranquillity are thus not equally attended from the White House.

This misallocation of confidence itself has a consequence. If energy and activism from the White House only elevates and produces democratic progress, any barriers to the exercise of "presidential leadership" are rendered illogical and unnecessary. Why, if activist presidents have left the nation with emancipation proclamations, and civil rights acts, and voting rights acts, erect any restraints on presidential activism at all? Of course, the question proceeds from an error in logic—an assumption that when presidents are not leading (that is, when they are not activist in the approved fashion) they are political nullities. Again, here, a more instrumental definition of leadership as it relates to the presidency would attract attention to activist presidential practices that work contrary to "the realization of . . . real change." Such a departure from the directional bias of leadership defined would serve to reassert the logic of those in Philadelphia who constructed a national government not on a principle of leadership, but on standards of balance and counterpoise.

A final distortion of the common directional component of leadership proceeds accordingly: a lack of attention to active presidential efforts to weaken movements for racial equality fosters an underappreciation of the durability and tenacity of those who pressed for change. Not only did they labor against a multitude of the kinds of problems that confront any large-scale voluntary organization, they also battled powerful political actors, armed with the coercive authority of the state. A principal lesson of this case, then, has been that monumental political change comes only at the expense of many lifetimes of labor, devoted to surmounting overwhelming obstacles.

The elevation of those presidents who eventually embraced racial advance to the stature of "Great Emancipators" thus tends to bring full circle the presidency's role as an instrument of political conservation. If common perceptions are that important political change derives principally from the active sponsorship of an Abraham Lincoln, a John Kennedy, or a Lyndon Johnson, the incentives for individuals to participate in wide-scale political action are depressed just as they are when presidents actively apply their executive, legislative and rhetorical powers to retarding mass politics. In effect, the way that presidential behavior is remembered—the way that it becomes a part of our everyday discourse and the way that it is encoded into our political culture—subtly but forcefully influences the ways that contemporary Americans see fit to channel their own behavior.

Although my primary purpose in this study has not been to address directly the question of presidential *effectiveness* in establishing a sense of futility, it should be noted here that even slight contributions in discouraging collective action could exert a significant influence on the overall organizational effort. As Jack H. Nagel has noted, "For most people the calculus of collective action yields net incentives to participate that, at best, barely exceed zero; therefore, even slight governmental pressure on the cost side of the scale tips the balance toward passivity."[92] Presidentially sanctioned pressure on activists for racial equality conforms to Nagel's general rule.

Over the last three decades American political culture has become increasingly democratized.[93] As evidence, joining the presidential monuments in Washington is a slab of granite cutting into the earth near Lincoln's Memorial honoring each of the nearly 58,000 Americans who sacrificed their lives in the Vietnam War. Just across the Mall, a troop of stone footsoldiers commemorates the extraordinary sacrifice of the ordinary fighting man and woman in Korea. Further, Dr. King's own work is also enshrined with a federal holiday in January of each year. But, unlike the revolutionary toppling of Lenin statuary across the Soviet steppe, Americans did not mark their newest democratic reformation by razing the shrines devoted to their public icons. They simply erected new ones alongside the old.

Accordingly, the messages conveyed to those who today are shaped by the force of that culture are less simple than they once were. The accommodation of many stories, many sacrifices, and many commitments, takes on a complexity missing when the stories, sacrifices and commitments deemed worth remembering are few, prominent, and comforting. Yet such complexity is hardly original to our time. The very framers of the American Constitution wrestled earnestly with efforts to reconcile commitments to republicanism and strong central authority, to democracy and diversity. The government they created, as their critics were eager to point out, did not bear the virtue of simplicity of design, nor did it conform to recognized patterns of self-government. Moreover, it has revealed itself to be remarkably malleable over time, bending and twisting to meet unforeseen exigencies in ways that make its shape even more difficult to apprehend.

A great virtue of governance under presidential direction is its simplicity of design in action and comprehension. The framers recognized those qualities and yet elected to discard them in favor of a complex construction repeatedly derided in their day as a "heterogeneous phantom."[94] Yet they had their reasons.

In late May 1922, a crowd gathered at the newly extended west end of the Mall in Washington to dedicate the recently completed monument to the memory of Abraham Lincoln. The featured speaker on that occasion was the thirteenth man to follow Lincoln into the presidency, another Republican, but one whose legacy would fall far short of the mark established by the party's first representative in the White House.[95] In retrospect, the comments offered by Warren Harding betray markings of a confessional. But Harding also spoke to an enduring verity of American politics.

> Abraham Lincoln was no superman. Like the great Washington, whose monumental shaft towers nearby as a fit companion to the memorial we dedicate today . . . Lincoln was a very natural human being, with the frailties mixed with the virtues of humanity. There are neither supermen nor demi-gods in the government of kingdoms, empires, or republics. It will be better for our conception of government and its institutions if we will understand this fact.

PREFACE

1. Quoted in James Madison, *Notes of Debates in the Federal Convention of 1787* (New York: Norton, 1987), p. 421.

2. For a creative discussion of societal boundaries, and of conflicts over inclusion and exclusion, see Constance Perin, *Everything in Its Place: Social Order and Land Use in America* (Princeton: Princeton University Press, 1977); and Perin, *Belonging in America: Reading Between the Lines* (Madison: University of Wisconsin Press, 1988).

INTRODUCTION

1. Sanford Levinson, *Constitutional Faith* (Princeton: Princeton University Press, 1988).

2. This issue is addressed in Herbert J. Storing, "Slavery and the Moral Foundations of the American Republic," in Robert H. Horwitz, ed., *The Moral Foundations of the American Republic*, 3d ed. (Charlottesville: University Press of Virginia, 1986), pp. 313–32.

3. When I use the term "citizen" or "citizenship" in this work, I am referring not to a strict, legalistic concept, but to a broader notion, implying a full range of participatory privileges for the citizen. Judith N. Shklar finds both voting and earning essential elements to a broadly interpreted definition. See *American Citizenship: The Quest for Inclusion* (Cambridge: Harvard University Press, 1991). See also Morris Janowitz, *The Reconstruction of Patriotism: Education for Civic Consciousness* (Chicago: University of Chicago Press, 1983), ch. 1.

4. I borrow the word "liminal" from Anne Norton, who says that it "corresponds roughly to the terms 'marginal' and 'peripheral,' designating an individual (and more often) a group, whose inclusion in the community is ambiguous. Such groups are subordinated within, or excluded from, economic, social, and political structures." She credits her use of the term to anthropologist Victor Turner. See Norton, *Alternative Americas: A Reading of Antebellum Political Culture* (Chicago: University of Chicago Press, 1986), p. 12.

5. It is hoped that in some respects the results of this study can be generalized to the larger class of behavior described above, the overall expansion of membership privileges that has characterized American political development.

6. Clinton Rossiter, *The American Presidency*, 2d ed. (New York: New American Library, 1960), pp. 117, 121.

7. Michael Nelson observes that despite the many differing models of presidential power—some asserting the inherent vigor, others the inherent weakness of the modern institution—a common feature "has been a recurring, if sometimes implicit, celebration of presidential strength." See "Evaluating the Presidency," in Nelson, ed., *The Presidency and the Political System*, 4th ed. (Washington: CQ Press, 1995), p. 9.

8. The classic treatment of the phenomenon addressed here is James Sterling Young, *The Washington Community 1800–1828* (New York: Columbia University Press, 1966).

9. As this book was being prepared for press, a fourth presidential monument— to Franklin D. Roosevelt—was dedicated, filling space between the memorials to Lincoln and Jefferson.

10. Recent history has produced a noticeable trend toward increased democratization of the nation's commemoratives. The most prominent examples of this trend on the Mall are the placement and architecture of the Vietnam War Memorial and the Korean War Memorial. Yet as Washington architect Paul B. Spreiregen has written, these war monuments "are either modest in size or positioned so as not to challenge" the core Mall monuments. Thus, their presence does little to detract from the messages those other monuments communicate. See Spreiregen, "One Mall, Indivisible: A World War II Memorial Is a Good Idea—But the Location Is All Wrong," *Washington Post*, July 6, 1997, C5.

11. I am not claiming here that these figures are memorialized solely on the basis of their service in the presidency. Rather my argument is that it is striking that in a democratic polity only those who have served in this position seem worthy of the nation's highest expressions of lasting esteem, *and* that this practice may have profound implications for how our polity views its political institutions.

12. The analogous nature of the Mall is identified in Allan Greenberg, "Peter Charles L'Enfant's Plan for Washington, D.C.," unpublished typescript, 1989.

13. For a more extensive treatment of this general phenomenon see Bruce Miroff, "Monopolizing the Public Space: The President as a Problem for Democratic Politics," in Thomas E. Cronin, ed., *Rethinking the Presidency* (Boston: Little, Brown, 1982), pp. 218–32.

14. George J. Olszewski, *History of the Mall: Washington, D.C.* (Washington: U.S. Department of the Interior, National Park Service, Office of History and Historic Architecture, 1970).

15. The number of visitors to the Constitution's vault in the National Archives is routinely well below that of visits to other monuments in the capital.

16. See Robert K. Merton, "Manifest and Latent Functions," in Merton, ed., *Social Theory and Social Structure* (New York: Free Press, 1968), pp. 73–138.

17. The conventional place for honoring nonpresidential achievement has been the postage stamp, the province of actors, musicians, and other cultural icons. These, importantly, tend to be less enduring commemoratives than the others, in addition to being culturally second-tier.

18. I should note here that after completing the original version of this work, I encountered references to "monumental presidents," in Philip Abbott, *Strong Presidents: A Theory of Leadership* (Knoxville: University of Tennessee Press, 1996), pp. 19–23 ff. Abbott's usage is similar, but not identical, to that employed here.

19. For evidence that Lincoln's humility is central to the public use of his memory, see Senator Alan Simpson's (R-Wy) essay commemorating Lincoln's birth, "A Comfort to Our Historical Memory," *Washington Post*, February 12, 1995, C7.

20. For more on what the social psychologists term "attribution theory," see Sonja M. Hunt, "The Role of Leadership in the Construction of Reality," in Barbara Kellerman, ed., *Leadership: Multidisciplinary Perspectives* (Englewood Cliffs, N.J.: Prentice-Hall, 1984), pp. 157–78.

21. These biases are not wholly absent from studied accounts of American politics, either. See, for example, Thomas E. Cronin, "The Textbook Presidency and Political Science," reproduced in U.S. Congress, *Congressional Record*, 1970 vol. 116, pp. 517102–15. Senate, 91st Cong., 2d sess. A more accessible, but less extensive, version appears in Cronin, *The State of the Presidency* (Boston: Little, Brown, 1975), ch. 2. For more recent commentary, see J. M. Sanchez, "Old Habits Die Hard: The Textbook Presidency Is Alive and Well," *PS: Political Science and Politics* 29 (March 1996): 63–66.

22. I do not intend to provide other than superficial documentation here to sustain this proposition. However, ample anecdotal evidence gives me confidence that the proposition is fundamentally sound. For example, during the many years that this manuscript was in preparation, hardly a week passed without someone asking the question, "What are you working on?" My standard response was, "A study of the presidency and movements for racial equality." Inevitably the questioner would reply with some variation of, "Oh, so your looking at Lincoln? Kennedy? Johnson?" (I should note that no violence would be done to my theory by adding Harry Truman to the short list, as some are inclined to do.)

23. Kennedy used that phrase in a September 22, 1962 statement commemorating the one-hundredth anniversary of the Emancipation Proclamation. See *Public Papers of the Presidents of the United States: John F. Kennedy, 1962* (Washington: U.S. GPO, 1963), p. 702.

24. To borrow Bruce Miroff's phrasing, in dealing with racial inequality presidents have confronted the problem of creating "effective techniques for the exercise of White House leverage" over a movement's internal affairs. Miroff, "Presidential Leverage over Social Movements: The Johnson White House and Civil Rights,"

Journal of Politics 43 (February 1981): 11.

25. For more bibliographic information on the literature on social movements, see my concluding chapter.

26. Illustrative of these are James MacGregor Burns, *Roosevelt: The Lion and the Fox* (New York: Harcourt, Brace and World, 1956); Arthur M. Schlesinger Jr., *A Thousand Days: John F. Kennedy in the White House* (Boston: Houghton Mifflin, 1965); and the entire University Press of Kansas series on individual administrations.

27. Among the texts in this category are Donald J. Lisio, *Hoover, Blacks, & Lily-Whites: A Study of Southern Strategies* (Chapel Hill: University of North Carolina Press, 1985); Robert Fredrick Burk, *The Eisenhower Administration and Black Civil Rights* (Knoxville: University of Tennessee Press, 1984); and Carl M. Brauer, *John F. Kennedy and the Second Reconstruction* (New York: Columbia University Press, 1977).

28. Miroff, "Presidential Leverage over Social Movements," p. 3. He goes on to note that a single case study can be useful "in generating new hypotheses and in revealing the limitations or inadequacies of prevailing theoretical formulations."

29. I am especially indebted to Professors Michael F. Holt and Richard E. Neustadt—historian and political scientist respectively—for revealing to me the value of expanding my study of each movement beyond the confines of a single presidency.

30. Illustrative of these are Ruth P. Morgan, *The President and Civil Rights: Policy-Making by Executive Order* (New York: St. Martin's Press, 1970), and Steven A. Shull, *The President and Civil Rights Policy: Leadership and Change* (New York: Greenwood Press, 1989). A fourth type of work has also been used extensively here: movement histories. These are legion, and do not commonly concentrate on the presidency, but they have been invaluable in building a narrative scheme to cover the vast period of American history examined here. A representative sampling of these includes Gilbert Hobbs Barnes, *The Antislavery Impulse, 1830–1844* (New York: Harcourt, Brace and World, 1964); Richard Kluger, *Simple Justice: The History of Brown v. Board of Education and Black America's Struggle for Equality* (New York, Vintage Books, 1977); and Taylor Branch, *Parting the Waters: America in the King Years, 1954–63* (New York: Simon and Schuster, 1988).

31. After the original version of this study was completed (as a doctoral dissertation), historian Kenneth O'Reilly produced a parallel work entitled *Nixon's Piano: Presidents and Racial Politics from Washington to Clinton* (New York: Free Press, 1995), the first comprehensive assessment of the subject ever published. I make no attempt in these pages to offer a point-by-point comparison of the particulars of our two works, although our ultimate conclusions are roughly the same: presidents have commonly fought racial advance. However, two significant distinctions merit attention here. First, despite the scope of his subtitle, O'Reilly devotes fewer than fifty pages to the nineteenth-century presidency; in my work, the scales are tilted much more heavily in that direction. Second, and more importantly, O'Reilly writes as an historian. Thus, the framework he brings to the subject differs from that of the political scien-

tist. Much of my work here is devoted to explaining the contextual factors giving shape to presidential behavior over the long scope of American history. Those factors are not central to O'Reilly's work, which focuses instead on the moral choices presidents have made. He accordingly claims that "In the history of American racism, stateways have influenced folkways far more deeply than the reverse" (pp. 11–12), a conclusion at odds with my understanding of politics in general and this issue in particular.

32. James W. Ceaser, *Presidential Selection: Theory and Development* (Princeton: Princeton University Press, 1979); Richard Ellis and Aaron Wildavsky, *Dilemmas of Presidential Leadership: Washington through Lincoln* (New Brunswick, N.J.: Transaction, 1989); Richard J. Ellis, "What Can 19th-Century Presidents Teach Us About the Twentieth-Century Presidency?" (paper delivered at the 1990 annual meeting of the American Political Science Association, San Francisco, August 30–September 2, 1990); Jeffrey K. Tulis, *The Rhetorical Presidency* (Princeton: Princeton University Press, 1987); Stephen Skowronek, "Presidential Leadership in Political Time," in Nelson, ed., *The Presidency and the Political System*, and "Notes on the Presidency in the Political Order," *Studies in American Political Development*, vol. 1 (New Haven: Yale University Press, 1986), pp. 286–302; Sidney M. Milkis and Michael Nelson, *The American Presidency: Origins and Development, 1776–1993* (Washington D.C.: Congressional Quarterly Press, 1994).

33. Ellis, "What Can 19th-Century Presidents Teach Us About the Twentieth-Century Presidency?" pp. 4–9.

34. See Richard E. Neustadt and Ernest May, *Thinking in Time: The Uses of History for Decision-Makers* (New York: Free Press, 1986).

35. Clinton Rossiter outlined ten "major roles [the president] plays in the sprawling drama of American government." He alternately uses the term "function" or "duty" for role, and he defines all these as simply "those tasks we call upon the President to perform." The nation-keeping role is not identified as such by Rossiter, but it resembles in some respects what he calls "Protector of the Peace." Rossiter, *American Presidency*, pp. 14–38.

36. Kenneth M. Stampp suggests that such a role, given general popular receptivity to the notion of disunion (under the appropriate circumstances), was not much in evidence before the nullification crisis of the 1830s. However, I am doubtful that those who preceded Jackson in the president's chair would have treated actual prospects for disunion any differently than he did, despite the unsettled question of the right to secede. See Stampp, "The United States and National Self-determination," in Gabor S. Boritt, ed., *Lincoln, The War President: The Gettysburg Lectures* (New York: Oxford University Press, 1992), pp. 126–29.

37. These are essentially the constitutional bases wherein Lincoln found the "war power," with special emphasis on the oath of office. For a broad discussion of the constitutional roots of what he terms the president's "emergency prerogative," see Arthur M. Schlesinger Jr., "War and the Constitution: Abraham Lincoln and Franklin D.

Roosevelt," in Boritt, ed., *Lincoln, the War President*, pp. 147–78. A thoroughgoing critique of such expansive notions of presidential authority appears in Raoul Berger, *Executive Privilege: A Constitutional Myth* (Cambridge: Harvard University Press, 1974).

38. The preeminence of foreign policy concerns—of a sense of vulnerability to foreign powers—among those who met to frame the new Constitution is maintained in Paul A. Varg, *Foreign Policies of the Founding Fathers* (Baltimore: Penguin Books, 1970), ch. 4, and in Julian P. Boyd, *Number 7: Alexander Hamilton's Secret Attempts to Control American Foreign Policy* (Princeton: Princeton University Press, 1964), Foreword. The importance of a *presidential* remedy for those seeking to correct this existing weakness in foreign affairs is asserted in Boyd and in Charles C. Thach Jr., *The Creation of the Presidency, 1775–1789: A Study in Constitutional History* (Baltimore: Johns Hopkins University Press, 1969, reprint of 1923 edition), pp. 17, 61–75.

39. Other students of the presidency have noted the importance of Shays's Rebellion in motivating the convention to adopt a stronger executive. See Thach, *The Creation of the Presidency*, pp. 16–24; Richard M. Pious, *The American Presidency* (New York: Basic Books, 1979), pp. 19–20, 23; Milkis and Nelson, *The American Presidency*, pp. 9–10, 31.

40. Flexner, *George Washington and the New Nation (1783–1793)* (Boston: Little, Brown, 1970), p. 100.

41. Flexner, *George Washington*, p. 101. Madison's notes from the convention further indicate the prominence of Shays's Rebellion in the minds of the gathered delegates; it was directly referred to on at least nine occasions, and the subject of domestic violence in general at least six other times. James Madison, *Notes of Debates in the Federal Convention of 1787* (New York: Norton, 1987). See the "General Index," pp. 664, 673.

42. Alexander Hamilton, James Madison, John Jay, *The Federalist Papers* (New York: New American Library, 1961). The quote is taken from No. 16 (p. 117), authored by Hamilton.

43. *The Federalist Papers*, pp. 83–84.

44. *The Federalist Papers*, No. 23, p. 153.

45. The words here are from Publius's third voice, John Jay. *The Federalist Papers*, No. 3, p. 42.

46. It might reasonably be objected here that Article I, Section 8 of the Constitution grants to Congress control of the militia for such purposes. That objection will be addressed shortly.

47. *The Federalist Papers*, pp. 69, 423, 449.

48. James Thomas Flexner, *George Washington: Anguish and Farewell (1793–1799)* (Boston: Little, Brown, 1972), p. 162.

49. Quoted in Bennett Milton Rich, *Presidents and Civil Disorder* (Washington: Brookings Institution, 1941), p. 10.

50. There were two such proclamations. The language quoted in this paragraph is taken from the first, issued on September 15, 1792. The latter came almost two years afterward—August 7, 1794—suggesting that Washington's earlier actions were somewhat fruitful, if ultimately dismissed. See James D. Richardson, ed., *A Compilation of the Messages and Papers of the Presidents* (New York: Bureau of National Literature, 1897), pp. 116–17, 150–52.

51. See Washington's Fourth Annual Address, in Richardson, ed., *Messages and Papers*, p. 119.

52. Whether the antitax protesters were wholly defeated is a matter about which historians disagree. Some argue that although the nature of the protests quietened considerably in the aftermath of the militia incursion, the whiskey excise tax was still not paid as the law demanded, especially in the nation's westernmost areas. See Mary K. Bonsteel Tachau, "A New Look at the Whiskey Rebellion," in Steven R. Boyd, ed., *The Whiskey Rebellion: Past and Present Perspectives* (Westport, Conn: Greenwood Press, 1985), pp. 97–118.

53. These acts are discussed by Edward S. Corwin in *The President: Office and Powers, 1787–1984*, fifth revised edition by Randall W. Bland, Theodore T. Hindson, and Jack W. Peltason (New York: New York University Press, 1984), p. 153. The original sources are 1 Stat. 264 and 1 Stat. 424.

54. Corwin, *The President*, p. 153. Corwin also claims a second significant change in 1795, writing that the president "was authorized to call forth the militia to aid a state in suppressing 'domestic violence,' a provision that evidently assumes a close identity between 'domestic violence' and 'insurrection,' and in so doing enlarges the possible realm of martial law." I have been unable to confirm independently the author's claim, as the 1795 act does not contain the language to which Corwin refers. If confirmed, the claim would merely strengthen further my argument about loosened restraints on nation-keeping behavior in the presidency.

55. For more on the issue of averting crisis, see Russell L. Riley, "The Limits of the Transformational Presidency," paper prepared for presentation at a conference entitled "Presidential Power: Forging the Presidency for the 21st Century," Columbia University, New York, November 15–16, 1996.

56. A brief account of the Alien and Sedition Acts appears in Richard Hofstadter, *The Idea of a Party System: The Rise of Legitimate Opposition in the United States, 1780–1840* (Berkeley: University of California Press, 1969), pp. 102–20.

57. It should be noted here that there has been something of an ebb and flow of sensitivity on the question of race. Some challenges to the prevailing order have not elicited very strong reactions precisely because the privileged position of whites in the United States has been so powerful, and thus challenges have been treated as mere nuisances. Objectively minor changes in the relative status of blacks and whites, however, have had profound effects on the majority community's willingness to tolerate questioning of its privileged position.

58. This logic was at the heart of Lincoln's willingness to break with forms of the Constitution to save the Union. "[M]y oath to preserve the constitution to the best of my ability, imposed upon me the duty of preserving, by every indispensable means, that government—that nation—of which that constitution was the organic law. Was it possible to lose the nation, and yet preserve the constitution? By general law life *and* limb must be protected; yet often limb must be amputated to save a life; but a life is never wisely given to save a limb." Don E. Fehrenbacher, ed., *Abraham Lincoln: Speeches and Writings, 1859–1865* (New York: Library of America, 1989), p. 585.

59. It should be noted here that the two faces of this role are closely interrelated, inasmuch as at least part of the presidential impulse to protect existing societal structures is derived from an interest in maintaining peace and security. Those who engage in serious efforts to change dearly held conventions—contrary to majority will—routinely incite strong, often violent, backlash. Thus, presidents have an incentive to suppress efforts that might set off such violence.

60. In this work I deal mainly with the barriers to collective action purposely erected by those who benefited from the status quo. For a seminal discussion of inherent barriers to mobilization, see Mancur Olson Jr., *The Logic of Collective Action: Public Goods and the Theory of Groups* (Cambridge: Harvard University Press, 1965). On barriers in general, see Russell L. Riley, "On Political Institutions and Race in America," paper presented at the Southern Political Science Association annual meeting, Tampa, November 4, 1995.

61. Quoted in Doris Kearns, *Lyndon Johnson and the American Dream* (New York: Harper and Row, 1976), p. 161.

62. Skowronek, *The Politics Presidents Make: Leadership from John Adams to George Bush* (Cambridge: Belknap Press of Harvard University Press, 1993). Skowronek's book has been awarded both the Neustadt Prize and the Greenstone Prize by the American Political Science Association (APSA), annually given to the author of the best new contribution in the fields of presidential research and history and politics respectively, and his work has been the subject of roundtable discussions by panels convened by the APSA and the Western Political Science Association.

63. Skowronek, "Response [to Peri E. Arnold, Sidney M. Milkis, and James Sterling Young]," *Polity* 27, no. 3 (Spring 1995): 521.

64. Skowronek, *The Politics Presidents Make*, pp. 4, 15, 20.

65. Skowronek is not very precise about these distinctions, about the limits of his theory. Indeed, his general account of the order-shattering imperatives of the institution (provided in part 1 of the book) tend to be overly expansive, making it difficult for the reader to detect clearly a focus on the *political* dimension. For example, he claims that the presidency is "an office that routinely disrupts established power arrangements and continually opens new avenues of political activity for others" (p. 15). How does an institution given to *political* disruption uproot "established power arrangements" and patterns of political participation that are deeply rooted in social

and economic factors that reside largely outside the realm of institutional politics? The simple answer is that presidents *routinely* do not. And on those rare occasions when presidents do pursue such change, it is seldom the politics they make that initiate the disruption of the established order.

66. Skowronek, *The Politics Presidents Make*, p. 17.

67. Skowronek does assert that, at some level, the presidency is an "*order-affirming* institution." But he repeatedly argues that "the disruptive effects of the exercise of presidential power must be *justified* in constitutional terms broadly construed as the protection, preservation, and defense of values emblematic of the body politic" (p. 20; my emphasis). That this search for justification might be evidence of a polity more interested in preservative rather than disruptive behavior from their presidents is not fully attended.

1. THE ORIGINS AND POLITICS OF ABOLITION

1. Cited in Dumas Malone, *Jefferson and His Time: The Sage of Monticello* (Boston: Little, Brown, 1981), pp. 335–36. Jefferson likened the effect to a "firebell in the night."

2. This is hardly a comprehensive presentation of the origins and development of abolitionism, and is not intended as such. Rather, it is a selective sketch the uninitiated reader will find useful as a primer for much of what follows.

3. Richard E. Neustadt, *Presidential Power and the Modern Presidents: The Politics of Leadership from Roosevelt to Reagan* (New York: Free Press, 1990), p. xxi.

4. It is acknowledged here that by linking the origins of the antislavery movement to Garrison and *The Liberator* I am venturing into an historical minefield. Historians generally agree that Garrison played a central role in the movement— some claim him as the central figure—but no consensus exists on his importance relative to other actors, especially those in the West whose contemporaneous advancement of antislavery thought differed more in style than substance from Garrison's work. My attention will be on the interplay of forces between movement and reaction, which escalated over the decades, terminating in civil war. The evidence is compelling that, because of his extremism, no figure exceeded Garrison in establishing a reaction against abolitionism; this is a point which even detractors, such as Gilbert Hobbs Barnes, concede. Garrison is important here not because of any role he may or may not have played in building organizations or bringing recruits to the cause— he shared that role with many—but because the South perceived and reacted primarily to abolitionism of the Garrisonian school, at least in the movement's formative years. This set a recognizable chain of events in motion that cannot be tied as closely to any other antislavery figure. For a classic text suggesting the primacy of others than Garrison in advancing abolitionism, see Barnes, *The Antislavery Impulse, 1830–1844* (New York: Harcourt, Brace and World, 1964).

5. Leonard L. Richards, "The Jacksonians and Slavery," in Lewis Perry and Michael Fellman, eds., *Antislavery Reconsidered: New Perspectives on the Abolitionists* (Baton Rouge: Louisiana State University Press, 1979), p. 106. See also William W. Freehling, *The Road to Disunion: Secessionists at Bay, 1776–1854* (New York: Oxford University Press, 1990), pp. 133–34.

6. For commentary on the importance of what preceded Garrison, see Ronald G. Walters, "The Boundaries of Abolitionism," in Perry and Fellman, eds., *Antislavery Reconsidered*, pp. 3–23. See also Louis Filler, *The Crusade Against Slavery: 1830–1860* (New York: Harper Torchbooks, 1963), p. 13.

7. For more on Garrison's early work, prior to *The Liberator*'s establishment, see Charles A. Madison, *Critics and Crusaders: A Century of American Protest* (New York: Henry Holt, 1947), pp. 14–19.

8. In researching this work I read extensively in *The Liberator*, examining over half of all issues published to map the development of antislavery action from 1831 to 1865. I concentrated my reading more heavily in the movement's early years, and I looked principally for material on its relationship to national political institutions.

9. Barnes, *Antislavery Impulse*, p. 51.

10. Aileen S. Kraditor offers a similar characterization of Garrison's primary intentions, but one that differs in important respects from that presented here. See Kraditor, *Means and Ends in American Abolitionism: Garrison and His Critics on Strategy and Tactics, 1834–1850* (New York: Pantheon Books, 1969), p. viii.

11. *The Liberator*, January 1, 1831, p. 1.

12. See Freehling, *Road to Disunion*, chs. 7–11.

13. Freehling, *Road to Disunion*, p. 159.

14. It should be noted here that Leonard L. Richards argues that it was the assault on colonization that actually precipitated the major northern reaction against the abolitionists discussed later. See Richards, *"Gentlemen of Property and Standing": Anti-Abolition Mobs in Jacksonian America* (London: Oxford University Press, 1970), ch. 2.

15. *The Liberator*, February 18, 1832, p. 25. Such sentiments later were at the heart of Frederick Douglass's claims about the rightful place of African Americans in the United States. See Benjamin Quarles, "Abolition's Different Drummer: Frederick Douglass," in Martin Duberman, ed., *The Antislavery Vanguard: New Essays on the Abolitionists* (Princeton: Princeton University Press, 1965), pp. 123–34.

16. Charles A. Madison noted that *The Liberator* had only 500 subscribers at the end of its first year, and only about 2,000 by 1834. He further claims that of this latter number, "no more than a fourth were whites." However, during this era subscribers represented only a fraction of the readership of a given newspaper. Most newspapers were in a sense anthologies, relying on articles clipped from other publications in much the same way that contemporary papers rely on wire services for much of their news. Thus, a colorful editor, like Garrison, might expect his pieces to be reprinted

many times over, if only as a matter of curiosity. Madison, *Critics and Crusaders*, p. 18.

17. *The Liberator*, July 30, 1831, p. 121. This emphasis was shared by both the Garrisonians and that large group of evangelical abolitionists in the West usually thought at odds with Garrison, associated with Theodore Dwight Weld. For an extensive, if overly partisan, view of Weld and the western abolitionists, see Barnes, *The Antislavery Impulse*.

18. *Third Annual Report of the American Anti-Slavery Society* (New York, 1836), p. 83. Later this point would be supplemented with an argument for positive, political responsibility, in which the North, because of its unwillingness to break its civil ties with the South, was viewed as giving military support for an evil southern regime, for the suppression of the slaves' rightful demands for freedom.

19. Cited in *The Liberator*, July 2, 1831, p. 106.

20. The history of church conflict on slavery during this era closely parallels that obtaining in the political arena, and makes for fascinating reading and analysis. Of special importance is the "coming out" movement, the theoretical justifications for which were intimately related to the later push for leaving existing political parties. For a discussion of "coming out" of the churches see Carleton Mabee, *Black Freedom: The Nonviolent Abolitionists from 1830 Through the Civil War* (New York: Macmillan, 1970), esp. chs. 9–14.

21. Perhaps the most important philosophical difference between the Garrisonians and Weld's evangelical abolitionists arose over the attitude the converted should take toward the South. Weld's followers adopted a charitable course of hating the sin while loving the sinner. The Garrisonians were more condemnatory, declaring the slave-holder himself evil. Both groups intended the same end of converting the southern slaveholder, but one felt it could be best accomplished with benevolence, the other with fire and brimstone. Further, the logical connection of means to ends—of northern conversion leading to emancipation—was never as clearly conceived among the evangelicals as with the Garrisonians. After working with Weld for several years, one prominent abolitionist still could anxiously solicit from him "a plain common Sense view of *how* emancipation and abolition are to be brought about by the correction of public sentiment at the North. . . . Can you not furnish me some *facts* pertinent to . . . the *effectiveness* of Northern abolition on the South? They will be thankfully recd." Barnes, *Antislavery Impulse*, p. 248.

22. That historiographical distinction between the Garrisonians and the so-called "political" abolitionists—those who later departed from Garrison to work primarily through the institution of political parties—is thus unfortunate, for it implies that the Garrisonians were not political. This is true only if one accepts a severely confined definition of politics as limited to action directed through accepted institutional channels using traditional means. Protest or movement activists commonly seek redress through mass organization because they believe conventional channels are dead ends. The Garrisonians, finding little hope for pursuing their ends through

usual means, resorted to alternative means, thus redefining what was in fact "political." It is true that by the late 1830s Garrison's idealism led him to a harsher critique of government that might be described as anarchic, but this was a later development and did not fully reverse the effects of his early labors to work through human institutions that he considered inherently fallible. See Richard H. Sewell, *Ballots for Freedom: Antislavery Politics in the United States, 1837–1860* (New York: Norton, 1976), pp. 24–33. See also Kraditor, *Means and Ends,* pp. 118–19. On the distinction between movement politics and the conventional politics of bargaining, see Bruce Miroff, "Presidential Leverage over Social Movements: The Johnson White House and Civil Rights," *Journal of Politics* 43 (February 1981): 5–6.

23. Garrison's original but abandoned intention to establish *The Liberator* in Washington, not Boston, also testifies to this often-ignored aspect of his labors. "Political Suggestions," *The Liberator,* December 20, 1834, p. 203; "To the Public," *The Liberator,* January 1, 1831, p. 1.

24. William Jay to the *New-York Emancipator,* reprinted in *The Liberator,* June 29, 1833, p. 102.

25. Perhaps the most eloquent and sophisticated exponent of moral suasion was Wendell Phillips. For a thorough (albeit later) statement of Phillips' thinking on this subject, see his 1852 address to the Massachusetts Antislavery Society, entitled "Public Opinion," in Phillips, ed., *Speeches, Lectures, and Letters* (Boston: James Redpath, 1863). See also Irving H. Bartlett, "The Persistence of Wendell Phillips," in Duberman, ed., *The Antislavery Vanguard,* pp. 102–22.

26. See Kraditor, *Means and Ends,* p. 79.

27. "Prospectus of The Liberator, A weekly Journal Published in Boston, Mass.," *The Liberator,* May 28, 1831, p. 87.

28. *The Liberator,* April 14, 1832, p. 57.

29. "Prospectus of The Liberator, A weekly Journal Published in Boston, Mass.," *The Liberator,* May 28, 1831, p. 87.

30. "Judge Thacher's Charge. Number V.," attributed to "Z.Z.," *The Liberator,* September 22, 1832, p. 149.

31. "Mr. Child's Speech [to the New England Anti-Slavery Society]," *The Liberator,* August 3, 1833, p. 121.

32. Richards, "The Jacksonians and Slavery," p. 107.

33. Not everyone agreed that Congress did in fact have the authority to outlaw slavery in the District, based on the agreements made with Maryland and Virginia for the cession of their slaveholding territory for creating the nation's capital.

34. "Constitution of the American Anti-Slavery Society," reprinted in part in William Jay, *Miscellaneous Writings on Slavery* (Boston: John P. Jewett, 1853), p.125.

35. *The Liberator,* January 1, 1831, p. 1.

36. In the main, electioneering was viewed by Garrisonian abolitionists as a morally corrupting activity. Divisions over this question eventually occasioned a

split among those active in the movement, with one faction supporting organized electoral activity and the other eschewing it. See Sewell, *Ballots for Freedom*, ch. 2.

37. Barnes, *Antislavery Impulse*, pp. 29–37. See also "Anti-Slavery Movements in Great Britain," *The Liberator*, June 25, 1831, p. 101; Howard R. Temperly, "British and American Abolitionists Compared," in Duberman, ed., *Antislavery Vanguard*, pp. 343–61.

38. *The Liberator*, June 18, 1831, p. 97. Because petitioning required an active organizational force, women, whose political activity at the time was severely circumscribed by law and custom, were especially useful to the movement in helping to gather signatures. Later, when Congress and state legislatures began to refuse to receive antislavery petitions, one argument used by those speaking against such gag rules was that they unfairly restricted the already-limited degree of political action acceptable for women. The role of women in the movement eventually became a major point of contention for those who wished to make more mainstream efforts to affect emancipation, and thus who believed that the active involvement of women unnecessarily alienated prospective supporters. On this issue, see " 'Am I Not a Woman and a Sister?' Abolitionist Beginnings of Nineteenth-Century Feminism," in Perry and Fellman, eds., *Antislavery Reconsidered*, pp. 252–83.

39. According to some analysts, one of the strongest sources of opposition to northern abolitionism was the New England trader, whose financial ties to the southern slave led him into a conservative stance on the issue of slavery—he may not have supported the institution as such, but his fiscal conservatism would not allow him to place at risk southern business. On this matter, see Richards, *"Gentlemen of Property and Standing,"* ch. 5.

40. *The Liberator*, March 26, 1831, p. 49.

41. "What Shall Be Done?" *The Liberator*, August 7, 1831, p. 121. Also suggested here were further appeals to the clergy to condemn slavery, efforts to remove from the Constitution that provision allowing slave representation in Congress, and the creation of "at least one hundred periodicals over the land, expressly devoted to the cause of emancipation."

42. The emergence of this and other more localized organizational structures is a useful datum about the development of the abolitionist movement. However, none of these structures, nor the sum of them, can be taken as representative of, or proxy for, the movement in its entirety. Sidney Tarrow has observed, as a general matter, that "Most people do not actually *join* an SMO [social movement organization], but participate episodically in collective actions that it sponsors. Unlike the case of interest group participation, these occasional participants are likely to be outside the range of the resources that movement organizers can muster and may not even be aware of the role of the organization in mounting them." Tarrow's observations readily apply to the case of the early abolitionists. Sidney Tarrow, *Struggle, Politics, and Reform: Collective Action, Social Movements, and Cycles of Protest* (Ithaca: Western

Societies Program, Occasional Paper No. 21, Cornell University, 1989), p. 20.

43. In the parlance of later students of mass behavior, the early abolitionists acknowledged the importance of developing social movement organizations to coordinate efforts to bring about desired change. On this general subject, see, for example, John D. McCarthy and Mayer N. Zald, "Resource Mobilization and Social Movements: A Partial Theory," in Zald and McCarthy, eds., *Social Movements in an Organizational Society: Collected Essays* (New Brunswick, N.J.: Transaction Books, 1987), pp. 20–21; Tarrow, *Struggle, Politics, and Reform*, pp. 18–22; Jo Freeman, "Resource Mobilization and Strategy: A Model for Analyzing Social Movement Organization Actions," in Zald and McCarthy, eds., *The Dynamics of Social Movements: Resource Mobilization, Social Control, and Tactics* (Cambridge: Winthrop, 1979), pp. 167–89.

44. Barnes, *Antislavery Impulse*, pp. 88–89, 150–51.

45. Barnes, *Antislavery Impulse*, p. 77; *The Liberator*, March 29, 1834, p.50.

46. *Annual Report of the American Anti-Slavery Society* (New York, 1835), pp. 37, 83.

47. "Plan of Cooperation Between the American and the New England Anti-Slavery Societies," *The Liberator*, February 14, 1835, p. 26; *Third Annual Report of the American Anti-Slavery Society* (New York, 1836), p. 26. Some states worked extremely hard to organize and take advantage of latent community sympathies. In 1838 the Massachusetts Anti-Slavery Society adopted a plan entitled "The Work to be Done," detailing an organizational arrangement reaching from the state to the county, from the county to the city, and from the city to the local school district, and covering activities such as membership recruitment, maintenance of antislavery libraries, and fund-raising. Reprinted in *The Liberator*, July 13, 1838, p. 112.

48. *First Annual Report of the American Anti-Slavery Society* (New York, 1834), p. 66.

49. Quoted in Irving H. Bartlett, *Wendell Phillips: Brahmin Radical* (Westport, Conn.: Greenwood Press, 1973), p. 102.

50. For a discussion of those internal divisions that did open in the late 1830s, see Kraditor, *Means and Ends*, ch. 3.

51. The dynamic at work here mirrors that which Dennis Chong has found in the later civil rights movement. Until some sense of efficacy was established, it was difficult for organizers to convince prospective participants that there were any real advantages to protest behavior. The occasioning of southern reaction may have been of itself sufficiently gratifying to motivate participation among some otherwise disposed to apathy. See Chong, *Collective Action and the Civil Rights Movement* (Chicago: University of Chicago Press, 1991), pp. 11, 79, 90. I will say more about this in my concluding chapter.

52. Reprinted in *The Liberator*, September 21, 1833, p. 151.

53. Actually many northern politicians with interests in national security were acutely aware of this vulnerability, as it remained a ripe target for exploitation by hostile foreign powers.

54. Southern accounts of the era are somewhat schizophrenic. Mixed in with

expressions of grave concern over the meddling of the abolitionists were reports dismissive of their activity. The latter were probably offered primarily in hopes of deflating any movement progress with ridicule, but in the context of the larger, more worried reaction, such ridicule takes on the character of whistling in the dark.

55. See the brief accounts of the Turner revolt in Louis Filler, *Crusade Against Slavery*, pp. 52–55; W. Sherman Savage, *The Controversy over the Distribution of Abolition Literature 1830–1860* (Jefferson City, Mo: Association for the Study of Negro Life and History, 1938), pp. 1–3.

56. For commentary on how the abolitionists responded to the matter of slave revolts, see Mabee, *Black Freedom*, pp. 51–70.

57. It should be noted, however, that in succeeding months Garrison's pacifist inclinations were frequently reflected. For example, that September he began running a series of dialogues among a group of fictitious slaves under the title "The Art of Preventing Slave Insurrections." Confronting two men who contemplate rebellion, Alfred, who, importantly, reads and understands the Bible, counsels patience, based in part on the peaceful work he knows is being done by the abolitionists. Alfred exhorts, "While others are thus engaged for us, it should be our care to avoid all acts of violence, and to display a meek and benevolent temper." *The Liberator*, September 24, 1831, p. 153.

58. "Walker's Appeal. No. 1," *The Liberator*, January 8, 1831, p. 6; "The Insurrection," *The Liberator*, September 2, 1831, p. 143. Walker's *Appeal*, a pamphlet first published in 1829 by the free Negro David Walker, was openly supportive of slave rebellion, and thus was especially alarming to the slaveholders. Garrison disapproved of Walker's proposed methods, but could not escape being linked with him in the southern mind. He ruefully recognized that his commentary was being perceived in the South as more promotion than prophecy.

59. He published many of the death threats he received in order to show the extent of southern depravity. See, for example, "Threats to Assassinate," *The Liberator*, September 9, 1831, p. 145.

60. Cited in "Incendiary Publications," *The Liberator*, October 8, 1831, p. 161.

61. Noted, for example, in *The Liberator*, January 7, 1832, p. 3; Richards, *"Gentlemen of Property and Standing,"* pp. 16–17. See also Fawn M. Brodie, "Who Defends an Abolitionist?" in Duberman, ed., *The Antislavery Vanguard*, p. 58.

62. Madison, *Critics and Crusaders*, p. 19. See also Savage, *Controversy over the Distribution of Abolition Literature*, pp.3–8, for an extensive array of provisions enacted in the South after the Turner insurrection to prevent further slave violence.

63. As we shall see, it was at this level of the dispute—between a small morally based interest in New England and a regional interest in the slaveholding South— that national political institutions were first called into service as organs of conflict resolution.

64. Cited in "Incendiary Publications," *The Liberator*, October 8, 1831, p. 161.

65. *The Liberator*, April 7, 1832, p. 55.

66. *New-York Journal of Commerce*, reprinted as "The Meeting Called by Gentlemen from the South," *The Liberator*, July 26, 1835, p. 118.

67. This final point is the focus of Richards in *"Gentlemen of Property and Standing,"* ch. 2.

68. From the *Boston Daily Atlas*, as quoted in *The Liberator*, August 28, 1832, p. 118. Emphasis in the original.

69. Richards, *"Gentlemen of Property and Standing,"* p. 16, ch. 3.

70. In effect, many sympathizers joined because they were offended by the South's violation of what David B. Truman has called "the rules of the game." For Truman's treatment of this general phenomenon, see *The Governmental Process: Political Interests and Public Opinion* (New York: Knopf, 1951), pp. 512–24.

71. It may be that the abolitionists' opponents recognized the value of such a strategy before they themselves did. Northern opponents often cautioned against mob violence not on its own grounds, but because "men will become [Garrison's] friends out of hatred to mobs." *Boston Recorder*, cited in *The Liberator*, October 21, 1835, p. 185.

72. From Phillips' lecture on "Disunion" delivered in the Music Hall in Boston, January 20, 1861. See Wendell Phillips, *Speeches, Lectures, and Letters* (Boston: James Redpath, Publisher, 1863), p. 348.

73. See Bartlett, *Wendell Phillips*, pp. 48–51.

74. Phillips, *Speeches, Lectures, and Letters*, pp. 213–14, 217.

75. *Third Annual Report of the American Anti-Slavery Society* (New York, 1836), p. 66.

76. *Annual Report of the American Anti-Slavery Society* (New York, 1834), p. 61.

2. A THIRTY YEARS "WAR": THE PRESIDENCY AND THE ABOLITIONISTS

1. Theodore J. Lowi, *The Personal President: Power Invested, Promise Unfulfilled* (Ithaca: Cornell University Press, 1985), p. 40.

2. In this instance, I find myself sharing Stephen Skowronek's view of the importance of the presidency to the politics of this era. *The Politics Presidents Make* (Cambridge: Belknap Press of Harvard University Press, 1993).

3. Although a grouping of this nature is useful for purposes of explanation, I should not be read as suggesting that the categories utilized here are exhaustive.

4. Leonard L. Richards, *"Gentlemen of Property and Standing": Anti-Abolition Mobs in Jacksonian America* (London: Oxford University Press, 1970), p. 7. Some of Jackson's critics blamed his style of politics for a general tone of lawlessness.

5. Figures from the *Second Annual Report of the American Anti-Slavery Society* (New York, May, 1835), p. 48; *Third Annual Report of the American Anti-Slavery Society* (New York, May 1836), p. 35. Leonard L. Richards reports that the extraordinary

increase in publications was due both to increased funding by New York's Tappan brothers and to a revolution in print technology associated with the invention of the steam press. *"Gentlemen of Property and Standing"*, pp. 71–73.

6. For the reaction of southern papers, see William Sherman Savage, *The Controversy Over the Distribution of Abolition Literature, 1830–1860* (Washington, D.C.: Association for the Study of Negro Life and History, 1938), pp. 13–15.

7. Huger to Samuel L. Gouverneur, August 1, 1835, in Frank Otto Gatell, ed., "Postmaster Huger and the Incendiary Publications," *South Carolina Historical Magazine* 64 (October 1963): 194–95; Clement Eaton, "Censorship of the Southern Mails," *The American Historical Review* 48 (January 1943): 266–67; *Third Annual Report of the American Anti-Slavery Society* (New York, May 1836), pp. 42–43; Savage, *Distribution of Abolition Literature*, pp. 27–29; William W. Freehling, *Prelude to Civil War: The Nullification Controversy in South Carolina, 1816–1836* (New York: Harper and Row, 1966), pp. 340–41. See also Defensor, *The Enemies of the Constitution Discovered, or, An Inquiry into the Origin and Tendency of Popular Violence* (New York: Leavitt, Lord, 1835), pp. 11–31; and Robert V. Remini, *Andrew Jackson and the Course of American Democracy, 1833–1845*, vol. 3 (New York: Harper and Row, 1984), pp. 258–63.

8. Huger to Gouverneur, August 8, 1835; Huger to Gouverneur, August 6, 1835; Gouverneur to Huger, August 8, 1835, all in Gatell, ed., "Postmaster Huger," pp. 197–99.

9. Kendall to the Postmaster of Charleston, August 4, 1835, reproduced in James Parton, *Life of Andrew Jackson*, vol. 3 (New York: Mason Brothers, 1860), pp. 586–87. See also the account in Savage, *Distribution of Abolition Literature*, pp. 15–26.

10. Savage, *Distribution of Abolition Literature*, pp. 14–15.

11. Jackson to Kendall, August 9, 1835, in John Spencer Bassett, ed., *Correspondence of Andrew Jackson*, vol. 5, (Washington D.C.: Carnegie Institute, 1931), pp. 360–61.

12. *Richmond Enquirer* and *Richmond Whig* articles reprinted as "Public Meeting at Richmond" in *The Liberator*, August 22, 1835, p. 133.

13. Eaton, "Censorship of the Southern Mails," pp. 267–68.

14. Kendall to Gouverneur, August 22, 1835, cited in Defensor, *Enemies of the Constitution Discovered*, pp. 21–22; Savage, *Distribution of Abolition Literature*, pp. 19–22.

15. The sentiments expressed in the letters to Huger and Gouverneur were formalized into departmental policy later that year, when Kendall stated in the postal department's annual report that local postmasters should follow state law in determining how to dispose of questionable documents. Again, this did not comply precisely with Jackson's directive that subscribers be guaranteed delivery, but Jackson made no effort to counter this order, either.

16. Quoted in *The Liberator*, September 26, 1835, p. 153. See also Eaton, "Censorship of the Southern Mails," p. 267; Savage, *Distribution of Abolition Literature*, pp. 15, 29–35.

17. The American Anti-Slavery Society declared the preceding May that its papers were not intended for slaves, and it issued a "Clarification Statement" in early September, expressly reiterating its belief in state sovereignty, its strenuous opposition to slave insurrection, its refusal to send its publications to slaves, and its support for the continuation of the federal Union. Savage, *Controversy over the Distribution of Abolition Literature*, p. 12; "Clarification Statement for the American Anti-Slavery Society," reprinted in *The Liberator*, September 12, 1835, p. 143.

18. James D. Richardson, ed., *A Compilation of the Messages and Papers of the Presidents* (New York: Bureau of National Literature, 1879), pp. 1394–95.

19. Jackson's most prominent biographer, Robert V. Remini, has stated that "Jackson's attitude and response to this incident have been unfairly criticized. For one thing he has been charged with calling abolitionist tracts 'unconstitutional and wicked.' He did no such thing. He called [in the seventh state of the Union message] the attempt to foment insurrection and servile war 'unconstitutional and wicked.'" Remini's point, however, is woefully compromised by his inability to cite an instance in which Jackson himself did not equate abolitionist tracts with servile war. Their very conflation in Jackson's mind undergirded his entire response to the problem, treating it as a case more of preserving the peace than of protecting civil liberties. See Remini, *Andrew Jackson*, p. 261.

20. Cited in *The Liberator*, October 10, 1835, p. 164. See also the *New York Evening Post* story cited in Savage, *Distribution of Abolition Literature*, pp. 14–15.

21. This reaction, and indeed the entire furor caused by the president's message, is overlooked by Jeffrey K. Tulis in his treatment of Jackson in *The Rhetorical Presidency*. Despite the formal, written, "reasoned" nature of the presentation—a state of the Union message—the rhetoric employed was no less inflammatory than much of what was being shouted from soapboxes in meeting halls throughout the country. Admittedly, Jackson did not, as he did in his letter to Kendall, call for executing those found guilty of fostering "servile war," but the passionately moral overtones of his message are unmistakable. Tulis, *The Rhetorical Presidency* (Princeton: Princeton University Press, 1987), pp. 73–75.

22. The Executive Committee's letter is reprinted in full as an appendix to William Jay's, "A View of the Action of the Federal Government, in Behalf of Slavery" in his *Miscellaneous Writings on Slavery* (Boston: John P. Jewett, 1853), pp. 364–69.

23. The limits acknowledged here are reminiscent of those encountered in the wake of the Alien and Sedition controversy described in the Introduction.

24. Remini, *Andrew Jackson*, p. 263.

25. Barnes, *The Antislavery Impulse*, pp. 100–104. Barnes notes that the decision to reduce proselytizing the South through the mails was accompanied by a determination to increase the number of lecturers circulating through the North and the West supported by the movement. The AASS never again published as many periodicals as it did in 1835.

26. *The Liberator*, February 11, 1837, p. 27.

27. Report of the *Boston Daily Advocate*, filed on February 6, 1837, reprinted in *The Liberator*, February 18, 1837, p. 30.

28. The most extensive treatment of the gag rule comes in William Lee Miller, *Arguing About Slavery: The Great Battle in the United States Congress* (New York: Knopf, 1996). See also William W. Freehling, *The Road to Disunion: Secessionists at Bay, 1776–1854* (New York: Oxford University Press, 1990), chs. 16–19; Robert P. Ludlum, "The Antislavery 'Gag-Rule': History and Argument," *Journal of Negro History* 26 (April 1941), pp. 203–43; James M. McPherson, "The Fight Against the Gag Rule: Joshua Leavitt and Antislavery Insurgency in the Whig Party, 1839–1842," *Journal of Negro History* 48 (July 1963), pp. 177–95; George C. Rable, "Slavery, Politics, and the South: The Gag Rule as a Case Study," *Capitol Studies* 3 (Fall 1975), pp. 69–87.

29. Van Buren's position did not come as a complete surprise to those who had followed closely his career and campaign. In a letter to North Carolinians widely publicized during the 1836 campaign, Van Buren indicated that he felt congressional action restricting slavery in the District of Columbia was ill-advised. He expressed an abiding interest in "arrest[ing] all agitation upon this disturbing subject." He also had a record of support for Jackson's postal service policy relating to abolitionism. Rable, "Slavery, Politics, and the South," pp. 77–82, 86–87; John Niven, *Martin Van Buren: The Romantic Age of American Politics* (New York: Oxford University Press, 1983), pp. 398–400; Van Buren's letter reprinted in *The Liberator*, April 23, 1836, p. 66.

30. Thomas Hart Benton, *Thirty Years' View*, vol. 2 (New York: D. Appleton, 1858), pp. 7–8.

31. Richardson, ed., *Messages and Papers*, p. 1535.

32. On a personal level, this impulse was probably especially strong in a talented and ambitious figure just recently freed from the frustrations of his constitutionally imposed role as understudy to the dominant political presence of his era. Benton observed of Van Buren's inaugural ceremonies, "For once, the rising was eclipsed by the setting sun." *Thirty Years' View*, vol. 1, p. 735.

33. "The pledged veto was not a necessity," wrote Benton, "but a propriety;—not necessary, but prudential." In other words, it made no real difference in relation to congressional action, but it did send a valuable signal to the agitators. Benton, *Thirty Years' View*, vol. 2, p. 9.

34. The efficacy of Van Buren's pledge, considered in isolation, was questionable. During nearly every session of his presidency Congress got entangled in the petition matter, despite Van Buren's posture. However, his pronouncement may well have been a contributing factor in some abolitionists' later decisions to enter more fully the world of party politics, thereby contributing to the fragmentation of the movement described below. In any event, I am less concerned here with the efficacy of a particular presidential action against the movement than the fact that the effort to suppress access was made and contributed to the overall political defense against agitation. As president, Martin Van Buren was no friend of those pushing for liberation of the enslaved. Barnes, *Antislavery Impulse*, p. 119.

35. I am indebted to Professor Sidney M. Milkis for suggesting to me the importance of connecting this episode with Van Buren's party-building aspirations. An extensive discussion of Van Buren's theory of political parties as instruments of rechanneling conflict in constructive directions appears in James W. Ceaser, *Presidential Selection: Theory and Development* (Princeton: Princeton University Press, 1979), ch. 3.

36. Barnes, *Antislavery Impulse*, chs. 14–16. On the abolitionists' commitment to decentralization and equality, see *The Liberator*, October 13, 1837, p. 165; Richard Ellis and Aaron Wildavsky, "The Cultural Role of the Abolitionists in the Coming of the Civil War," typescript, University of California-Berkeley, 1988.

37. Leonard L. Richards holds that "only two major obstacles stood in the way of antislavery agitation": primitive communications networks and politicians. "The Jacksonians and Slavery," in Lewis Perry and Michael Fellman, eds., *Antislavery Reconsidered: New Perspectives on the Abolitionists* (Baton Rouge: Louisiana State University Press, 1979), pp. 107–8.

38. For a discussion of the internal debate on political action, see Richard H. Sewell, *Ballots for Freedom: Antislavery Politics in the United States, 1837–1860* (New York: Oxford University Press, 1976), ch. 2.

39. Further, Garrison had pragmatic reasons for acting as he did. He saw prospects for *losing* rather than gaining support, because any choice of party affiliation or coalition would automatically alienate partisans of opposition parties.

40. The electoral weapon of choice for the purists was a policy of vote "scattering," an individualistic approach in which each voter went to the polls and wrote-in the name of one he knew to be committed to the cause—perhaps his neighbor—without engaging in any organized effort to get that person elected.

41. Originally published in *The Friend of Man*, reprinted in *The Liberator*, September 7, 1838, p. 141.

42. For example, Garrison's desire to allow women to play an advanced part in the movement was not tolerated by those who pursued change through electoral politics, because they saw equal treatment of women as alienating of prospective support on the issue of slavery. See Aileen S. Kraditor, *Means and Ends in American Abolitionism: Garrison and His Critics on Strategy and Tactics, 1834–1850* (New York: Pantheon Books, 1969), ch. 3.

43. Freehling, *Road to Disunion*, p. 294; *The Liberator*, December 11, 1840, p. 196.

44. Freehling, *Prelude to Civil War*, p. 328; Ellis and Wildavsky, "A Cultural Analysis" p. 24. The most prominent of these antebellum polemicists was George Fitzhugh, who did not, however, publish his central work until 1857. See Fitzhugh, *Cannibals All! or Slaves Without Masters*, ed. by C. Vann Woodward (Cambridge: Belknap Press of Harvard University Press, 1960).

45. E. E. Schattschneider, *The Semisovereign People: A Realist's View of Democracy in America* (New York: Holt, Rinehart, and Winston, 1960), pp. 4–5.

46. My account of the period leading up to the Texas revolution is sketchy. For more details see Randolph B. Campbell, *An Empire for Slavery: The Peculiar Institution in Texas* (Baton Rouge: Louisiana State University Press, 1989), chs. 1 and 2.

47. Quoted in William J. Cooper Jr., *The South and the Politics of Slavery, 1828–1856* (Baton Rouge: Louisiana State University Press, 1978), p. 196.

48. Abolitionist Benjamin Lundy wrote of the Texas revolution: "It is susceptible of the clearest demonstration, that the immediate cause and leading object of the contest originated in a settled design, among the slaveholders of [the United States], (with land speculators and slave traders,) to wrest the large and valuable territory of Texas from the Mexican Republic, in order to re-establish the SYSTEM OF SLAVERY; to open a vast and profitable SLAVE-MARKET therein; and, ultimately, to annex it to the United States." Lundy, *The War in Texas: A Review of Facts and Circumstances Showing that This Contest Is a Crusade . . . to Reestablish, Extend, and Perpetuate the System of Slavery and the Slave Trade* (Philadelphia, 1837), p. 3. Cited also in Campbell, *An Empire for Slavery*, pp. 35–36.

49. Major L. Wilson, *The Presidency of Martin Van Buren* (Lawrence: University Press of Kansas, 1984), pp. 149–53.

50. *The Liberator*, February 16, 1838, p. 26; March 30, 1838, p. 51.

51. Benton, *Thirty Years' View*, vol. 1, pp. 667–69.

52. Wilson, *Martin Van Buren*, p. 149.

53. A third candidate, as we will see, is Pierce's decision to embrace the Kansas-Nebraska Act, reversing the Missouri Compromise.

54. For commentary on the full implications of the accident of Harrison's death, see Freehling, *Road to Disunion*, p. 393.

55. Here Stephen Skowronek's logic about *political* disruption is especially relevant.

56. Cooper, *The South and the Politics of Slavery*, p. 183.

57. Merrill D. Peterson, *The Great Triumvirate: Webster, Clay, and Calhoun* (New York: Oxford University Press, 1987), p. 312; Cooper, *The South and the Politics of Slavery*, pp. 176–81.

58. Moreover, it is worth mentioning here that an "accidental" president may be deprived of certain kinds of reliable cues that a conventionally elected president counts on to get an accurate reading as to what specific steps his nation-keeping responsibilities require of him. "Accidental" presidents, then, are perhaps more vulnerable to mistakes in judging those requirements. Too, "accidental" presidents may be generally less politically astute, and are almost assuredly less able to stand against questionable advice offered by powerful advisors, formal or informal. Indeed some historians have argued that Tyler succumbed to just such vulnerabilities in approaching Texas as he did, mistakenly aggravating sectional jealousies that might have been better left alone. See Freehling, *Road to Disunion*, pp. 393, 398–401.

59. Freehling, *Road to Disunion*, p. 369.

60. This entire episode is discussed at length in Freehling, *Road to Disunion*, chs. 20–25. The quoted material appears on p. 397.

61. Freehling, *Road to Disunion*, pp. 397–98.

62. "A characteristic of the annexation propaganda flowing from Tyler circles was its selectivity as to audience." Frederick Merk, *Fruits of Propaganda in the Tyler Administration* (Cambridge: Harvard University Press, 1971), p. 31.

63. Merk, *Fruits of Propaganda in the Tyler Administration*, p. 98. Walker's letter is conveniently reproduced in full in an appendix to this volume, pp. 221–52.

64. Freehling notes that such arguments were also persuasive among some southern audiences, which too worried about the future presence of blacks in their midst. *Road to Disunion*, pp. 418–25.

65. Peterson, *The Great Triumvirate*, pp 347–49; Cooper, *The South and the Politics of Slavery*, pp. 103–18, 188–89.

66. Merk, *Slavery and the Annexation of Texas*, pp. 61–69, 85–92, 113–20.

67. Cooper, *The South and the Politics of Slavery*, pp. 191–92.

68. Florida would be added that same year as the twenty-seventh state, and also a slave state.

69. Richardson, ed., *Messages and Papers*, pp. 2227, 2231.

70. Merk, *Slavery and the Annexation of Texas*, p. 181.

71. *The Liberator*, March 5, 1847, p. 38.

72. Paul H. Bergeron, *The Presidency of James K. Polk* (Lawrence: University Press of Kansas, 1987), p. 67.

73. For instance, during this period the *Charleston Courier* proclaimed, "Every battle fought in Mexico, and every dollar spent there, but insures the acquisition of territory which must widen the field of southern enterprise in the future. And the final result will be to readjust the whole balance of power in the confederacy so as to give us control over the operations of the government in all time to come." Quoted in Hubert Howe Bancroft, *History of California*, vol. 6, in *The Works of Hubert Howe Bancroft*, 23 vols. (San Francisco: History Company Publishers, 1888), p. 338.

74. Correspondence with the author, December 20, 1996, p. 9.

75. Milo Milton Quaife, ed., *The Diary of James K. Polk During His Presidency* (New York: Kraus, 1970), vol. 2, p. 75. The editor of these diaries writes in an accompanying biographical sketch that Polk "totally failed to perceive the relation between his policy of territorial expansion and the rising tide of agitation over slavery" (p. xxx). This seems to be a stunning fault in a president commonly designated by historians as one of the century's most astute.

76. Bergeron, *The Presidency of James K. Polk*, p. 68.

77. Richardson, ed., *Messages and Papers*, p. 2230.

78. Cooper, *The South and the Politics of Slavery*, p. 241.

79. Quoted in Freehling, *Road to Disunion*, p. 461.

80. Discussions of efforts to rally southern opinion versus the invigorated north-

ern effort against extension can be found in Peterson, *The Great Triumvirate*, ch. 8, and Freehling, *Road to Disunion*, ch. 27. See also Cooper, *The South and the Politics of Slavery*, p. 238.

81. Bergeron, *The Presidency of James K. Polk*, p. 204.

82. This position had practical consequences at that moment as decisions were then being made about the disposition of Oregon, which rested entirely above the 36°30' parallel. Polk signed the organizational bill for Oregon, in August 1848, only after clarifying in an executive message to Congress that he did so because that area met the Missouri Compromise restrictions. Polk's message is found in Richardson, ed., *Messages and Papers*, pp. 2456–60.

83. Bergeron, *The Presidency of James K. Polk*, p. 208.

84. Peterson, *The Great Triumvirate*, pp. 426–28; Freehling, *Road to Disunion*, pp. 479–80; McPherson, *Battle Cry of Freedom*, pp. 57–58; Eric Foner, *Free Soil, Free Labor, Free Men: The Ideology of the Republican Party Before the Civil War* (London: Oxford University Press, 1970), pp. 138–39; George M. Fredrickson, ed., *William Lloyd Garrison* (Englewood Cliffs, N.J.: Prentice-Hall, 1968), pp. 52–55.

85. Quaife, ed., *Diary of James K. Polk*, vol. 3, p. 502.

86. "In the [1848] election, the Free-Soilers polled almost 300,000 votes in all, and in New York alone about six thousand more than Lewis Cass, the regular Democratic candidate. Since both major contestants had, without New York, the same number of electoral votes, the 36 votes of that state [disproportionately drawn from the Democrats] decided the election and gave the Presidency to the Whig candidate, Zachary Taylor." Stefan Lorant, *The Presidency: A Pictorial History of Presidential Elections from Washington to Truman* (New York: Macmillan, 1951), pp. 186–87.

87. Evidence of inclinations toward independence can be found in Bancroft, *History of California*, vol. 5, pp. 191–223, 600; vol. 6, pp. 279–80, 347.

88. Quaife, ed., *Diary of James K. Polk*, vol. 4, pp. 136–38; McCoy, *Polk and the Presidency*, p. 159.

89. For evidence of Polk's concerns about prospects of losing California, see Quaife, ed., *Diary of James K. Polk*, vol. 4, pp. 231–33.

90. It should be noted here that this compromise was not, all things considered, a transcendent victory for the antislavery movement. At the most basic level the southwestern lands question constituted an elaborate diversion from the central concerns of the abolitionists: the eradication of slavery where it already existed. This fact renders the concessions that the free states won in the Southwest meager, but not inconsequential. Both sides recognized this to varying degrees. *Liberator* editorials of the period commonly exhorted true believers not to lose sight of the ultimate goal: "The Wilmot Proviso, though we should hail its adoption by Congress as a sign of antislavery progress, is not the great issue before the country. That issue is, the immediate and entire abolition of slavery on every inch of American soil" (February 4, 1848, p. 26). Some southerners recognized the positive effects of keeping opponents tied up

out West rather than in their own backyards. Calhoun once observed in this regard, "It is a true maxim to meet danger on the frontier, in politics as well as war." Quoted in Benton, *Thirty Years' View*, vol. 2, p. 698.

91. Quaife, ed., *Diary of James K. Polk*, vol. 4, pp. 293, 299–300.

92. Richard E. Neustadt, *Presidential Power and the Modern Presidents* (New York: The Free Press, 1990), pp. xx-xxi.

93. Quaife, ed., *Diary*, vol. 4, p. 376.

94. Quoted in Holman Hamilton, *Zachary Taylor: Soldier in the White House* (Indianapolis: Bobbs Merrill, 1951), p. 225.

95. Freehling, *The Road to Disunion*, pp. 491–92.

96. Freehling, *The Road to Disunion*, p. 492.

97. Peterson, *The Great Triumvirate*, p. 456.

98. Freehling, *The Road to Disunion*, pp. 490–91.

99. Quoted in Hamilton, *Zachary Taylor*, p. 335.

100. Indeed, although the dispute was primarily over honest, good-faith differences in how to resolve a vexing problem, Clay claimed that the president was making "open, undisguised war" on his package, and it was Taylor's White House that derisively termed Clay's an "omnibus" bill. Quoted in Peterson, *The Great Triumvirate*, p. 471.

101. Many historians have speculated as to what might have happened had Taylor lived and prevailed on the territorial matter. Armed conflict may have resulted—the Texas-New Mexico border situation was almost at a boiling point—bringing civil war in 1850 rather than 1861. The conventional wisdom is that war at that time, as opposed to later, would have benefited the South, since much of the northern industrial growth which paved the way for the Union war machine during the Civil War was to develop in the 1850s. Holman Hamilton, however, suggests that this thinking is flawed in two ways. First, had the president continued with his firm stand, the South may have acquiesced, as they had under Andrew Jackson. According to this reasoning, a firm stand in 1850 may thus have spared the nation civil war. Second, had the South decided to fight, they were not the unified front they would present a decade later. Subsequently, they may not have proved to be the formidable opponent they would later become. These arguments are presented in Hamilton's *Zachary Taylor*, ch. 32.

102. Peterson, *The Great Triumvirate*, p. 473.

103. K. Jack Bauer, *Zachary Taylor: Soldier, Planter, Statesman of the Old Southwest* (Baton Rouge: Louisiana State University Press, 1985), p. 301.

104. "The Compromise of 1850 substantially embodied the resolutions Clay had introduced in February." Peterson, *The Great Triumvirate*, p. 475.

105. Peterson, *The Great Triumvirate*, p. 473.

106. Perhaps the best illustration of this was Herbert Hoover's fate in the 1932 election, driven by his failure to take drastic action to save the nation's economy. Examples are hard to come by, because few are elevated to the presidency without a

refined sense of how to read compelling signals in the political environment, especially those related to system-threatening problems.

107. Cited in Benson Lee Grayson, *The Unknown President: The Administration of Millard Fillmore* (Washington D.C.: University Press of America, 1981), p. 49.

108. David M. Potter, *The Impending Crisis 1848–1861* (New York: Harper and Row, 1976), p. 114.

109. "Most of the country gave a sigh of relief," according to James M. McPherson. See his *Battle Cry of Freedom: The Civil War Era* (New York: Oxford University Press, 1988), p. 75.

110. Martin B. Duberman, *Charles Francis Adams, 1807–1886* (Boston: Houghton Mifflin, 1961), p. 179.

111. *New York Independent*, reprinted in *The Liberator*, March 8, 1850, p. 37.

112. Bauer, *Zachary Taylor*, p. 302. Ironically, those who for so long had looked to preserve states' rights sought an expansion in the scope of federal authority on the fugitive slave question. See Larry Gara, *The Liberty Line: The Legend of the Underground Railroad* (Lexington: University of Kentucky Press, 1961), p. 127.

113. David M. Potter writes of Clay's provisions, "implicitly they promised what no act of legislation really could promise—namely that the crusade against slavery would die down for lack of issues on which to feed." *The Impending Crisis*, p. 100.

114. *The Liberator*, September 27, 1850.

115. The folklore surrounding the Underground Railroad tends to distort somewhat the essential elements useful for my account. Apparently there never was a well-developed, systematic nationwide network of abolitionists engaged in spiriting northward fugitive slaves. Rather, most fugitives were on their own through the most dangerous part of their journeys through the South, and only found episodic help once they entered the free states. There was also disagreement among abolitionists about how much encouragement to give fleeing slaves. However, records clearly show that assistance to fugitives was a priority among many antislavery activists, and that escape itself constituted an act with substantial political consequences. For a thorough account of the folklore and historic evidence about the Underground Railroad, see Gara, *The Liberty Line*.

116. Gara, *The Liberty Line*, pp. 131, 138–39.

117. Gara, *The Liberty Line*, p. 135.

118. Richardson, ed., *Messages and Papers*, pp. 92–93, 138–39.

119. Reprinted in *The Liberator*, March 7, 1851, p. 38.

120. John W. Burgess, *The American History Series: The Middle Period, 1817–1858* (New York: Charles Scribner's Sons, 1897), pp. 370–72.

121. Richardson, ed., *Messages and Papers*, pp. 105–06, 109–10.

122. Filler, *The Crusade Against Slavery*, p. 204; Potter, *The Impending Crisis*, pp. 133–34. Fillmore also sent troops into Pennsylvania in 1851 to find those responsible for the death of a slaveholder searching for his runaway. Unable to locate precisely the

responsible party, the administration brought treason charges against a number of locals suspected of knowledge of the earlier crime. The charges were ridiculed by defense attorneys and subsequently dropped. McPherson, *Battle Cry of Freedom*, pp. 84–85.

123. Potter, *The Impending Crisis*, p. 143. Harriet Beecher Stowe's book, published in serial form in 1851, and in book form a year later, created a sensation among its northern readership. Potter suggests that Stowe's account, absent the "vituperation" of the abolitionists, made converts of some the latter may never have reached otherwise.

124. Richardson, ed., *Messages and Papers*, p. 2755.

125. Cited in McPherson, *Battle Cry of Freedom*, p. 118.

126. Richardson, ed., *Messages and Papers*, pp. 2735, 2755.

127. Roy F. Nichols, *Franklin Pierce: Young Hickory of the Granite Hills* (Philadelphia: University of Pennsylvania Press, 1958), pp. 361–62; Filler, *The Crusade Against Slavery*, pp. 213–17.

128. McPherson, *Battle Cry of Freedom*, p. 120.

129. Filler, *The Crusade Against Slavery*, pp. 215–17.

130. For details on the role of the railroads in reopening the territorial issue, see Potter, *The Impending Crisis*, ch. 7. On the Kansas-Nebraska Act, see Freehling, *Road to Disunion*, chs. 30–31.

131. Freehling, *Road to Disunion*, pp. 552–56.

132. Nichols, *Franklin Pierce*, p. 323.

133. Nichols, *Franklin Pierce*, p. 337; David Herbert Donald, *Charles Sumner and the Coming of the Civil War* (Chicago: University of Chicago Press, 1960), p. 253.

134. Potter, *The Impending Crisis*, pp. 162–64.

135. Skowronek, *The Politics Presidents Make*, p. 192.

136. Potter, *The Impending Crisis*, p. 167.

137. Potter, *The Impending Crisis*, p. 174.

138. Nichols, *Franklin Pierce*, pp. 319–21; Skowronek, *The Politics Presidents Make*, pp. 190–91. For Pierce's own comments in this regard, see the case he made for popular sovereignty in his third annual message (1855), in Richardson, ed., *Messages and Papers*, pp. 2877–82.

139. Freehling, *Road to Disunion*, pp. 536–37.

140. Richardson, ed., *Messages and Papers*, pp. 2877, 2882–83.

141. McPherson, *Battle Cry of Freedom*, p. 123. See also Potter, *The Impending Crisis*, p. 161.

142. Holt, *The Political Crisis of the 1850s* (New York: Wiley, 1978), p. 147 (emphasis added). See also Nichols, *Franklin Pierce*, p. 323.

143. Both cited in Sewell, *Ballots for Freedom*, pp. 256–57.

144. Freehling, *Road to Disunion*, pp. 554–55.

145. Nichols, *Franklin Pierce*, p. 338.

146. Cited in Elbert B. Smith, *The Presidency of James Buchanan* (Lawrence:

University Press of Kansas, 1975), p. 17. The election of 1856 was the first in which the new Republican party produced a presidential candidate, and Buchanan's election can, in part, be attributed to a fractured electorate searching for realignment in the wake of the Whigs' passing. See James L. Sundquist, *Dynamics of the Party System: Alignment and Realignment of Political Parties in the United States*, rev. ed. (Washington D.C.: Brookings Institution, 1983), ch. 5.

147. Smith, *The Presidency of James Buchanan*, p. 24.

148. Cited in Smith, *The Presidency of James Buchanan*, p. 26.

149. Richardson, ed., *Messages and Papers*, p. 2962.

150. McPherson, *Battle Cry of Freedom*, p. 165; Kenneth M. Stampp, *America in 1857: A Nation on the Brink* (New York: Oxford University Press, 1990), pp. 273–75.

151. Stampp, *America in 1857*, pp. 281–89.

152. For a brief discussion of the constitution's terms, see Smith, *The Presidency of James Buchanan*, p. 39.

153. Stampp, *America in 1857*, p. 282. Stampp argues here (p. 285) that Buchanan finally gave in due less to external pressure than to an internal sympathy with the slaveholders, and because of an interest in moving the Kansas question off the agenda as quickly as possible. In this instance, then, it would seem that he errantly traded off the long-run for the short. Others argue that Buchanan's positioning on Kansas had all along derived primarily from political considerations. He apparently believed that a popular vote there would result in a free soil decision, and thus by standing with the Lecompton convention he could avoid alienating both slave and free interests. Once it became apparent that the convention would not allow a free popular vote, the president decided the best course was to get the fight behind him as quickly as possible, and that meant above all else avoiding another constitutional convention. See Smith, *The Presidency of James Buchanan*, pp. 33–42.

154. McPherson, *Battle Cry of Freedom*, pp. 165–67.

155. Richardson, ed., *Messages and Papers*, p. 3010.

156. McPherson, *Battle Cry of Freedom*, p. 226; Phillip Shaw Paludan, *The Presidency of Abraham Lincoln* (Lawrence: University Press of Kansas, 1994), pp. 22–23.

157. Stampp, *America in 1857*, p. 311.

158. Smith, *The Presidency of James Buchanan*, p. 46.

159. Cited in Stampp, *America in 1857*, p. 331. Stampp concludes his work with this quote, followed by: "Let him be remembered, then, for that!"

160. Quoted in McPherson, *Battle Cry of Freedom*, p. 166.

161. Smith, *The Presidency of James Buchanan*, p. 127.

162. Richardson, ed., *Messages and Papers*, pp. 3157–58.

163. Richardson, ed., *Messages and Papers*, p. 3169.

164. Smith, *The Presidency of James Buchanan*, p. 151.

165. Richardson, ed., *Messages and Papers*, pp. 3158–59.

166. Indeed, according to Lincoln's thought, because the rebellion was unconsti-

tutional, the Union actually was *not* dissolved by southern secession. See his inaugural address, reprinted in Don E. Fehrenbacher, ed., *Abraham Lincoln: Speeches and Writings, 1859–1865* (New York: Library of America, 1989), p. 220.

167. Fehrenbacher, ed., *Speeches and Writings*, p. 196.

168. Fehrenbacher, ed., *Speeches and Writings*, p. 358.

3. THE MAKING OF A GREAT EMANCIPATOR

1. For Lincoln's explanation of his position, see Robert W. Johannsen, ed., *The Lincoln-Douglas Debates of 1858* (New York: Oxford University Press, 1965), passim.

2. David Herbert Donald, *Lincoln* (New York: Touchstone, 1996), pp. 226, 234, 269.

3. His predictions of an "irrepressible conflict" over the issue, and his association in popular thinking (largely undeserved) with John Brown, reduced his appeal among "old Whig conservatives" and border state voters. James M. McPherson, *Battle Cry of Freedom: The Civil War Era* (New York: Oxford University Press, 1988), pp. 198, 211, 216–17.

4. Quoted in Richard Hofstadter, *The American Political Tradition and the Men Who Made It* (New York: Vintage Books, 1973), p. 165.

5. For material on Lincoln's campaign commitments on the slavery question, see Hofstadter, *The American Political Tradition*, p. 141; George M. Fredrickson, "A Man But Not a Brother: Abraham Lincoln and Racial Equality," in *The Arrogance of Race: Historical Perspectives on Slavery, Racism, and Social Inequality* (Middletown, Conn.: Wesleyan University Press, 1988), p. 58; McPherson, *Battle Cry of Freedom*, pp. 178–89; Don E. Fehrenbacher, ed., *Abraham Lincoln: Speeches and Writings, 1832–1858* (New York: Library of America, 1989), p. 426; Don E. Fehrenbacher, ed., *Abraham Lincoln: Speeches and Writings, 1859–1865* (New York: Library of America, 1989), p. 157; Thomas Hudson McKee, ed., *The National Conventions and Platforms of All Political Parties, 1789 to 1905*, 6th ed. (Baltimore: Friedenwald, 1906), pp. 13–14.

6. David M. Potter, *Lincoln and His Party in the Secession Crisis* (New Haven: Yale University Press, 1962), p. 42; James Brewer Stewart, *Joshua R. Giddings and the Tactics of Radical Politics* (Cleveland: Press of Case Western Reserve University, 1970), p. 273.

7. Hofstadter, *The American Political Tradition*, p. 171.

8. William Best Hesseltine, quoted in Hans L. Trefousse, *Lincoln's Decision for Emancipation* (Philadelphia: Lippincott, 1975), p. 107.

9. The story of Lincoln's odyssey from nonextensionist to emancipator has been the subject of such extensive scholarship that there is little new or novel in the way of particulars I can add to it. However, the purpose of this chapter is to place Lincoln's efforts in the context of a struggle that had been waged for over thirty years. The usefulness of this treatment, then, is twofold: to document the resistance to change Lincoln evidenced—thus connecting him with presidents before and after—and to establish for the record that his movement toward emancipation culminated under

great duress. These factors will be important when I examine how popular portraits of presidential "leadership" diverge from historical particulars in a recognizable pattern.

10. *Richmond Enquirer*, quoted in *The Liberator*, January 6, 1860, p. 1.

11. *Charleston Mercury*, reprinted in *The Liberator*, July 27, 1860, p. 117.

12. Quoted in McPherson, *Battle Cry of Freedom*, pp. 230–31.

13. Phillip Shaw Paludan, *The Presidency of Abraham Lincoln* (Lawrence: University Press of Kansas, 1994), pp. 32, 69–70.

14. Donald, *Lincoln*, p. 270.

15. Quoted in McPherson, *Battle Cry of Freedom*, p. 231.

16. McPherson, *Battle Cry of Freedom*, p. 256.

17. *The Liberator*, January 4, 1861, p. 2.

18. *Frankfort* (Ky.) *Commonwealth*, reprinted in *The Liberator*, November 9, 1860, p. 177.

19. Paludan, *The Presidency of Abraham Lincoln*, p. 29.

20. Lincoln's union-saving inclinations had a long provenance, and tended to supersede all other considerations, including, on some occasions, the expansion of slavery. David Herbert Donald writes, "Lincoln's commitment to maintaining the Union was absolute." See Donald, *Lincoln*, pp. 180–81, 269.

21. Donald, *Lincoln*, p. 342.

22. Fehrenbacher, ed., *Speeches and Writings, 1859–1865*, p. 215. Lincoln continued in this vein by also pledging fidelity to the Constitution's fugitive slave provision.

23. Fehrenbacher, ed., *Speeches and Writings, 1859–1865*, p. 260.

24. Clinton Rossiter, *Constitutional Dictatorship: Crisis Government in the Modern Democracies* (New York: Harcourt, Brace and World, 1963), pp. 224–30.

25. Fehrenbacher, ed., *Speeches and Writings, 1859–1865*, p. 224.

26. T. Harry Williams contended that most radical Republicans—he called them "Jacobins"—were not true abolitionists. Rather, "more than slavery they hated its political representatives, the proud cavaliers who had dominated Congress in the fifties." The distinction is useful, but not important for my purposes, inasmuch as the policy prescriptions during war were practically indistinguishable. Williams, *Lincoln and the Radicals* (Madison: University of Wisconsin Press, 1941), pp. 4–6.

27. Cited in Trefousse, *Lincoln's Decision for Emancipation*, p. 18.

28. Cited in Williams, *Lincoln and the Radicals*, p. 25.

29. Trefousse, *Lincoln's Decision for Emancipation*, pp. 19–20.

30. Trefousse, *Lincoln's Decision for Emancipation*, pp. 20–21.

31. Trefousse, *Lincoln's Decision for Emancipation*, pp. 21–23. Privately, the president indicated that slaves escaping to Union lines ought not be returned. Donald, *Lincoln*, p. 343.

32. Williams, *Lincoln and the Radicals*, pp. 26–27; Trefousse, *Lincoln's Decision for Emancipation*, pp. 22–23.

33. Fehrenbacher, ed., *Speeches and Writings, 1859–1865*, p. 266. This course was representative of Lincoln's behavior during the first year of the conflict, when he was still committed to fighting a limited war. A full-scale commitment to total war—only a part of which was emancipation—arose only after the president became convinced that Union victory required that the South be wholly conquered. See James M. McPherson, "Lincoln and the Strategy of Unconditional Surrender," in Gabor S. Boritt, ed., *Lincoln, The War President: The Gettysburg Lectures* (New York: Oxford University Press, 1992), pp. 31–62.

34. Paludan, *The Presidency of Abraham Lincoln*, p. 87.

35. Lincoln to Orville H. Browning, in Fehrenbacher, ed., *Speeches and Writings, 1859–1865*, pp. 268–69.

36. Quoted in Donald, *Lincoln*, p. 315.

37. Paludan, *The Presidency of Abraham Lincoln*, p. 88.

38. Williams, *Lincoln and the Radicals*, pp. 41, 48–50.

39. Williams, *Lincoln and the Radicals*, pp. 50–51.

40. Donald, *Lincoln*, p. 326; Trefousse, *Lincoln's Decision for Emancipation*, pp. 26–27.

41. Williams, *Lincoln and the Radicals*, pp. 136–37.

42. Williams, *Lincoln and the Radicals*, pp. 137–38. See also Lincoln's "Proclamation Revoking General Hunter's Emancipation Order," in Fehrenbacher, ed., *Speeches and Writings, 1859–1865*, pp. 318–19.

43. Paludan, *The Presidency of Abraham Lincoln*, p. 125.

44. Donald, *Lincoln*, p. 342.

45. Williams, *Lincoln and the Radicals*, p. 64.

46. Williams, *Lincoln and the Radicals*, p. 82

47. McPherson, *Battle Cry of Freedom*, pp. 494–96. See also Kenneth M. Stampp, "The United States and National Self-determination," in Boritt, ed., *Lincoln, The War President*, p. 136; Paludan, *The Presidency of Abraham Lincoln*, p. 124.

48. In two places he did make a veiled reference to the topic. He noted, in criticism of the southern declaration of independence, the omission of the words "all men are created equal." Perhaps more importantly, he tried to reassure those in rebellion of how they would be treated upon returning to the fold. He said that he "probably will have no different understanding of the powers, and duties of the Federal government, relatively to the rights of the States, and the people, under the Constitution, than that expressed in the inaugural address." Fehrenbacher, ed., *Speeches and Writings, 1859–1865*, pp. 259–60.

49. Williams, *Lincoln and the Radicals*, p. 157.

50. Donald, *Lincoln*, pp. 343–48; Paludan, *The Presidency of Abraham Lincoln*, pp. 126–28.

51. This should not be interpreted as suggesting that Lincoln treated the secessionists with a light hand. He recognized that his moderation in trying to define an

enduring settlement would only be attractive to the South if it were contrasted with the alternative of a well-fought war. Thus, before he called Congress into session, he unilaterally imposed a blockade of southern ports and called up state militias to suppress the rebellion. Rossiter, *Constitutional Dictatorship*, pp. 225–28.

52. John Hope Franklin, *The Emancipation Proclamation* (Garden City, N.Y.: Doubleday, 1963), p. 22; Stephen B. Oates, *Abraham Lincoln, The Man Behind the Myth* (New York: Harper and Row, 1984), pp. 103–4; Donald, *Lincoln*, pp. 342–48.

53. Donald, *Lincoln*, p. 343.

54. *The Liberator*, December 6, 1861, p. 194.

55. David Herbert Donald notes that this was the first message calling for some form of emancipation ever sent by a president to Congress. Donald, *Lincoln*, p. 346.

56. Donald, *Lincoln*, pp. 346–48.

57. Shortly thereafter, slavery was abolished in the national territories. Again, Lincoln approved, although this time (perhaps because the number of people affected was so small) there were no colonization or compensation clauses. Fehrenbacher, ed., *Speeches and Writings, 1859–1865*, pp. 307–8; Williams, *Lincoln and the Radicals*, pp. 158–61; Donald, *Lincoln*, p. 348.

58. See Paludan, *The Presidency of Abraham Lincoln*, pp. 133–35.

59. The Crittenden Resolution had been adopted just after the Union rout at Bull Run as a means of unifying northern opinion behind a shaky war effort. The radicals passively consented, fearful of being seen as obstacles in defeating a southern menace. They did not allow the resolution, however, to interfere with their efforts to make slavery a war aim. Paludan, *The Presidency of Abraham Lincoln*, pp. 82–83.

60. Williams, *Lincoln and the Radicals*, pp. 160–62.

61. Indeed, he angered many radicals by later returning with the signed bill a veto message indicating what he would have done had they not complied with his demands altering the measure. This they considered gratuitous. Trefousse, *Lincoln's Decision for Emancipation*, p. 37.

62. McPherson, *Battle Cry of Freedom*, p. 500.

63. Cited in Williams, *Lincoln and the Radicals*, p. 167.

64. McPherson, *Battle Cry of Freedom*, p. 500.

65. Trefousse, *Lincoln's Decision for Emancipation*, pp. 18–19.

66. It was at this time, under these circumstances, that he countermanded General Hunter's emancipation order in the field. Trefousse, *Lincoln's Decision for Emancipation*, pp. 32–33.

67. Trefousse, *Lincoln's Decision for Emancipation*, pp. 30–31.

68. McPherson, *Battle Cry of Freedom*, p. 503.

69. Quoted in Donald, *Lincoln*, p. 317. These remarks came in relation to the president's decision to relieve Fremont of his command after his emancipation order.

70. "When, in March, and May, and July 1862 I made earnest, and successive appeals to the border states to favor compensated emancipation, I believed the indis-

pensable necessity for military emancipation, and arming the blacks would come, unless averted by that measure. They declined the proposition; and I was, in my best judgment, driven to the alternative of either surrendering the Union, and with it, the Constitution, or of laying strong hand upon the colored element. I chose the latter." Fehrenbacher, ed., *Speeches and Writings, 1859–1865*, p. 586.

71. McPherson, *Battle Cry of Freedom*, p. 554.

72. Quoted in Donald, *Lincoln*, p. 363.

73. Franklin, *Emancipation Proclamation*, pp. 34–39.

74. Lincoln did issue a "Proclamation of the Act to Suppress Insurrection" in late July, essentially publicizing this first paragraph of his proposed emancipation proclamation, and thus expressing an intent to enforce the second Confiscation Act. Franklin, *Emancipation Proclamation*, p. 44.

75. Franklin, *Emancipation Proclamation*, pp. 39–42.

76. For the loyal slave states he proposed a constitutional amendment ending slavery. Paludan, *The Presidency of Abraham Lincoln*, pp. 147–48.

77. Cited in McPherson, *Battle Cry of Freedom*, p. 510.

78. "Address on Colonization to a Committee of Colored Men, Washington D.C.," in Fehrenbacher, ed., *Speeches and Writings, 1859–1865*, pp. 353–57.

79. David Herbert Donald writes of this incident, "No doubt he expected his proposal to be rejected." Although he gives no direct evidence to support that interpretation, he suggests that Lincoln took this very public approach as a means of preparing non-radical publics for the dramatic action he was about to take with the Emancipation Proclamation. See Donald, *Lincoln*, pp. 368–69.

80. *The Liberator*, August 29, 1862, p. 139; September 5, 1862, p. 141.

81. Cited in McPherson, *Battle Cry of Freedom*, p. 509.

82. McPherson, *Battle Cry of Freedom*, pp. 544–45; Franklin, *Emancipation Proclamation*, pp. 46–48.

83. Franklin, *Emancipation Proclamation*, pp. 48–50.

84. There was, in fact, a principled reason for this course of action. Lincoln believed that he was empowered, because of the war emergency, to take action in the executive arena that was denied Congress by the Constitution.

85. McPherson, *Battle Cry of Freedom*, p. 558; Franklin, *Emancipation Proclamation*, pp. 61–62.

86. Franklin, *Emancipation Proclamation*, p. 67.

87. Franklin, *Emancipation Proclamation*, pp. 70–73.

88. Franklin, *Emancipation Proclamation*, pp. 84–86.

89. The connection of this proposal to earlier efforts in the United States to adopt programs of gradual emancipation is made in David Brion Davis, "The Emancipation Moment," in Boritt, ed., *Lincoln, The War President*, pp. 73–75.

90. Fehrenbacher, ed., *Speeches and Writings, 1859–1865*, pp. 406–9.

91. Donald, *Lincoln*, p. 397.

92. *The Liberator*, December 5, 1862, p. 194; December 12, 1862, p. 198.

93. Hofstadter, *The American Political Tradition*, p. 171.

94. See Franklin, *Emancipation Proclamation*, ch. 4.

95. Quoted in Hofstadter, *The American Political Tradition*, p. 169.

96. Paludan, *The Presidency of Abraham Lincoln*, p. 188.

97. "Reluctantly, and after great hesitation, Lincoln turned to the one source of manpower he had vowed he would never use: African-Americans." Donald, *Lincoln*, p. 429. See also Paludan, *The Presidency of Abraham Lincoln*, p. 155.

98. Stephen Oates writes, "The Proclamation had indeed liberated Abraham Lincoln, enabling him to act more consistently with his moral convictions." *Abraham Lincoln*, p. 118.

99. David Herbert Donald records two relevant occasions on which Lincoln confronted the question of allowing the South to return to the Union with slavery intact, his emancipation order notwithstanding. On the first, in August 1864, the president was attempting to coax from Jefferson Davis an offer of peace, and he wished to set aside whatever obstacles might prevent that. On the second, in February 1865, the president pursued a similar course during and just after negotiating sessions with Confederate Vice President Alexander H. Stephens. Whether Lincoln's position here was merely a bargaining ploy—perhaps he expected no reply and thus was merely trying to embarrass the rebels as unwilling to negotiate—cannot be known because the confederates never made a proposal for peace in response to the president's proposition. They never called what might have been a bluff. But it does seem clear from the record that at least in the first instance Lincoln was genuinely conflicted, even at that late date, over whether he ought to insist on abolition as the price of peace and reunion. See Donald, *Lincoln*, pp. 526–27, 557–61.

100. On the practical side, Congress had already passed one measure, the Wade-Davis bill, insisting on abolition as a condition of peace. Lincoln vetoed this legislation, primarily to maintain executive control of reconstruction policy. Also, Lincoln felt sure that he would lose the service of 200,000 black troops if he reversed his course. On the moral side, he believed he would be "damned in time and eternity" if he turned his back on those who had left their masters to aid the war effort. Donald, *Lincoln*, pp. 511, 527.

101. Donald, *Lincoln*, pp. 522–45. Lincoln cultivated carefully the support of Garrison and other abolitionists in the 1864 campaign. Paludan, *The Presidency of Abraham Lincoln*, pp. 271–72.

102. Donald, *Lincoln*, p. 504.

103. Oates, *Abraham Lincoln*, pp. 116–17.

104. Fehrenbacher, ed., *Speeches and Writings, 1859–1865*, p. 586.

105. Fehrenbacher, ed., *Speeches and Writings, 1859–1865*, p. 585. In a similar vein, Lincoln also said that "certain proceedings are constitutional when, in cases of rebellion or Invasion, the public safety requires them, which would not be constitutional

when, in absence of rebellion or invasion, the public Safety does not require them."
Quoted in Arthur M. Schlesinger Jr., "Abraham Lincoln and Franklin D. Roosevelt,"
in Boritt, ed., *Lincoln, The War President*, p. 159.

106. Quoted in Donald, *Lincoln*, p. 364.

107. James MacGregor Burns, *Leadership* (New York: Harper and Row, Publishers,
1978), p. 18.

108. Rossiter, *Constitutional Dictatorship*, p. 223. See also Paludan, *The Presidency
of Abraham Lincoln*, chs. 4, 16.

109. The potential for some kind of meaningful empowerment of the presidency
on the question of slavery had not gone completely unrecognized before the Civil
War. John Calhoun had predicted it, and accordingly proposed the erection of barriers to guard against its occurrence. Toward this end, he produced a novel argument
in favor of a dual executive, designed so that the North and South would each be represented in the presidency, with each serving as a check on the other. Also, John
Quincy Adams delivered a floor speech to the House of Representatives in 1836, correctly predicting that the exercise of war powers would provide the necessary
empowerment of the national government to liberate the slaves. Adams's speech was
reprinted, among other places, in *The Liberator*, June 18, 1836, p. 97. Calhoun's argument appears in *A Disquisition on Government and Selections from the Discourse*
(Indianapolis: Bobbs-Merrill, 1953), pp. 100–104.

110. Phillip Shaw Paludan's admiring portrait of Lincoln focuses on a fundamental unity he finds in the president's Union-saving and slave-freeing purposes. My
argument here mirrors his to the extent that I claim an indispensability of a relatively
unified Union—which I take as Lincoln's preeminent purpose—to the ultimate task
of emancipation. I find less convincing Paludan's assertion that Lincoln deserves
credit as a liberator because "The Union that Lincoln wanted to save was not a union
where slavery was safe. He wanted to outlaw slavery in the territories and thus begin
a process that would end it in the states." (Paludan, *The Presidency of Abraham
Lincoln*, p. xv). Whether noncoercive gradualism, through a quarantine, would have
brought slavery to an end with the same finality as the radical, coercive measures
adopted for that purpose is more a leap of faith than a conclusion demonstrably ver-
ifiable from evidence. (The South's reaction against Lincoln's election cannot be
taken as probative evidence that they equated a peaceful quarantine with slavery's
ultimate demise. Their reaction was largely related to their being cast as a pariah, *and*
to suspicions that a quarantine might lay the groundwork for later military action.)
Indeed, that the reign of Jim Crow, farm tenantry, and debt peonage endured for
another century suggests that the process of gradual emancipation may have been
vastly more gradual—and less emancipatory—than anyone would have imagined.
We can establish with certainty Lincoln's direct connection to liberation only beginning in mid-1862, when he altered the purposes of the war. Before then, Union-saving and direct emancipation Lincoln judged to be antagonistic ends.

4. FROM RECONSTRUCTION TO THE GREAT DEPRESSION: LATENCY YEARS

1. The citation is from one of the Lincoln-Douglas debates, which appears in T. Harry Williams, ed., *Abraham Lincoln: Selected Speeches, Messages, and Letters* (New York: Holt, Rinehart and Winston, 1957), p. 72.

2. Gunnar Myrdal, *An American Dilemma: The Negro Problem and Modern America* (New York: Harpers, 1944), p. xli.

3. For a discussion of how the problems of reconstruction looked prospectively to those involved in bringing the Civil War to a conclusion, see Phillip Shaw Paludan, *The Presidency of Abraham Lincoln* (Lawrence: University Press of Kansas, 1994), chs. 12–16.

4. John Hope Franklin argues that the period of reconstruction was actually much shorter than is conventionally asserted. "The fact is that few troops were left in the South in 1877 and only three states could be considered 'unredeemed' by this time." Thus, this unusual interval of commitment to making racial advances was, in fact, more abbreviated than commonly thought. See Franklin, *Reconstruction After the Civil War*, 2d. ed. (Chicago: University of Chicago Press, 1994), p. 191. For other treatments of the politics of race and reconstruction, see Eric Foner, *Reconstruction: America's Unfinished Business, 1863–1877* (New York: Harper and Row, 1988), and Richard N. Current, ed., *Reconstruction: 1865–1877* (Englewood Cliffs, N.J.: Prentice-Hall, 1965).

5. C. Vann Woodward notes that the collapse of political equality in the South did not occur promptly with the Compromise of 1877. Rather, segregation–and the formal Jim Crow laws that mandated it—did not emerge fully until around the turn of the century. The door to these changes was opened, however, when northern troops were withdrawn from their southern posts. *The Strange Career of Jim Crow*, 2d rev. ed. (New York: Oxford University Press, 1966). See also Woodward's *Reunion and Reaction: The Compromise of 1877 and the End of Reconstruction* (Garden City, N.Y.: Doubleday Anchor Books, 1956).

6. This claim is not intended to diminish the importance of the end of slavery. Liberation, of course, was a meaningful act. But the reality of emancipation did not include the emergence of social, civil, or political equality for most freedmen. It is that reality that is of paramount interest here. See Franklin, *Reconstruction After the Civil War*, chs. 11–12.

7. Woodward, *Jim Crow*, p. 32.

8. Woodward, *Jim Crow*, pp. 32–33.

9. W. E. B. Du Bois, *Black Reconstruction in America* (Millwood, N.Y.: Kraus-Thomson, 1976), pp. 694–702; Foner, *Reconstruction*, pp. 608–10.

10. Pete Daniel, "The Metamorphosis of Slavery, 1865–1900," *Journal of American History* 66 (1979): 88–99; Donald G. Nieman, ed., *From Slavery to Sharecropping:*

White Land and Black Labor in the Rural South, 1865–1900 (New York: Garland, 1994); Edward Royce, *The Origins of Southern Sharecropping* (Philadelphia: Temple University Press, 1993).

11. It would be an oversimplification to claim that these three figures exhaust completely the roster of key African-American leaders of the period. I cite them here because my research indicates that, at least from the vantage point of the White House, they were the most influential.

12. Fourteen volumes of Washington's writings (with a cumulative index) are available in Louis R. Harlan, ed., *The Booker T. Washington Papers* (Urbana: University of Illinois Press, 1972–1989). Biographies include Louis R. Harlan, *Booker T. Washington: The Making of a Black Leader, 1856–1901* (New York: Oxford University Press, 1972); Harlan, *Booker T. Washington: The Wizard of Tuskegee, 1901–1915* (New York: Oxford University Press, 1983); and Basil Mathews, *Booker T. Washington: Educator and Interracial Interpreter* (Cambridge: Harvard University Press, 1948).

13. Du Bois's views can be found in Herbert Aptheker, ed., *The Complete Published Works of W. E. B. Du Bois* (Millwood, N.Y.: Kraus-Thomson, 1982–1986). Biographies include Manning Marable, *W. E. B. Du Bois: Black Radical Democrat* (Boston: Twayne, 1986), and David Levering Lewis, *W. E. B. Du Bois: Biography of a Race, 1868–1919* (New York: Henry Holt, 1993).

14. For a brief but useful discussion of these distinctions, see Thomas E. Harris, *Analysis of the Clash Between Booker T. Washington and W. E. B. DuBois* (New York: Garland, 1993).

15. Myrdal, *An American Dilemma*, pp. 720–35.

16. Richard Kluger, *Simple Justice: The History of Brown v. Board of Education and Black America's Struggle for Equality* (New York: Vintage Books, 1975), p. 100.

17. In 1934, Du Bois left the NAACP's employ, having lost a longtime internal struggle to keep print agitation as prominent a part of the organization's activities as litigation, the preferred route of the more conservative black elites. Kluger, *Simple Justice*, pp. 96–104, 165–66.

18. Turner's career and thought are extensively chronicled in Edwin S. Redkey, *Black Exodus: Black Nationalist and Back-to-Africa Movements, 1890–1910* (New Haven: Yale University Press, 1969). Garvey's writings are available as Robert A. Hill, ed., *The Marcus Garvey and Universal Negro Improvement Association Papers*, 9 vols. (Berkeley: University of California Press, 1983–1995). Biographies include E. David Cronon, *Black Moses: The Story of Marcus Garvey and the Universal Negro Improvement Association* (Madison: University of Wisconsin Press, 1981), and Rupert Lewis, *Marcus Garvey: Anti-Colonial Champion* (Trenton, N.J.: Africa World Press, 1988).

19. Hugh Hawkins, ed., *Booker T. Washington and His Critics: Black Leadership in Crisis*, 2d ed. (Lexington, Mass.: Heath, 1974), p. xi.

20. George Sinkler, *The Racial Attitudes of American Presidents, from Abraham*

Lincoln to Theodore Roosevelt (Garden City, N.Y.: Anchor Books, 1972), p. 459. It should be added that no violence is done to Sinkler's conclusions by extending them as commentary on presidencies from Taft through Hoover, too.

21. Bruce Miroff writes, "An administration will want to cast in a favorable light those [movement] leaders—usually moderates—who sympathize with the concerns of the White House and work comfortably with it. In power struggles between moderates and militants in a social movement, the White House may use its resources to boost the moderates' attractiveness." Miroff, "Presidential Leverage over Social Movements: The Johnson White House and Civil Rights," *Journal of Politics* 43 (February 1981): 14.

22. I have borrowed the terms "psychological" and "tangible" preferment from Randall B. Ripley, who uses them to describe the tools available to congressional party leaders for establishing party loyalty in Congress. See Ripley, *Congress: Process and Policy* (New York: Norton, 1988), ch. 6.

23. The text of these remarks, in draft and final form, is found in Harlan, ed., *The Booker T. Washington Papers*, vol. 3, pp. 578–87. The quotation appears on page 586.

24. Cited in Sinkler, *Racial Attitudes of American Presidents*, p. 271.

25. Myrdal, *An American Dilemma*, p. 727. The presence of this dynamic greatly aided presidents who sought to use the stature of the office to make leaders of the preferred kind of black figure. Indeed, when black communities began to sense white manipulation of their leadership later in the struggle, the presidential effort to keep the race issue from the national agenda was immensely complicated. The correlation between presidential favors and community standing became highly unpredictable, especially frustrating Kennedy and Lyndon Johnson.

26. Samuel R. Spencer Jr., "The Achievement of Booker T. Washington," reprinted in Hawkins, ed., *Washington and His Critics*, p. 173.

27. Louis R. Harlan, "The Secret Life of Booker T. Washington," in Hawkins, ed., *Washington and His Critics*, pp. 183–203. Harlan amply documents the extensive network of spies and press agents in the employ of Washington's "Tuskegee Machine." "Here," Harlan observes, "both white and black enemies were made to feel the secret stiletto of a Machiavellian prince."

28. Du Bois's review of Washington's *Up From Slavery* appeared in 1901, and included seeds of a critique of Washington's philosophy that would fully bloom within two years' time, during Roosevelt's first term. Du Bois's 1903 publication of *The Souls of Black Folk* became widely known for its respectful but blistering attack on Washington's "policy of submission." "The black men of America," proclaimed Du Bois, "have a duty to perform, a duty stern and delicate,—a forward movement to oppose a part of the work of their greatest leader." That review and *The Souls of Black Folk* are conveniently reprinted in Eric J. Sundquist, ed., *The Oxford W. E. B. Du Bois Reader* (New York: Oxford University Press, 1996). The quoted material is taken from pp. 127, 131.

29. Lewis L. Gould, *The Presidency of Theodore Roosevelt* (Lawrence: University Press of Kansas, 1991), p. 22.

30. It is notable that Washington's *political* consultations brought little southern protest; it was the *social* dimension of a black man dining in the White House that provoked a backlash. A lengthy account of this affair (and the folklore that arose from it) appears in Willard B. Gatewood Jr., *Theodore Roosevelt and the Art of Controversy: Episodes of the White House Years* (Baton Rouge: Louisiana State University Press, 1970), ch. 2.

31. See August Meier, "Booker T. Washington and the 'Talented Tenth,'" reprinted in Hawkins, ed., *Washington and His Critics*, pp. 127–38.

32. Sinkler, *Racial Attitudes of American Presidents*, pp. 427–28.

33. Elliott M. Rudwick, *W. E. B. Du Bois: A Study in Minority Group Leadership* (Philadelphia: University of Pennsylvania Press, 1960), p. 142. Taft's preference for Washington's way over Du Bois's is asserted also in Paolo E. Coletta, *The Presidency of William Howard Taft* (Lawrence: University Press of Kansas, 1973), pp. 29–30.

34. This trend continued even after Washington's death. In late 1917, for example, a long-time Washington intimate, Emmett J. Scott, was appointed Special Assistant to Wilson's secretary of war, charged with helping the administration deal with the peculiar problems of fighting for democracy abroad during a time when its fruits were denied African Americans at home. Charles Flint Kellogg, *NAACP: A History of the National Association for the Advancement of Colored People* (Baltimore: Johns Hopkins University Press, 1967), p. 258.

35. John B. Kirby, *Black Americans in the Roosevelt Era: Liberalism and Race* (Knoxville: University of Tennessee Press, 1980), p. 5. Nancy J. Weiss has come to the same general conclusion: "The Harding and Coolidge administrations appointed few blacks to federal posts and failed to reverse the policies of civil service segregation that had begun under Woodrow Wilson. During the Coolidge administration, there were fewer blacks holding presidential appointments than there had been in the Roosevelt-Taft era; seven months before Coolidge left office, there were only 77 more blacks working for the federal government than there had been when he became president in 1923. While Harding and Coolidge both spoke out against lynching, the NAACP's battle to secure federal anti-lynching legislation found little support in the White House. . . . Except for a handful of congressmen and senators, few public figures in the 1920s cared very much about black rights." *The National Urban League, 1910–1940* (New York: Oxford University Press, 1974), pp. 145–46.

36. Nancy J. Weiss writes, "The Republicans seemed more interested in cultivating the lily-white constituency in the South than in courting the black vote." Weiss, *The National Urban League*, p. 145. See also Donald J. Lisio, *Hoover, Blacks, & Lily-Whites: A Study of Southern Strategies* (Chapel Hill: University of North Carolina Press, 1985).

37. Excerpts reprinted in the *Congressional Record*, 71 Cong., 2d sess., vol. 72, p. 1930.

38. For details of the African-American role in the Parker nomination fight, see

Richard L. Watson Jr., "The Defeat of Judge Parker: A Study in Pressure Groups and Politics," *Mississippi Valley Historical Review* 50 (1963): 213–34; Rona Hirsch Mendelsohn, "Senate Confirmation of Supreme Court Appointments: The Nomination and Rejection of John J. Parker," *Howard Law Journal* 14 (1968): 105–48; Walter White, "The Negro and the Supreme Court," *Harper's Monthly Magazine* (January 1931), pp. 238–46. See also Walter White, "Statement of Walter White, Secretary [of the] National Association for the Advancement of Colored People," in Committee on the Judiciary, United States Senate, *Hearing Before the Subcommittee of the Committee on the Judiciary: Confirmation of Honorable John J. Parker to be an Associate Justice of the Supreme Court of the United States* (Washington D.C.: U.S. GPO, 1930): 74–79. The *Congressional Record* of the period (vol. 72, parts 7–9) also contains material relevant to this episode.

39. Lisio, *Hoover, Blacks, & Lily-Whites*, pp. 217–18. Hoover managed to retain substantial black support in the 1932 election, primarily because African Americans feared the southern orientation of Franklin Roosevelt's campaign. Of special concern was the placement of Texan John Nance Garner a proverbial "heartbeat away" from the presidency, in service with a man whose physical capacity to serve was already in some quarters suspect. This subject is explored in Lisio's ch. 21.

40. This was the precursor of the Federal Bureau of Investigation (FBI).

41. Max Lowenthal, *The Federal Bureau of Investigation* (Westport, Conn.: Greenwood Press, 1971 [reprint]), pp. 3–5.

42. The degree of direct presidential involvement in subsequent episodes of political surveillance by the Bureau is often very difficult to establish, largely because of the sensitive nature of such operations. Judicious use of presidential and agency archives—which was not possible for this study—would reveal with some degree of accuracy how frequently and how directly later presidents were involved in similar instances, but it is entirely likely that records were not made on certain cases. This study relies on the available secondary literature on the subject—which is more episodic than comprehensive—to make general claims about the nature of presidential involvement in bureaucratic political suppression. The origins of the Bureau are addressed here principally to show how thoroughly consistent acts of political suppression are with the Bureau's original character, and to establish the centrality of the presidency in what I believe to be a seminal episode.

43. Theodore Kornweibel, ed., *Federal Surveillance of African Americans (1917–1925): The First World War, The Red Scare, and the Garvey Movement* (Frederick, Md.: University Publications of America, 1985), "Introduction" (to Microfilmed Collection), pp. xi, xiv. See also Kornweibel, *No Crystal Stair: Black Life and the Messenger, 1917–1928* (Westport, Conn.: Greenwood Press, 1975), chs. 1–3.

44. A combination of the Wilson administration's pro-segregationist policies and its perceived hypocrisy with respect to the promotion of liberty led to a dramatic escalation of black protest, much of it associated with what some have termed a "new

Negro journalism." The ascendancy of these forces, aided in part by a black population newly urbanized and inducted into American industrial life, marked the end of a period of relative ascendancy for Booker Washington's teachings among African Americans. His passive, agrarian-based solutions for the American dilemma became quickly antiquated for an increasingly urbanized and frustrated black population.

45. Kornweibel, "Introduction," p. xiii.

46. Richard Gid Powers, *Secrecy and Power: The Life of J. Edgar Hoover* (New York: Free Press, 1987), p. 128.

47. Cited in John Hope Franklin, *From Slavery to Freedom: A History of Negro Americans*, 5th ed. (New York: Knopf, 1980), pp. 350–51.

48. Franklin, *From Slavery to Freedom*, p. 355. A full explication of Du Bois's views on Garvey appears in his essay "Back to Africa," which is reprinted as "Marcus Garvey" in Sundquist, ed., *The Oxford Du Bois Reader*, pp. 265–76.

49. John Hope Franklin writes of the NAACP's shortcomings in this regard, "Despite their vigorous efforts, [they] . . . failed to reach more than a small minority of blacks and whites. . . . Negroes on the lower social and economic levels were inclined to regard such organizations as agencies of upper-class blacks and liberal whites who failed to join hands with them in their efforts to rise." *From Slavery to Freedom*, pp. 353–54.

50. Kornweibel, "Introduction," p. xii.

51. In January 1920, the Justice Department examined Garvey's work and concluded that he was the "foremost pro-negro agitator in New York. It is apparent, however," continued an internal memorandum, "that his pro-negroism is secondary to his scheme for the solicitation of subscriptions for stock in the Black Star Line." Since Garvey's work, then, was seen as essentially commercial in nature—and thus the antithesis of the radicalism of the Bolsheviks—the federal surveillance network did not at first intrude aggressively into his business. Judith Stein, *The World of Marcus Garvey* (Baton Rouge: Louisiana State University Press, 1986), p. 200.

52. Judith Stein argues that the absence of a sizable black middle class placed insurmountable limits on what the UNIA could accomplish—the enterprise was, therefore, doomed from the outset. *The World of Marcus Garvey*, ch. 7.

53. Kornweibel, *No Crystal Stair*, p. 140.

54. An extensive account of the "Garvey Must Go" effort appears in Kornweibel, *No Crystal Stair*, ch. 5.

55. Stein, *The World of Marcus Garvey*, p. 167.

56. Stein, *The World of Marcus Garvey*, p. 186.

57. Powers, *Secrecy and Power*, p. 128.

58. Stein, *The World of Marcus Garvey*, p. 206.

59. Lisio, *Hoover, Blacks, & Lily-Whites*, p. 222; Powers, *Secrecy and Power*, p. 163.

60. Powers, *Secrecy and Power*, pp. 162–63.

61. Kluger, *Simple Justice*, p. 100.

62. It should be added here that, in the main, the association's subsequent influence was to become felt not in the legislative or executive branches, but in the nation's courtrooms. Although the Parker battle signaled for the NAACP an unparalleled prominence among African-American organizations, it did not indicate the advent of a perpetual legislative force. Indeed, because of repeated frustrations in the legislative arena— for example in failing to have enacted a national anti-lynching law— the NAACP's leadership decided to concentrate on litigation, sensing that incremental, case-by-case offensives using a Constitution they believed favored them promised greater progress than appeals to a Congress dominated by southerners. That preference for litigation was to become a distinguishing feature of the NAACP through the 1960s. See Kluger, *Simple Justice*, passim.

63. Attentive Republican leaders worried that as many as nine states might swing Democratic as a result of African-American disaffection with the Parker nomination. Watson, "The Defeat of Judge Parker," p. 221.

64. See Myrdal, *An American Dilemma*, p. 192.

65. See W. E. B. Du Bois, "The Migration of the Negroes," *The Crisis* (June 1917), reprinted in Charles Van Doren, ed., *The Negro in American History: A Taste of Freedom, 1854–1927* (New York: Encyclopaedia Britannica Educational Corporation, 1969), pp. 51–52.

66. This growth was not immediate and unlimited, as the urban ghetto produced its own set of barriers. Harris, *Booker T. Washington and W. E. B. DuBois*, pp. 19–20.

5. THE RISE OF BLACK POLITICAL POWER: ROOSEVELT AND TRUMAN

1. Frank Freidel writes, "The fact that every black moving to the North, and some moving into southern cities like Houston, was gaining access to the ballot, gave Roosevelt a new incentive to make overtures toward blacks. In a close election their votes could be important." Freidel, *Franklin D. Roosevelt: A Rendezvous with Destiny* (Boston: Little, Brown, 1990), p. 520.

2. Nancy J. Weiss, *Farewell to the Party of Lincoln: Black Politics in the Age of FDR* (Princeton: Princeton University Press, 1983) p. 266. Weiss here is characterizing the reasoning of Tommy Corcoran.

3. The period during which that logic prevailed actually goes beyond the period under study in this chapter. Eisenhower also confronted it. And since Kennedy is a transitional figure, I treat his administration in a succeeding chapter.

4. Joseph P. Lash, *Eleanor and Franklin: The Story of Their Relationship Based on Eleanor Roosevelt's Private Papers* (New York: Norton, 1971), pp. 512–13, 516. For contrasting portraits of Roosevelt's personal disposition toward African Americans, see Mary McLeod Bethune, "My Secret Talks with FDR," *Ebony* (April 1949), pp. 42–51, and "The Secret Papers of FDR," *Negro Digest* (January 1951), pp. 3–13. Both are conveniently reprinted in Bernard Sternsher, ed., *The Negro in Depression and War:*

Prelude to Revolution 1930–1945 (Chicago: Quadrangle Books, 1969). See also Arthur M. Schlesinger Jr., *The Age of Roosevelt: The Politics of Upheaval* (Boston: Houghton Mifflin, 1960), pp. 430–31; Freidel, *Franklin D. Roosevelt*, pp. 244–45.

5. Robert S. McElvaine, *The Great Depression: America, 1929–1941* (New York: Times Books, 1984), p. 188. Before the New Deal, the author reports, no black delegates had *ever* been seated by the party convention.

6. Quotation is attributed to Wendel Philips Dabney in Ernest M. Collins, "Cincinnati Negroes and Presidential Politics," *Journal of Negro History* 41 (April 1956): 131–32.

7. Moreover, the conservative backlash against Roosevelt for not more aggressively excluding African Americans contributed to a sense that even minor advances were meaningful tokens of friendship. Freidel, *Franklin D. Roosevelt*, p. 245.

8. Weiss, *Farewell to the Party of Lincoln*, pp. 36–37. See also Raymond Wolters, *Negroes and the Great Depression: The Problem of Economic Recovery* (Westport, Conn.: Greenwood, 1970).

9. I also include under this general heading the administration's purely *political* initiatives toward buttressing the liberal wing of the Democratic Party at the expense of the conservative. The death of the two-thirds rule, the court-packing scheme, and the attempted purge of the party in 1938 (and even to some extent the mild efforts to bring an end to the poll tax) all were aimed at undermining the conservative opposition to New Deal principles. None of these initiatives was pursued with African Americans specifically in mind. Indeed, some evidence suggests that some of them were constructed in part by fencing African Americans *out*. Of the court-packing plan, Oswald Garrison Villard protested, "If I were a Negro I would be raging and tearing my hair over this proposal. Woodrow Wilson introduced segregation in the departments in Washington; . . . a future Woodrow Wilson could pack the Supreme Court so that no Negro could get within a thousand miles of justice." And Roosevelt's chosen candidates in 1938 may have had preferable records on such New Deal issues as the wages and hours bill, but racial liberalism apparently was not a requisite qualification. William E. Leuchtenburg, *Franklin D. Roosevelt and the New Deal, 1932–1940* (New York: Harper Torchbooks, 1963), pp. 235, 268. See also Freidel, *Franklin D. Roosevelt*, p. 520.

10. John B. Kirby, *Black Americans in the Roosevelt Era: Liberalism and Race* (Knoxville: University of Tennessee Press, 1980), p. 106. Overall, black employees in the federal government increased from 50,000 in 1933 to over 200,000 in 1946. Morrison, "Secret Papers of FDR," in Sternsher, ed. *The Negro in Depression and War*, p. 71.

11. See Kirby, *Black Americans in the Roosevelt Era*, ch. 6.

12. Roosevelt refused, for example, directly to address the subject of lynching in his 1935 annual message, telling a disappointed Walter White of the NAACP that his one sentence on crime in that speech was sufficient on the subject. Roosevelt's most

notable utterance on black concerns came in an October 1936 speech at Howard University: "Among American citizens, there should be no forgotten man and no forgotten race." The politics of that election season undoubtedly shaped the president's remarks. Lash, *Eleanor and Franklin*, p. 517; Morrison, "The Secret Papers of FDR," in Sternsher, ed., *The Negro in Depression and War*, p. 70; Leslie H. Fishel Jr., "The Negro in the New Deal Era," *Wisconsin Magazine of History* 48 (Winter 1964): 116.

13. This openness to associating with African Americans publicly did not occur immediately, and it seems to have correlated directly with the president's electoral needs. Frank Freidel notes that FDR became significantly more accessible to black leaders just before the 1940 and 1944 elections. See Freidel, *Franklin D. Roosevelt*, pp. 356, 521.

14. See Lash, *Eleanor and Franklin*, ch. 44.

15. Weiss, *Farewell to the Party of Lincoln*, p. 157.

16. Lash, *Eleanor and Franklin*, p. 514.

17. Doris Kearns Goodwin, *No Ordinary Time: Franklin and Eleanor Roosevelt: The Home Front in World War II* (New York: Simon and Schuster, 1994), pp. 162–63.

18. Quoted in John A. Salmond, "The Civilian Conservation Corp and the Negro," *Journal of American History* 52 (June 1965): 84–85. Salmond also notes (pp. 86–87) that the CCC enforced segregation in their camps even in states where governors preferred to integrate.

19. McElvaine, *Great Depression*, pp. 189–90. See also Fishel, "The Negro in the New Deal Era," pp. 111–115

20. FDR's reform efforts also were charged with the same deficiency. The centerpiece of the so-called Second New Deal, the Social Security Act, did not cover almost 90 percent of African Americans, because of exclusions for domestic and farm laborers. Gareth Davies and Martha Derthick assert, however, that such limitations were less the product of racial prejudice than of rational conclusions that domestic and farm labor were not well suited for that kind of social insurance program. See Raymond Wolters, "The New Deal and the Negro," in John Braeman, Robert H. Bremner, and David Brody, eds., *The New Deal: The National Level* (Columbus: Ohio State University Press, 1975), pp. 194–95; Gareth Davies and Martha Derthick, "Race and Social Welfare Policy: The Social Security Act of 1935," *Political Science Quarterly*, 112 (Summer 1997): 217–35. On black opposition to the Social Security Act, see Charles V. Hamilton and Dona L. Hamilton, "The Dual Agenda: Social Policies of Civil Rights Organizations, New Deal to the Present," paper prepared for the 1991 annual meeting of the American Political Science Association, Washington, D.C., August 29–September 1, 1991.

21. It should be noted here that some New Dealers did mimic the token-oriented appointments practices of their Republican predecessors. Those friendly to African Americans were distressed, for example, to find that Frances Perkins had hired a black North Carolinian to handle racial matters in the Labor Department, an

appointee deemed by critics to be "a white man's nigger if ever there was one." Quoted in Lash, *Eleanor and Franklin*, p. 514.

22. Kirby, *Black Americans in the Roosevelt Era*, p. 108. Another scholar claims that each appointee was expected to become a "booster for the New Deal." Weiss, *Farewell to the Party of Lincoln*, p. 43.

23. In another case, the NAACP's Walter White left his post on the Virgin Islands Advisory Council in protest over Roosevelt's refusal to endorse publicly an anti-lynching bill then being subjected to a southern filibuster. Kirby, *Black Americans in the Roosevelt Era*, pp. 121–39; James H. Brewer, "Robert Lee Vann, Democrat or Republican?: An Exponent of Loose-Leaf Politics," *Negro History Bulletin* 21 (February 1958): 100–103, reprinted in Sternsher, *The Negro in Depression and War*; Lash, *Eleanor and Franklin*, pp. 517–18.

24. Kirby, *Black Americans in the New Deal*, pp. 148, 110.

25. Lash cites Henry Wallace as a case in point. See *Eleanor and Franklin*, pp. 521, 528.

26. Reported in Kirby, *Black Americans in the Roosevelt Era*, p. 109.

27. Wolters, "The New Deal and the Negro," p. 201.

28. Even among the most progressive whites in the administration, there was a general consensus that the fundamentals of southern segregation were not to be disturbed. Lash, *Eleanor and Franklin*, p. 513.

29. Evidence indicates that many southerners otherwise supportive of segregation found the practice of lynching offensive and believed federal intervention would be a useful prophylaxis. Erwin D. Hoffman reported that two prominent South Carolina newspapers, the *Columbia Record* and the Charleston *News and Courier* backed efforts to end lynching while defending Jim Crow. Presidents unwilling to intervene on this issue—where black lives were at stake—were even less enthusiastic about engaging in potentially calamitous fights to secure for African Americans liberty and the right to pursue happiness. See Hoffman's "The Genesis of the Modern Movement for Equal Rights in South Carolina, 1930–1939," *Journal of Negro History* 44 (October 1959): 346–69, reprinted in Sternsher, ed., *The Negro in Depression and War*. For a discussion of the reasons the antilynching campaign became the NAACP's principal political concern, see Weiss, *Farewell to the Party of Lincoln*, ch. 5.

30. Goodwin, *No Ordinary Time*, p. 447.

31. Richard Gid Powers, *Secrecy and Power: The Life of J. Edgar Hoover* (New York: Free Press, 1987), pp. 228–33; Kenneth O'Reilly, "A New Deal for the FBI: The Roosevelt Administration, Crime Control, and National Security," *Journal of American History* 69 (December 1982): 638–58.

32. As an example, see the information Eleanor got through back channels in relation to a 1941 strike, involving black workers, at a Ford assembly plant in Dearborn, Michigan. Goodwin, *No Ordinary Time*, pp. 227–29.

33. Joseph P. Lash wrote that her efforts "to bring the Negroes' plight to the attention of her husband and his cabinet colleagues . . . was a lonely enterprise." *Eleanor*

and Franklin, p. 512. Eleanor's labors in the civil rights arena are a central theme in Goodwin, *No Ordinary Time*.

34. Lash, *Eleanor and Franklin*, p. 519.

35. "It was useful for the President to have his wife serve in these varying capacities, absorbing some of the criticism, supplying him with information he could get from no other source, and sparking his conscience, when that was needed. This relieved the President from having to punctuate his speeches and press conferences with references to the Negro." Fishel, "The Negro in the New Deal Era," p. 116.

36. Joseph P. Lash wrote of Eleanor, "What she did as a matter of heart and moral courage turned out [by the 1936 election] to be astute politics, although that had not been her motivation." He makes no surmise, however, about Franklin's motivation for indulging her inadvertently astute politics. *Eleanor and Franklin*, p. 521. Doris Kearns Goodwin notes the political rewards of Eleanors labors in *No Ordinary Time*, pp. 164–65.

37. Lash, *Eleanor and Franklin*, p. 528.

38. Roosevelt cited in Wolters, "The New Deal and the Negro," p. 201; Thomas cited in Kirby, *Black Americans in the Roosevelt Era*, p. 77. See also Weiss, *Farewell to the Party of Lincoln*, pp. 104–7. This deniability generally worked well for the president, probably because of the conventional perceptions of marriage and of the inferior role of women in the workplace. One wonders if Bill Clinton, an ardent reader of presidential history, appropriated the analogy of Eleanor and Franklin on race when he placed his wife in charge of the administration's health care initiative. If so, he displayed a weak understanding of the context within which that relationship took place, and of the crucial distinctions between his project and that of FDR.

39. Goodwin concludes otherwise, asserting that FDR never interfered with Eleanor's work in the civil rights arena. *No Ordinary Time*, p. 164.

40. Lash, *Eleanor and Franklin*, p. 517.

41. My claim here merely is that the president intended to use his wife to the extent possible to work, at the margins, perhaps, to shape the dynamic of black political action. I do not maintain that he succeeded either in completely controlling Eleanor or in managing how her work molded black activism. Joseph P. Lash argues that when the president "laid down the law, she generally let the matter rest there," but "Not always." That her relationship may have been a clumsy tool for him does not diminish the importance of his reliance on that tool in the first instance. Lash, *Eleanor and Franklin*, p. 519.

42. The portrait of White painted here draws on details in Kirby, *Black Americans in the Roosevelt Era*, pp. 175–86.

43. Lash, *Eleanor and Franklin*, pp. 526–27.

44. See Kirby, *Black Americans in the Roosevelt Era*, pp. 85–6.

45. See Herbert Garfinkel, *When Negroes March: The March on Washington Movement in the Organizational Politics of the FEPC* (Glencoe, Ill.: Free Press of Glencoe, 1959), p. 41.

46. For a contemporary account of the extent to which the prospects of war pre-occupied Washington during these days before Pearl Harbor, see Anne O'Hare McCormick's article in *The New York Times Magazine*, March 9, 1941. Excerpts reprinted in *The New York Times Magazine*, April 14, 1996, pp. 87–88.

47. Burns, *Roosevelt: The Soldier of Freedom* (New York: Harcourt Brace Jovanovich, 1970), pp. 123–24.

48. Cited in Dalfiume, "The 'Forgotten Years' of the Negro Revolution," *Journal of American History*, LV (June 1968): 90–106, reprinted in Sternsher, *The Negro in Depression and War*, p. 299.

49. Sternsher, "Introduction," *The Negro in Depression and War*, p. 6. Lerone Bennett later claimed simply, "Pearl Harbor had killed or, at least, had seriously wounded Uncle Tom." *Confrontation: Black and White* (Chicago: Johnson, 1965), p. 184.

50. Cited in Dalfiume, "The 'Forgotten Years,' " p. 94. The author arrays a variety of similar citations as evidence that these sentiments were not isolated.

51. Quoted in Garfinkel, *Why Negroes March*, p. 17.

52. Goodwin, *No Ordinary Time*, pp. 165–67, 246–47.

53. Louis C. Kesselman, *The Social Politics of the FEPC: A Study in Reform Pressure Movements* (Chapel Hill: University of North Carolina Press, 1948), p. 7.

54. Dalfiume, "The 'Forgotten Years,' " p. 92.

55. Quoted in Jervis Anderson, *A. Philip Randolph: A Biographical Portrait* (New York: Harcourt Brace Jovanovich, 1972), p. 248. Emphasis added.

56. Paula F. Pfeffer, *A. Philip Randolph, Pioneer of the Civil Rights Movement* (Baton Rouge: Louisiana State University Press, 1990), p. 18

57. Pfeffer, *A. Philip Randolph*, p. 21.

58. A detailed account of this meeting and its aftermath appears in Goodwin, *No Ordinary Time*, pp. 167–72.

59. Quoted in Weiss, *Farewell to the Party of Lincoln*, p. 277.

60. Weiss, *Farewell to the Party of Lincoln*, pp. 278–79.

61. Herbert Garfinkel writes, "Even these concessions were obtained as a conse-quence of much pressure and negotiation with the White House." *When Negroes March*, p. 21. See also Goodwin, *No Ordinary Time*, pp. 171–72.

62. Garfinkel, *When Negroes March*, p. 37.

63. *When Negroes March*, p. 48.

64. Although Randolph was the focal point, it should be noted here that mass protest meetings were also held by such groups as the NAACP, testifying to the wide-spread acceptance of that new tactic. Dalfiume, "The 'Forgotten Years,'" p. 98.

65. Quoted in Garfinkel, *When Negroes March*, pp. 56–57.

66. Cited in Wolters, *Negroes and the Great Depression*, p. xii.

67. In the late 1930s, Dr. Ralph Bunche wrote, the "NAACP does not have a mass basis. It has never assumed the proportions of a crusade, nor has it attracted the

masses of the people to its banner. It is not impressed upon the mass consciousness, and it is a bald truth that the average Negro in the street has never heard of the Association nor any of its leaders." In 1941, Roy Wilkins, an NAACP official, echoed those claims in an internal memorandum, saying that "we recognize our lack of skill at mass appeal, and I believe we are on our way to doing something about it." Bunche quoted in Wolters, *Negroes and the Great Depression*, pp. 357–58; Wilkins in Gunnar Myrdal, *An American Dilemma: The Negro Problem and Modern Democracy* (New York: Harper and Brothers, 1944), p. 836.

68. Anderson, *A. Philip Randolph*, p. 250.

69. Cited in Garfinkel, *When Negroes March*, p. 60.

70. Ted Morgan, *FDR: A Biography* (New York: Simon and Schuster, 1985), p. 594.

71. Goodwin, *No Ordinary Time*, p. 252.

72. Russell L. Riley, "The Limits of the Transformational Presidency," paper prepared for presentation at a conference entitled "Presidential Power: Forging the Presidency for the 21st Century," Columbia University, November 15–16, 1996.

73. Quotes appear in Goodwin, *No Ordinary Time*, p. 163. Parenthetically, Roosevelt's claim is a useful datum about the relationship of personal motive and presidential behavior. The nation-keeping constraints on a president operating in a political culture heavily mortgaged to racial inequality usually rendered personal motives largely inoperative. This was true even on an issue like lynching, which was so repugnant that many hard-core segregationists condemned it. Small wonder, then, that progress on jobs, voting, and social desegregation usually met with official presidential indifference or strategic resistance, unless, as was sometimes the case, wartime necessity—nation-keeping at its most fundamental level—required change. If black soldiers were needed to win the war, or if continuing segregation proved to be a rich target for enemy propagandists, *then* the strictures on presidential behavior might relax enough to permit concessions to an African-American minority. Otherwise, the tools, as FDR admitted, were relatively meager.

74. Burns, *Soldier of Freedom*, p. 123.

75. Kesselman, *Social Politics of the FEPC*, p. 16. The author's commentary here is made regarding the initial president's committee; thus the reference to a two-year life span. In 1943 the FEPC was reconstituted under a new executive order—under duress from black groups—but the second iteration was no more effective than the first. Despite pressures for a permanent FEPC, the wartime version was killed by Congress in 1945. See Garfinkel, *When Negroes March*, chs. 4–6.

76. Burns, *Soldier of Freedom*, p. 462. Burns elsewhere wrote, "[Roosevelt] seemed reluctant to spend any of his own personal capital to mobilize support for the committee, even within the government, or to give much time to the problem" (p. 265). One occasion when FDR did intervene to support the FEPC came in a 1944 transit system strike in Philadelphia. There, the president moved the army in to operate the

streetcars and threatened to draft white workers who refused to work alongside blacks. As Doris Kearns Goodwin notes, this was done to reopen the "fourth largest war-production center" in the country, and markedly contrasted with an earlier FEPC decision—with presidential acquiescence—sanctioning segregated shipyards in Mobile, Alabama. See Goodwin, *No Ordinary Time*, pp. 444, 537–41.

77. Richard M. Dalfiume, *Desegregation of the U.S. Armed Forces: Fighting on Two Fronts, 1939–1953* (Columbia: University of Missouri Press, 1969), pp. 117–20.

78. Weiss, *Farewell to the Party of Lincoln*, p. 36 (see note 4).

79. Garfinkel, *When Negroes March*, pp. 105, 203 (see note 45).

80. Garfinkel, *When Negroes March*, p. 90.

81. Morgan, *FDR*, p. 595.

82. Robert K. Carr, *Federal Protection of Civil Rights: Quest for a Sword* (Ithaca: Cornell University Press, 1947), pp. 24–25, 56.

83. Sidney Fine, *Frank Murphy: The Washington Years* (Ann Arbor: University of Michigan Press, 1984), ch. 6.

84. Brian K. Landsberg, *Enforcing Civil Rights: Race Discrimination and the Department of Justice* (Lawrence: University Press of Kansas, 1997), p. 9.

85. Carr, *Federal Protection of Civil Rights*, p. 25. Mark V. Tushnet echoes this claim, noting that Murphy's recent loss of the Michigan governor's race motivated him to find some way to restore his good name among the Democratic Party's liberals. Tushnet, *Making Civil Rights Law: Thurgood Marshall and the Supreme Court, 1936–1961* (New York: Oxford University Press, 1994), p. 49.

86. In a public report on Department of Justice activities issued in July 1939, Murphy remarked that the office had been created at the president's order. None of the principle students of the unit have established any firm roots for that claim. See J. Woodford Howard Jr., *Mr. Justice Murphy: A Political Biography* (Princeton: Princeton University Press, 1968), p. 205.

87. Freidel, *Franklin D. Roosevelt*, p. 247. Later, Roosevelt *informally* directed the Justice Department to investigate suspected lynchings. Carr, *Federal Protection of Civil Rights*, p. 164.

88. Richard Kluger, *Simple Justice: The History of Brown v. Board of Education and Black America's Struggle for Equality* (New York: Vintage Books, 1975), p. 234. See also Carr, *Federal Protection of Civil Rights*, pp. 83–84, 94, 148, 178, 198–99.

89. In developing this account, I have tended to rely on scholarship that focuses on political pressures as the central motivating force in explaining Truman's actions on civil rights. Some find such treatments insufficiently attentive to the force of Truman's own personal ideological commitments on the race issue. I do not claim here that Truman was unsympathetic to the cause of racial equality as an individual, only that his conception of the possible—and his preferred timing—differed signif- icantly from that of leading African-American activists. That they wanted more, and faster, would have created severe pressures on him to act whether he was fundamen-

tally sympathetic or not. For a portrait that is critical of those who understate the import of Truman's own disposition, see Dalfiume, *Desegregation of the U.S Armed Forces*, chs. 7–9.

90. William C. Berman, *The Politics of Civil Rights in the Truman Administration* (Columbus: Ohio State University Press, 1970), p. 6; Donald R. McCoy and Richard T. Ruetten, *Quest and Response: Minority Rights and the Truman Administration* (Lawrence: University Press of Kansas, 1973), pp. 11–12.

91. Aldon D. Morris, *The Origins of the Civil Rights Movement: Black Communities Organizing for Change* (New York: Free Press, 1984), p. 78.

92. Henry Lee Moon, *Balance of Power: The Negro Vote* (Garden City, N.Y.: Doubleday, 1948), p. 198. The logic of Moon's argument, while compelling in 1948, would within two decades lose its potency. With the onset of substantial white backlash in the North, the arithmetic of electoral politics changed; by then, additions to a candidate's column from a unified black public often entailed substantial subtractions through the departure of disenchanted white voters nationwide.

93. McCoy and Ruetten, *Quest and Response*, pp. 97–98.

94. McCoy and Ruetten, *Quest and Response*, pp. 11, 17.

95. It should be noted here that attentive southerners of that day also recognized the general source of Truman's movement toward a civil rights agenda. "It is perhaps the irony of political development," proposed University of Kentucky Professor Jasper B. Shannon, "that the electoral college, which is preserved partly on the argument of state's rights, should have produced this peculiar twist which tends to protect minorities. May not the South and other so-called old American sections come to see that the electoral college exaggerates the importance of minorities and pressure groups beyond their actual proportions in the entire nation? Will the South be compelled to advocate abolition of the electoral college and the enfranchisement of all its voters to redress the present regional balance against it in the presidential sweepstakes?" Shannon, "Presidential Politics in the South," *Journal of Politics* 10 (1948): 470. Shannon's argument mimicked, in a modified fashion, those earlier offered by John Calhoun, regarding the need for modifications in presidential electoral structures to secure the South's place in the Union. Indeed, it was during Truman's presidency that vigorous southern reaction to black activism began its resurgence.

96. Berman, *The Politics of Civil Rights*, p. x.

97. Dalfiume, *Desegregation of the U.S. Armed Forces*, pp. 134–35.

98. Robert J. Donovan, *Conflict and Crisis: The Presidency of Harry S. Truman, 1945–1948* (New York: Norton, 1977), pp. 30–32.

99. Cited in Berman, *The Politics of Civil Rights*, p. 38.

100. Dalfiume, *Desegregation of the U.S. Armed Forces*, pp. 132–34; Donovan, *Conflict and Crisis*, pp. 243–45.

101. Donovan, *Conflict and Crisis*, pp. 244–45.

102. Berman, *The Politics of Civil Rights*, pp. 50–52; McCoy and Ruetten, *Quest and Response*, pp. 49–50.

103. Donovan, *Conflict and Crisis*, p. 333.

104. Executive Order 9008, reprinted in The President's Committee on Civil Rights, *To Secure These Rights: The Report of the President's Committee on Civil Rights* (Washington D.C.: U.S. GPO, 1947), p. viii.

105. Barton J. Bernstein, "The Ambiguous Legacy: The Truman Administration and Civil Rights," in Bernstein, ed., *Politics and Policies of the Truman Administration* (Chicago: Quadrangle Books, 1972), p. 278.

106. McCoy and Ruetten, *Quest and Response*, pp. 53–54; Berman, *The Politics of Civil Rights*, p. 58.

107. Quoted in McCoy and Ruetten, *Quest and Response*, p. 81.

108. *Public Papers of the Presidents of the United States: Harry S. Truman, 1947* (Washington D.C.: U.S. GPO, 1963), p. 312.

109. Barton J. Bernstein, "The Ambiguous Legacy," p. 279.

110. The Justice Department attorney who drafted the brief later said that he believed "Tom Clark made the decision to put the government into *Shelley*," the lead housing case before the Supreme Court. Drafting of the brief began shortly *after* the President's Committee on Civil Rights issued its report. Kluger, *Simple Justice*, pp. 252–53.

111. The President's Committee, *To Secure These Rights*.

112. Berman, *The Politics of Civil Rights*, pp. 70–72. Evidence does indicate that the president himself disagreed with some of the policy prescriptions advanced by the committee.

113. McCoy and Ruetten, *Quest and Response*, pp. 86, 94; Berman, *The Politics of Civil Rights*, pp. 72–73.

114. Richard E. Neustadt, "Congress and the Fair Deal: A Legislative Balance Sheet," in Richard Abrams and Lawrence W. Levine, eds., *The Shaping of Twentieth Century America* (Boston: Little, Brown, 1965), p. 574.

115. Barton J. Bernstein notes the diversionary purposes to which such committees are often put in American politics, but he argues that Truman foreclosed many possible options by naming "prominent men of liberal faith" to his committee, appointees who in effect committed the president to a course of action he could reject only at enormous political costs. Bernstein, "An Ambiguous Legacy," p. 277.

116. McCoy and Ruetten, *Quest and Response*, p. 94.

117. Robert J. Donovan writes of the White House reaction to the report, "Truman wanted the support of white southerners. He wanted the black vote. The dilemma of reconciling these objectives was discussed in the White House for weeks." The political calculus, then, became a controlling factor. *Conflict and Crisis*, p. 336.

118. David McCullough traces the memorandum's initial draft to James A. Rowe Jr., a former Roosevelt aide. Rowe's authorship was concealed from Truman because

of the president's animus toward Rowe's law partner, Thomas Corcoran. McCullough, *Truman* (New York: Simon and Schuster, 1992), p. 590.

119. Truman's veto of the Taft-Hartley bill was another manifestation of the president's decision to follow the recommendations of this group.

120. Cited in McCullough, *Truman*, p. 590.

121. Sidney M. Milkis focuses on a fourth factor in their logic, the secular movement away from party-centered politics toward presidency-centered politics. Concern with that long-term trend, Milkis argues, also moved a perceptive James Rowe (and subsequently Clifford) to suggest a reorientation of presidential campaign politics. They urged a greater reliance on "pressure groups" rather than on the decaying party organization such groups were superceding (and which, probably not coincidently, spoke with a heavy southern accent). There was thus, in Milkis's view, a virtue to the Rowe-Clifford recommendations beyond their specific relevance to the 1948 elections. Even Milkis concedes, however (apropos of my argument), that "Rowe and Clifford had persuaded [Truman] that he could move more aggressively on civil rights in 1947 and 1948 and still hold the party together, but he learned that was not true." Their errors in execution in the short-run, which are important for my story here, do not undermine the long-term validity of their assessment of the state of presidency-party relations. See Milkis, *The President and the Parties: The Transformation of the American Party System since the New Deal* (New York: Oxford University Press, 1993), pp. 154–59.

122. McCullough, *Truman*, pp. 590–92; Berman, *The Politics of Civil Rights*, pp. 79–82. It is worth asking what Truman might have done had his advisers not so seriously erred on this third point. Truman may then have decided (a) to steer a moderate middle course, deemphasizing civil rights, or (b) to galvanize conservative forces to his side, leaving Dewey and Wallace to fight over and split the liberal vote. Under these alternative scenarios, Truman might have taken great advantage from sitting on the committee report.

It may be claimed that what Clifford and his colleagues were doing was merely dressing up their own policy preferences in a language suited to get Truman to go where he was already inclined. If that was the case, it is still worth noting the indispensability of political calculus in establishing the president's path.

123. Berman, *The Politics of Civil Rights*, pp. 81–82.

124. *Public Papers, 1948*, pp. 121–26; cited in Berman, *The Politics of Civil Rights*, pp. 84–85. Truman had also made reference to the relevance of Cold War politics in his earlier Lincoln Memorial address to the NAACP. See also Donovan, *Conflict and Crisis*, p. 334; Robert Cushman, "Our Civil Rights Becomes A Major World Issue," *New York Times Magazine*, January 11, 1948.

125. McCoy and Ruetten, *Quest and Response*, p. 102. See also Clifford's remarks to Mark Stern, presented in Stern, "Lyndon Johnson and the Democrats' Civil Rights Strategy," paper prepared for the annual meeting of the American Political Science Association, Atlanta, August 31–September 3, 1989, p. 4.

126. Robert J. Donovan writes that the president's special message on civil rights—drafted "in order to counterbalance [Henry] Wallace's appeal to blacks"— "opened a fissure in the political landscape that Truman had not foreseen." *Conflict and Crisis*, pp. 352–53.

127. "Truman canceled his original plan to send such legislation to Capitol Hill because the South was manifesting much greater resistance to his February 2 message than he or Clifford had anticipated. Unwilling to alienate that section any more than absolutely necessary, Truman now retreated somewhat from his more advanced position in order to protect his flank against the possibility of a southern revolt." Berman, *The Politics of Civil Rights*, p. 95.

128. Berman, *The Politics of Civil Rights*, p. 102.

129. Berman, *The Politics of Civil Rights*, p. 95.

130. McCullough, *Truman*, pp. 638–40; Berman, *The Politics of Civil Rights*, pp. 111–12.

131. These orders had been prepared long before then. This suggests that the timing of their issuance deserves some higher level of scrutiny than might otherwise be the case.

132. Garfinkel, *When Negroes March*, p. 161.

133. The president was forced to be especially sensitive to Randolph's pressures, because he needed all the support he could get to revive the selective service during peacetime. Truman's initial recommendation to Congress had no provisions for desegregation, and thus incurred the wrath of congressional liberals who viewed it as a shrinking departure from previously established positions. Donovan, *Conflict and Crisis*, pp. 390–91.

134. Berman, *The Politics of Civil Rights*, pp. 119, 239. For an extensive treatment of this episode, which concurs with Berman's assessment, see Pfeffer, *A. Philip Randolph*, ch. 4.

135. In a 1973 oral history interview, Clifford held that he eventually modified his advice to Truman in recognition of the great "risk in alienating the South." See Kenneth O'Reilly, *Nixon's Piano: Presidents and Racial Politics from Washington to Clinton* (New York: Free Press, 1995), pp. 157, 455.

136. Berman, *The Politics of Civil Rights*, p. 129. On the importance of the liberal civil rights plank in the Democratic platform, David McCullough writes: "[W]hether Truman and his people appreciated it or not, Hubert Humphrey had done more to reelect Truman than would anyone at the convention other than Truman himself." *Truman*, p. 640.

137. Shannon, "Presidential Politics in the South," p. 470. The demographics of political power in Congress did not favor African Americans as they did in the electoral college. Thus, the pressure politics that worked well in the executive arena failed to create much immediate movement within Congress. McCoy and Ruetten, *Quest and Response*, pp. 176–77.

138. Truman's liberal critics often seemed inattentive, however, to the limits on what the president could do. Thus, Truman often found it necessary to remind them of the relative dearth of political and institutional tools available to the president for wringing action from a reluctant Congress. McCoy and Ruetten, *Quest and Response*, pp. 23–24, 42, 182.

139. "The spur of the civil-rights advocates was compelling, but the bridle of their opponents was almost proportionately discouraging." McCoy and Ruetten, *Quest and Response*, p. 351

140. I hasten to add here that the metaphor is not applicable to the institution across the entire range of issues that might confront the polity. I think it is apt in this case because it highlights the inseparability of the president's problem with that of the nation as a whole on this issue.

141. For example, the seniority rule was not adopted expressly for nation-keeping purposes, but to protect the southern voice in the affairs of state. Its centrality to the way Washington works has tended to require, then, presidential attention to that regional voice, *especially* in those instances where it has been clear and strong. The resulting effect is to ensure that no president, however tin his political ear, could mistakenly move ahead on a policy that might so violate southern sensibilities as to provoke internal convulsions. In this regard a biological metaphor may be more illuminating than a nautical one. Such forces serve the body politic as a fever does the body corporeal: it can provide a valuable signal that something more fundamental is wrong.

142. Robert J. Donovan, *Tumultuous Years: The Presidency of Harry S. Truman, 1949–1953* (New York: Norton, 1982), pp. 118–19.

143. Quoted in Berman, *The Politics of Civil Rights*, p. 150. Wilkins's remark was made in 1952.

144. Berman, *The Politics of Civil Rights*, p. 148.

145. Berman, *The Politics of Civil Rights*, pp. 148–49.

146. Kluger, *Simple Justice*, pp. 558–61. Although the evidence indicates that Truman himself was usually not directly a party to the decision to submit such briefs—not even in a case with the gravity of *Brown*—he does deserve some credit for placing sympathetic administrators in positions where they could act, and allowing them the freedom to do so. Truman's attorney general, Tom Clark, later did credit Truman directly with the first-term decision to intervene in the *Shelley* case, but documentary evidence is apparently unavailable to corroborate his account. See Donovan, *Conflict and Crisis*, p. 335, footnote 9.

147. As we shall see later, it was this very factor that encouraged the NAACP, under Thurgood Marshall's direction, to parallel Walter White's political activism with initiatives in the courts.

148. Quoted in Berman, *The Politics of Civil Rights*, p. 160.

149. Bernstein, "The Ambiguous Legacy," p. 293.

150. Berman, *The Politics of Civil Rights*, p. 168.

151. For example, Truman's unwillingness to press the Democratic leadership in Congress to punish its partisans who had strayed to the Dixiecrat standard seemed to betray to some his continuing unwillingness to put his presidency fully on their side. Further, in May 1949, Truman included three measures on a list of "must" bills sent to Congress: consent to the North Atlantic Pact, extension of the Reciprocal Trade Agreement program, and repeal of Taft-Hartley. This array of priorities outraged many liberals and African Americans. See McCoy and Ruetten, *Quest and Response*, p. 181.

152. In response, "Negro leaders . . . and their white allies realized sadly that Truman's efforts were not fully in the struggle for equality." Berman, *The Politics of Civil Rights*, p. 180.

153. Berman, *The Politics of Civil Rights*, p. 168.

154. O'Reilly, *Nixon's Piano*, pp. 150–52.

155. Harry S. Truman, *Memoirs by Harry S. Truman: Volume 2, Years of Trial and Hope* (Garden City, N.Y.: Doubleday, 1956), p. 183.

156. Truman, *Years of Trial and Hope*, p. 183; O'Reilly, *Nixon's Piano*, p. 154. O'Reilly's depiction of the Truman presidency, in chapter 4 (entitled "Cold Warriors"), is especially perceptive.

157. O'Reilly, *Nixon's Piano*, pp. 154–55. Those Cold War concerns actually cut both ways. Racial inequality undermined the nation's strength on distant horizons, contributing to a reformist impulse, but the furtive presence of the enemy within undermined the president's confidence in many who agitated for change at home. That a president is expected to attend to nation-keeping responsibilities does not mean that those requirements are always clearly defined.

158. Berman, *The Politics of Civil Rights*, p. 180.

159. O'Reilly, *Nixon's Piano*, p. 162.

160. Quoted in McCoy and Ruetten, *Quest and Response*, pp. 286–87.

161. Berman, *The Politics of Civil Rights*, p. 179.

162. See, for example, Richard M. Freeland, *The Truman Doctrine and the Origins of McCarthyism* (New York: Schocken, 1974).

163. Quoted in Bernstein, "The Ambiguous Legacy," p. 300.

164. McCoy and Ruetten, *Quest and Response*, pp. 263–66. These authors found, for example, that possession of recorded music by Paul Robeson was sufficient cause for employees to be placed in a suspect category.

165. It is doubtful that Truman had the legal authority to follow Roosevelt's lead in issuing an executive order reconstituting an FEPC. Congress had expressly proscribed such authority—absent expressed legislative approval—in ending the immediate postwar battle over an FEPC. Bernstein, "The Ambiguous Legacy," p. 298.

166. Quoted in Berman, *The Politics of Civil Rights*, p. 187.

167. Quoted in Berman, *The Politics of Civil Rights*, p. 197.

6. RACE RETURNS TO CENTER STAGE: THE EISENHOWER YEARS

1. A common method of self-defense employed by Eisenhower when asked during the 1952 campaign about specific racial issues was to claim, "I have not even thought about" it. Richard Kluger, *Simple Justice: The History of Brown v. Board of Education and Black America's Struggle for Equality* (New York: Vintage Books, 1975), pp. 664–65.

2. Chester J. Pach Jr. and Elmo Richardson write, "Civil rights, in short, revealed more dramatically than any other issue the shortcomings of Eisenhower's philosophy of government restraint." Even Eisenhower's generally favorable biographer, Michael S. Mayer, concludes, "While individual acts of bigotry or discrimination never failed to invoke his horror, he could not translate his reaction to specific instances into outrage at the larger issues of racial injustice in American society." Pach and Richardson, *The Presidency of Dwight D. Eisenhower* (Lawrence: University Press of Kansas, 1991), p. 137; Mayer, "Regardless of Station, Race, or Calling: Eisenhower and Race," in Joann P. Krieg, ed., *Dwight D. Eisenhower: Soldier, President, Statesman* (New York: Greenwood Press, 1987), p. 39.

3. Toward the end of his tenure, Eisenhower wrote to his principal black appointee—E. Frederic Morrow—a letter that hints at apologia, rooted in the claim that "Our Nation can never be run by one man." Morrow, *Black Man in the White House: A Diary of the Eisenhower Years by the Administrative Officer for Special Projects, the White House, 1955–1961* (New York: Coward-McCann, 1963), frontispiece.

4. National Association for the Advancement of Colored People, *90 Years + 10 = Freedom: NAACP Annual Report, Forty-fifth Year, 1953*, p. 38.

5. National Association for the Advancement of Colored People, *The Year of the Great Decision: NAACP Annual Report, Forty-sixth Year, 1954*, p. 41. See also Merlo J. Pusey, *Eisenhower the President* (New York: Macmillan, 1956), pp. 291–92.

6. In his memoirs, Herbert Brownell—who was the major activist of the administration in the realm of civil rights—claims that the Eisenhower he encountered just before the 1952 presidential campaign was "in accord with the pro-civil rights stance of the Republican party. . . . I felt that Eisenhower's heart was in the right place on civil rights, but [he] signaled to me that he would not lead the charge to change race relations fundamentally in the United States." Herbert Brownell with John P. Burke, *Advising Ike: The Memoirs of Attorney General Herbert Brownell* (Lawrence: University Press of Kansas, 1993), pp. 98–99.

7. For a related claim about the broader contours of the Eisenhower program, see Pusey, *Eisenhower the President*, p. 216.

8. Robert Fredrick Burk, *The Eisenhower Administration and Black Civil Rights* (Knoxville: University of Tennessee Press, 1984), ch. 3.

9. Cited in Burk, *Eisenhower Administration*, pp. 45–46. Burk later comments (p. 49), "In addressing the District's racial problems, Eisenhower saw his primary duty

not as the extension of capital home rule but rather the upgrading of the image of the 'citadel of democracy' through unobtrusive executive actions."

10. The administration's preoccupation with the propaganda or public relations aspects of the racial problem, and its general deficiency of real curiosity about the full extent of racial prejudice in American society, is a central theme in Burk, *Eisenhower Administration*, chs. 2–6.

11. Burk, *Eisenhower Administration*, p. 28; Pach and Richardson, *Dwight D. Eisenhower*, p. 138.

12. Those Republicans with especially good political ears—and those concerned about the long-term health of the party beyond the Eisenhower presidency—tended to stake out positions on civil rights far in advance of the president. This is a central thesis of J. W. Anderson, *Eisenhower, Brownell, and the Congress: The Tangled Origins of the Civil Rights Bill of 1956–1957* (University: University of Alabama Press for the Inter-University Case Program, 1964).

13. Although the administration frequently touted its successful work in combating discrimination in the District of Columbia, its success was not truly extensive. An inadvertently piercing commentary on this point appears in the memoirs of Eisenhower's highest ranking black aide, E. Frederic Morrow, in his account of the indignities visited on an African American public official trying to find adequate housing in the Washington of Eisenhower's time. See Morrow, *Black Man in the White House*, pp. 82–84, 164.

14. NAACP, *Annual Report, 1953*, pp. 38–39. The Association's 1954 *Annual Report* (p. 41) claimed that "Some of [Eisenhower's] efforts were impeded, if not sabotaged, by subordinates in the administration, who for one reason or another, sought to retard the pace of the President's . . . action."

15. Pach and Richardson, *Dwight D. Eisenhower*, p. 140.

16. Eisenhower, *The White House Years: Waging Peace, 1956–1961* (Garden City, N.Y.: Doubleday, 1965), pp. 151–52.

17. NAACP, *Annual Report, 1954*, p. 45.

18. The quotation is from the Bible, the Book of Amos 5:24. This was one of Dr. Martin Luther King Jr.'s favorite passages, and it now adorns the face of the Civil Rights Memorial in Montgomery, Alabama. Taylor Branch, *Parting the Waters: America in the King Years, 1954–63* (New York: Simon and Schuster, 1988), p. 141.

19. Steve Lawson, *Black Ballots: Voting Rights in the South, 1944–1969* (New York: Columbia University Press, 1976), pp. 141–42.

20. This reaction came from a branch of the administration said by one close observer to be "more eager to promote a definitive resolution of the matter than was the [Chief] Executive." Kluger, *Simple Justice*, pp. 650–51.

21. The story of the development and execution of that strategy is extensively reported in Richard Kluger's nearly 800-page treatment, *Simple Justice*.

22. Kluger, *Simple Justice*, p. 284.

23. Despite the brief's favorable view of overruling *Plessy*, NAACP representatives were disappointed with it, because they felt it left the Supreme Court too many other easier exits. Kluger, *Simple Justice*, pp. 558–60.

24. Dwight D. Eisenhower, *Ike's Letters to a Friend, 1941–1958*, Robert Griffith, ed. (Lawrence: University Press of Kansas, 1984), p. 186.

25. Robert H. Ferrell, ed., *The Eisenhower Diaries* (New York: Norton, 1981), pp. 246–47. The diary entry is from July 1953.

26. The Southern Manifesto, signed by the overwhelming majority of southern members of Congress in the immediate aftermath of the *Brown* decision, is conveniently reprinted in Brownell, *Advising Ike*, pp. 359–63.

27. Cited in Burk, *Eisenhower Administration*, p. 135.

28. Actually, Eisenhower declared that *both* of his mistakes as president were seated on the Supreme Court, referring to his appointees Warren and William Brennan. Quoted in Henry J. Abraham, *Justices and Presidents: A Political History of Appointments to the Supreme Court*, 2d ed. (New York: Oxford University Press, 1985), p. 263. A slightly different assertion appears in William Bragg Ewald, Jr. *Eisenhower the President: Crucial Days, 1951–1960* (Englewood Cliffs, N.J.: Prentice-Hall, 1981), p. 85.

29. Brownell, *Advising Ike*, p. 191.

30. Burk, *Eisenhower Administration*, pp. 135–36.

31. Brownell, *Advising Ike*, pp. 193–94.

32. Burk, *Eisenhower Administration*, pp. 141, 166. Brownell's memoirs confirm the extent to which he found it necessary, as one who believed segregation was unconstitutional, to shield Eisenhower and to bring him along slowly on the race question, emphasizing primarily the president's *duty* to support the work of the Court. Brownell, *Advising Ike*, ch. 11.

33. Burk, *Eisenhower Administration*, pp. 141–42. William Bragg Ewald vigorously disputes the notion that Eisenhower staged the dinner for such purposes, but concedes that the president, "in a moment of thoughtless candor," addressed the "southern horror of adolescent miscegenation." Ewald, *Eisenhower the President*, pp. 82–83. See also Brownell, *Advising Ike*, p. 174.

34. According to Pach and Richardson, Eisenhower saw the result "not as a great victory over a moral evil, but as a tragic and destructive mistake." *Dwight D. Eisenhower*, p. 143.

35. Jackson was alleged to have challenged the court accordingly in 1832 in the case of *Worcester v. Georgia*. Henry Abraham, while conceding that Jackson allowed the court's ruling to be openly flouted, believes that Jackson did *not* make the statement commonly attributed to him: "Well, John Marshall has made his decision, now let him enforce it." Abraham, *Justices and Presidents*, p. 94.

36. Kluger, *Simple Justice*, pp. 558–61; Burk, *Eisenhower Administration*, pp. 136–37.

37. Kluger, *Simple Justice*, p. 727.

38. Kluger, *Simple Justice*, pp. 726–27.

39. Burk, *Eisenhower Administration*, pp. 148–50. Michael Mayer holds that Eisenhower's premier contributions to civil rights advances came with his federal judicial appointees, especially in the South, where the ensuing struggle took place for making good on the Supreme Court's ruling. "Eisenhower was nothing if not a gradualist," Mayer writes, "which is perhaps why he made his greatest contribution through the appointment of judges." Mayer, "Eisenhower and the Southern Federal Judiciary: The Soboloff Nomination," in Shirley Anne Warshaw, ed., *Reexamining the Eisenhower Presidency* (Westport, Conn.: Greenwood Press, 1993), pp. 57–83.

40. Quoted in Kluger, *Simple Justice*, p. 735.

41. It should be noted here that the president did mount some token efforts to give life to the Court's orders. For example, the day after the initial ruling was handed down, Eisenhower pressed to have schools, theaters, and restaurants within the District of Columbia integrated.

42. Cited in Burk, *Eisenhower Administration*, p. 144. Suspicions about the president's position on *Brown* may have derived in part from a correct public reading of the president's own privately expressed views. Eisenhower confidentially groused about the Court's rulings, sentiments that publicly leaked several years later when he complained about the justices' political "stupidity." Disclosure of these comments occasioned a public apology from the White House. Burk, *Eisenhower Administration*, p. 171.

43. Burk, *Eisenhower Administration*, pp. 145–50, 153.

44. For an account of the unfolding of that initiative, see Donald W. Jackson and James W. Riddlesperger Jr., "The Eisenhower Administration and the 1957 Civil Rights Act," in Warshaw, ed., *Reexamining the Eisenhower Presidency*, pp. 85–101.

45. Brownell's position in advance of the rest of the administration, including the president, is discussed in Ewald, *Eisenhower the President*, pp. 203–8.

46. Anderson, *Eisenhower, Brownell, and the Congress*, pp. 3–4; Lawson, *Black Ballots*, p. 150.

47. Anderson, *Eisenhower, Brownell, and the Congress*, pp. 22–24.

48. Pach and Richardson, *Dwight D. Eisenhower*, p. 146.

49. Pach and Richardson write: "Eisenhower hoped to silence demands for strong action against white southern intransigence [on school desegregation] by sending a civil rights bill to Congress in 1956. The heart of the measure was greater federal protection of voting rights." *Dwight D. Eisenhower*, p. 145. The same case is made in Robert Fredrick Burk, "Dwight D. Eisenhower and Civil Rights Conservatism," in Krieg, ed., *Dwight D. Eisenhower*, pp. 53–54. See also Lawson, *Black Ballots*, p. 165.

50. Burk, *Eisenhower Administration*, pp. 155–58. It should be noted that the administration received some encouragement to pursue this path by the fact that many civil rights activists also saw enfranchisement as crucial in the struggle for equal standing. Where they generally disagreed with Eisenhower was in his use of

voting rights as a substitute for—not a supplement to—vigorous enforcement of school desegregation. See Aldon D. Morris, *The Origins of the Civil Rights Movement: Black Communities Organizing for Change* (New York: Free Press, 1984), pp. 101–12.

51. Burk, *Eisenhower Administration*, pp. 155, 159–60, 170; Branch, *Parting the Waters*, pp. 191, 199.

52. Branch, *Parting the Waters*, pp. 181–82.

53. Both quotes appear in Burk, *Eisenhower Administration*, pp. 160–61.

54. Minutes of the cabinet meeting are quoted in Branch, *Parting the Waters*, p. 182.

55. Anderson, *Eisenhower, Brownell, and the Congress*, pp. 28–40; Pach and Richardson, *Dwight D. Eisenhower*, pp. 145–46; Lawson, *Black Ballots*, pp. 150–55.

56. He "had no license from the White House to go so far," claims a close student of this episode. "In his astonishingly bold tactics, Brownell had deliberately jeopardized his own office to get this set of powerful bills introduced; it appeared that he had, as a cabinet member, overstepped the line that divided initiative from insubordination." Anderson, *Eisenhower, Brownell, and the Congress*, pp. 40–43. See also Brownell, *Advising Ike*, pp. 219–20.

57. Anderson, *Eisenhower, Brownell, and the Congress*, pp. 135–39; Lawson, *Black Ballots*, pp. 161–62.

58. On that confusion, see Jackson and Riddlesperger, "The Eisenhower Administration and the 1957 Civil Rights Act," pp. 90–92.

59. Liberal activist Joe Rauh later remarked, "To give the devil his due he got us the first civil rights bill since Reconstruction, but he also took out its teeth." Quoted in Milton Viorst, *Fire in the Streets: America in the 1960s* (New York: Simon and Schuster, 1979), p. 238. Close observers of LBJ's Senate career note that, although presidential aspirations drove him to enter the fray on behalf of a civil rights bill, he was largely motivated, too, by fears that the South could no longer completely fight off Republican administration advances toward racial equality. Johnson and Sam Rayburn worried that a southern filibuster might fail, or that, in succeeding, it might occasion such a negative reaction nationwide that cloture rules would be forever loosened. For these reasons, LBJ sought to "transform the Eisenhower bill into the Johnson bill." His movement was essentially reactive in nature. See the discussion in Rowland Evans and Robert Novak, *Lyndon B. Johnson: The Exercise of Power* (New York: Signet Books, 1966), ch. 7. (The quote cited above appears on p. 137.) For a succinct discussion of the differing interpretations of Johnson's behavior, see Jackson and Riddlesperger, "The Eisenhower Administration and the 1957 Civil Rights Act," pp. 89–90, 92–93, 99–100.

60. Lawson, *Black Ballots*, pp. 165–200; Pach and Richardson, *Dwight D. Eisenhower*, pp. 147–48; Morrow, *Black Man in the White House*, pp. 165–68. The amendment held that jury trials would be required when the penalty for criminal contempt charges might be in excess of $300 or 45 days in jail.

61. Pach and Richardson, *Dwight D. Eisenhower*, pp. 148, 155–57; Lawson, *Black Ballots*, pp. 203–247.

62. Quoted in Kluger, *Simple Justice*, p. 727.

63. Burk, *Eisenhower Administration*, p. 166; *Dallas Morning News*, August 23, 1956, editorial page (unnumbered).

64. See Stanley I. Kutler, "Eisenhower, the Judiciary, and Desegregation: Some Reflections," in Gunter Bischof and Stephen E. Ambrose, eds. *Eisenhower: A Centenary Assessment* (Baton Rouge: Louisiana State University Press, 1995), pp. 90–91.

65. A brief account of the Mansfield case is included in Anderson, *Eisenhower, Brownell, and the Congress*, pp. 128–30. See also Burk, *Eisenhower Administration*, pp. 167–73.

66. *Washington Post*, September 1, 1956, p. 39; September 2, 1956, p. A-12; September 5, 1956, p. 9.

67. *Washington Post*, September 1, 1956, p. 39; *Dallas Morning News*, August 30, 1956, p. 2; August 31, 1956, pp. 1–2; September 1, 1956, p. 3.

68. *Dallas Morning News*, August 31, 1956, pp. 1–2; September 1, 1956, pp. 1, 3; September 2, 1956, D-1; September 5, 1956, p. 1.

69. *Dallas Morning News*, September 1, 1956, p. 1; September 5, 1956, p. 2; September 7, 1956, editorial page [unnumbered].

70. A crucial subtext to the administration's actions in Mansfield was the 1956 election. The Texas conflict erupted as the ink was barely dry on newspapers announcing Eisenhower's renomination at the San Francisco Cow Palace. The presidential election was to occur only two months later. Consequently, an issue that the White House had labored extensively to neutralize threatened to explode at the most inopportune time. Further, Eisenhower had a unique opportunity to solidify Republican gains in the South by keeping Texas Governor Shivers happy, as Shivers intended to support Eisenhower against his own party's candidate in the fall election. Subsequently, the White House was apprehensive that Shivers and Eisenhower would find themselves at odds over Mansfield. They did not. *Dallas Morning News*, September 7, 1956, p. 1.

71. *Dallas Morning News*, September 5, 1956, p. 1; September 6, 1956, p. 1 [early and late editions], September 7, 1956, editorial page [unnumbered]; *Washington Post*, September 6, 1956, pp. 1, 24.

72. "Orval Faubus and the Shadow of History," *Washington Post*, January 25, 1993, p. B1; Eisenhower, *Waging Peace*, p. 165.

73. Faubus highlighted the importance of political considerations in Eisenhower's thinking in his scrapbook *cum* memoir, *Down From the Hills* (Little Rock: Pioneer Press, 1980), p. 223. He writes, noting the relevant differences between Mansfield and Little Rock: "Texas was a large state with a powerful governor not bound to either party, with a large number of electoral votes that could be numbered in either polit-

ical column. The defiance of the federal court order at Mansfield occurred while a campaign for the presidency was under way.... Arkansas was a small state with a governor supporting unequivocally the Democratic nominee for president in 1956, and a small number of electoral votes already counted in the Democratic column. Therefore, [Arkansas] was a good place for the Justice Department to inject its authority, Brownell to show his colors, and the national Democratic liberals to make statements."

74. Burk, *Eisenhower Administration*, pp. 176–77. Governor Faubus later justified his actions partly on the grounds that the school board itself was far from unanimous in its initial position, and thus its membership, and the school superintendent, welcomed the political cover his intervention provided. Faubus, *Down From the Hills*, pp. 199–204.

75. The Justice envoy was Arthur Caldwell. Faubus details the encounter in *Down From the Hills*, pp. 197–98.

76. Faubus's interpretation of the president's intentions for Little Rock also derived from remarks Eisenhower delivered in June 1957 at the National Governor's Conference, a speech Faubus termed "one of the strongest states rights speeches I have ever heard." See Faubus, *Down From the Hills*, pp. 182, 249.

77. Burk, *Eisenhower Administration*, p. 158.

78. In his memoirs, Brownell makes much of this distinction between Mansfield and Little Rock. He argues that since the district court responsible for executing *Brown* II in Texas had not invited the administration to be a party to the conflict, the president was correct to stay out. He admits, however, that others in his own Justice Department felt that the administration was overly timid in this approach, evidently reasoning that the president's own conception of his enforcement powers with respect to a judgment of the Supreme Court ought to play at least as prominent a role as the district court's conception. Apparently the administration was spared a Little Rock in 1956 because the district court in Mansfield refused to hold the local school board's feet to the fire on its earlier desegregation order (perhaps because the NAACP dropped the matter when no White House help was forthcoming), avoiding confrontation by conceding the issue. Brownell, *Advising Ike*, pp. 204–16.

79. Burk, *Eisenhower Administration*, pp. 177–78.

80. Burk, *Eisenhower Administration*, pp. 178–79.

81. Eisenhower was vacationing in Newport and did not wish to be seen interrupting his vacation to deal with Faubus. Brief accounts of the subsequent meetings appear in Burk, *Eisenhower Administration*, pp. 179–82, and Pach and Richardson, *Dwight D. Eisenhower*, pp. 150–52. See also Faubus, *Down From the Hills*, ch. 12.

82. Burk, *Eisenhower Administration*, pp. 182–83.

83. Pach and Richardson, *Dwight D. Eisenhower*, p. 153; Burk, *Eisenhower Administration*, pp. 184–85.

84. Dwight D. Eisenhower, "The Eisenhower Address on Little Rock, September

24, 1957," in Henry Steele Commager, ed., *The Struggle for Racial Equality: A Documentary Record* (Gloucester, Mass.: Peter Smith, 1967), p. 86. See also Brownell, *Advising Ike*, p. 375.

85. David J. Garrow, *Bearing the Cross: Martin Luther King Jr. and the Southern Christian Leadership Conference* (New York: Vintage Books, 1986), p. 119.

86. Ambrose cited in Pach and Richardson, *Dwight D. Eisenhower*, p. 154.

87. Eisenhower, *Waging Peace*, p. 171.

88. Branch, *Parting the Waters*, p. 224. See also Eisenhower, *Waging Peace*, p. 169.

89. Brownell's memorandum recapitulates the oral advice he gave Eisenhower during the days of the Little Rock crisis. The memo is conveniently reprinted as "Brownell Opinion to Eisenhower on Little Rock School Desegregation," in Brownell, *Advising Ike*, pp. 365–84.

90. Brownell's memo cited the relevance in this regard of Article VI, clause 2: "This Constitution, and the Laws of the United States which shall be made in Pursuance thereof . . . shall be the supreme Law of the Land."

91. Eisenhower, "The Eisenhower Address on Little Rock," p. 87.

92. Eisenhower, *Ike's Letters to a Friend*, p. 193.

93. The Mansfield case indicates, however, that the president was willing to tolerate a fairly high level of peaceful resistance to orders of the court. The social fabric-destroying character of violent opposition was what most concerned him.

94. Brownell, *Advising Ike*, p. 219.

95. Eisenhower, *Waging Peace*, p. 168.

96. Eisenhower, "Address on Little Rock," p. 88. See also "Brownell Opinion to Eisenhower," in Brownell, *Advising Ike*, pp. 381–82.

97. Of course, that international threat cut both ways. Eisenhower was ever sensitive to prospects that the NAACP and other organizations were being infiltrated by communists. Some black activists, including Thurgood Marshall, cooperated privately with the administration to try to prevent any possible infiltration from damaging their efforts. *Washington Post*, December 8, 1996, A4. See also Eisenhower, *Waging Peace*, p. 152.

98. Carl M. Brauer writes, "The Little Rock Crisis did not initiate a change of policy . . . [T]he administration still sought to avoid any involvement in the racial issue." *John F. Kennedy and the Second Reconstruction* (New York: Columbia University Press, 1977), p. 5.

99. Burk, *Eisenhower Administration*, pp. 196, 201.

100. Garrow, *Bearing the Cross*, pp. 90, 133–35.

101. Branch, *Parting the Waters*, pp. 216–18; Burk, *Eisenhower Administration*, p. 112.

102. During his remarks, the president had counseled the editors to "be patient" in their pursuit of equal rights, instruction that did not at all sit well with Eisenhower's audience. On African-American sensitivity to such counsel, see

Morrow, *Black Man in the White House*, p. 58.

103. Pach and Richardson, *Dwight D. Eisenhower*, pp. 155–56; Burk, *Eisenhower Administration*, p. 238; Morrow, *Black Man in the White House*, pp. 218, 228; Garrow, *Bearing the Cross*, p. 106.

104. The years from 1956 to 1960 were a time of much soul-searching by southern civil rights leaders, as they sought to find some way to apply what they had learned in Montgomery to the entirety of segregation in the South. See Branch, *Parting the Waters*, chs. 6–7; Morris, *Origins of the Civil Rights Movement*, passim.

105. On the emergence and development of this form of protest, see Martin Oppenheimer, *The Sit-In Movement of 1960* (Brooklyn: Carlson, 1989).

106. Morris, *Origins of the Civil Rights Movement*, p. 201.

107. Morris, *Origins of the Civil Rights Movement*, chs. 3–6. Conventional accounts of the civil rights movement usually cite the Greensboro sit-in as the beginning of massive civil disobedience in America. See, for example, Branch, *Parting the Waters*, ch. 7; Burk, *Eisenhower Administration*, p. 253.

108. Burk, *Eisenhower Administration*, p. 253.

7. EMANCIPATION, ACT II: PRESSURES AND CONVERSION

1. For purposes of this analysis, I treat Johnson's administration as an extension of Kennedy's. Thus, Johnson's embrace of civil rights came only after his participation in an administration earlier committed to keeping civil rights advances under control. A similar approach is taken by Bruce Miroff in his seminal article, "Presidential Leverage over Social Movements: The Johnson White House and Civil Rights," *Journal of Politics* 43 (February 1981): 2–23.

2. Democrat Harry McPherson has written, "Kennedy's success among Negroes in 1960 had surprised me. He had never been outspoken about civil rights, and Nixon, with his progressive rulings during the filibuster debates and his chairmanship of a government fair-employment committee, was at least an equal friend to black aspirations." McPherson, *A Political Education: A Washington Memoir* (Boston: Houghton Mifflin, 1988), p. 193. See also Mark Stern, "Lyndon Johnson and the Democrats' Civil Rights Strategy," paper prepared for the annual meeting of the American Political Science Association, Atlanta, August 31–September 3, 1989, p. 6.

3. Both Eisenhower's chief black aide, E. Frederic Morrow, and Martin Luther King Jr., had a generally favorable assessment of Nixon's performance as vice president. See Morrow, *Black Man in the White House: A Diary of the Eisenhower Years by the Administrative Officer for Special Projects, The White House, 1955–1961* (New York: Coward-McCann, 1963), pp. 41, 133–34, 240–41, 293; David J. Garrow, *Bearing the Cross: Martin Luther King Jr. and the Southern Christian Leadership Conference* (New York: Vintage Books, 1986), pp. 90–91, 94–95, 118–19.

4. Nicholas Katzenbach later recalled that at the beginning of the Kennedy term neither Robert nor John knew any African Americans personally. Gerald S. and Deborah H. Strober, eds., *"Let Us Begin Anew": An Oral History of the Kennedy Presidency* (New York: HarperCollins, 1993), pp. 274, 278. See also Richard Reeves, *President Kennedy: Profile in Power* (New York: Simon and Schuster, 1993), p. 62.

5. Taylor Branch, *Parting the Waters: America in the King Years, 1954–63* (New York: Simon and Schuster, 1988), p. 306.

6. Theodore C. Sorensen reports that Kennedy considered "the approach of many single-minded civil rights advocates"—presumably including King— "uncomfortable and unreasonable." *Kennedy* (New York: Harper and Row, 1965), p. 471. See also Stephen B. Oates, *Let the Trumpet Sound: The Life of Martin Luther King Jr.* (New York: Harper and Row, 1982), pp. 158–59; Garrow, *Bearing the Cross*, p. 143.

7. Branch, *Parting the Waters*, pp. 306–8.

8. For recollections of this episode by key participants, see the oral history excerpts printed in Strober and Strober, eds., *"Let Us Begin Anew,"* pp. 34–37

9. Arthur M. Schlesinger Jr., *Robert Kennedy and His Times* (New York: Ballantine Books, 1978), pp. 233–35; Theodore H. White, *The Making of the President, 1960* (New York: Pocket Books, 1961), p. 385.

10. Robert Fredrick Burk, *The Eisenhower Administration and Black Civil Rights* (Knoxville: University of Tennessee Press, 1984), pp. 259–60; White, *Making of the President, 1960*, p. 387; Morrow, *Black Man in the White House*, p. 296. Burk writes, "Without his margin of black support, Kennedy could not have carried the key states of Illinois, Michigan, New Jersey, Texas, and South Carolina. In contrast, Nixon's level of black support represented a disappointing slippage of between 5 and 10 percent from the Republican figures of 1956" (p. 260).

11. Reeves, *President Kennedy*, p. 60.

12. I will thus argue that although the increased effort to keep black constituents happy was not unimportant, it did not constitute a distinction in kind from the efforts of Kennedy's predecessors until much later. In other words, a New Frontier in civil rights *did* emerge, but not until important events in 1963 ushered it in.

13. Arthur M. Schlesinger Jr., *A Thousand Days: John F. Kennedy in the White House* (Boston: Houghton Mifflin, 1965), pp. 931–32. See also Strober and Strober, eds., *"Let Us Begin Anew,"* p. 272; Reeves, *President Kennedy*, p. 63.

14. The validity of this point may more clearly emerge by noting that these areas of executive activity had identifiable roots in the Roosevelt and Truman presidencies.

15. Carl M. Brauer, *John F. Kennedy and the Second Reconstruction* (New York: Columbia University Press, 1977), pp. 69–71.

16. The dynamics of that organizational subversion are fairly straightforward. The elevation of black appointees to visible posts within the administration helped to create a large reservoir of goodwill among African-American publics. Later, when those such as King—and even the NAACP itself—tried to rouse mass pressure by attacking

the president, they found that the president had largely inoculated himself from such assaults in part because of his record of appointments. "I attacked John Kennedy for ten minutes," Roy Wilkins once told colleagues who had suggested assailing the president, "and everyone sat on their hands. Then I said a few favorable words about the things he had done, and they clapped and clapped." Quoted in Schlesinger, *Thousand Days*, p. 950.

17. *Washington Post*, September 6, 1956, p. 1.

18. Kennedy's general approach to the role of rhetoric is touched on in Jeffrey K. Tulis, *The Rhetorical Presidency* (Princeton: Princeton University Press, 1987), pp. 190–91.

19. Brauer, *Second Reconstruction*, pp. 74–75. The president was generally very reluctant to make use of rhetoric during periods of high tension such as the crisis at Oxford, Mississippi, in fear that his constitutional obligations to enforce court orders would require him to make statements that provoked a reaction he in fact wished to discourage. See Reeves, *President Kennedy*, pp. 357–58.

20. Garrow, *Bearing the Cross*, p. 154. Kennedy thus fell very much in the tradition of Franklin Roosevelt, who reproved Herbert Hoover for allowing the Bonus Army protests of 1932 to degenerate into armed conflict, rather than meeting with its leaders to hear their grievances. "What Hoover should have done was to have . . . sent out coffee and sandwiches and asked a delegation in," Roosevelt explained to presidential aid Rex Tugwell. Tugwell, *The Brains Trust* (New York: Viking Press, 1968), p. 359.

21. Wofford initially encouraged the president to make routine use of his office for such meetings, both to keep black leaders satisfied and to keep the profile of such meetings as low as possible. "[T]he way to avoid 'summit meetings' with big delegations and great expectations and possible disappointments is to hold occasional informal meetings," Wofford wrote. Brauer, *Second Reconstruction*, pp. 71–74. Garrow, *Bearing the Cross*, p. 170; Reeves, *President Kennedy*, pp. 100–101.

22. Victor S. Navasky, *Kennedy Justice* (New York: Atheneum, 1971), pp. 108–11.

23. Martin Luther King Jr., *Why We Can't Wait* (New York: Signet Books, 1963), pp. 20, 30–31.

24. Quoted in Garrow, *Bearing the Cross*, p. 170.

25. Brauer, *Second Reconstruction*, pp. 43, 205.

26. Kennedy, according to Nicholas Katzenbach, "was always conscious of the closeness of the election, I always thought too conscious." Quoted in Strober and Strober, eds., *"Let Us Begin Anew"*, p. 277.

27. Such tensions—which have been commonplace in the political history of parties in the United States—are often inexplicably overlooked by those who seek pseudo-parliamentary government, i.e., *"party* government," here. For a critique of such thinking, see James Sterling Young and Russell L. Riley, "Party Government and Political Culture," paper prepared for the American Political Science Association, annual meeting, San Francisco, August 30–September 2, 1990.

28. On this idea of forced leadership, see Russell L. Riley, "The Limits of the

Transformational Presidency," paper prepared for a conference entitled "Presidential Power: Forging the Presidency for the 21st Century," Columbia University, New York, November 15–16, 1996.

29. James Peck, *Freedom Ride* (New York: Simon and Schuster, 1962), pp. 114–16.

30. Quoted in Garrow, *Bearing the Cross*, p. 156.

31. Peck, *Freedom Ride*, pp. 116–30. There was some episodic harassment of the Freedom Riders before they reached Atlanta, but nothing on the scale of violence experienced in Alabama.

32. On the administration's failure to take note of the advanced warnings of the Ride, see the comments of James Farmer, Burke Marshall, and Nicholas Katzenbach, in Strober and Strober, eds. *"Let Us Begin Anew,"* pp. 293–94.

33. Reeves, *President Kennedy*, pp. 123, 125–26.

34. Branch, *Parting the Waters*, pp. 433–36, 451.

35. Reeves, *President Kennedy*, p. 124.

36. Garrow, *Bearing the Cross*, pp. 154–56.

37. Branch, *Parting the Waters*, pp. 429–30; Peck, *Freedom Ride*, pp. 130–38. In this instance the president found his own rhetorical support for civil rights coming back to haunt him. One of the Riders explained to Seigenthaler that they intended to "show those people in Alabama who think they can ignore the President of the United States." Quoted in Reeves, *President Kennedy*, p. 126.

38. Quoted in Branch, *Parting the Waters*, p. 443. The telephone call was tapped in Alabama by administration critics, who leaked Kennedy's remarks to the local press, seriously undermining his reputation in the South.

39. Branch, *Parting the Waters*, p. 441; Clayborne Carson, *In Struggle: SNCC and the Black Awakening of the 1960s* (Cambridge: Harvard University Press, 1981), p. 35.

40. Garrow, *Bearing the Cross*, p. 157.

41. Garrow, *Bearing the Cross*, pp. 157–59; Reeves, *President Kennedy*, pp. 127–31.

42. *Parting the Waters*, p. 469.

43. The conversation is described in Garrow, *Bearing the Cross*, pp. 159–60.

44. "The state officials . . . wanted to stage an extravagant show in order to advertise that interracial travelers could not survive with anything less." Branch, *Parting the Waters*, pp. 469–72.

45. On the international relations dimension of Robert Kennedy's response to the Freedom Riders, see Strober and Strober, eds., *"Let Us Begin Anew,"* p. 297; Reeves, *President Kennedy*, pp. 132–33.

46. By the time of his conversation with King, Robert Kennedy had lost patience with the Freedom Riders. He was especially angered when, after he had carefully negotiated to get the first group into Mississippi safely, others followed, threatening to recreate the entire episode. He went so far as to issue a press release calling the follow-up Riders "curiosity seekers, publicity seekers, and others who are seeking to serve their own causes." Brauer, *Second Reconstruction*, pp. 100–8; Garrow, *Bearing the Cross*, pp. 156–60.

47. Cleveland Sellers and Robert Terrell, *The River of No Return: The Autobiography of a Black Militant and the Life and Death of SNCC* (Jackson: University of Mississippi Press, 1990), ch. 4; Carson, *In Struggle*, pp. 37–38.

48. See "Student Nonviolent Coordinating Committee Statement of Purpose," printed in Joanne Grant, ed., *Black Protest: History, Documents, and Analyses, 1619 to the Present*, 2d ed. (New York: Faucett Premier, 1968), pp. 289–90.

49. "The Freedom Ride brought national attention to the southern movement, but it also exacerbated both student distrust of King's personal commitment and organizational competition among the civil rights groups." Garrow, *Bearing the Cross*, pp. 159, 161. See also Branch, *Parting the Waters*, pp. 466–67.

50. Branch, *Parting the Waters*, p. 477–78; Garrow, *Bearing the Cross*, p. 161.

51. See John Lewis's remarks in Strober and Strober, eds., *"Let Us Begin Anew"*, p. 297.

52. Quoted in Branch, *Parting the Waters*, p. 414. The text of Robert Kennedy's address appears in Henry Golden, *Mr. Kennedy and the Negroes* (Greenwich, Conn.: Crest Books, 1964), pp. 218–26.

53. See the discussion of Marshall's role as a mediator in Brauer, *Second Reconstruction*, ch. 6. Note especially pp. 152, 155, 178.

54. Details of events in Albany appear in Garrow, *Bearing the Cross*, ch. 4.

55. Branch, *Parting the Waters*, pp. 554–55.

56. Branch, *Parting the Waters*, pp. 603–7; Garrow, *Bearing the Cross*, pp. 203–4.

57. Details on the Meredith controversy are found in Russell H. Barrett, *Integration at Ole Miss* (Chicago: Quadrangle Books, 1965). See also Branch, *Parting the Waters*, ch. 17.

58. See Reeves, *President Kennedy*, pp. 356–64.

59. The intervention in Oxford occurred only one month before the 1962 midterm elections. Although Kennedy had feared the popular reaction to use of troops against American citizens, his pollster Louis Harris measured a sizable jump in Democratic prospects just after this episode. "I am frank to say that I have never seen the temper and mood change so drastically as this election outlook," Harris reported. "Every Democrat running for major office should put front and center that this country needs firm and resolute leadership such as the President demonstrated in the Mississippi case." Reeves, *President Kennedy*, p. 364.

60. Mark Stern, *Calculating Visions: Kennedy, Johnson, and Civil Rights* (New Brunswick, N.J.: Rutgers University Press, 1992), pp. 63–67.

61. Brauer, *Second Reconstruction*, p. 112.

62. Doug McAdam, *Political Process and the Development of Black Insurgency, 1930–1970* (Chicago: University of Chicago Press, 1982), pp. 170–71. See also Oates, *Let the Trumpet Sound*, p. 176.

63. Garrow, *Bearing the Cross*, pp. 161–62, 658. Taylor Branch claims that the VEP was "pursued . . . with a vengeance" by the Kennedys. *Parting the Waters*, p. 478.

64. Branch, *Parting the Waters*, p. 479.

65. Branch, *Parting the Waters*, pp. 478–482; Garrow, *Bearing the Cross*, pp. 162–63, 658.

66. Mark Stern takes an opposing view. He argues that "early on, the administration was aware that the voting-rights drive as a tactic to control black activism would have only limited success." *Calculating Visions*, p. 65.

67. Martin Luther King Jr., in a 1960 "Meet the Press" interview, had declared to a national audience that the right to vote was *the* principal aim of the movement. He added some components to the movement's agenda in a February 1961 article for *The Nation*, but he claimed once again that equal voting rights should be the first major item on the president's agenda. Garrow, *Bearing the Cross*, pp. 134, 154.

68. Brauer, *Second Reconstruction*, p. 116.

69. Branch, *Parting the Waters*, p. 625. It should also be noted here that the administration's interest in favoring King publicly escalated dramatically by 1963, largely because by then more radical African-American factions, including the Nation of Islam, were gaining in strength.

70. Strober and Strober, eds., *"Let Us Begin Anew,"* p. 313.

71. These associates were Stanley Levison and Hunter Pitts "Jack" O'Dell. See Michael Friedly and David Gallen, *Martin Luther King Jr.: The FBI File* (New York: Carroll and Graf, 1993), ch. 2.

72. James Baldwin, originally appearing in *Harper's Magazine* (February 1960), under the title "The Dangerous Road Before Martin Luther King." This essay has been reprinted as "The Highroad to Destiny," in Lincoln, ed., *Martin Luther King Jr.*, pp. 90–112. The quoted material is taken from pp. 107–9.

73. This general problem is also addressed in Miroff, "The Johnson White House and Civil Rights," pp. 11, 15–16.

74. Branch, *Parting the Waters*, pp. 485–86.

75. It should be noted here that King himself recognized that the battle for equal rights would continue on other fronts even as he endorsed participation in the Voter Education Project.

76. King's mediatory burdens are assessed in August Meier, "On the Role of Martin Luther King," *New Politics* 4 (Winter 1965): 52–59. This essay is conveniently reprinted, and aptly retitled, "The Conservative Militant," in C. Eric Lincoln, ed., *Martin Luther King Jr.: A Profile* (New York: Hill and Wang, 1970), pp. 144–56.

77. See comments by Julian Bond in Strober and Strober, eds., *"Let Us Begin Anew,"* p. 311.

78. Ralph David Abernathy, *And the Walls Came Tumbling Down* (New York: HarperPerennial, 1990), pp. 230–31.

79. All quotes taken from Garrow, *Bearing the Cross*, p. 228 (emphasis in the original).

80. King aide Andrew Young later credited Shuttlesworth with getting King into Birmingham. David Garrow goes so far as to say that King could not avoid going to

Birmingham, because of the momentum of events there. Garrow's characterization suggests the extent to which even King himself was being swept along by popularly based forces over which he had little direct control. *Bearing the Cross*, p. 229.

81. Garrow, *Bearing the Cross*, ch. 5.

82. Quoted in Brauer, *Second Reconstruction*, p. 238. In a little over a two-month period of time after the settlement in Birmingham, 758 racial demonstrations occurred in the United States, bringing 14,733 arrests in 186 communities. Branch, *Parting the Waters*, p. 825.

83. Garrow, *Bearing the Cross*, p. 265.

84. Brauer, *Second Reconstruction*, pp. 233, 241–44. Baldwin's essay originally appeared in *The New Yorker*, and was reprinted as "Down at the Cross," in Baldwin's *The Fire Next Time* (New York: Dell, 1964), pp. 23–141. King's letter subsequently appeared in King, *Why We Can't Wait*, ch. 5. See also Oates, *Let the Trumpet Sound*, p. 225; Reeves, *President Kennedy*, pp. 497–98.

85. Quoted in Brauer, *Second Reconstruction*, p. 243. Other accounts of that meeting appear in Strober and Strober, eds., *"Let Us Begin Anew,"* pp. 289–93.

86. Garrow, *Bearing the Cross*, p. 268; Brauer, *Second Reconstruction*, pp. 241–42.

87. Branch, *Parting the Waters*, p. 807.

88. Brauer, *Second Reconstruction*, p. 240.

89. Reeves, *President Kennedy*, pp. 488–93.

90. The partisan political dimension of the pressure on Kennedy was also important, and is often overlooked. Through 1963, Nelson Rockefeller, then governor of New York and widely known to harbor presidential aspirations, maintained a vigorous campaign of support for civil rights across the country. His private wealth placed him at a distinct advantage in winning friends among the movement, because he was frequently able to aid the efforts of King and others financially without confronting the usual checks of the political system. King himself was not above raising Rockefeller's name with the Kennedys to shake their political sensibilities. Given the precarious state of his electoral coalition, the president could not afford to ignore the potential consequences of Rockefeller's work. Indeed, when he was later apprised that Barry Goldwater would be the likely 1964 Republican nominee, the president exclaimed, "I can't believe we will be that lucky." Quoted in Brauer, *Second Reconstruction*, p. 299. See also Branch, *Parting the Waters*, pp. 488–89, 699–700, 787, 789; Reeves, *President Kennedy*, pp. 465, 468.

91. "The situation was rapidly reaching a boil," noted Theodore Sorensen, "which the President felt the federal government should not permit if it was to lead and not be swamped." Quoted in Brauer, *Second Reconstruction*, p. 246.

92. Brauer, *Second Reconstruction*, pp. 259–60.

93. Garrow, *Bearing the Cross*, pp. 267–69. Richard Reeves argues that the decision came after Birmingham had calmed down, as the administration began directly confronting the problem of integrating the University of Alabama, and indirectly con-

fronting prospects of occupying the South to ensure the execution of federal court orders. Several close observers of these events saw in them the seeds of a second civil war. Reeves, *President Kennedy*, pp. 500–515.

94. Branch, *Parting the Waters*, pp. 822–23; Reeves, *President Kennedy*, p. 521.

95. The text of Kennedy's speech is found in Harry Golden, *Mr. Kennedy and the Negroes*, pp. 213–18.

96. Brauer, *Second Reconstruction*, p. 263. See also Garrow, *Bearing the Cross*, p. 269.

97. Civil rights protests did not entirely cease in the wake of the speech. See Reeves, *President Kennedy*, p. 525.

98. Reeves, *President Kennedy*, pp. 524–25.

99. Stern, "Lyndon Johnson and the Democrats' Civil Rights Strategy," p. 9.

100. Brauer, *Second Reconstruction*, pp. 271–73; Garrow, *Bearing the Cross*, pp. 271–72; Branch, *Parting the Waters*, pp. 833–41.

101. Later, as Kennedy became convinced that the march would be well behaved, he publicly endorsed it. Garrow, *Bearing the Cross*, pp. 271–72, 278.

102. Garrow, *Bearing the Cross*, pp. 280–86. See also Milton Viorst, *Fire in the Streets: America in the 1960s* (New York: Simon and Schuster, 1979), pp. 228–30; Reeves, *President Kennedy*, pp. 581–82.

103. Branch, *Parting the Waters*, p. 851. See also Brauer, *Second Reconstruction*, pp. 286–88; Garrow, *Bearing the Cross*, pp. 272–73.

104. Strober and Strober, eds., *"Let Us Begin Anew,"* p. 268.

105. Branch, *Parting the Waters*, pp. 906–9; Friedly and Gallen, *The FBI File*, pp. 36–43.

106. One of the administration's actions that especially outraged civil rights activists was Robert Kennedy's announcement of federal criminal indictments against a group of Albany, Georgia demonstrators, on relatively obscure charges related to organizing boycotts. Given the administration's earlier disinterest in using federal law to aid those who protested segregation in Albany, King and others were incensed at the Justice Department's open zeal in pursuing these later prosecutions. Branch, *Parting the Waters*, pp. 866–68.

107. Branch, *Parting the Waters*, p. 901.

108. Brauer, *Second Reconstruction*, pp. 312–13; Garrow, *Bearing the Cross*, p. 307. In the Deep South, conversely, some—for the very same reason—greeted the news of Kennedy's death as occasion for holiday. Marshall Frady, *Wallace* (New York: Meridian Books, 1976), p. 142. See also Carolyn Pratt and Robert E. Lane, "Patterns of Closure: College Students' Return to Political 'Normalcy,'" in Martha Wolfenstein and Gilbert Kliman, eds., *Children and the Death of a President: Multi-Disciplinary Studies* (Garden City, N.Y.: Anchor Books, 1966), pp. 189–90.

109. White, *Making of the President*, pp. 206–12; Stern, *Calculating Visions*, pp. 27–32, 150–51. For a nuanced discussion of how Johnson dealt with the issue of race as a mem-

ber of Congress from a southern state, see McPherson, *A Political Education*, ch. 5.

110. Johnson, for example, agreed (against the counsel of adviser James Rowe) to chair the President's Committee on Equal Employment Opportunity, and on at least one occasion he urged Kennedy to be more aggressive in using the presidency to advance a civil rights agenda. See Walt Rostow's comments in Strober and Strober, eds., *"Let Us Begin Anew,"* p. 288. See also Reeves, *President Kennedy*, pp. 504–5.

111. For a rich and penetrating analysis of the Johnson administration's relationship with African Americans, see Miroff, "Presidential Leverage Over Social Movements: The Johnson White House and Civil Rights," pp. 2–23.

112. Those critics who took their soundings of Johnson based on his work in watering down the Eisenhower administration's civil rights initiatives of the 1950s looked at the right evidence, but came to the wrong conclusions. Johnson's early, active involvement in civil rights as majority leader derived not from an interest in retarding racial equality, but from a politically motivated desire to get some kind of legislation passed appealing to Democratic constituencies outside his native South. In other words, the power of Johnson's presidential ambitions drove him to secure passage of historic, if modest, civil rights statutes when most southern legislators refused to touch anything hinting of compromise on the question of race. Stern, *Calculating Visions*, pp. 117–20, 129, 133–49. See also Doris Kearns, *Lyndon Johnson and the American Dream* (New York: Signet, 1976), pp. 198–99.

113. Stern, *Calculating Visions*, pp. 160–62; Miroff, "The Johnson White House and Civil Rights," p. 8.

114. Richard N. Goodwin, *Remembering America: A Voice from the Sixties* (Boston: Little, Brown, 1988), pp. 256–57. One may reasonably question Goodwin's accuracy in recounting a direct quote, without any apparent reference material, twenty-four years after the fact, but the essence of the comment attributed to Johnson is entirely consistent with other, more carefully documented presidential statements of the time.

115. Miroff, "The Johnson White House and Civil Rights," p. 9.

116. Quoted in Charles and Barbara Whalen, *The Longest Debate: A Legislative History of the 1964 Civil Rights Act* (New York: Mentor Books, 1985), p. 80.

117. Stern, *Calculating Visions*, pp. 164–65.

118. Whalen and Whalen, *Longest Debate*, pp. 81–82 (emphasis in the original). Farmer fell out of favor later for refusing to endorse a moratorium on street demonstrations. On this point, see Miroff, "The Johnson White House and Civil Rights," pp. 13–16.

119. Stern, *Calculating Visions*, p. 166.

120. On the complexities of the FBI's position in relation to the civil rights movement—including the evident dissonance of maintaining efforts to undermine at once the movement and the Ku Klux Klan—see William W. Keller, *The Liberals and J. Edgar Hoover: Rise and Fall of a Domestic Intelligence State* (Princeton: Princeton

University Press, 1989). See also David J. Garrow, *The FBI and Martin Luther King Jr.* (New York: Penguin Books, 1981).

121. The pernicious effects of FBI surveillance on King's psyche, and on the movement at large, is a central feature of the discussion in Garrow, *Bearing the Cross*, chs. 6–7. It should also be noted here, however, that the movement's relatively low profile in Washington politics at this time also derived from the SCLC's active choice to continue investing its energies in local-based protests in the South, including a poorly rewarded campaign in St. Augustine, Florida. Thus, both endogenous and exogenous factors played important parts in the movement's relative quiescence.

122. Whalen, *Longest Debate*, p. 82.

123. Charles Whalen, "Johnson and the Civil Rights Act of 1964," in Kenneth W. Thompson, ed., *Portraits of American Presidents*, vol. 5, *The Johnson Presidency: Twenty Intimate Perspectives of Lyndon B. Johnson* (Lanham, Md.: University Press of America, 1986), pp. 70–73; Stern, *Calculating Visions*, pp. 168–85; Whalen and Whalen, *Longest Debate*, pp. 188–203; Kearns, *Lyndon Johnson and the American Dream*, p. 200.

124. Quoted in Whalen, *Longest Debate*, p. 230.

125. Garrow, *Bearing the Cross*, pp. 339–40.

126. The other possible candidate for such honors would be the Supreme Court's *Brown* decision, although that ruling required subsequent execution by President Eisenhower to come fully into effect. For commentary on the on-going debate about *Brown*'s legacy, see Walter Dellinger, "A Southern White Recalls a Moral Revolution," *Washington Post*, May 15, 1994, p. C1.

127. Historians disagree over precisely the level of commitment Johnson brought to voting rights reform as he entered his full term as president. Some, including Richard Goodwin, and his wife Doris Kearns, argue that Johnson had no intention of producing voting rights reform in 1965. Others, including David J. Garrow in his book *Protest at Selma*, contend that Johnson began laying the groundwork for the voting rights act immediately after the 1964 election. Johnson takes that same position in his memoirs. The president apparently sanctioned efforts within the Justice Department to begin drafting legislative proposals on the subject in November 1964. However, there does seem to be a consensus that the president did not expect to move actively on voting rights as quickly as King wanted. Thus, King precipitated presidential action, and remarkably quick congressional consent. In the words of Steven F. Lawson, "Circumstances in Selma, Alabama, altered the timetable and content of the [administration's] legislative considerations," alterations conceded to King. Lawson, *Black Ballots*, p. 308; Garrow, *Protest at Selma: Martin Luther King Jr., and the Voting Rights Act of 1965* (New Haven: Yale University Press, 1978), chs. 2, 4; Lyndon Baines Johnson, *The Vantage Point: Perspectives of the Presidency, 1963–1969* (New York: Holt, Rinehart and Winston, 1971), pp. 160–61; Goodwin, *Remembering America*, pp. 317–18; Kearns, *Lyndon Johnson and the American Dream*, pp. 238–39. See also Stern, *Calculating Visions*, pp. 184, 186, 210–17.

128. Quoted in Garrow, *Bearing the Cross*, p. 338; Miroff, "The Johnson White House and Civil Rights," p. 12.

129. For details on the party-building initiative, see Miroff, "The Johnson White House and Civil Rights," pp. 16–18.

130. To the extent that Johnson was successful in achieving a cessation of protests in 1964, it was largely because he convinced most key civil rights activists that Barry Goldwater would benefit in that November's election from any signs of civil unrest. See Garrow, *Bearing the Cross*, p. 343.

131. Brief accounts of the MFDP fight include Rowland Evans and Robert Novak, *Lyndon B. Johnson: The Exercise of Power* (New York: New American Library, 1966), pp. 475–80; Garrow, *Bearing the Cross*, pp. 340–50, 358.

132. For details on events in Mississippi of that year, see Sally Belfrage, *Freedom Summer* (New York: Viking Press, 1965).

133. Viorst, *Fire in the Streets*, p. 263.

134. "The President had hoped the 1964 Civil Rights Act would be the last word in such legislation for several years to come." Evans and Novak, *The Exercise of Power*, p. 518. See also Viorst, *Fire in the Streets*, p. 255.

135. On the one occasion during this period when something approaching a race-based emergency arose—the high profile disappearance in Mississippi of three civil rights workers (Michael Schwerner, Andrew Goodman, and James Chaney)—the Johnson administration and the FBI took extraordinary steps to intervene in order to keep the situation from escalating into broader bloodshed. Viorst, *Fire in the Streets*, pp. 258–59.

136. Miroff, "The Johnson White House and Civil Rights," pp. 12–13; Garrow, *Bearing the Cross*, p. 343.

137. "I have never seen such just really blatant use of power," proclaimed one sympathetic Democratic delegate of the Johnson team's behavior at that convention. For example, in one crucial instance, when MFDP delegate Fannie Lou Hamer was in the middle of riveting, televised testimony to the credentials committee, the president hastily convened an impromptu press conference to get the cameras off her and onto himself. Garrow, *Bearing the Cross*, pp. 346–47; Viorst, *Fire in the Streets*, p. 263.

138. Sidney M. Milkis, *The President and the Parties: The Transformation of the American Party System Since the New Deal* (New York: Oxford University Press, 1993), p. 212; Viorst, *Fire in the Streets*, pp. 263–65. The hands-on approach the president took in this episode strongly contrasts with the episodic intervention made on behalf of the Civil Rights Act of 1964.

139. "Blacks and liberal whites had never worked more productively, or more harmoniously, than in the first months of the Johnson presidency. On the surface the spirit of the March on Washington flourished, but the experience in Atlantic City would shatter that illusion. . . . Militant blacks had acquired a new orthodoxy, and declared that you could never trust a 'dirty white liberal.' . . . For SNCC, the chief villain at Atlantic

City was, of course, Lyndon Johnson." Viorst, *Fire in the Streets*, pp. 235, 237, 267–70.

140. Stephen B. Oates writes that before the 1965 act, "SCLC's only recourse had been to file [voting rights] suits with the Justice Department, but eight years of case-by-case litigation in the federal courts had convinced King of the ineffectiveness of that approach . . . . In Alabama, 80.7 percent of the eligible Negro voters were still not registered." *Let the Trumpet Sound*, p. 325.

141. Ralph David Abernathy explains the interrelationship between the two main sets of issues concerning the activists at that time, and thus the need to secure suffrage reform: "If public transportation and public accommodations were to remain equally accessible to blacks . . . then *local* authorities would have to share the responsibility for seeing that their states and communities created a climate in which the law was obeyed" (emphasis added). Abernathy, *Walls Came Tumbling Down*, p. 298.

142. Garrow, *Bearing the Cross*, p. 368; Miroff, "The Johnson White House and Civil Rights," pp. 11–12.

143. Abernathy, *Walls Came Tumbling Down*, pp. 298–99.

144. Abernathy, *Walls Came Tumbling Down*, p. 300.

145. Garrow, *Bearing the Cross*, p. 379; Abernathy, *Walls Came Tumbling Down*, pp. 302–4; Oates, *Let the Trumpet Sound*, pp. 326–28.

146. Garrow, *Bearing the Cross*, p. 390. King later claimed, "We are going to bring a voting bill into being in the streets of Selma" (p. 394).

147. It was at the beginning of the Selma campaign that the FBI's most egregious assault on King's civil liberties occurred. Hoover had one of his top aides manufacture a composite tape from bugs in various locations—apparently capturing King in a variety of compromising settings—and sent it to King's home, along with a crudely constructed letter anonymously suggesting suicide as the only way to avert public humiliation. There is no evidence to suggest that the president had knowledge of this incident, although he certainly knew that some embarrassing product of FBI surveillance was making the rounds in Washington officialdom, and that King was increasingly despondent over Hoover's private war against him. King's inner circle suspected Johnson's complicity in the bugging. Ralph Abernathy, on occasionally finding a transmitter, entertained King's young aides by addressing "Mr. President" through it. Oates, *Let the Trumpet Sound*, pp. 331—34; Garrow, *Bearing the Cross*, pp. 372–78; Abernathy, *Walls Came Tumbling Down*, pp. 309–12.

148. Garrow, *Bearing the Cross*, pp. 378–80.

149. Quoted in Garrow, *Bearing the Cross*, pp. 385–87.

150. Garrow, *Bearing the Cross*, p. 690; Oates, *Walls Came Tumbling Down*, pp. 343–44.

151. Garrow, *Bearing the Cross*, pp. 387–88, 395.

152. Garrow, *Bearing the Cross*, pp. 398–99; Abernathy, *Walls Came Tumbling Down*, pp. 325–33.

153. Garrow extensively discusses the importance of media messages in creating

national pressure for presidential action in *Protest at Selma*, chs. 3–5.

154. Oates, *Let the Trumpet Sound*, p. 349.

155. The text of the Voting Rights Act is included in Henry Steele Commager, ed., *The Struggle for Racial Equality: A Documentary Record* (Gloucester, Mass.: Peter Smith, 1972), pp. 214–16.

156. Evans and Novak, *The Exercise of Power*, p. 517.

157. Oates, *Let the Trumpet Sound*, p. 354. Indeed, the bill the House passed was even more expansive than the president's proposal. It would have disallowed the use of poll taxes in state and local elections, a provision the administration challenged as unconstitutional. To get the bill out of conference, King endorsed the Senate's more modest provision. Garrow, *Bearing the Cross*, p. 435; Oates, *Let the Trumpet Sound*, p. 369.

158. The president also, because of Governor George Wallace's refusal to guarantee the safety of the marchers, provided federalized National Guard troops to guard the parade route from Selma to Montgomery. Garrow, *Bearing the Cross*, pp. 410–11.

159. Quoted in Garrow, *Bearing the Cross*, p. 407.

160. A lightly edited text of Johnson's address is found in Commager, ed., *Struggle for Racial Equality*, pp. 208–13. See also Goodwin, *Remembering America*, pp. 324–39.

161. Garrow, *Bearing the Cross*, pp. 408–9.

8. THE PRESIDENCY, LEADERSHIP, AND THE STRUGGLE FOR RACIAL EQUALITY

1. William Faulkner, *Requiem for a Nun* (New York: Random House, 1951), p. 92.

2. Higham makes a sophisticated and persuasive case about historical trends in race relations in "America's Three Reconstructions," *New York Review of Books*, November 6, 1997, pp. 52–56. I simply believe that he mischaracterizes the nature of Truman's gamble.

3. Richard E. Neustadt, *Presidential Power and the Modern Presidents: The Politics of Leadership from Roosevelt to Reagan* (New York: Free Press, 1990), pp. ix, 6.

4. Merrill D. Peterson, *Lincoln in American Memory* (New York: Oxford University Press, 1994).

5. Rossiter, *Constitutional Dictatorship: Crisis Government in the Modern Democracies* (New York: Harcourt, Brace, and World, 1963), ch. 15.

6. *Washington Post*, June 12, 1993, p. B1; June 22, 1993, p. A18; July 1, 1993, p. A22.

7. Charles A. and Mary R. Beard, *The Rise of American Civilization* (New York: Macmillan, 1930), part 2, p. 100.

8. David B. Truman, *The Governmental Process: Political Interests and Public Opinion* (New York: Knopf, 1951), pp. 48–49.

9. Sonja M. Hunt, "The Role of Leadership in the Construction of Reality," in Barbara Kellerman, ed., *Leadership: Multidisciplinary Perspectives* (Englewood Cliffs, N.J.: Prentice-Hall, 1984), p. 171.

10. Ambrose's comments were offered in response to reviewer Henrik Bering-Jensen's questions about the accuracy of a then-emerging tendency among Nixon biographers to find in Nixon's presidency an activist, progressive domestic strain. Ambrose was critical. *Washington Times*, July 10, 1991, p. E2.

11. A major corrective did appear as my study was being completed, in Kenneth O'Reilly, *Nixon's Piano: Presidents and Racial Politics from Washington to Clinton* (New York: Free Press, 1995). Another useful study, examining a single case, is Bruce Miroff, "Presidential Leverage Over Social Movements: The Johnson White House and Civil Rights," *Journal of Politics* 43 (1981): 2–23.

12. Matthew Holden Jr., "The Presidency and Constitutional Change in the Twentieth Century: The Racial Component," *PRG Report: Newsletter of the Presidency Research Group* (Washington D.C.: American Political Science Association, Fall 1993), pp. 7–8.

13. Most of the literature on individual administrations does reflect the tension between movements and the single presidents under examination. However, few scholars have worked to piece together composite portraits based on the ample biographical studies already in existence, and those who have looked at civil rights as a presidential issue have done so by examining a time frame in which the incentive structures of American politics had already dramatically shifted to reward presidential advances on civil rights. These individual studies, then, however accurate they may be for their given frames of time, tend to understate important dynamics over time. One exception to this general rule is George Sinkler's *The Racial Attitudes of American Presidents, from Abraham Lincoln to Theodore Roosevelt* (Garden City, N.Y.: Anchor Books, 1972). However, Sinkler's study ends before the era of modern presidents.

14. Richard P. Longaker, *The Presidency and Individual Liberties* (Ithaca: Cornell University Press, 1961), pp. 1–12.

15. Ruth P. Morgan, *The President and Civil Rights: Policy-Making by Executive Order* (New York: St. Martin's Press, 1970), Preface and Introduction; Steven A. Shull, *The President and Civil Rights Policy: Leadership and Change* (New York: Greenwood Press, 1989), Preface, chs. 1–2. Quote is on page 28.

16. See, for example, Jack Walker, "Origins and Maintenance of Interest Groups in America," *American Political Science Review*, 77 (1983): 390–406.

17. Carol McClurg Mueller, "Building Social Movement Theory," in Aldon D. Morris and Mueller, eds., *Frontiers in Social Movement Theory* (New Haven: Yale University Press, 1992), pp. 3–4. This volume contains a series of fifteen essays examining and evaluating the various strengths and weaknesses of resource mobilization (RM) theory. It should be noted here that even some of RM's strongest critics still accept as legitimate the theory's central focus on resources as a means of understanding the emergence and structure of social movements. I find particularly useful the political process model offered by Doug McAdam. McAdam's alternative still holds resources as central to understanding social movement development, but he

differs with many RM theorists over where those resources originate, and especially over the receptivity of the established political order to social change. He posits, consistent with my findings, that established elites "share an abiding conservatism that does not predispose them to initiate any insurgent activity that might conceivably prove threatening to their interests." McAdam, *Political Process and the Development of Black Insurgency, 1930–1970* (Chicago: University of Chicago Press, 1982), p. 35. For a recent application of this model in political science, see Anne N. Costain, *Inviting Women's Rebellion: A Political Process Interpretation of the Women's Movement* (Baltimore: Johns Hopkins University Press, 1992).

18. One of my criticisms of RM theory is that its proponents have not developed a consensus roster of resource categories commonly mobilized by movements. In the absence of such a precise list, I have constructed my own here, derived from three sources: the empirical content of my cases; a selective borrowing from the available literature on social movements; and the more refined work on political resources found in the literature on interest groups. See Ralph H. Turner, "Collective Behavior and Resource Mobilization as Approaches to Social Movements: Issues and Continuities," in Louis Kriesberg, ed., *Research in Social Movements, Conflicts, and Change: A Research Annual*, vol. 4 (Greenwich, Conn.: JAI Press, 1981), p. 18; McAdam, *Political Process*, pp. 43–48; Norman J. Ornstein and Shirley Elder, *Interest Groups, Lobbying, and Policymaking* (Washington D.C.: Congressional Quarterly Press, 1978), ch. 3.

19. I should note here that I have adopted these categories for heuristic purposes alone. Each of my general categories could include a number of relevant subcategories that might, under alternative constructions, be moved to another general category, or be elevated to a standing category itself. My central aim in asserting the existence of these categories is to afford one kind of simple analytic window onto presidential-movement relations, as an alternative to the chronological account that went before. Another variation on categorizing general governmental responses, which rests somewhere between the chronological and the simple five-category schema offered here, appears in Gary T. Marx, "External Efforts to Damage or Facilitate Social Movements: Some Patterns, Explanations, Outcomes, and Complications," in Mayer N. Zald and John D. McCarthy, eds., *The Dynamics of Social Movements: Resource Mobilization, Social Control, and Tactics* (Cambridge, Mass.: Winthrop, 1977), pp. 94–125.

20. I use the term "movement" in this section as shorthand for all the collective action efforts toward racial equality discussed in this study. Clearly during much of the period under review here—for example, during the time from Reconstruction through the 1920s—no real movement as such existed. However, the resource mobilization problems discussed here affected those activists in the pre-movement environment as thoroughly as they did later activists, perhaps more so. Thus, adherence to a strictly defined use of the term "movement" here is not essential.

21. Marx, "External Efforts to Damage or Facilitate Social Movements," p. 124.

22. Alternatively, to further the seminal metaphor authored by Bruce Miroff, as presidents have tried to exercise leverage over social movements, they have sought their fulcrum in movement leaders. "Presidential Leverage Over Social Movements," pp. 2–23.

23. For a discussion of the subtle appeal of recognition by political elites, see McAdam, *Political Process*, pp. 25–29.

24. Sociologist Doug McAdam has called this process of coming to a sense of political empowerment "cognitive liberation." See his *Political Process*, pp. 48–59.

25. Schattschneider, *The Semisovereign People: A Realist's View of Democracy in America* (New York: Holt, Rinehart and Winston, 1960), p. 2. Schattschneider's work informs a central part of the analysis in David J. Garrow's *Protest at Selma: Martin Luther King Jr. and the Voting Acts Right of 1965* (New Haven: Yale University Press, 1978), ch. 7.

26. Similar intent—that is, encouraging public and private efforts at intimidation—were behind efforts in the 1950s, by southern legislatures, to compel organizations such as the NAACP to make public their membership rosters. In recognition of the threat posed to the free exercise of the right to assembly, the Supreme Court outlawed such attempts in *NAACP v. Alabama* (1958).

27. Dennis Chong, *Collective Action and the Civil Rights Movement* (Chicago: University of Chicago Press, 1991), pp. 11, 79, 90. The original source for the quote is Barry, *Sociologists, Economists, and Democracy* (Chicago: University of Chicago Press, 1978), p. 30.

28. See Randolph B. Campbell, *An Empire for Slavery: The Peculiar Institution in Texas, 1821–1865* (Baton Rouge: Louisiana State University Press, 1989).

29. Indeed, the entire drama of western expansion that occurred during the twenty-five years before the advent of the Civil War makes for a fascinating application of Schattschneider's theory, although he makes no mention of it in his classic text *The Semisovereign People*.

30. Jeffrey K. Tulis, *The Rhetorical Presidency* (Princeton: Princeton University Press, 1987).

31. This renders very difficult content analysis of political rhetoric on race. Conventional studies that rely on the identification of certain keywords risk understating the degree of relevant commentary on racial issues unless a very sensitive effort is undertaken to recognize code words or ghost topics that allow communication on race absent direct mention of it. For one example of an effort to map racial commentary using a conventional set of keywords, see Shull, *The President and Civil Rights Policy*, pp. 36, 41–67.

32. This dissonance between rhetoric and practice may have important ramifications for students of presidential rhetoric, who often reveal an inclination to reify rhetoric as policy. In the case of racial activism, presidential rhetoric frequently took

on an advanced cast precisely to *avoid* more substantive changes in policy.

33. McAdam, *Political Process*, pp. 48–51; Frances Fox Piven and Richard A. Cloward, *Poor People's Movements: Why They Succeed, How They Fail* (New York: Pantheon Books, 1977), p. 4.

34. The federal government's unwillingness or inability to protect interstate travel by itinerant abolitionists within the southern states gave added importance to the decision not to try to protect the mails.

35. Indeed, movements often arise precisely because the fiscal resources that might allow their participants to pursue effective action in conventional political spheres are not available to them. Thus, they must seek out alternative mechanisms for redress of those grievances. Booker T. Washington and Marcus Garvey subscribed to this logic and accordingly sought economic advance, expecting that course to preface racial advance through the usual conventions of American politics, including electoral influence and lobbying.

36. Marx, "External Efforts to Damage or Facilitate Social Movements," p. 100.

37. Van Buren did not completely break new ground in this regard, as Andrew Jackson had already used his veto for political purposes. I should note here, however, that it was also highly unusual that Van Buren took the occasion of his inaugural address to announce his position, rather than awaiting an opportunity for a special message to Congress on the issue.

38. Note here also the efforts by Franklin Pierce to direct decision making on the slavery issue out of Washington, to deny antislavery advocates the fruits of their victory in converting the House of Representatives to their cause.

39. It should be added that in Roosevelt's case these pressures were supplemented with direct threats to his presidential standing by the March on Washington Movement, which effectively testified to the mass power newly activated blacks could wield.

40. Figures cited in McAdam, *Political Process*, p. 78. McAdam's table shows black migration from the South to be 407,000 from 1930 to 1940, and 1,599,000 from 1940 to 1950.

41. Evidence suggests that much of this migration might have occurred even in the absence of war, as southern agricultural practices—especially the dependence on cotton—was undergoing a transformation beginning in the 1920s. However, the timing of presidential concessions on race with this increased migration needs to be noted here, as does the general absence of any effort to curb that movement. Given the breadth of control the government exercised over the nation's economy during the war, it should also be noted that its powers to restrain migration went unused in relation to African Americans.

42. McAdam, *Political Process*, pp. 78–80.

43. Russell L. Riley, "On Political Institutions and Race in America," paper delivered at the Southern Political Science Association Annual meeting, Tampa, November 4, 1995.

44. In this way the two faces of the nation-keeping role are shown to be intimately related. Forcing change in accepted cultural institutions on a nation unprepared for it risks destroying the nation in violent reaction. Thus, presidents committed to national peace and security find ample incentives to preserve prevailing social institutions and structures.

45. Richard Robert Madden, *Memoirs, Chiefly Auto-biographical from 1798 to 1886*, T. M. Madden, ed. (London: Wards and Downey, 1891), p. 96.

46. Don E. Fehrenbacher, ed., *Abraham Lincoln: Speeches and Writings, 1859–1865* (New York: Library of America, 1989), p. 358.

47. Martin Shefter makes the same case in his essay, "International Influences on American Politics," in Lawrence C. Dodd and Calvin Jillson, eds., *New Perspectives on American Politics* (Washington D.C.: CQ Press, 1994), pp. 319, 323. See also John David Skrentny, "The Effect of the Cold War on African-American Civil Rights: America and the World Audience, 1945–1968," *Theory and Society* 27 (1998): 237–85; Azza Salama Layton, "The International Context of U.S. Civil Rights Politics: The Dynamics Between Race Policies and International Politics, 1941–1960," paper presented at the American Political Science Association annual meeting, Washington D.C., August 27–31, 1997.

48. It is the *enduring* nature of that peace and security that is crucial here. Presidents confronted a variety of challenges to domestic tranquillity before the sixties of each century, and responded by quashing those agitating for black equality. A nation-keeping institution would follow that course under these circumstances because the prevailing nature of public opinion was such that repelling change rather than advancing it was more likely to still conflict. Once the legitimacy of claims to equality became more widely accepted, however, to have openly suppressed those advocating change was to invite continuing or escalated conflict. Under these conditions, sympathetic presidents saw the necessity of vigorously investing their powers of persuasion in the cause of equality so as to establish a new consensus, which produced the only foreseeable prospects for securing the Union and a lasting peace.

49. Cited in Richard Hofstadter, *The American Political Tradition and the Men Who Made It* (New York: Vintage Books, 1974), p. 171.

50. Thomas G. Dyer, *Theodore Roosevelt and the Idea of Race* (Baton Rouge: Louisiana State University Press, 1980), pp. 150, 153. Dyer explains that Roosevelt's position on women derived in part from his concerns about "race suicide," diminished birth rates that would allow allegedly inferior races eventually to outnumber white America.

51. Henry F. Pringle, *Theodore Roosevelt: A Biography* (New York: Harcourt, Brace, and World, 1956), pp. 331–33.

52. Paolo E. Coletta, *The Presidency of William Howard Taft* (Lawrence: University Press of Kansas, 1973), p. 35.

53. Sally Hunter Graham, "Woodrow Wilson, Alice Paul, and the Woman Suffrage

Movement," *Political Science Quarterly* 98, no. 4 (Winter 1983/84): 674, 678.

54. Woodrow Wilson, "Appeal for Woman Suffrage," in Ray Stannard Baker and William E. Dodd, eds., *The Public Papers of Woodrow Wilson: War and Peace: Presidential Messages, Addresses, and Public Papers (1917–1924)* (New York: Harper), vol. 1, pp. 263–67. See also Christine Lunardini and Thomas Knock, "Woodrow Wilson and Woman Suffrage: A New Look," *Political Science Quarterly* 95, no. 4 (Winter 1980/81): 668.

55. Alexander Hamilton, James Madison, and John Jay, *The Federalist Papers* (New York: New American Library, 1961), p. 269.

56. "Leaders of the new nation sought from the outset to subject Indians to a paternal presidential authority." Michael P. Rogin, *Fathers and Children: Andrew Jackson and the Subjugation of the American Indian* (New York: Knopf, 1975), p. 188.

57. Francis Paul Prucha, *The Great Father: The United States Government and the American Indians,* abridged ed. (Lincoln: University of Nebraska Press, 1986), pp. 64, 78.

58. Rogin, *Fathers and Children,* p. 121.

59. James D. Richardson, ed., *A Compilation of the Messages and Papers of the Presidents* (New York: Bureau of National Literature, 1897), p. 1117.

60. Rogin, *Fathers and Children,* pp. 121–33, 197, 296–99, 304–7.

61. Richardson, ed., *Messages and Papers,* p. 1083.

62. These actions are extensively documented in Rogin, *Fathers and Children,* ch. 7.

63. Quoted in Rogin, *Fathers and Children,* p. 233.

64. T. Harry Williams, Richard N. Current, and Frank Freidel, *A History of the United States Since 1865,* 3d ed. (New York: Knopf, 1969), p. 87.

65. Bennett Milton Rich, *Presidents and Civil Disorder* (Washington D.C.: Brookings Institution, 1941), pp. 84–85.

66. Williams, Current, and Freidel, *History of the United States,* p. 87.

67. *Appendix to the Annual Report of the Attorney-General of the United States for the Year 1896* (Washington D.C.: GPO, 1897), p. 61.

68. See Robert Higgs, *Crisis and Leviathan: Critical Episodes in the Growth of American Government* (New York: Oxford University Press, 1987), pp. 91–97.

69. Arthur M. Schlesinger Jr., *The Age of Roosevelt: The Coming of the New Deal* (Boston: Houghton Mifflin, 1959), chs. 6–10, 23–25; James Morone, *The Democratic Wish: Popular Participation and the Limits of American Government* (New York: Basic Books, 1990), p. 160.

70. See Arthur M. Schlesinger Jr., *The Age of Roosevelt: The Politics of Upheaval* (Boston: Houghton Mifflin, 1960); Alan Brinkley, *Voices of Protest: Huey Long, Father Coughlin, and the Great Depression* (New York: Vintage Books, 1983).

71. Edward S. Corwin, *Total War and the Constitution* (New York: Knopf, 1947), p. 91. Corwin's remark echoed that of Mr. Justice Murphy in his dissenting opinion in *Korematsu v. United States* (1944), 323 U.S. 214 at 235. On this episode, see also Clinton Rossiter, *Constitutional Dictatorship: Crisis Government in the Modern Democracies*

(New York: Harcourt, Brace, and World, 1963), pp. 280–85; Morton Grodzins, *Americans Betrayed: Politics and the Japanese Evacuation* (Chicago: University of Chicago Press, 1949); and Richard P. Longaker, *The Presidency and Individual Liberties* (Ithaca: Cornell University Press, 1961), pp. 26–29.

72. Quoted in Jacobus tenBroek, Edward N. Barnhart, and Floyd W. Matson, *Prejudice, War, and the Constitution* (Berkeley: University of California Press, 1975), p. 110.

73. On the character of the perceived military threat, see tenBroek, Barnhart, and Matson, *Prejudice, War, and the Constitution*, pp. 292–93; Longaker, *The Presidency and Individual Liberties*, pp. 26–28.

74. Quoted in tenBroek, Barnhart, and Matson, *Prejudice, War and the Constitution*, p. 89.

75. The Supreme Court did strike down two California state laws that further intruded on the liberties of Japanese Americans. That they did so highlights the importance of the war emergency concerns underlying the Court's ruling in the federal cases, as those concerns could not properly be said to apply in the state setting. See tenBroek, Barnhart, and Matson, *Prejudice, War, and the Constitution*, pp. 304–7. On the congressional and judicial role in this entire affair, see Grodzins, *Americans Betrayed*, chs. 11–12.

76. This quote is taken from King's "I Have a Dream" speech, reprinted in Richard C. Sinopoli, *From Many, One: Readings in American Political and Social Thought* (Washington D.C.: Georgetown University Press, 1997), p. 307.

77. Sam Howe Verhovek, "In Poll, Americans Reject Means But Not Ends of Racial Diversity," *New York Times*, December 14, 1997, p. 1.

78. Quoted in Gerald S. and Deborah H. Strober, *"Let Us Begin Anew": An Oral History of the Kennedy Presidency* (New York: HarperCollins, 1993), p. 277.

79. O'Reilly, *Nixon's Piano*, pp. 299, 318–19 (emphasis added).

80. This dynamic is at the heart of Kenneth O'Reilly's view of the presidency, especially in the post-civil rights years. See *Nixon's Piano, passim*.

81. O'Reilly, *Nixon's Piano*, p. 420; "Rift Between Blacks, Whites Is Tearing at the Heart of America," *Washington Post*, October 17, 1995, p. A13.

82. See, for example, Professor Derrick Bell's op-ed essay, "A Commission on Race? Wow." *New York Times*, June 14, 1997, p. 23.

83. Clinton confidante Harold Ickes—a longtime liberal activist and son of a New Deal Cabinet member famously friendly to black interests—observed that "If there is a true north to Bill Clinton, it is race. I never had any doubt in my mind where he stood on this issue." Michael Lewis, "Clinton's Garbage Man," *New York Times Magazine*, September 21, 1997, p. 88. See also Garry Wills, "The Clinton Principle," *New York Times Magazine*, January 19, 1997, p. 31.

84. At the outset I should note the tentative nature of such an exercise. It is difficult to make claims for the generalizability of refinements in a field in which the cen-

tral topic has no widely agreed-on definition (one study found 130) and few agreed-on boundaries. James MacGregor Burns, *Leadership* (New York: Harper Torchbooks, 1978), p. 2

85. The text is Dinesh D'Souza, *Ronald Reagan: How an Ordinary Man Became an Extraordinary Leader* (New York: Free Press, 1997). The quoted comments appear in Joan Didion, "The Lion King," *New York Review of Books*, December 18, 1997, p. 14.

86. This construction appears in Jones, *The United States Congress: People, Place, and Policy* (Homewood, Ill.: Dorsey Press, 1982), p. 357. Jones also finds presidential preeminence in the area of program implementation.

87. The change orientation is not nearly so prominent in the literature produced by anthropologists, sociologists, and psychologists. A convenient anthology providing evidence of this distinction is Barbara Kellerman, ed., *Leadership: Multidisciplinary Perspectives*. Quote is taken from Kellerman, "Leadership as a Political Act," p. 71 (emphasis in the original).

88. Bert Rockman, *The Leadership Question* (New York: Praeger, 1984), p. 20. Rockman admits that this "natural way" is not without complications—especially in how change is conceived—but the emphasis throughout is on how leadership can provide direction. He is more sensitive than many others to the preservative component of presidential action, but the emphasis in his work is more on leadership as an act of mobility than as an act of stasis.

89. Stephen Skowronek, *The Politics Presidents Make: Leadership from John Adams to George Bush* (Cambridge: Belknap Press of Harvard University Press, 1993) p. vii.

90. In one specific manifestation of this general tendency, historian LaWanda Cox has argued, "To credit Lincoln [with emancipation] is a reminder that presidential leadership can be critically important in affecting social change." The general works of political science cited here seem to indicate that such a reminder is unnecessary. Indeed, in a political culture inclined toward presidential attribution, it is something of a redundancy. Cox, "Lincoln and Black Freedom," in Gabor S. Boritt, ed., *The Historian's Lincoln* (Urbana: University of Illinois Press, 1988), p. 182.

91. Burns, *Leadership*, pp. 457–62.

92. Jack H. Nagel, *Participation* (Englewood Cliffs, N.J.: Prentice-Hall, 1987), p. 47.

93. See, for example, James W. Ceaser, *Presidential Selection: Theory and Development* (Princeton: Princeton University Press, 1979), ch. 6; Samuel P. Huntington, *American Politics: The Promise of Disharmony* (Cambridge: Belknap Press, 1981), ch. 7.

94. Quoted in Herbert J. Storing, *What the Anti-Federalists Were For* (Chicago: University of Chicago Press, 1981), p. 54.

95. The text of Harding's address can be found in Richardson, ed., *Messages and Papers*, pp. 9127–9132. The quote used here appears on p. 9130.